When Falls the Coliseum

a journal of American culture (or lac k thereof)

Also by Scott Stein

Lost

When Falls the Coliseum

a journal of American culture (or lac k thereof)

from the files of
www.WFtheColiseum.com

edited by
Scott Stein and C.P. Kaiser

When Falls the Coliseum: a journal of American culture (or lack thereof) copyright © 2001 by WFtheColiseum.com, inc. All graphics are the property of WFtheColiseum.com, inc. Printed in the United States of America. All rights reserved. All literary works herein are copyright © 1999-2001 by their respective authors, and are used here by permission of each copyright holder. This book contains satire, fiction, opinion, and humor. The opinions expressed by individual writers herein do not necessarily reflect the views of Free Reign Press, Inc., or WFtheColiseum.com, inc., its writers, or its editors. Responsibility for each essay rests with its author. Names, characters, and incidents are either the product of the authors' imaginations or are used fictitiously, and any similarity to actual persons, living or dead, events, or locales is entirely coincidental, except in cases of public or newsworthy figures or events being satirized or discussed in opinion pieces. All quotations from and references to other published or copyrighted works in this book are covered by fair use provisions that allow for freedom of speech and the expression of political ideas, or are from work in the public domain. In all cases effort has been made to credit the original sources. No part of this book may be used, transmitted, or reproduced in any way whatsoever without express written permission except in the case of brief quotations embodied in critical articles or reviews.

"The Last Peanut" was first published in *Art Times*; "The Stacker" was first published in *The G.W. Review;* "Garghibition" was first published in *Liberty*.

Cover illustration and design and interior book design by Andrew Turner. Interior graphics by Andrew Turner, with additional graphics by Jodi Vinaccia.

Free Reign Press, Inc.
Langhorne, Pennsylvania
October, 2001

Publisher's Cataloging-in-Publication

When falls the coliseum : a journal of American culture (or lack
  thereof) / from the files of www.WFtheColiseum.com ; Edited
  by Scott Stein and C.P. Kaiser. - 1st ed.
    p. cm.
    ISBN 0-9701554-1-7

  1. United States–Civilization. 2. United States–Civilization–Fiction. 3. United States–Politics and government. 4. United States–Politics and government–Fiction. 5. Religion–United States. 6. Religion–United States–Fiction.   I. Stein, Scott, 1971-   II. Kaiser, C.P.

E169.1.W442001   973.9
                QBI01-700581

Dedication

This book is dedicated to my parents, Cheryl and David Stein, for creating a home where laughter, debate, and love reigned; and, of course, to Andee.
- Scott Stein

This book is dedicated to Eva: my rock, my inspiration, my pillow.
- C.P. Kaiser

Acknowledgements

WFtheColiseum.com, inc. is grateful to C.P. Kaiser, for his editorial vision and passion; Andrew Turner, for bringing us to cyber-life with his talents; Andee Stein, for her sharp editorial eye; all of our contributors, for their creativity and energy; Jodi Vinaccia, for graphic design and advice; Scott Brandt and Tal Marnin, our attorneys; Wayne Kellner, our accountant; and, most of all, our readers, for speaking up.

**While stands the Coliseum, Rome shall stand;
When falls the Coliseum, Rome shall fall;
And when Rome falls—the World.**

– Lord Byron

Contents

Introduction   1

Jody Lane
People are Idiots   2
And I am related to every one of them.

Scott Stein
The Last Peanut   3
Even worse than banning them on airplanes.

Bob Sullivan
Top Ten Rejected Major League Baseball Expansion Teams   6

C.P. Kaiser
Reach Out and Punch Someone   7
Ring, Ring. Hello, do you have any toilet paper over there?

David "Preacher" Slocum
American-Americans   10
Lose the hyphen.

Scott Stein
That Other National Pastime   11
It isn't what you think.

Ari McKee
The Gods Are Taking a Meeting   12
Three cheers for polytheism.

Marni Schwartz
Eyes Wide Shut? They Should Be   14
Kubrick's final masterpiece isn't one.

Suzanne Hakanen
And the Beating Goes On   16
The difference between the candidates.

Scott Stein
Life Might Imitate Art, But it isn't Worth as Much (Just Ask NATO)   19
To be or not to be ... aw, just bomb the place.

Kevin Bolshaw
Squirrel-Buggery   21
Why there is next to no litter on the mountain.

C.P. Kaiser
Churchgoing Man Kills 13   23
What some people learned in Sunday school.

Scott Stein
Who's Your Daddy?   27
I'll have the McBroccoli with cheese.

Bob Sullivan
Have Guns, Will Travel   29
The vandals never steal the handle when you need them to.

Robert L. Hall
This Is Your Brain, Unplugged   33
Turn off to turn on.

Andrew Turner
Why I Haven't Solved World Hunger   35
Oh, the humanity.

Scott Stein
Baseball Players Deserve the Money 36
Got a problem with that? Stay home.

Robert O'Hara
Recipe for Continuing To Collect Unemployment 42

C.P. Kaiser
Seventh-Inning Stench 43
Is that odor coming from the field or the stands?

Scott Stein
If a Tree Falls In the Woods... 45
... get the hell out of the way.

Suzanne Hakanen
**The History of Inhalation In the U.S.
(As Chronicled By Mothball Product Labels)** 47
Warning: May cause Saturday night fever.

Eva Marie Tremoglie
Feeding the Bloodlust of the Rabble 49
Capital punishment and our schizophrenic culture.

Jody Lane
Headline News from the 21st Century 52
Y2K was only the beginning.

Scott Stein
"Literally" Decimated, Figuratively Speaking 54
Now you've gone and made Superman angry.

C.P. Kaiser
The Beeper 57
She loves that buzz.

Alastair MacDonald Black
If It Bleeds, It Leads 58
A relatively innocent bystander's report from Seattle.

Scott Stein
Fluidity of Thought 60
Leaps and tangents on the arts.

Ari McKee
We Are *Too* a Men's Magazine 62
Keeping the "ass" in class.

Chuck Sheehan
Furry Doorstops and Quieter Kids 65
Cure your barking and screeching ills.

Scott Stein
The Spice of Life ... and Death 67
These teens had the munchies something awful.

C.P. Kaiser
The Animal Network 68
Monkeys can type Hamlet, but can they direct it?

Rev. Angeline E.M. Theisen
Fair is Better than Equal 70
If we got what we deserved...

Scott Stein
Infidel 72
If ignorance is bliss, meet a very happy man.

Bob Sullivan
Top Ten Easiest Jobs in the World   **74**

Robert O'Hara
In Hitler's Defense   **75**
Political correctness is alive and well.

Suzanne Hakanen
**Recipe for Surviving Thanksgiving
with Your Mother**   **77**

Scott Stein
Making Change   **78**
Brother, can you spare a quarter?

C.P. Kaiser
If Boys Will Be Boys, Why Can't Girls Be Girls?   **82**
If he's a stud, why is she a slut?

Jeffrey Scheuer
Hooked: A Journal of Addiction and Malediction   **84**
Have a coke and a smile.

Scott Stein
Alzheimer's, Max and Flo   **88**
A spatial love poem worth remembering.

Jeff Podell
A Choice? Maybe. But Whose?   **89**
Abortion rights or states' rights?

Bob Sullivan
Top Ten Thoughts That Make Your Dog Smile   **93**

Scott Stein
40,000 Lies About the Culture of Violence   **94**
Get out your abacus.

Alex Joseph
Fatness   **96**
She will never be thin.

Jody Lane
Everything a Really Big Fking Idiot Needs to Know
About Drugs and Alcohol**   **98**
Coming soon to a bookstore near you!

Bob Sullivan
The Matrix and the Culture of Violence   **100**
Shiny, happy bullets.

Scott Stein
In the Morning, After Breakfast   **102**
What a writer should write about.

Robert L. Hall
The Two Religions   **104**
Sight for the blind.

Jason Stein
Gang Bang, Anyone?   **111**
Not as much fun as it sounds.

C.P. Kaiser
Deciphering Dot-com Ad Speak   **113**
Detail-oriented, self-starter wanted.

Scott Stein
Bruce Springsteen's "The Ghost of Tom Joad" and the Problem of Barbra Streisand   115
Born to run, but not for office.

Cassendre Xavier
Who Is God?   118
Or, more correctly, who isn't?

David "Preacher" Slocum
Shotguns and Rifles and Pistols, Oh My!   119
Who needs a gun when you can dial 911?

Scott Stein
Conspiracy   121
The truth might be out there, but they can't find it.

C.P. Kaiser
(un)-Sound Bytes   124
Not your standard headline news.

Ari McKee
Scared Straight (Well, Mostly)   126
A proposal from the hopelessly alert and reality-based.

Scott Stein
Absolute Denial   128
I'm fairly certain it's very unique.

Rev. Angeline E.M. Theisen
The Weekly Challenge   130
Saturday night special.

Robert O'Hara
Where my Marsupials at?   133
A cool cat or a hot dog?

C.P. Kaiser
Vaginal Ghosts   135
Let's baptize the hell out of them.

Scott Stein
Garghibition   137
A tall tale from a short man.

Bob Sullivan
All Hail the New Quayle!   140
Be compassionated. Vote for Bush.

David "Preacher" Slocum
Recipe for Brewing the Perfect Liberal   142

C.P. Kaiser
Legislators with Gonadal Dysfunction   143
An apple a day isn't supposed to keep babies away.

Scott Stein
Let Them Eat (Their Own) Cake   145
Half-baked ideas about tax cuts.

Bob Sullivan
Top Ten Signs You're Getting Old   148

Ari McKee
Can't We Wait Until His Head's a Little Bigger?   149
Modern maternity martyrdom.

Ron Schorr
Circus Crap 151
The smelliest show on earth.

Scott Stein
A Talking Ass, or a Braying Mule? 152
Literal truth and the Torah.

Robert L. Hall
Blame Game Justice 156
The genes made me do it.

C.P. Kaiser
Alcohol Problem? Break Out the Leeches and the Bible 158
Try getting your HMO to cover a change of heart.

Alex Joseph
Sheep 161
A unique story. A unique story.

Scott Stein
If At First You Don't Succeed... 164
Murder and attempted murder are the same crime.

David "Preacher" Slocum
Insert Foot 166
I get along with people.

Katherine Hauswirth
Punch Drunk 167
Priceless lessons.

Scott Stein
Thoughts on the Death of Nafés Johnson 169
It was an education.

C.P. Kaiser
Just Another Bloody Mess 172
Sour milk? Wilting flowers? Here's why.

Suzanne Hakanen
A Kill-Halloween Party 174
Maybe you should skip this house.

Scott Stein
The Same River Twice 176
A whale of a fish story.

C.P. Kaiser
Homeless, Not Heartless 183
Don't make it easy to ignore the destitute.

Ari McKee
Why Vote? That's What Electors Are For 185
Non-voters count as much as voters do.

Scott Stein
Prideless, and Proud of It 187
Join the one-man march.

Amy Boshnack
Recipe for Getting to Work by Public Transportation 189

David "Preacher" Slocum
Affirmative Action: Is It Working If I'm Not? 191
I had a dream. Then I woke up.

Jody Lane
The Mechanics of Humility 193
Blood is thicker than oil.

Jason Stein
The Temp 196
The American way.

Scott Stein
Recipe for Exhibition in the Museum of Modern Art 198

Bob Sullivan
Scam the Sham and the Pharaohs 199
Someone let the lobbyists into the penthouse.

Cassendre Xavier
I'm Not Seeking a Husband, Just a Well-Trained Boyfriend 202
Learning the art of maybe.

Scott Stein
The Politics of Star Trek: Peace on Earth, Klingon Racism, and Bleeding-Heart Vulcans 204
Live long and prosper, or we'll bust a phaser in your ass.

Jody Lane
The Committee (A Fairy Tale) 207
Where there's smoke, there's firing.

C.P. Kaiser
When Murder Becomes a Footnote 209
When is it TIME to applaud the Third Reich?

Helen Cates
Blame It on Uncle Sam 212
In the Navy, you can drink the seven seas.

Scott Stein
And the Loser Is... 214
American Beauty, the Oscars, and the oppressed suburbs.

David "Preacher" Slocum
The Confederate Flag Debate in South Carolina: Heritage or Hate? 217
Should any group have a monopoly on the past?

Bob Sullivan
Top Ten Signs Your Favorite Presidential Candidate is on Drugs 221

C.P. Kaiser
Getting Laid Was Never So Easy 222
Some suggestions from a grammar slut.

Scott Stein
Kangaroo Court 224
A wild tail.

Ari McKee
The Slow Food Movement 226
People with more time than sense.

Helen Cates
How About Keeping the Sex in Sexual Harassment? 228
Some people like the attention.

Scott Stein
I Passed on Passover, But Happy Easter 231
Forget the locust and frogs ... beware the wrath of mothers.

Robert L. Hall
One Word: Responsibility 233
Just say no. Really.

C.P. Kaiser
Enough Male Bashing 235
Another shot won't help this sot.

Scott Stein
A Second Chance 237
The heroics of Roberto the Clown.

Ari McKee
Supreme Being, Your Party Is Waiting for You at Baggage Claim 242
A mixed marriage.

Jason Stein
Taxed to the Max 244
Do I get to keep any of my money?

Jody Lane
Recipe for Holiday Peace 245

C.P. Kaiser and Scott Stein
To email or Not to e-mail 246
What would Shakespeare do?

Ari McKee
Help for the Reluctantly Human 250
Homo Sapiens are animals too.

Helen Cates
The Empty Bed 252
Dirty hands, priced to sell.

Scott Stein
Keep (All) Your Laws Off My Body 254
Listen to the bumper sticker.

David "Preacher" Slocum
Screw Who You Want, But Shoot Who We Tell You 256
The problem with don't ask, don't tell.

Robert O'Hara
Six Innings of Freedom 258
Sometimes it's more than a game.

Cassendre Xavier
Why Do Gay Men Have Such Small Dogs and Lesbians, Large Ones? 261
You are what you walk.

Scott Stein
Ask Marilyn About the Big Bang and the Difference Between Faith and Science 262
We're not in Kansas anymore.

Suzanne Hakanen
Acting Assistant Executive Associate Manager 269
The Kroc of meaningless titles.

Bob Sullivan
Making the Most of Your Take-Home Pay 271
What to do with the surplus.

Scott Stein
Boos for the Boss? 273
No, they're saying Broooooce!

Jared Boshnack
America's Sport 275
Baseball, football, or basketball?

C.P. Kaiser
I Thank God the Tornado Didn't Suck Me Up ...
Too Bad About My Neighbors, Though 277
What students should really be praying for.

Scott Stein
An Open Letter to the Dirty Bastard
Who Stole My Car 292
1989 - 2000 R.I.P.

Ari McKee
In Praise of Short Men 294
Costanza! Costanza! Oh, baby!

Willie, for C.P. Kaiser
If I Had Balls, I'd Be Licking Them 296
A dog's work is never done.

Scott Stein
The Stacker 298
He was the greatest ever.

About the Contributors 300

Introduction

Welcome to *When Falls the Coliseum: a journal of American culture (or lack thereof)*. This book can best be described as a conversation about America. A sometimes loud conversation. An often funny one. And, some might be bold enough to suggest, an important one. We are not that bold. It would be pretentious to claim that this conversation is the voice of America. It would also be inaccurate, implying that America speaks with one voice. The writers of *When Falls the Coliseum* certainly do not. The disclaimer, "Opinions expressed herein do not necessarily reflect the views of the editors" has perhaps never been more appropriate.

Be warned that free speech is the guiding principle of the Web site from which this book was born. Contributors with very different perspectives were recruited, and humor and debate are to be found here in abundance. About the only speech prohibited by *When Falls the Coliseum* is boring speech. Many of our readers got in on the action, and their responses to essays can also be found in this book. A few arguments ensued, but at least no punches were thrown. If you have no sense of humor, are easily offended, or think certain topics should not be discussed, put this book down now. Visit the self-help aisle instead. There's probably something there for you. If you disagree with or are offended by some of what you read here, good. It means our contributors did their jobs, and made you think.

When Falls the Coliseum is full of humor and satire, vigorous discussion, energetic short fiction, reviews, occasional strangeness, and more loudmouthed opinions than you can shake a big stick at, if you are the sort who shakes sticks (we gave up the practice ourselves several years ago, along with walking softly). Some of our writers might be defined as liberal, conservative, or libertarian, some as Christian, Jewish, or atheist. Others don't own dictionaries and can't say for sure what they are. Some are writers by trade; some actually work for a living. Some are motivated by high political and philosophical ideals; some just hate bad service at restaurants and think you need to hear about it. They come from all corners of the fruited plains, and all of them are, like everyone else in this country, sure they're right.

Many of the essays and stories in this book are short. This is, after all, a journal of *American* culture. So you can sneak in a quick read during the commercial break of your favorite sitcom. We can't promise that reading this book will offset the side effects of that glowing box and its laugh track calling to you from the living room, but we can promise you a literary good time and lots of genuine laughs. If you enjoy this book, then check out the newest additions to www.WFtheColiseum.com. The conversation isn't over yet.

Jody Lane
People are Idiots

Recently, I received an e-mail forwarded by a relative that claimed I was somehow "related to one out of every six people on the planet." No, I did not attempt to test the validity of the theory myself by actually determining my relationship to any one randomly chosen person on a planet of six billion. I have never been very good at math. I really didn't have that much time to devote to it, and, well (OK, damn it), I guess some would say I'm just plain lazy.

There are highly qualified professional people who have spent years in Ivy League colleges, followed by prestigious think-tank assignments and top-level positions in the public and private sectors, people who are paid very well to do that kind of stuff. Who am I to question them? But just because I haven't checked it out and confirmed it for myself doesn't mean that I am not concerned by the implications.

The truly disturbing part about this hypothesis, aside from the obvious indications of rampant global incest, is that, coupled with the sad fact that nine out of 10 of my *known* relatives are proven idiots, I could very well be related to nearly a billion more. And out of a population of six billion, could I possibly be the only one with idiot relatives? I think not. How many idiots are *you* related to?

Keeping the math as simple as possible, for my sake, let's investigate this more closely, shall we?

If I am related to a billion idiots, and 10 of my friends are related to about a half-billion idiots apiece (because no one can be related to as many idiots as I am), give or take a few thousand, that equals six billion idiots. Wow! The idiots do add up quickly. That is the entire world's population. Granted, we'll have some shared relatives that will reduce the number of individual idiots that we are uniquely related to, as well as the number of idiots that we each descend from. Since we are keeping it simple, that's of no consequence and we'll just assume that all of our ancestors were idiots and that we have at least one shared relative, which would make each of us distantly related to one another and our respective idiot relatives.

Science! Science has proven what I have suspected for years: People are idiots and I am related to every one of them!

Scott Stein
The Last Peanut

It occurred to little Jimmy Peter one August morning, after the electricity went and video games with it, that he hadn't even opened the chemistry set he'd received from his parents for Christmas.

In the backyard Jimmy tested the Bunsen burner's flame on the chemistry set's instruction book. He smiled with satisfaction as the fifty-five pages of red warnings in 11 languages burned away. No sooner had Jimmy mixed a clear liquid with a thick blue, added just a dash of salt, and heated the concoction, than a monstrous orange cloud wafted from his test tube and was picked up by the wind and carried away. The cloud continued to expand as it departed. He stared at it for a second, but the whole thing rather bored Jimmy, and he went inside to play with the dog.

The cloud soon covered the East coast of the United States, reached the West coast within hours, and had crossed the Pacific by dark. Air raid sirens and emergency broadcast systems around the world were dusted off as people taped their windows and fought over bread and bottled water at the supermarkets. Lines for gas backed traffic up for miles and the price for a gallon nearly doubled. Industry insiders blamed increased demand, but Democrats pointed to a corrupt capitalist economy and decreased support for school lunch programs. Senior Republicans noted that this could all have been avoided if only more people owned guns and taxes were lower.

No one claimed responsibility for the cloud, but by morning there were theories. It was the first strike in a Holy War against the West, or sex, or poorly written sitcoms. This was clearly the work of the religious right, who would never be satisfied until the Ten Commandments were tattooed on the back of every infant's hand at birth. Or it was the Democrats, who were using scare tactics to take money from the nation's struggling corporate executives in order to give poor children the same chance as rich kids to view pornography. The militias warned of UN troops amassing on our northern border—the orange cloud could just be a diversion. Maybe it was a message from outer space, or an unexpected result of greenhouse gases. Some said the Day of Judgment was upon us, others were confirmed in their belief of a Jewish conspiracy, and more than a few were sure the earth was fighting back after years of abuse and that all the endangered species would soon rise up and take control of the world's nuclear arsenals. A woman in Idaho who saw the Virgin Mary in her frozen waffles every other Thursday knew from a reliable source that the orange cloud was Satan's work.

Everyone prepared for the end. Did it matter if this catastrophe was the result of affirmative action, which certainly put unqualified people in charge of dangerous chemicals? And why hold a grudge against wealthy, industrialized nations, just because of their obsession with progress and their disregard for its consequences? None of this would have happened if only everyone spoke English, but now wasn't the time to start problems. So what if the Israelis blamed the Arabs, and fat people blamed thin people, and all of this could be traced, if one looked hard enough, to a dirty joke told by a man to another man in the presence of a woman on the floor of an automobile assembly line? The orange cloud was coming for them all. The cloud penetrated every home, every bomb and emergency shelter, every office, every school. But no one died. No one even got sick. The cloud dissipated, and blue once again dominated the sky. There was wild celebration in the streets, world peace, random acts of kindness, and alternate side of the street parking was suspended.

Then the cloud's evil was realized. Calls came in from farmers all over the world. There were no peanuts. They were gone, melted away. The cloud had left the humans unharmed. The peanuts weren't as lucky. Peanut farmers and peanut manufacturers were ruined, stocks plummeted, brokers threw themselves from office windows or else were gunned down by disgruntled clients. Wasn't this another sign of a federal government, some Republicans wondered, that had spiraled out of control? The medical community was outraged—how could the peanut's untapped medicinal potential be recovered? Hadn't anyone heard of the peanut's ability to cure cancer? And what about the poor? the Democrats asked. Didn't anyone know that peanuts were their main source of protein? Wasn't this just an attempt to keep down developing nations, who depended on the money produced from peanuts for military power? And let's not even mention elephants. How would they survive?

Answers. The nation, the world, demanded an explanation. Satellite spy photography, the FBI, a well-trained German shepherd, a three-minute call to the Psychic Hotline, and a spot on *Unsolved Mysteries* soon traced the orange cloud to little Jimmy Peter's backyard, and he was immediately arrested along with his parents. Accusations of treachery, of treason, soon fell away, and it became clear that Jimmy had acted alone. Daytime talk shows and respected nightly news programs interviewed his teacher, his doctor, the ice cream man in Jimmy's neighborhood, examined the comb his barber used a week earlier on Jimmy's head, checked for radical literature in his school's library. Standardized tests revealed nothing, though a fight he had in the school cafeteria in the first grade indicated hostility and aggressiveness, if not proving the intent to destroy the world's peanut crop.

Parents, they were the problem. Not enough love, or they didn't read to him when he was in the womb, or they neglected to buy him a pony even though he really wanted one and promised to look after it. Jimmy Peter's perversity had to be connected with having two first names. If not that, at least his mother was at fault for trying marijuana once before she met Jimmy's father. Not that good old Dad was off the hook. Wasn't it Mr. Peter who made Jimmy wash behind his ears before going to bed? How could such people be allowed to have children?

What kind of parents bought their kid a chemistry set, anyway? What was wrong with television and computer games? Environmentalists demanded that chemistry sets be outlawed, or at least a five-day waiting period be established, so a background check and mental stability test could be performed before purchases. The National Chemistry Association called the demand political grandstanding, noting that chemicals don't kill peanuts—

people do. Besides, they said, when chemistry sets are outlawed, only outlaws will have chemistry sets.

Just when it seemed that all was lost, it was announced that a peanut had survived the orange cloud. There was one peanut left, and it was apparently immune to the effects of little Jimmy Peter's experiment. The world held its breath. The last peanut was immediately transported by ground, escorted by helicopters, army jeeps, and a New York City cab driver, to Washington, D.C., where it was presented to the assembled leaders of the world. Scientists explained that they could engineer peanuts from the lone survivor. The new peanuts would have the same immunity. In almost no time, they assured the many presidents, prime ministers, kings, evil dictators, and military strong men in attendance, the world's peanut supply would be replaced.

The investigation had uncovered no malice, no intent, on Jimmy's part, and had concluded that it was just an accident born from the natural curiosity of an eight-year-old boy. What a learning experience, the President thought, to allow the boy to acknowledge his mistake to all the world. There would be photo opportunities, and the President would be portrayed as a forgiving, sensitive man. It was an election year, and Congress agreed. Both parties were sure they had decided to forgive Jimmy first. There were protests from the peanut industry, claims of exploitation from child welfare groups, movie offers from four major studios. Jimmy and his parents were brought into the great hall.

They were led to the podium, where the last peanut sat on a plate beneath a crystal cover. Cameras were trained on Jimmy, who had to stand on a chair to reach the podium's microphone. Before the apology, the President asked everyone to close their eyes and bow their heads in silent prayer, to give thanks to whomever they thanked when great tragedy is averted. The room was still, the universe at peace, leaders from every nation in the world prayed together.

Just then, as he quietly removed the crystal cover from the plate, it occurred to little Jimmy Peter that he'd never even tasted a peanut.

Bob Sullivan
Top Ten Rejected Major League Baseball Expansion Teams

10. The Vermont Teddy Bears
9. The Lansing Boils
8. The Pittsburgh Pansies
7. The West Virginia Cousins
6. The San Francisco Smoothboys
5. The Albuquerque Herky-Jerkies
4. The Baton Rouge Applicators
3. The Tennessee Waltzers
2. The Salt Lake City Bigamists

And the Number 1 Rejected Major League Baseball Expansion Team is...

1. The Winston-Salem Phlegm

C.P. Kaiser
Reach Out and Punch Someone

When we talk about progress, we need to distinguish between technical and personal, because, unfortunately, technical advancement doesn't always promise personal improvement. This is no more evident than with cell phone (ab)users. The newest rage (double entendre intended) is commuters, shoppers, symphony patrons, etc., punching out their cell-phoned brethren who haven't the couth to speak softly or privately. How many times have you huffed silently as your self-important neighbor on the bus, train, or subway nibbled on his Nokia loud enough to crack your dentures, or, at least, offend your decency? I've seen entire boxcars of passengers become as stony faced as Joan Rivers after someone's cell phone conversation became a loud recounting of sexual exploits.

At a recent theater performance, while waiting in the intermission restroom line, several of us were witness to an incredible spectacle. Not only was this guy blabbering on his cell phone about something that could have waited, but he then took said precious conversation into the stall with him and continued to blabber. One patron of the arts remarked, "Let's hope he flushes that damn phone down, too."

My wife was in a stall recently when a voice wafted over the top, inviting her to comment on her day. She thought, Do I know this person? Is she talking to me? And then she realized that her bladder-relieving companion was on a cell phone. My wife said this woman must have been double jointed because she griped and wiped without missing a beat.

Do cell phones really fulfill a need, or do they, like so many other new technologies, merely offer a cure to an anxiety they themselves create? The feeling that we have to be connected all the time, the fear of being unavailable, has developed in direct proportion to the technology that is its remedy. According to one survey, 39% of people said they would answer a cell phone call in the bathroom; the survey didn't note how many people would *call* from the crapper. But I've heard stories of salespeople making calls from the stalls.

"Not long ago, everyone was commenting on how the Walkman privatized the public world, turning people inward so they could waltz or rock through their community without being a part of it," writes syndicated columnist Ellen Goodman. "Well, the mobile phone promotes a verbal gated community; you can shut out everyone around you. It's become a personal accessory that allows the oblivious to live in their own world."

But cell phoners are *not* living in their own world and that's what disgruntled bystanders are trying to teach them. Reports of violence against cellular loudmouths are making national headlines. One report from the Associated Press says that doctors in Toronto have treated both mobile phone talkers and irritated bystanders for black eyes and cracked ribs after eruptions of cell phone rage. In those incidents, I imagine the person with the cell phone called 911.

Last year, a Hiroshima man angered by a conductor's request to stop using his cellular phone retaliated by jumping off the train and blocking the tracks of an oncoming train, which had to slam on its brakes. He demanded money for the phone interruption. Police charged him with extortion. The most celebrated cell phone rage incident, however, has to be when actor Laurence Fishburne, as Othello on Broadway, broke character and asked an audience member to please turn off the fucking phone.

Again, Ellen Goodman writes: "I admire the guerrilla tactic of the New York commuter who sat beside so many lawyers conducting business that he finally made a tape recording that blared, 'Your attorney-client privilege is no longer privileged!'"

Cell phone rage may very well become the social controversy of the new millennium. The battle lines seem to have been drawn. On one side, you have people who embrace constant communication; on the other, you have people who want their personal boundaries respected. Caught in between are the business owners and public officials who are trying to accommodate everyone.

Some businesses and public places have devised ways to deal with the phenomenon. Signs stating No Cell Phones are springing up all over, including in restaurants, theaters, museums, libraries, hospitals, and doctors' offices. There are even Cell Phone Free Zones being designated, such as on the San Francisco to Sausalito ferries.

It's hard to believe that San Francisco Mayor Willie Brown, a one-man corporate band, would do anything to upset the Starbucks crowd, but he's come perilously close with his ban of cell phones from city hall meetings. And a number of fine eating establishments in the Bay Area have banned cell phones as well, including Berkeley's Chez Panisse (whose chef Alice Waters single-handedly started the fresh, locally-grown veggie craze in the 1970s).

To combat the recent rash of commuter/consumer rage against the wireless machines, several manufacturers have started campaigns to educate cell phone users about etiquette. In July, Nokia handed out Quiet Zone stickers as part of Cell Phone Courtesy Week in San Diego.

The number of cell phone users is nearing 100 million and at any moment 10% of them are offending someone. Cell phones have been called the boom boxes of the '90s, as far as their annoying presence in normally quiet settings. They're also being referred to as the cigarettes of the new millennium, because users are being forced more and more to occupy "exempt" spaces, out of the way of offended bystanders.

What seems to annoy people most, perhaps, is not the disturbance of sound waves as much as the disturbance of the social hierarchy. The cell phone has a way of minimizing the importance of the group. A guy on his cell phone is basically telling people around him that they don't matter, that he must be very important. "No other technology allows you to be elsewhere so casually while in the company of others," says Lavi Lewis in Air Canada's *en Route* magazine. "Cellphone Guy does more than just erode the line between the public and the private. He continually makes a statement on his surroundings, blind to his effect on others, until everyone around him feels subtly rebuffed."

We all know that Cellphone Guy or Girl isn't any more important or busy or focused than the rest of us, and that's probably what makes us mad. *We* can wait to call our friends, *we* can leave work in the office, and *we* can keep our private business private. So why can't Cellphone Guy? "He's just a modern-day overgrown teenager," Lewis says, "who's figured out how to leave the house while remaining in his bedroom."

In an Internet poll listing the top 200 most annoying uses of cell phones, the winning entry was for the call in the movie theater that begins with "Oh, nothing. You?" My favorite, though, was number 8. That's the couple comparing prices in two grocery stores on their phones. At 87 cents a minute, they're saving 5 cents on cornflakes. Now, *they* really do deserve to be punched out.

David "Preacher" Slocum
American-Americans

There is a disturbing trend in America, one that seems harmless on the face of it but is indicative of greater ills.

In the early '60s, groups like the Black Panthers and the Nation of Islam were searching for an identity, while at the same time distancing themselves from mainstream America. They disdained the terms *Negro* and *colored* as demeaning and coined the designation *African-American*.

They embraced their African roots and the heritage that they felt America had kept from them. In the still openly racist era of the 1960s, this was seen by many blacks as a way to show solidarity and present a unified face to the world. The whites of the time saw this as yet another way that blacks were different and were sure that this was a fad that would fade in time.

It didn't fade. In fact, Americans of Mexican descent, Italian descent, and Irish descent picked it up. Today, you would be hard pressed to find an ethnic group that does not identify itself primarily by its ethnic roots.

Doesn't sound like a calamity, does it?

The problem is that the identity of the individual is being absorbed into the sub-group. People are beginning to believe that their worth as individuals, their futures, and their pasts are connected only to their ethnic identity. They are forgetting that, first and foremost, they are Americans.

America has long prided itself on being a melting pot of ethnic diversity (even if it has not always been equal to this ideal), a place where people could come together and become Americans despite their differences. People the world over risked life, limb, and fortune to travel to America, secure in the knowledge that this was the greatest country in the world. More recently, Americans have turned those welcome arms into barbed-wire barriers and armed patrols. We are turning away immigrants by the boatload.

We have stopped being one great nation, united against the world, and have become a nation of sects. We have so divided ourselves that the emphasis is not on the plurality of being American, but on our individual heritage. Mexican-Americans are Mexican first, African-Americans are African first, and few are those who even call themselves just Americans.

It used to be a matter of pride to be an American. When we pulled Europe's ashes out of the fires of World Wars I and II, we marched down the streets with our heads held high, proud that we were Americans.

When we stopped being proud of being just ordinary Americans and instead embraced our hyphenated status, we lost something precious. We stopped looking out for our neighbors and started looking inward, concentrating not on what we owe to the society that embraced our differences, but on what that society owes us.

Scott Stein
That Other National Pastime

It is a sunny summer day on Manhattan's West Side, and the sidewalks are teeming with people on their way to the park or walking for its own sake. The air is still, yet fresh, and even white clouds don't dare challenge the clear blue sky. It is a day to be outside and breathing deep.

Today, despite roaring cars and more than a few honking horns directed at the rushing people ignorant or blind to instructions from traffic lights, New York is at peace, maybe for the first time—ever. Just as I realize that I am a privileged witness (along with perhaps nine million others) to an occurrence as rare to New Yorkers as snow is to residents of Miami Beach, the peace is shattered.

A couple on a two-seated bicycle barrels through the intersection I have just crossed and jumps the curb. Everyone darts left and right but one man, strolling still as if the city hadn't shrugged off its peace like a too large coat. The bicycle hits him from behind, its front wheel finding a comfortable spot on the back of his calf. The bicycle is stopped; its momentum has shifted to the man.

He is hopping on his left leg, the one the bicycle has spared, and he is cursing. But he has not fallen to the ground or been run over—he is fortunate to be uninjured. The man does not feel fortunate and glances back at the couple on the bicycle now at rest with accusatory eyes, but says nothing.

The couple, a man and woman in khakis, is sorry. They didn't mean to hit the man. They didn't mean to hit anyone. But these two-seated bicycles are as hard to maneuver as you'd guess. Is he OK? Can they do anything to help?

The man isn't listening. He's already on his way again. Limping. He has important plans—that much is indisputable. With effort he limps another five feet and turns into a doorway. Only five feet from his destination and a bicycle slams his leg. Dumb luck.

But the proud American is determined and not easily deterred, and limps right through the doorway of the shop with a blackened window that keeps minors and the easily offended from seeing the products offered for sale inside. In bright green letters on the window are the words: Adult Videos.

Which only goes to show that—forget about baseball—what Americans really love is their pornography.

Ari McKee
The Gods Are Taking a Meeting

Do you yearn for a time when things were simple and straightforward, when folks listened to a higher authority and obeyed holy writ without question? Do you long for the old-time religious faith of your forefathers? We're talking *real* old-time, you understand. Not those Johnny-come-latelies, the Druids, or even that new group, what are they again—Christians? Forget the fly-by-night Buddhists or those postmodernist Muslims. I mean *way* back. Back to the good old days when the gods were in business and that meant business.

That's right, gods with an "s." It's time to bring gods, lots of gods, back into the classroom. It's not such a farfetched idea. Thanks to Disney every school kid knows Hercules, son of Zeus and Hera. We've never forgotten Poseidon, god of the sea and the only person not afraid of Shelly Winters. You'll be acquainted with the whole clique before you know it.

Naturally, we'll have to do a little modifying to bring them up to speed. They may be immortal, but they're not exactly up-to-the-minute. For example, protecting hunters isn't the full-time job it used to be. The goddess Diana might be interested in taking over holiday shopping or personal injury lawsuits. Hermes, the messenger god, could branch out into telecommunications. Martha—oops, I mean Minerva, the Roman goddess of handicrafts—I can see her expanding across the whole interior design and do-it-yourself realm. She could get somebody under her who just did decks. Homedepoteus, maybe.

OK, it's starting to become obvious that everything I know about ancient history is on Fox right after *X-Files*, but that doesn't mean I'm not a true believer. Over the years, I've come to see that polytheism can explain everything. Like how I never win anything, even gumballs, but how all of last winter I was enveloped in a state of parking grace with space after space of unoccupied asphalt opening up just for me, right next to the handicapped spot. Or how I am always, *always* on the bad side of the Leaving-Your-Headlights-On god, but how the Locking-Your-Keys-Inside-The-Car god has never once dissed me. Or how Aphrodite, the goddess of love, made it possible for my husband and I to perform our conjugal duties, day after day and week after week—to completion—for *two solid years* without the baby waking up. It was uncanny. It almost makes up for the grocery goddess, Demeter, that bitch, who gives me a bad shopping cart every time.

If you think about it, polytheism would answer a lot of eternal theological questions, like the whole "bad things happening to good people" problem. Plane crash? The god of air travel just woke up on the wrong side of the temple. Natural disaster? Some jerk, probably Ares, left the seat up at Mount Olympus and Gaea, the earth goddess (never a stable personality to begin with), has a little venting to do. Each god is different, they're all flawed, every one of them has a bone to pick.

The main argument against a classical comeback is that the ancient gods weren't always fair and just, but it's important to remember that this was the *ultimate* market economy. Simple equation: six crispy virgins buys you one decent harvest. If the gods never delivered on these deals, they'd put themselves right out of business. Of course, like any trading venture, there're risks. Occasionally, mortals encountered "I'll scratch your back, you smite mine" circumstances, but it was nothing that a couple of barbecued oxen couldn't fix.

Then that goody-goody Moses came along with He Who Cannot Be Bribed and everything went to hell. All that omnipotence was consolidated into one hard-to-reach central office (Um, excuse me? *When* did you say that switchboard would be up? Wasn't it right after the Dark Ages?) run by those ingratiating seraphim who only tell Him what He wants to hear. We've all heard the rumors about the complaint box being emptied every morning before the Big Guy comes in. We've even tried apologizing for the Age of Reason. We got nowhere. What's a mortal to do?

Go on. Start small. Burn a dollar bill in an ashtray for Eros while your date's in the restroom. Make a discreet toast to Dionysus at the bar. Who's to say? It couldn't hurt. Still skeptical? Of course there's no proof, but who has proof of anything B.C.? Who knows if Rome fell? Maybe it was pushed! Just think about it. If it's too weird, don't even consider them "gods." Think of them as a holy human relations department. Just like personnel, they're folks who can't take credit for the whole system, but who have the power to make you wish you only lived as long as your average 3rd century gladiator. So, in a situation where another futile memo would be appropriate, instead take a personal leave day and cremate two ritually-slaughtered chickens and a bushel of bulgur wheat. Go on—light the pyre, offer up a prayer to the god or two of your choice, and watch things finally start to go your way. That is, if your particular god feels like it, if he hasn't just broken up with his sister, for example, or if you're not standing next to someone he's trying to kill.

On second thought, maybe this isn't such a good idea. Too many variables. In fact, it all makes me a little nostalgic for the *real* good old days, when you could just threaten someone with a pterodactyl femur and that would be the end of it.

Marni Schwartz
Eyes Wide Shut? They Should Be

It had been advertised as Stanley Kubrick's posthumous masterpiece. Advertisements spoke of the movie using modest words like *decadent, sensual, divine,* and *spellbinding*. It starred Tom Cruise and Nicole Kidman, beautiful people loved by Hollywood and, supposedly, the rest of the world. But what is the real deal on Kubrick's *Eyes Wide Shut*?

I went to see *Eyes Wide Shut* during a late afternoon showing on the Saturday of its opening weekend. The theater was large and crammed full of people. Due to the early afternoon show time there was a strong smell of vinegar and oatmeal, the perfume of the perspiring elderly. The other patrons were speaking to each other in the hushed buzzing sound that only occurs in movie theaters, as Kenny G blared from the speakers, while a hundred people tried to unscramble Blair Underwood's name and decide if they should go out to the lobby and grab themselves a snack. The theater did not promote jingling cans for any foundation, so the movie began quickly.

The movie opened on a nude scene of Nicole Kidman; there was a lot of salivation in the audience, but before judging it as sexual arousal I remembered the age of my movie-going compatriots. We were introduced to Tom and Nicole as a, gasp, married couple. Chris Issak sang "Baby Did a Bad, Bad Thing" as the sex symbols dressed and had casual conversation. The music ebbed and the audience got a glimpse of Nicole Kidman on the toilet. Nicole Kidman on the toilet? Does that image evoke sexuality? Does the American—scratch that—international entertainment audience really want to see a redhead on the toilet? Do we stay up at night wondering if Nicole Kidman wipes herself from front to back, or back to front? These are the questions that I was faced with during the first ten minutes of *Eyes Wide Shut*.

After the couple left their home to attend a black-tie party, I lost track and interest in this movie. The following two hours were a blur of nudity, only female nudity aside from a few shots of Mr. Cruise's back, and profanity. Let me clarify something: I am a child of the seventies. I have grown up with nudity, violence, cursing, and a basic NC-17 world. But the sheer quantity of profanity and the cherub-faced actors spouting it shocked me. The constant nudity ceased overwhelming me after an hour—from that point on I expected all of the women onscreen to be nude. After I came back from a run to the bathroom, I was astounded to find the audience still clothed.

Eventually, after what felt like hours, the movie came to an abrupt close. The last word of Kubrick's final piece was *fuck*. That's right, *fuck*. Nicole Kidman turns her face toward her husband, of the screen and (formerly) of the real world, and tells him that they need to fuck. Not have sex, not make love, no horizontal mambo, not even a request to create the beast with two backs. With that word leaving Nicole Kidman's mouth and reverberating through the theater, the screen turns black.

The theme music played and the credits rolled. The theater was silent; no one was moving. After a solid thirty seconds, which seems like hours when you are sitting in a theater with a few hundred people, we began to shuffle out. As we stood outside in the sun, our eyes adjusting to the light, people began talking. They spoke in the tones of the elderly. That is, they spoke at a normal volume, parroting the naughty words, like *fuck*, *naked*, and *sex*.

Eyes Wide Shut was quite a snappy title; I applaud Kubrick for that. However, I feel that the rest of his movie was no more than over three hours of filthy language, naked women, countless sexual positions, and fake shots of Greenwich Village filmed in England. For some people this alone constitutes a reason to see this movie. To those people, I say it's not worth it. You can see all the naked pictures of Nicole Kidman on the Internet, and learn the rest through careful reading of the *Kama Sutra* and *Hooked on Phonics* (the *Goodfellas* edition).

The real deal on *Eyes Wide Shut* is that beneath all of the vulgarity it is a boring movie with a pseudo-symbolic plot and message that gets lost in a sea of breasts and Hollywood icons. I hope Stanley Kubrick is remembered for *Dr. Strangelove* and *A Clockwork Orange* instead. Kubrick was an incredible man with a creative mind that opened the motion-picture field to many new ideas and lines of thought. Perhaps Kubrick's final film will spawn more new views into filmmaking. Maybe the future holds more scenes of women urinating and propositioning men in toy stores. If this is so, I only have one suggestion: For the love of God, throw something in for the ladies. Perhaps the three hours would have gone by faster if I could have seen a few male provocative poses—we all need a piece of the pie sometime or another.

Suzanne Hakanen
And the Beating Goes On

The Time: Any election year
The Place: Any strategic location for a presidential debate
The Event: A debate
The Participants: SAL SIDESTEP and SIDNEY SKIRT, two presidential hopefuls

SIDESTEP: I think the biggest problem facing the United States today is violence. My first priority is to set up a task force to curb violence, because my platform is strictly and rigorously opposed to violence.

SKIRT: Well, my platform is also opposed to violence. I question your plan to set up a task force to curb violence because this task force, no doubt, will be violent. I am opposed to using violence to curb violence. I'm for peace.

SIDESTEP: I'm for peace too. That's why I want to set up an anti-violence task force.

SKIRT: Well, I'm *really* against violence because I'm not only anti-violence, I'm anti the anti-violence task force. What I support is the pro-peace task force, which, you must realize, is much more anti-violence than an anti-violence task force could ever be.

SIDESTEP: The ultimate goal of the anti-violence task force is peace.

SKIRT: Well, if you were as much against violence as I am, you would find an anti-violent vehicle for dealing with violence.

SIDESTEP: I told you that I'm against violence, so now I'll tell you what I'm for, and what the American public is for: more police. My platform totally supports increasing the police presence in our cities and towns. Nothing says "peacetime" like an increased police presence.

SKIRT: Not only would I put more police in the cities and towns, I'd put them in the sports arenas and the public transportation depots. I'm for peace in the streets, on the turf, and in the subway.

SIDESTEP: This issue of police support really points to another issue: children. I am for protecting our children. Increasing police presence in our cities and towns is the best way to protect our children, and I'm going to make that one of my top priorities: protecting our children through an increased police presence. Along with lower taxes.

SKIRT: As a father of five, I can honestly say that there is nothing more important to me than child safety. I'm talking about safety from crime, from kidnappers and pedophiles, from fire, from toys that have small removable parts that could become lodged in a child's throat. My agenda focuses on controlling and eliminating these dangers, thus creating a safer environment for our children. That's what's most important to me: the children. I also plan to cut federal taxes.

SIDESTEP: The best way to protect the children is to educate them, and if I've said this once, I've said it a thousand times: I support education and I will do everything in my power to make sure every child gets a thorough, comprehensive, government-sponsored education. Provided for by a generous, though less tax-generated, federal budget.

SKIRT: If you asked my constituents to choose an adjective to describe me, no doubt they'd pick "Pro-Education." If I'm elected president, I'm sure I'll be known for generations as "The Education President." I'm for education and I've always been for education and for people who stand for education. If you want to know what I'm against, I'll tell you what I'm against. I'm against drugs.

SIDESTEP: I'm against drugs and I'm against people who sell drugs. Especially people who sell drugs to children. What I'm for is an increased police presence to arrest drug dealers and put them in jail. I'm also for offering rewards to people who turn in drug dealers. That and lower taxes.

SKIRT: Well, I'm really for educating children about drugs and about what can happen to them if they sell drugs. Remember when you were a kid and the policeman came to your school with a big case with samples of little pills and pot and all the drugs that are bad for kids? I'll create an increased police presence, thus providing children with more education about the effects of drug use. This action will address my top priorities: education, drugs, police, and children. And taxes.

SKIRT: I'm against drugs but I'm also against the illegal search and seizure of drugs.

SIDESTEP: Well, I'm against anything illegal!

SKIRT: You know what I'm really against? I'm really against illegal dumping of toxic waste in the environment. You know, that's a really important issue that just does not receive enough press coverage: the environment.

SIDESTEP: I'm really for cleaning up the environment. One way to eliminate illegal dumping of toxic waste in the environment is to increase police presence in remote areas where criminals usually dump toxic waste. I'm not only for peace in the streets, I'm for clean in the green.

SKIRT: You know what I am really against? Serial killers. I am so totally against serial killers. You know, the remote areas that are popular toxic-waste dumping grounds are also used as body-disposal sites by serial killers. If I'm elected, I'll make sure those police in remote areas are doing double duty: not only will they monitor illegal toxic waste dumping, but they'll keep an eye out for serial killers too.

SIDESTEP: I'm against serial killers, but I'm for the victims of serial killers. The families of the victims of serial killers, I mean. I'm for supporting the families of victims of serial killers.

SKIRT: I'm for finding a cure for cancer, AIDS, and the common cold.

SIDESTEP: I'm for keeping diseases like smallpox, anthrax, and leprosy from rearing their ugly heads in the continental United States.

SKIRT: I'm against all diseases.

SIDESTEP: I'm against social diseases including poverty, crime, tax evasion, and fraud.

SKIRT: I'm against global warming, rainforest destruction, acid rain, and using children as unwitting test subjects for experimental drugs.

SIDESTEP: Well, I am really for the environment and I am going to make that one of my priorities: the environment. That and lower taxes...

And the beating goes on and on and on and on...

Scott Stein
Life Might Imitate Art, But it isn't Worth as Much (Just Ask NATO)

A question often posed by amateur philosophers and people with too much time on their hands is, If you had to choose to rescue one thing from a burning building, and in the building was a baby and the sole existing copy of the complete works of William Shakespeare, which would you save?

This passes for profundity among those whose only other big dilemma is whether taking another bong hit will interfere with making it to class the next morning. It's the perfect mental challenge for stoned undergraduates or pseudo-intellectual graduate students, since, like college, it bears little relation to real life. Unfortunately, people trained by questions such as these run the world.

In a low point for even the human species, this hypothetical question was made real and answered by NATO's air campaign against Yugoslavia in 1999. Throughout the conflict, whenever a stray NATO missile took out the Chinese embassy or portions of various hospitals or residential neighborhoods, NATO and the United States hurriedly apologized. But the allies with their shield of moral certainty pointed out each time that, though these errors were regrettable, there was a substantial difference between themselves and the Serbs, who killed innocent people intentionally and not because smart bombs just weren't as smart as everyone remembers them being.

Justifications were not limited to misfires and bad aim. After taking out a bridge or office building with very expensive missiles and killing innocent civilians, NATO defended the attacks as being on "legitimate military targets." Yugoslav President Milosevic's home was also a legitimate military target. Though a residence, NATO claimed it was being used as a command and control center for the Serbian military, and blew it up.

Like the many who lost their lives on the legitimate target of a bridge or in office buildings, the presidential residence's servants and groundskeepers and other ordinary people not responsible for mass killings were torn to pieces or burned alive by NATO missiles. Legitimate targets are legitimate targets, and there were no apologies from NATO or the United States for the deaths their missiles brought.

However, another presidential residence was not a legitimate target, because it contained an original painting by Rembrandt. No other reason was given for targeting one home and not the other; both functioned as residences for Milosevic, both could be seen as command and control centers, and destroying both would contribute to the regime's sense of insecurity and might hurt the Serbs' morale. One contained only human beings and the other contained a few feet of canvas, probably a pretty frame, and a small amount of paint arranged in a pattern pleasing to the eye and perhaps the soul. NATO chose to spare the canvas and exterminate the people.

A very valuable work of art by a very famous painter was judged to be more important than human life, innocent of the crimes for which this non-declared war was supposedly being fought. NATO undermined its claim to the moral highroad in this instance as surely as in any other in the conflict.

Which brings us back to our hypothetical question and our stoned undergraduates who one day might go on to make decisions for NATO or the United States. Anyone who chooses to save the complete works of William Shakespeare over a baby doesn't deserve to read *Hamlet*, and is incapable of appreciating it anyway. No one with any understanding of real art would choose a painting as the reason to save some people and kill others.

No painting is more important than human life. Anyone who claims otherwise is missing the point of art in the first place. Art exists because of humans and is created by humans. To have lasting value, art must give joy to humans and/or enlighten them about what being human means. Human life is the point of art, not the other way around.

To write the way Shakespeare did, to deal in humanity with such honesty and beauty and drama, one must have a perfect sense of the value of human life, even given its failings. If he were alive to know about the choosing of a Rembrandt over human life, of his own works over an innocent baby, Shakespeare's response might once again capture the wonder of the potential of humanity mixed with even greater sadness and outrage at its continued failure to live up to it:

> What a piece of work is a man! How noble in reason! How infinite in faculty! In form, in moving, how express and admirable! In action how like an angel! In apprehension how like a god! The beauty of the world! The paragon of animals! And yet, to me, what is this quintessence of dust? Man delights not me; no, nor woman neither.... (*Hamlet*)

Kevin Bolshaw
Squirrel-Buggery

It happened on the next to last day; Angus and I were walking back to our lean-to late in the afternoon hoping to roll a fat one and relax our aching joints on our air mattresses when we spied two big ugly burr heads in flannel shirts burying some orange peels in the dirt under their lean-to. There were a couple of chip bags and beer cans scattered about so we stopped to share the code of the "pack in and pack out" wilderness with them.

"You shouldn't bury that there, buddy."

"Why not, it's biodegradable," said jock number one, revealing a sizable gap between his front teeth and the piggy close-set eyes of the hopelessly inbred.

"Well, it takes many years to go. Besides, it could attract animals to your lean-to."

"I'm not afraid of no bears."

Angus assumed a serious look. "Tell him, Jeremy."

"It's not the bears, it's the squirrels."

"Squirrels?! Right."

"No, really, they'll get your food. And they can be rabid."

"Oh, thank you for your cautionary tale, Mr. Woodsman." Smoke, laughter, and the fetid stench of Slim Jims issued forth from the gaping maw of the second goober. I said nothing more, and we walked away.

"Why didn't you tell him?" asked Angus as we settled ourselves down, swinging our feet back and forth in front of the lean-to.

"Let them find out the hard way," I sneered.

Fifteen minutes later the screams began. There was a growing rustling in the brush and the guy with the gap teeth came down the path. He appeared to be floating off the ground about six inches, but in reality he was supported by a herd of squirrels. He screamed as his head bounced off one of the many granite boulders along the trail. He passed us almost before we knew it, headed up the trail toward the Saddle. We would not have been sure except his orange hunter's cap fell off, marking his passage. Soon after, his buddy puffed up.

"Did you see which way he went?"

"Yup."

"C'mon, we gotta go get him, we gotta find him!"

"No sense in running," I said. "You'll never catch him. Get the ranger. Tell him to call for help, enough for a carryout rescue."

"B-B-But that's only for life-threatening injuries!"

"That's right. Don't worry, we'll find him. They're usually just off the trail in these cases. Angus, get the first aid kit. Now, go get the ranger."

We set off at a brisk clip toward the Saddle and after about twenty minutes we heard the horrible screams, the kind that can only be the result of squirrel-buggery, the most fiendish of all of cruel Mother Nature's punishments. The bloodcurdling wails spurred us to greater speed, and our heads were filled with gory visions of what we might find.

We followed the howls to a flat spot along the trail and plunged off into a thicket on the side nearest Hamelin Peak. In a small clearing we observed a dreadful example of wilderness justice: The poor sod from lean-to one was being held face down by thirty or so of the usually cute and shy red squirrels from the Chimney Pond campground while a long line of their fellows were taking turns diving into his rectum from an overhanging birch bough. The pants had been neatly scissored from knee to belt loop. Each squirrel leapt headlong into his poopchute, teeth gnashing and clawed forelegs flailing. By the time we got there, the damage was considerable, more than a flagrant litterbug deserved, so I pulled my portable air horn from my pocket and loosed a blast.

"Alright, you rotten bastards, that's enough!" The vengeful rodents scattered, but not before making a few menacing surges toward us. I covered the half-delirious camper with my sweater (vowing never to wear it again) and held his hand while Angus joyfully poured peroxide.

"You're lucky we got here," he crowed in his Australian accent, "you'd 'ave been a goner!"

We waited for the ranger and tried to ignore the moaning.

C.P. Kaiser
Churchgoing Man Kills 13

When 42-year-old Mark O. Barton went on a summer murder spree in Atlanta, Georgia, in 1999, bludgeoning his wife and children, shooting some co-workers, and finally killing himself, the print media chronicled the grisly affair detail by detail. First they described the murder scenes; then they delved into Barton's history, revealing a similar murder six years earlier in which his then wife and mother-in-law were bludgeoned to death; then they described the quiet Atlanta suburb where the Bartons lived. Inevitably, the stories would end with neighbors describing Barton as "a quiet, churchgoing man who stayed to himself."

Interesting that the mainstream media attributed little importance to Barton being a churchgoing man. Normally, the last few paragraphs of a newspaper account contain the least important information, ready to be deleted by a harried editor looking for advertising space. In many areas of the country, the reading public was possibly deprived of knowing that Mr. Barton was a churchgoing man. I think it's important that we know that after 42 years of Christian upbringing, after 42 years of viewing Jesus' asphyxiated, bloodied body spiked to a cross, after 42 years of threats of eternal damnation, this Christian man snapped.

Had Barton belonged to a less mainstream cult (one not as well accepted as a major Christian religion), I guarantee the headlines of each media report would have been: "Cult Member Kills 13." The media would have inundated us with cult experts gnawing on the dead bones of past religious discrepancies. We would have been subjected to old footage of Jonestown, Waco, and the Hale-Bopp suicides. Christian religious leaders would have seized the opportunity for big-time fundraising.

Why are lesser-accepted cults called to blame when a member goes on a violent rampage, but in this case, the Christian church is not? Who decides which churches are and are not cults? Should we not question a group that professes to eat the body and drink the blood of its leader? The number of murderers belonging to mainstream religious organizations far outnumbers those belonging to smaller cults. Yet, the perception is that these so-called cults are the more dangerous to society.

Imagine a newspaper account with this sentence in the last paragraph and no one batting an eyelash: "He was a quiet man who attended cult rituals regularly." It would never happen. It's an impossible scenario because our mainstream media has chosen to accept as normal the bloodthirsty rituals of Christian-based religions and ostracize and demonize those who choose to worship outside this mainstream.

Reader Comments

—hmargolit responds to "Churchgoing Man Kills 13" by C.P. Kaiser.

I disagree that Christian religions get a free ride in the press. You believe that there is very little reference to these religions by the media when a member goes astray or commits an evil deed. There has been no bigger spotlight by the media on church or organizational misdeeds and sexual deviation than that shone on the Catholic Church over the past decade. Also, how many times have we been bombarded by the media about financial corruption by various Christian sects?

I am not a Christian, but I really believe that Christianity has had nothing but bad press over the years. Catholicism, especially, has been maligned because of the doctrines and excesses of a minute number of priests. I believe that it is time to respect all beliefs, rituals, and doctrines, even those that we believe are ridiculous. If one person or a multitude believe in a religion that does not cause physical or mental harm, then we have no right to cast aspersions on that belief.

—C.P. Kaiser responds to hmargolit's comments on his "Churchgoing Man Kills 13."

I didn't say that Christian religions get a totally free ride in the press. I focused on one aspect of mainstream media coverage that I believe is biased against smaller bands of worshippers, namely, referring to them as *cults*, a derisive term when used in the mainstream media.

In the beginning centuries of the Christian era, the Romans referred to the followers of the teachings of Jesus of Nazareth as renegades, rebels, heretics, and cult members, because the new Christian religious practices fell outside accepted Roman religious behavior. But the cunning, greedy Catholic Church quickly appropriated the indigenous religious celebrations as its own and, within a relatively short time, Roman Catholicism became the accepted religion.

The problem with that scenario is that we are not the Roman Empire and we don't have a state-sanctioned religion (on paper anyway). So my main question is, where does the mainstream media get the right to slander some religious practices while upholding others? If we were truly a tolerant nation, David Koresh would be alive today—perhaps jailed on some weapons charges, but alive.

I applaud the reporting of sexual misconduct within the ranks of Catholic priests; I welcome investigative reports of financial misdeeds among the Christian power hierarchy. One has to wonder, however, why it's taken so long for these "sins" (the Vatican never calls them crimes) to be uncovered and revealed. I believe it is because the mainstream media has blessed the major Christian religions, which in turn wield their awesome power over government and community leaders, in effect, creating a "no-fly zone" in which no reporter may investigate.

I personally think all religion is shit, a byproduct of the paranoia and fear fed to the masses by those who wish to remain in power. I have a constitutional right to believe that, as do the mainstreamers have a right to their beliefs. However, I do believe that, if left unchecked, mainstream religions and their minions will degrade lesser-accepted religious practices. And that is what we must always guard against.

—Alex responds to "Churchgoing Man Kills 13" by C.P. Kaiser.

I must take issue with one of C.P. Kaiser's statements in his reply to a reader's comment. Mr. Kaiser wrote, "If we were truly a tolerant nation, David Koresh would be alive today—perhaps jailed on some weapons charges, but alive."

Actually, if we were a truly tolerant nation, or if our law enforcement agencies were run by people with a bit more common sense, David Koresh might be alive, but he would be serving several consecutive twenty-year sentences for raping the daughters of several of his followers, including a couple of victims as young as eleven. Or he might be dead at the hands of some of his less depraved fellow prisoners—men who rape little girls are often murdered in prison.

Either way, I'm getting sick and tired of articles about the Branch Davidian fiasco that ignore the fact that Koresh was not merely the leader of an apocalyptic cult but a child-molester. That to me is the single most salient aspect of the man, and while I grieve for his followers who died in the fire, and for the agents who were killed in the initial, misguided raid, I fondly hope that Koresh himself suffered as much pain and terror in the inferno he created as he had inflicted upon his victims.

—C.P. Kaiser responds to Alex's comments on his "Churchgoing Man Kills 13."

I'm all for the democratic judicial system prosecuting Koresh on rape, statutory rape, and child abuse charges, or any other violation of the law. I just have a problem with our government's method of serving its summons, the force, of which, is directly proportional to the mainstream's acceptance or disapproval of that particular group's beliefs and practices (witness the MOVE bombing by the Philadelphia police). When was the last time we sent FBI and ATF agents into a rectory to abscond a Catholic priest with a history of molesting young boys? I personally don't agree with Koresh's religious philosophy (or his love of the Second Amendment), but as I understand the law, there's nothing illegal about being the leader of an apocalyptic faith. And I believe it was Koresh's religious beliefs, not his sexual crimes, that drove our officials to send in an army of tax-supported armed thugs, who wanted just as much to rid their quiet communities of this so-called bizarre religious threat. If being an apocalyptic leader is that dangerous, our jails should be filled with reverends, bishops, cardinals, popes, and mother superiors (although plenty of those religionists populate our penal system, it is usually for reasons other than apocalypticism).

I don't want physically dangerous people living in my community if they pose an illegal or potentially illegal threat, and I wonder why it took the law so long to prosecute Koresh on several outstanding charges. But those FBI agents, the Bureau of Alcohol, Tobacco and Firearms, U.S. senators, congress people, attorney generals, and presidents work for me in my democracy. As naïve as that sounds, it's the principle I guard. If the custodians of my freedom are allowed to judge others by their religious beliefs, what will stop them from respecting mine if it diverges from their idea of normalcy? That's too much power. And too much power corrupts too much.

A democracy is supposed to protect its citizens from threats to their personal safety and freedom. It's not supposed to be the arbiter of its citizens' beliefs. Even given that Koresh started the fire and shot some of his congregants, my tax-supported militia and politicians misused their power. Koresh deserved a trial by his peers just like every other American does.

Scott Stein
Who's Your Daddy?

Seen on a motorcycle helmet, in block letters: Helmet laws suck.

The helmet in question hung from the handlebars of a Harley. It was a faceless model, obviously not designed for maximum safety. It probably just met the minimum requirements to be considered a helmet. The biker was with five friends, in New Hope, Pennsylvania, enjoying one of the last pleasant days of early October. Decades from his teenage years, when maybe raising a little hell was the usual routine, this was no lawless punk.

He and his friends, all closer to forty than thirty, reveled in the rumble of their hogs and had found happiness in their leather jackets. But no trouble followed them. Like many bikers and others visiting New Hope, they were there for a relaxing lunch, maybe a beer, and perhaps, without meaning any insult to their manly natures, a little shopping. Their lack of rebellious spirit was apparent when, seeing the sign prohibiting more than one vehicle per metered parking space, they moved their bikes from the traditional side-by-side biker parking arrangement and found individual spots, each sure to deposit the required money in the meter. Hell's Angels? I don't think so.

So why the objection to helmet laws in such bold terms? After all, any intelligent person knows that motorcycles are dangerous, and a helmet could save a life in an accident. In this case, I imagine the specifics of the laws were offensive to the man—he probably preferred to feel the wind in his hair and was annoyed by the hassle of carrying a helmet around. But the specifics of helmet laws were not the only reason for his proclamation in block letters against them. Could it have had something to do with his recognition that, as an adult, he no longer needed anyone to tell him what to do?

Children need parents to make certain decisions for them, because their limited experience, less than fully developed reasoning abilities, and acute physical vulnerability make them unqualified to understand and assume many risks. Children have no incomes to allow them to pay for insurance, and cannot be responsible for the monetary consequences of their actions. Children rightfully have limited legal rights, and cannot sign contracts or get married (in most states). Children are ... well, children, and they need mommy or daddy to take care of them and protect them.

Adults do not need parents. Most adults know that drinking to excess is unhealthy, know (at this point) that smoking cigarettes can lead to many health problems, understand that not wearing helmets or seat belts is dangerous. Adults also know that red meat isn't as good for them as broccoli, chocolate is not in and of itself a food group, and using condoms can help prevent sexually transmitted diseases.

"But they do not know it," you argue. "If they did, more of them would wear seatbelts or eat broccoli or use condoms. The poor uneducated masses need the government to set standards."

I will grant you that some people continue to need basic information, and if you want to expend your own resources and energy making sure all painfully dumb and willfully ignorant adults know broccoli is better for them than bacon, I would applaud your noble crusade. But I hope you're not disappointed when, despite the newly educated citizenry, bacon remains the more popular cheeseburger topping. Don't give up. One day we'll all be ordering Big Macs with broccoli on top.

More people die every year as a result of poor diets and obesity and not exercising than not wearing helmets or seat belts, and that was true before seat belt and helmet laws went into effect.

Why not outlaw cake? Yes, cake. Obesity is dangerous. It kills people. For their own protection, destroy all the cake. Or, to be fair to thin people and children, require licensing for cake consumption. A yearly physical, at the taxpayers' expense, of course, can easily determine which people would be allowed to purchase cake. Make unauthorized consumption of cake a crime. Fat people eating cake might get a warning on the first offense, a ticket on the second, and finally, staying true to "three strikes and you're out," re-education and 20 sit-ups to life.

Paternalistic laws result in a nation of overgrown children. It is embarrassing that men and women call talk radio begging pseudo psychologists to tell them how to live their lives. "Dr. Laura, my father molests my son, but he's lonely and we feel bad not having him over for Thanksgiving. What should we do?"

Government is not here to protect us from ourselves. It is here, primarily, to protect us from each other. It exists to make sure I don't take your stuff or hurt you and you don't take my stuff or hurt me. The line needs to be clearly drawn—the government's responsibility and authority end when my actions only hurt myself. So drunk driving, not drinking, should be a crime. Surfing, skydiving, New York City softball leagues playing on asphalt, scuba diving, eating hot dogs from vendors on the street, and sitting too close to the television are dangerous activities. Should we outlaw all of them?

When society stops treating adults like children, maybe they will stop acting like children. If I am wrong, what is the worse that can happen? Are people going to eat more bacon?

Bob Sullivan
Have Guns, Will Travel

"Guns don't kill people—bullets do!
Guns just make them go real fast."

In the wake of the worst school shooting in American history—the April 20, 1999, tragedy at Columbine High in Littleton, Colorado—one might judge from the news coverage that the nation's newest pastime is debating the causes of violence in today's society. The two most popular culprits are the "culture of violence" and guns.

The problem with repeatedly mentioning the culture of violence and guns in the same breath is that they begin to take on a 50-50 level of importance, when the two couldn't be more unequal. For one thing, while there are some good films that help humanity, many of them completely nonviolent, there are no good or nonviolent bullets. Sure, there may be a bullet that stops someone from shooting even more bullets, but they are all intrinsically bad and destructive. While films may influence the violence, munitions *are* the violence.

Some claim the way to reduce the number of school shootings is to reduce the amount of violence in films and the other media, while others claim there is no connection. But I've never heard anyone suggest that the solution to violence in society is even more violence in our media. Yet there are actually large numbers of people buying into the premise that the solution to the proliferation of guns in our society is even more guns!

Every couple of years, particularly after an incident like Littleton or the shooting of President Reagan and James Brady, the House and Senate make a big show of passing groundbreaking gun-control legislation that, in the shell game that inevitably follows, gets so watered down and has so many loopholes inserted that the legislation becomes virtually meaningless. Just days after Littleton, Senate Republicans voted against mandatory background checks at gun shows, then voted for them, and then House Republicans delayed debate to give the NRA time to lobby and to let memories of Littleton fade a little.

Meanwhile, the real action is on the local level, where munitions makers are stimulating business by getting carrying concealed weapons (CCW) laws passed in more and more states. The ridiculous premise behind these laws is "an armed society is a polite society."

For years, local authorities would issue a few CCW permits to those with a legitimate reason to have them, such as private investigators and people who regularly carried valuables. These new laws have nothing to do with private home ownership, but with the ability of virtually anyone to carry heat, the advertising centering on new smaller guns, concealable, yet packing a wallop. Believe it or not, some of these CCW laws were passed *because* of the school shootings, with people suggesting that if every student or every teacher at these high schools had been packing, potential violent invaders would have thought twice about invading.

Of course, the presence of an armed guard at Columbine High didn't stop Harris and Klebold from killing 13 others. Since they were on a suicide mission (adolescents are 13 times more likely to commit suicide with a handgun in the home, and 32 times more likely if the gun is loaded), fear of death evidently wasn't much of a deterrent. The idea of all of the Columbine High students packing weapons is a microcosm of where these laws will lead. If all of the students had guns, any time anyone felt blind rage, any time the nerd accidentally cut off the steroidal jock on his way into the parking lot, any time anyone even thought someone else was about to draw first, any time a death had to be avenged, or someone accidentally dropped their piece, tragedy would result.

The cure is worse than the disease; for every life saved from invasion, five would be lost to homicide or suicide or accident. According to *The New England Journal of Medicine*, a gun in the home meant to protect family members is 43 times more likely to cause the death of a family member or friend than a criminal.

At an April 27, 1999, gun-control rally—exactly one week after Littleton, and about three weeks before Thomas Solomon's May 20th rampage in Conyers, Georgia—Hillary Clinton said, "Every day in America we lose 13 precious children to gun-related violence." Given the fact that Littleton involved 15 deaths—13 murders and two suicides—and given the fact that at least three children daily commit suicide with guns, one could say that a Littleton occurs every single day in the United States. The deaths just don't usually occur all at the same place. There were 23 injuries at Columbine, while the injury rate for the rest of the country is about five injuries for every fatality—so the national rate is much higher—and the Columbine deaths and injuries were all intentional—while the rest of the country suffers daily accidental deaths and injuries. Add to that the psychological damage to the physically uninjured Columbine students, students near other shootings, and students in general, and the total damage is incalculable.

Yet CCW laws continue passing, with Republican front-runner Texas Governor George W. Bush recently having signed one into law in Texas, calling it the kind of "reasonable" legislation he might support as President. Bush and the NRA also support state laws that would prevent local governments, such as cities, from suing gun manufacturers.

But the two more insidious local laws the NRA is backing are preemption laws and CCW reciprocity laws. Preemption laws are state laws prohibiting local governments from regulating firearms. State legislators and the NRA argue that they want to avoid a hodgepodge of different gun-law regulations that might inconvenience hunters as they transport their firearms through different jurisdictions in pursuit of their sport. It would make more sense to handle this concern with specific statutory language (as federal law does), rather than scrapping perfectly good laws passed by municipalities trying to fight crime on the local level.

Cities are particularly affected by the proliferation of guns, yet when they try to pass laws to get a handle on the situation, they constantly find themselves being trumped by legislators in the state capital. The states then pass no gun-control laws—instead they pass CCW laws—thereby preventing local governments from doing what the states refuse to do: pass decent controls over weapons that threaten public safety. If the NRA were really all that interested in public safety, they wouldn't be opposing the police on every issue from assault weapons to CCW laws to cop-killer bullets. CCW reciprocity laws allow licensed carriers of concealed weapons to carry their loaded hidden handguns into other states—in effect, a national CCW law.

If an armed society were really a polite society, the United States would be the most polite nation on earth. And what has the massive increase in the number of guns done for public safety so far? In 1995, firearms killed 35,957 Americans, including 5,285 children (for injuries, multiply by five). The whole NRA slant is, of course, the Second Amendment to the U.S. Constitution, thereby making it sacred text (even though the same document once condoned slavery).

Ah yes, the Second Amendment: the shell game at its most basic. As we hear ad nauseam, this amendment guarantees that "the right of the people to keep and bear arms, shall not be infringed." Period. As if half a sentence says the exact same thing as the whole sentence (looking under the second shell): "A well-regulated militia, being necessary to the security of a free State, the right of the people to keep and bear arms, shall not be infringed."

Now this was written right after we stole the country from its former owners, the British, and there was every chance that they, their allies, and their sympathizers still on American soil might be planning to steal it back again; after all, it's worth a fortune!

A militia is "a part of the organized armed services to be called only in emergency," and the question might arise whether the Founding Fathers meant that: (A) anyone could have a gun, (B) the reserves could have guns, or (C) any group (like the Michigan Militia) could have guns.

A basic tenet of law is, if you're unsure of a word's exact meaning, look for clues in the rest of the document—in context. In the Constitution itself, the word *militia* appears four times: once in Section 2, which names the President as the Commander-in-Chief of the militia of the several states when it's called into national service, and three times in Section 8, which says that Congress can call for the militia to execute the laws of the union, suppress insurrections, and repel invasions; that Congress should provide for the militia's organizing, arming, and discipline; and that the states should appoint officers and train the militia according to the discipline prescribed by Congress. (So, Michigan Militia, I guess this means that Bill is currently your boss.)

Retired Supreme Court Justice Warren Burger, never considered a liberal, called the NRA's Second Amendment argument "one of the greatest pieces of fraud—I repeat the word *fraud*—on the American people by special interests that I have ever seen in my lifetime." The NRA is also a big fan of the Declaration of Independence's "certain inalienable Rights [including] Life, Liberty and the pursuit of Happiness," saying that taking away guns is taking away both liberty and the pursuit of happiness. But remember: the proliferation of guns is taking away life—the first and most important of the three because, without it, the other two don't exist.

London doctor John Snow witnessed the four major cholera outbreaks in London between 1832 and 1866. At the time of the 1832 outbreak, nobody knew what caused the disease or how it was transmitted. Snow's theory of transmission, published in 1849, claimed cholera was contagious, that it caused a poison which spread through the body, and that the main mode of transmission were contaminated water supplies. During an 1854 outbreak near Cambridge and Broad Streets, over 500 cases of cholera were reported in 10 days. One version of the story has Snow deducing that the common thread in all these cases was water gotten from the Broad Street pump, so he immediately put up a sign to warn people not to use it. Not everyone obeyed the law, and people desperate for water kept using the pump. Snow tried more extreme measures—posting signs threatening prosecution, fencing off the area (the equivalent of reducing violence in the media or closing down Internet sites)—until he knew exactly what he had to do: he removed the pump handle.

Our only hope for ending gun violence is that people will wake up to the simple truth: Friends, we have an epidemic. It's time to remove the pump handle.

Robert L. Hall
This Is Your Brain, Unplugged

Two years ago I performed a simple task that saved my mental health: I turned off my television set. I have since had a life.

I know what you're thinking—and I thought the same thing too: Anyone who doesn't watch TV has got to be a Neanderthal. After all, if you're not plugged into your television, how do you possibly keep up with the latest crazes, political goings and comings, fashions, and Madison Avenue catch phrases?

Why did I turn off the boob tube? Because I was saturated with a veritable compost heap of bad taste and raunchy attitudes coming at me in the form of sitcoms, game show extravaganzas, lawyer melodramas, and hospital tragedies. I was quite frankly sick of the whole thing. So I ended it, with a simple click of the remote.

What happened?

The first thing was that I decided I could write scripts as well as those I had seen coming over the airwaves. So I started writing novels and short stories and discovered that I love writing, developing plots and characters, and feeling the pathos and ethos of the creative process. In fact, this very essay would have no life if it had not been for the blank stare of my black box.

Without the constant interruption of television, I began to look outside myself. I took over the leadership role of a youth program. I found out that a lot of kids are underprivileged and mistreated by their parents—either directly through abuse or indirectly through neglect. Up until then, I thought that only softhearted (and soft-brained) people ran those kinds of programs. I have since changed my opinion. Running that program also taught me to appreciate my own parents a lot more.

I also taught one semester of music appreciation at the local community college. It was a blast! I picked up some historical and musical facts that I had not known (or had forgotten) just from the research needed to teach others.

One of the things that I began to remember about music, and about art in general, was that great strides in the arts and literature are usually made in times of great world upheaval and turmoil. In times of plenty, there is little impetus to create or suffer for one's art. Isn't that what is happening now?

Experts call us a nation of couch potatoes, getting lazier, fatter, and more stupid, as well as lax in our jobs and our personal goal setting. We're unable to cogitate, read, speak articulately, or even express our emotions intelligently. All because we let the television do our thinking for us! We sit around like mindless zombies, grunting commercial slogans, laughing at retread jokes, and blandly accepting the opinions of others who don't know cogitate from Colgate.

I'm not telling you that television shows are depicting the wrong things. That's for you to decide. It's a matter of conscience. But I do want you to think. And the easiest way to think clearly, coherently, and intelligently, is to unplug!

So I beg you—unplug. Please ... for your sanity, your health, your family, and your future.

Join us! Join the living!

Andrew Turner
Why I Haven't Solved World Hunger

You can pay $6 for a shirt. You can get T-shirts for less. You can also buy a DKNY shirt for, like, $80 to $100. Or more.

Yet most shirts are based on classic patterns. These patterns say the shirt should have two sleeves, a neck hole, etc. The patterns are, naturally, altered to the tastes of the specific designer.

The shirts' styles vary widely—everybody knows this. Oh, the comfort of a well-fitting T-shirt. Ah, the luxury of a supple silk blend. The simple shirt could be the perfect item of clothing, except for one thing: Why is that stupid tag irritating the back of my neck? Don't clothing designers ever wear shirts?

An open request to all shirt manufacturers: Could you please stop putting that damn tag in the neckline of the shirt, please? Please? I mean, come on, what possible reason is there for putting it in that place?

I'm not going to forget who made the shirt. Besides, I bought it—you already have my money. And I'm not going to forget what size it is. Are you worried I might forget how to wash it? Put the fucking label somewhere else where it won't irritate my neck.

For the love of all things fabric, could someone please start a class action suit? I know there are people suffering all over the world. I know there are people starving. But I'm not one of those people, and maybe I could concentrate on helping them if it weren't for this tag scratching the back of my neck.

Scott Stein
Baseball Players Deserve the Money

When asked by a reporter what he thought about making more money than the President of the United States, Babe Ruth famously replied, "I had a better year." The reporters all laughed at the Babe's answer, and agreed that he had—a quaint scene.

Today, even mediocre baseball players fighting to stay on the roster routinely earn far more than the President, and every few weeks it seems a new record-breaking contract for an athlete in one sport or another makes the news. With each announcement of a $200-million ten-year deal there are short-lived outcries by fans and news commentators and the public-at-large. Some sports fans complain that a certain player isn't worth the money, or wonder what happened to playing for the "love of the game." But the larger concerns of fans and non-fans are ethical ones. Let's look at three typical objections:

1. *What does it say about us as a society that we pay athletes millions of dollars?*

It says nothing about us as a society that we pay athletes millions of dollars, because there is no *us*, and *we* don't pay anybody anything. Society is made up of individuals and, despite the wishes of advertising executives and the beliefs of certain social scientists, free will still exists and is the main driving force behind baseball players' salaries. It is the height of arrogance for intellectuals to point at the masses and declare the uneducated unable to resist advertising or evil marketing schemes. If asked, these same intellectuals will insist that they are not influenced by advertising, as if $100,000 in tuition is by itself an antidote to beer-selling frogs.

No committee of elites got together one day and decided that baseball players should make more money than other people. Their high salaries are simply a result of supply and demand, like the difference between the cost of a gallon of water and a gallon of diamonds. As long as enough individuals are willing to pay $40 or more to see a baseball game, watch baseball on television, and pay whatever is being charged for baseball jerseys and baseball cards, baseball income and salaries will continue to grow. If tomorrow enough individuals stopped paying attention to baseball, tuned out the games, didn't buy the magazines and the newspapers, didn't watch highlights of games they've already seen, then ticket prices, and salaries, would drop.

The people have spoken. They want players to make millions, and they gladly contribute to those salaries from their own hard-earned wages. They have it within their power not to participate; they can choose to value art, or community service, or fine wine. They do not. Those who value other things and choose not to contribute to the salaries of professional athletes have no cause to complain—it does not hurt them that other people spend their own money on sports (the scandal of using tax money to construct stadiums is another matter). Those who choose to pay the ticket prices also have no cause to complain, since they obviously think they are getting their money's worth, or else would not spend their money in this way. If baseball weren't worth it, people would not pay for it.

2. *Why should we pay a big dumb guy all that money just to hit a ball with a stick? It isn't brain surgery, after all.*

Hitting a ball with a stick isn't as easy as you might think. Go to a batting cage and try it some day. You won't even make contact with a 90-mph pitch down the middle of the plate, let alone on the corner—and forget about touching the curveball that follows. Hitting at the top of the major league level is a much rarer skill than performing brain surgery. It generates more money than brain surgery. It is valued more than brain surgery. It is therefore rewarded at a higher rate.

3. *Teachers are the real heroes—they deserve the millions of dollars.*

I set about answering this objection at my own peril—I am married to a talented teacher, and am myself a college professor. I have nothing but respect for those who take their duty seriously and apply with diligence and creativity their abilities and skills in the service of educating people. Several teachers, from the third grade through graduate school, have influenced me beyond my capacity to thank them, from encouraging me to love reading to encouraging me to think to encouraging me to write well.

But this has no bearing on baseball salaries. Compare the difficulty of succeeding as a baseball player, or any professional athlete, to becoming a teacher.

A large proportion of boys and more girls than ever before want to become professional athletes. If given their druthers, how many boys would grow up to be baseball players—all of them? Or all of them except those going on to be firefighters and astronauts? The competition for the few professional spots is intense—those not talented or skilled or dedicated enough are weeded out from the first little league game all the way through the minor and major leagues.

Would-be players take a huge risk by committing to a career with such long odds. They have no job security and tend to make very little money before it is over and they find themselves unqualified to do much but coach low-level baseball or start in another industry from scratch. These minor-leaguers play through injury, don't get sick days or good dental plans, travel on buses, and have little hope of ever realizing their dreams. Might we call them stupid for doing so? Perhaps. But should we be angry when one of them reaches the big time? Who would pursue such dreams if fame and fortune weren't dangled as potential rewards?

Look at actors, writers, and rock stars. Without the potential for big rewards, on both financial and personal levels, who would bother? Some people would still write and sing, but why risk the humiliation of failure and spend all the time and effort trying to reach an audience if there isn't the possibility of benefiting from that work? And why is the clamor always about athletes earning too much money? There can be no debating the skill of a professional athlete. No one gets to the pro ranks in any sport without being good enough to be there. No one is there because his or her father owns the team. If you suck at baseball and your father owns the Yankees, you don't get to play shortstop. The same cannot be said for getting the lead on *Beverly Hills 90210*.

Perhaps more people should be angry about the millions being made by untalented actors, and hack writers, and musicians who play no instruments, don't write songs, and can't sing. Are people not upset because they acknowledge the right of these "artists" to own and profit from their work? How is this different from athletes profiting from their hard work and genuine talents? I hate it when race is brought up as the explanation for everything, but can the complaining have something to do with the dominance of blacks in professional sports? Probably it has more to do with adults and their failed dreams, with bitterness at the banality of their lives: "Why should athletes get to live their dreams, when I have to work? They don't deserve the money—I'm the one dealing with these crazy kids in a hot school all day."

Yes, it takes skill and talent to be a good teacher, but too many teachers are neither skilled nor talented. Most people willing to go to college will be teachers if they want to be. They get their degree, pass certification, learn to write with chalk on a vertical board, and, unfortunately, for some that's it. Even for a bad teacher there is little risk, very strong job security, and a high likelihood of leading a stable life with a healthy standard of living and excellent benefits. No one is making millions, but no one is starving either.

Deserve has nothing to do with salary, if you are using the word to mean what people ought to value. If by *deserve* you mean salary should be based on one's contribution to the economy, on what people actually value, then there can be no question that baseball players deserve the money they make.

I defend capitalism because it is the only system of economics that places a premium on freedom and choice. That includes the freedom to value things that some might find undesirable, and the freedom to have bad taste. I am often appalled by the mediocrity people embrace and at what passes for culture when appealing to the lowest common denominator can mean the highest profit. I would like good teachers to be valued more. Good writers too, for that matter.

If baseball players make too much money, it is because of you. The same is true for bad books, dumb action movies, and television shows about lifeguards played by actors who obviously can't swim. But you don't have to buy those books or watch those movies. People need to understand that every time they spend money they are expressing their values. If it isn't worth it, then don't buy it. If it is worth it, then buy it and be happy you got what you paid for.

Whatever you do, please stop bitching about how much money a baseball player makes as you hand over $4 for a small popcorn at a $9 movie.

Reader Comments

—Martin Willett responds to "Baseball Players Deserve the Money" by Scott Stein.

Of course baseball players do not deserve the money. They are fulfilling a lifelong ambition. Think about it. Think about all the famous people who have a go at hitting the first ball before a big game. Think about how much people are prepared to pay to own a famous bat or ball. Then think how much the Yankees or the Cubs could charge for a place on the team. Major League Baseball players are being paid to do what millions would pay to do.

The money does not come from talent. It has no relation to talent whatsoever. If Babe Ruth had been twice as talented how much more money would he have earned? Who else was there to pay more to watch him? If he had been 10% less talented how much less would he have earned? If he had exactly the same talent but was overshadowed by 30 better players he would have earned much less. If he had lived in England instead, he might never have become a professional sportsman. From what I have seen of him in old films, he looked like a trade union leader.

Babe Ruth didn't earn the money, the crowd earned it. The enormous crowd paid modestly inflated prices to see him play. That money poured into the commercial operation around him. Then greed and envy ensured that the lion's share of the money went to Babe Ruth himself. I have no doubt that if he had to pay to play he would have done so. But he didn't.

Only a saint could see money being made out of his own talent without demanding a share. Anybody in the situation of generating money like that is going to want to believe that it is his or her talent that earns the money. They are wrong. Rap artists do not need three Ferraris to help them cope with the angst of having too much talent; they just need to remove their heads from their nether regions and wake up to reality. The world is big, there are a lot of people in it. If you have something that a lot of people are prepared to pay a modest amount for, you can channel large amounts of money in your direction.

Nobody paid $50,000 to watch Babe Ruth play. 50,000 people paid $1. That is the reality. Talent does not make people rich. People make people rich, and there are a lot of people. I think the people should ask for that money back. Nobody needs to be a millionaire in order to want to be a famous sportsman, pop star, supermodel, president of the U.S.A. or of a major company. Tax them, take our money back!

—Scott Stein responds to Martin Willett's comments on his "Baseball Players Deserve the Money."

How sad that "fulfilling a lifelong ambition" is looked down upon by Mr. Willett. No one should be punished for working hard to meet a goal and for being competent. If those that dedicate themselves and struggle to achieve excellence don't deserve the money, who does? The inept? The bitter? Is it more noble to hate one's job? If someone loves to bake, should he not be paid fair market value for his bread? If the bread is better than the competition's because of this passion for baking, does that mean the baker should give away his product? If millions choose to buy the baker's bread, how does that make him less deserving of the money? This line of thinking is corrupt, but how much people love or despise their jobs is irrelevant here.

Mr. Willett doesn't understand the free market, and doesn't seem to value the principle of freedom that makes the free market important.

What free people do with their money, as long as it does not directly and demonstrably infringe on the freedom of other people, is their business, and if some end up being rich because others overvalue their talents, great or small, then that is the price of freedom. The government that has a right to limit income and tell you how to run your business is the same government that tells you how to raise your kids, what religion to believe, what you can say and read, and who you can have sex with. Personal freedom requires economic freedom, to the greatest extent possible.

I agree that it is not mere talent that makes one rich; it is talent at doing something many people value. If people do not value knitting very much, there will not be many millionaire knitters, no matter how talented a particular knitter might be. This might seem unfair to Mr. Willett. Why should talented knitters be less rich than talented athletes? Because people are free to spend their money as they see fit. Enough of them value the experience that is baseball, and pay whatever is being charged to attend games and own souvenirs. They choose to do so, and are free not to pay if they do not want to.

But it is false to say that Babe Ruth's talent had no relation to his salary. Had he not been the best hitter in baseball, he would not have been the highest paid player. (That he looked like a trade union leader, though funny, does not change how truly talented he was.) The owner of the team was willing to pay Ruth a higher salary because Ruth's talent, his contribution to the team's ability to earn income, was worth it. He deserved it. Someone did decide to pay him a lot of money: the team's owner. Can Mr. Willett really argue, for example, that the immensely talented Tiger Woods has had no influence on the size of the viewing audience for professional golf? Woods is rich because of how much people value his talent.

The demand for good players, for the best players, drives the economy of sports. Competition for those players drives salaries up. The money comes from millions of people who give willingly toward the total, so they can participate in an activity—watching a good team play—that they enjoy. When they lose interest, they no longer pay. Many who were once sports fans no longer are, and choose to use their money in other ways. It is called freedom.

Mr. Willett tries to explain wealth as the channeling of money and as a mere consequence of there being a lot of people. He asks how many people were there to pay more to see Babe Ruth play—the answer is obvious. There were many more, as the continued explosive growth of the sports industry demonstrates. By improving the product, in terms of talent and presentation and technology, all the major sports have more fans and make more money than baseball did during Ruth's day.

Mr. Willett's analysis implies that there is only a certain amount of money to go around, and that by being paid a large salary, professional athletes and others are hurting the rest of us. But, even though our economy is really only partially capitalistic, it is not static. Wealth is created, not channeled. A side consequence is that this new wealth is then spent, making growth and the creation of still more wealth possible. Contrary to emotional propaganda and attacks on the "top one percent," redistribution of wealth by the government does not help people; it only encourages a closed system and limits the creation of new wealth. Just compare the lives of poor people in America to poor people living in nations with state-run economies (like India) to understand the benefits of capitalism and freedom.

But Mr. Willett's final comment is the most misguided: "Tax them, and take our money back!" If he or anyone else does not want a pop star, supermodel, actor, or athlete to have any of his money, he does not have to give it to them. If Mr. Willett does not buy women's magazines or products promoted by supermodels, then his money has not reached them. Only the money of people who bought those products contributed to the supermodel's wealth. It was their money, not Mr. Willet's or mine.

People didn't have to use their money this way, and they don't have to in the future. But asking for the money back in the form of taxes is to say, "I am a child, and was not free or was too dumb to make a decision to spend my money properly. I need the government to give me my money back, because I cannot be trusted to be responsible."

Is this the vision of humanity Mr. Willett has? If so, it is elitist, and sad. Mr. Willett seems to have rejected spending his money on pop culture and entertainment, so why does he assume others are incapable of making the same decision?

—David "Preacher" Slocum responds to "Baseball Players Deserve the Money" by Scott Stein.

Mr. Willett is way off the mark here. Baseball fans (among whose numbers I cannot be counted) pay to see talented athletes compete. They would not pay to see no-talent hacks that happened to have the money to purchase a spot on the team (what does he think baseball is, a presidential election?).

Robert O'Hara
Recipe for Continuing To Collect Unemployment

INGREDIENTS
20 resumés with your name misspelled
8 visible tattoos
5 four-letter words
4 years of imprisonment
3 non-visible tattoos
2 counts of statutory rape
2 short-sleeve dress shirts with accompanying sweaty armpit stains
2 ties (1 with a naked girl on it, 1 that ends 4 inches above navel)
1 year probation
¾ bottle of gin
½ front tooth

PREPARATION
1. Hand out 1 resumé with name misspelled at interview.

2. Before sitting down, turn around slowly, flexing your arms to display 8 visible tattoos.

3. When interviewer asks, "Tell me a bit about yourself?", mix in 4 years of imprisonment, 2 counts of statutory rape, and 1 year probation.

4. Sprinkle 5 four-letter words throughout the interview (you might want to use them all at once, but for better results, this recipe recommends throwing them in periodically).

5. When interview starts to slow, offer to show 3 non-visible tattoos (if the interviewer turns down the offer, expose non-visible tattoos anyway).

6. When asked why you were fired from your previous job, drink from the ¾ bottle of gin and explain, "I have no idea. You thirsty?"

7. Upon conclusion of the interview, high-five the employer and smile wide to display ½ front tooth.

Repeat above seven steps until resumés run out (20 times), alternating shirts and ties every other interview. Serves for about 6 months of unemployment payments (add or subtract a month based on leniency of government caseworker).

C.P. Kaiser
Seventh-Inning Stench

I resent those who insist that baseball is America's national pastime. Survey any 50 people crawling to work and barely one of them will have anything remotely to do with using a stick and ball on a regular basis (however, statistics gained in the S&M section of town may skew results).

The real national pastime is *watching* baseball or whatever other innocuous glandular joust your pituitary desires. We deceive our brains, create a sort of a cortexual *trompe l'oeil*, by calling someone else's job the national pastime. It gives us license to remain unconscious to our passivity, convincing ourselves that we are actually "involved" in sport, when in reality we are not at all involved in sport, unless you consider, as Machiavelli did, deception to be a sport (if that's the case, choose any of the following as candidates for the national pastime: politics, religion, corporate charity, or academia).

The sport of sport watching also creates a false sense of bonding among men. Where else will you see straight men "touching" each other but around a color TV ensconced with images of sweaty, uniformed gargantuans besting each other? The faux sportsman sports a faux emotional bond with his faux buddy by high-fiving, high-tenning, ass patting, backslapping, beer swilling, and female bashing all in the name of a fumble, an error, an ace, or a hat trick. In reality, they've shared nothing but space and time, and even that is up for debate.

The sports industry is a multi-billion-dollar-a-year enterprise. What is the average schmoe's contribution to that GNP? Money-wise? Nothing, except occasionally shelling out $75 for a stadium ticket where he slops down $20 beers and throws peanut shells at the troglodytes in front of him, or sometimes buying a franchised T-shirt made in East Timor by slave laborers suppressed by lopsided U.S. foreign (read *corporate*) policy. Sports' salaries are paid for by TV advertising revenues, which in return need passive consumers glued to the magic electron box. The powers that be prefer that we slouch on the couch and spout inane statistics about a ballplayer's shoe size in a year that didn't even get mentioned in the *Farmer's Almanac*. We, in turn, become *their* statistics.

Our game, truly, is nothing but watching, whether on the telly or in the arena or in newsprint; we are a nation of watchers. How many of us would survive even slow-pitch softball or touch football? We watch, period. We watch people slaughter each other inside a ring, smash each other on a gridiron, and slash deep gashes into opposing players' faces on the ice. We watch athletically gifted people attack referees and umpires because they disagree with a call.

What's worse is that this sporting deception leads to more serious lapses in judgment. For instance, we watch as the President of the United States sends bombs raining down upon unsuspecting countries; we watch as corporations receive big tax breaks at the expense of inner cities and then pollute the air and water of those cities with impunity; we watch as politicians of all stripes refuse to enact gun laws with real teeth; we watch millions of Americans remain in a sickly state because they can't afford health care; we watch it all, unless, of course, there's a good game on.

Sports might encourage a culture of violence (some reports indicate an increase in domestic violence on and around Super Bowl Sunday), but watching sports encourages a culture of passivity. Something somewhere has to suffer while we do our vicarious living through sports. Watching sports dulls the senses to the point that the aforementioned guilty can't even see their complicity. The national pastime, unfortunately, is nothing but watching time go by in a glandular stupor, a seventh-inning stench of sorts, where we are just too mesmerized by other's activities to act ourselves.

Scott Stein
If a Tree Falls In the Woods...

If a tree falls in the woods, and there is no one there to hear it, does it make a sound? This is an important question, but not for the reasons people seem to think.

Humanity has often used the question, among an arsenal of other long-standing weapons of mass-construction (such as religion), to place itself at the center of the universe. If a tree doesn't make a sound unless someone is there to hear it, doesn't that mean that sound happens *for* us? If the existence of sound depends on us, isn't reality itself dependent on people? Aren't we the reason there is a universe? And by the way, if we believe hard enough, maybe the sun will go back to revolving around the earth.

Often asked in hushed or haughty tones, to convey the metaphysical seriousness of the search for truth, or delivered with Seinfeld-esque knowing mockery of human rationality, to reveal the danger of trusting the senses, the question is thought by the general populace to have no answer. "There are some things we cannot know," they say, in awe of the feebleness of reason in the face of nature, with the pretend solitary and perpetually falling tree as evidence. Zen Buddhist monks reflect on questions such as these, known as koans, to clear the mind, to end a reliance on reason and enhance the power of intuition and the appreciation of the mystery of reality.

But there is no mystery here. As with many seemingly difficult philosophical questions, the answer is a matter of definition. The only legitimate purpose of the question is to point to the necessity of defining terms when making arguments or proofs or seeking evidence.

Some people dismiss an argument that focuses on defining terms as "splitting hairs" or "obsessing over semantics." My need to reiterate here that without clear words there cannot be clear concepts is an indication of the low level of rational thought in contemporary America. Our politicians and journalists and academics have gotten away with muddled expression for so long, we have accepted muddled thought as a given. What is the result? Politicians in debates who cannot even agree on the data they are arguing about, each accusing the other of having faulty or manipulated information. How many times are we going to hear, "You're distorting the truth," from all sides on an issue, before we recognize the importance of agreeing on ground rules and definitions and what counts as fact and evidence? That is the lesson the famous question teaches us.

If a tree falls in the woods, and there is no one there to hear it, does it make a sound? If sound is defined as "mechanical radiant energy that is transmitted by longitudinal pressure waves in a material medium (as air) and is the objective cause of hearing," then the answer is yes, it does make a sound. If sound is defined as "the sensation perceived by the sense of hearing; a particular auditory impression," then the answer is no, it does not make a sound.

We define sound as either a wave created or a wave received. For one to exist, people are not necessary, for the other, we are. The falling tree in the woods and the sound wave created care not for our definitions, and sound depends on us only if by our definition of *sound* it does.

Now, you might ask, hoping I can resolve all the mysteries of life at once, what is the sound of one hand clapping?

As a writer on an online magazine, I can answer that one as well: it is a lonely sound, my friends, a lonely sound.

Suzanne Hakanen
The History of Inhalation In the U.S.
(As Chronicled By Mothball Product Labels)

Year 1692
That whereas ye are afflicted by Moths, take these Crystals and scatter them thickly in the places at which your garments are kept. If the presence of Moths does not abate, prithee remove all vestiges to a strong box of Cedar. Pray keep Crystals away from Women, as their vapors create dizziness and hysterical pregnancy in all God's creatures and may lead to the practice of Witchcraft, whereas they should wear the Scarlet M. Sirs, you may use these precious Crystals also to clear the Sinus of hot air, and to make a Poultice healthy for breathing.

Year 1776
In order that We the People will enjoy a Life free from Moths, We hereby declare that all Moths are created equally destructive. And that We, in pursuit of Life, Liberty, and whole Garments, do hereby strike down these Moths of repression with these Balls. But in pursuit ye of pleasure, do inhale ye the vapors of such Balls.

Year 1865
For more than four score and seven years, mothballs have been a part of our history. And some would spurn the poisonous mothballs rather than let the coat survive, and others would accept mothballs rather than let it perish, and so out of the box the mothballs came and a country was divided.

Year 1920
Protect your lovely garments the easy way: with Mitchell's Mothballs! Just drop a few mothballs in each garment bag before sealing. Your coats and dresses will stay perfect for years to come! These lovely round mothballs are also an excellent substitute for pickled onions in gimlets, martinis, and all your favorite cocktails. Entertain the Mitchell's way!

Year 1929
You can't afford these mothballs. Try Sterno!

Year 1945
We regret having to use these mothballs, but if we had not, the moth problem would have gone on for much longer, and a lot more moths would have been killed. With each mothball purchase, we will donate 25% to the fund for surviving moths, those that have been crippled, maimed, or otherwise affected by this event. Caution: Inhalation of this product will live in infamy.

Year 1956
If we suspect these mothballs have been used in an unfriendly way, you will be asked to testify. You will not be under suspicion, but should be willing to testify about any Communist activity that you are aware of regarding these

mothballs, including communal huffing.

Year 1969
Scatter generously wherever moths are seen dancing. Inhale freely. Turn on a friend.

Year 1978
All insects, including moths, are fellow creatures, and should be treated with love and respect. (Lucky for us, moths don't eat polyester.) Inhalation may cause Saturday night fever.

Year 1985
To determine how many mothballs to use: Survey the space in your closet with a ruler. The value of the area of the closet is Set A. Take Set A, in inches, and convert to centimeters by dividing by 2.5. Multiply this number by 0.65 ounces, and you will have the weight of mothballs needed to properly treat your closet. Convert weight to mass (in grams), then measure the correct mass on a spring scale and transfer to a 2-liter soda bottle. Put the bottle in the corner of your closet. Ventilate properly (or just say no).

Year 1993
Conflict resolution is an important part of everyone's existence here on earth. Put yourself in the moth's shoes. If you were a moth, how would you feel?

Year 2000
This product is for the express use of killing moths, their offspring, and/or their eggs in clean, closed, airtight containers or closets. Any use of this product other than that which is specifically intended to kill moths, their offspring, and/or their eggs is strictly prohibited by law, and will be punished as such. Any non-moth insect injured by the use of this product is entitled to seek pecuniary damages in a court of law. Keep out of the reach of children, pets, and Bill Clinton (although he claims not to inhale).

Year 2002
Mothballs may not be right for everyone. Before using mothballs, speak with your insect control professional. Mothballs are not guaranteed to control every moth. People who are human should not use mothballs for food, seasoning, dietary supplements, or party favors. Women who are nursing should not rub mothballs on or around their breasts. Eating mothballs can cause upset stomach, blindness, and, in many cases, death. Therefore we urge you to limit your use of mothballs to that aimed at controlling destructive moths within closets and closed storage containers. Void where prohibited.

Eva Marie Tremoglie
Feeding the Bloodlust of the Rabble

Henry Blackmun, the former Supreme Court Justice who died recently, called the death penalty "a failed experiment." Justice Blackmun, who supported the death penalty early in his career, later realized this statute's inherent injustice, mainly its sanctioned use as a tool of oppression and racism. And in 1998, the American Bar Association said that it could not endorse the death penalty and called for a moratorium on the statute. The voices of Blackmun and the American Bar, voices that by no means could be called liberal, should resound to all Americans. It's time to recognize the intrinsic danger and unfairness of this so-called act of punishment.

What is the purpose of the death penalty? A deterrent? Is it my imagination that violent crimes continue to escalate? Am I having auditory hallucinations night after night when I hear Tom Brokaw regularly catalogue endless acts of horror? The deterrent notion has been dispelled many times by many studies. In fact, it's been shown that the rate for crimes that warrant the death penalty tends to be higher in those areas that have the death penalty.

So, if not a deterrent, then what? A tool of vengeance? That should disturb us all—that we have embedded in our so-called civilized society a revenge mechanism. You might disagree and believe that a just society has the right to exercise an eye-for-an-eye by sending a condemned person to death. But even if that is granted (it is not by me), who's really tipping the scales of this so-called justice? Who's calling the shots? You? Me? Are decisions being carried out fairly? When we see the disproportionate number of poor, black men who are on death row and hear legal voices such as Blackmun's and the Bar's denounce the death penalty, how can we not question who's running this show?

The *we* making these life and death decisions are the same people who own our public officials—the rich, white, male power structure. For the good ole patriarchy to hold on to all its goodies, it needs to control certain individuals (read: *minorities* and *women*). The masses will not be allowed to rise up. They'll be given low wage jobs, impossible living conditions, sub-par public education, no means to improve, and no health care, and then when those same individuals sell drugs as their only means of survival, they'll be locked up for years, even for misdemeanor offenses. (Of course, there's no thought given to that dirty idea of rehabilitation—witness the dismantling during the Nixon administration of government-funded college courses for inmates.) The only trade for our locked up young men to learn in our penal system is how to be better criminals. So, upon release, they commit more crimes, and the people call for their extermination. According to patriarchy in 2000, this is how a civilized society works.

The death penalty is an admission by our power structures that we are unable to control the problem of crime. Put more accurately, we are unwilling to treat the underlying problems that cause people to commit crimes. It is easier for politicians to increase penalties than to figure out how to decrease crime. The politicos look good to their constituents by passing ever-newer crime legislation. They won't spend money up front for education. Instead they spend it later to incarcerate uneducated, unemployed, or unemployable victims of our "just" system. If harsher laws have not made the problem go away, why do we keep passing harsher laws?

Our culture is schizophrenic. We say we stand for peace and freedom and the spread of benign democracy. Yet, our police shoot unarmed citizens, practice racial profiling, and shoot hoses of water at protestors seeking equity. Our leaders sanction torture, murder, and mayhem in countries that won't buy into our form of democratic capitalism. And our states say it's OK to kill a certain segment of the population through the death penalty. What do we expect from our young, impressionable males when we reinforce that the ultimate power lies in violence—state-sanctioned violence? To believe that we deter crime with the death penalty is as ludicrous as the belief that we keep peace by preparing for war.

In this country, the death penalty is a form of control. It controls and feeds the bloodlust of the rabble. It helps the public think that something is being done about crime, that their lives are safer now that a particular "monster" is not alive anymore. As long as people are distracted by the sound bites of political rhetoric, they'll continue to give credence to the death penalty's false sense of security. Justice Blackmun wasn't too proud to change his mind after a lifetime of advocating for the death penalty. Those who favor this inhuman act can learn from his change of heart.

Reader Comments

—David "Preacher" Slocum responds to "Feeding the Bloodlust of the Rabble" by Eva Marie Tremoglie.

First, Ms. Tremoglie makes the mistake of applying one man's very suspect change of heart to the motivations of the entire Bar Association on one hand, while labeling them (incorrectly in my opinion) as anti-liberal with the other. Not only is the ABA a liberal organization, they make their living pushing a liberal agenda on the American public. She then goes on to decry the deterrent factor of capital punishment and claim that the real reason behind the death penalty is vengeance. The response of everyone I know who read the above claim was, *So?*

Her ultra-liberal, racist, pro-communist leanings are made clear with the following: "The *we* making these life and death decisions are the same people who own our public officials—the rich, white, male power structure. For the good ole patriarchy to hold on to all its goodies, it needs to control certain individuals (read: *minorities* and *women*). The masses will not be allowed to rise up." Has anyone bothered to tell Ms. Tremoglie that communism is dead? Despite her wandering rhetoric, the truth is that the death penalty is hamstrung by the liberal left. It is not as effective as it should be because it takes 10 years or more to execute a criminal. What we need is not an immediate cessation of state-sponsored executions, but serious reform in the legal profession. We need to cut out the endless appeals and hold these executions in the town square, televising these events to every household in America.

—Bernd D. Ratsch responds to "Feeding the Bloodlust of the Rabble" by Eva Marie Tremoglie.

They have prisons that we have to pay for and this is where they "rehabilitate" the criminal. This means (in most cases) that a person can kill another, and sit in a cell watching cable TV, be fed for free, and never have to worry about taxes or mortgage payments again. It costs on the average $30 per day out of our taxpayers' pockets to keep a person in jail, let alone on death row. Let's see: $30 per day, multiplied by 365 days, times 80 years, equals $867,000. That's a nice retirement plan that just went down the tubes—and not into paying off our federal deficit. The death penalty isn't Disney Land for the inmate, but look at where the victim lives not: six feet under. You can say you can't condone the death penalty, or it's immoral, or whatever you may want to say, but I personally know someone whose life was eternally affected by a murderer. He also didn't condone the death penalty. His views changed overnight.

Jody Lane
Headline News from the 21st Century

Twenty-first Century Interrupted
We are sorry. Due to technical difficulties beyond our control, we are forced to interrupt the 21st century. Please be patient. We will resume programming you as soon as possible....

Common Cold Cured
The World Health Organization has announced that a promising new vaccine for the common cold has been discovered. Coupled with rest and heightened fluid intake, the vaccine is expected to cure those suffering from cold symptoms in seven to fourteen days. Prior to this medical breakthrough doctors were limited to prescribing rest and fluids to relieve symptoms which could remain for one to two weeks. Officials estimate that the vaccine, Bygbucksus Forbogusshotis, will be available to the public within eight to 12 years....

Dick Clark Thawed
Cryonically frozen in the last century, 187-year-old Dick Clark was thawed earlier today. Thousands of nostalgic fans attended the event in Times Square amid preparations for the annual New Year's Eve celebration. One unknown partygoer observed, "He doesn't look a day over 110...."

Race Riots on Mars
Peace talks on Mars were violently interrupted again this week when a shuttle bomb exploded outside the earth embassy. Although no specific group has come forward to claim responsibility for the act, a statement released by the Interplanetary Ethnicity Council suggests that several groups have been implicated, including: The Caucasian-Martian Coalition, The Afro-Martian League, Sons of the Asian-Martian Civil War, The Association for the Advancement of Martian Natives, and Anti-Earthling, Inc....

The Messiah Resigns
Jesus Christ has submitted his resignation to the powers that be. Top officials at the Pearly Gates have declined to relate specific reasons for the surprise decision, but sources close to the Savior state that he might just be looking for a real job. The Messiah's post officially ends in 30 days. Interested applicants may apply at....

FDA Recalls Clones
The Food and Drug Administration has issued an immediate recall of clones grown in a privately owned Washington laboratory. The clones are considered dangerous for exhibiting unnatural signs of mental activity and self-awareness. Gene donors who received their clones between the years 2072-2081 are urged to call 1-800-MY-DUM-BUDDY® as soon as possible to report their DumBuddy's® location. There will be a small fee for pickup and dis-

posal....

Unpopular Children's Puppet Mutilated

A large purple puppet with green spots was found mutilated in its home at the PBS building in New York. As the crime was clearly a misguided act of public service, authorities are not actively seeking suspects....

Violent Behavior Linked to Everything

An independent survey of two people conducted by the IWBS conclusively demonstrates that violent behavior is induced by everything. The participants, selected at random from the institute's two employees, were asked to answer the question: What causes violent behavior? Top officials at the Institute for Worthless and Biased Surveys stated that neither one of them was surprised by the results. See related story, "What Causes Cancer," on page 3A....

Scott Stein
"Literally" Decimated, Figuratively Speaking

"The offensive line is literally decimated by injury," the sportscaster says, and no one bats an eye. At the water cooler the next day, a few guys talking about the game lament the injured state of the hometown team. "Their offensive line is literally decimated by injury," one of them says, and they all shake their heads, agreeing with this grim assessment. Quietly, but not literally, the English language slumps against the water cooler and right there dies a slow death.

As nice as it might seem that sportscasters and American football fans are using big and complex-sounding words like *literally* and *decimated*, this doesn't bode well for the future of the English language. Both *literally* and *decimated* have specific functions and meanings, and the misuse of the former is reaching proportions that threaten to impede our language's capacity to allow people to communicate clearly with each other.

Decimated literally means that every tenth man has been killed. *Decimated* is properly used when discussing losses to war or disease. Our sportscaster is using *decimated* non-literally. He does not mean that 10% of the offensive line has been killed, nor does he even necessarily mean that 10% of the offensive line is out due to injury. He just means that many members of the offensive line are injured.

We might wish the sportscaster would choose his words more carefully, because there could be a major war or natural disaster or epidemic disease and segments of populations might indeed be decimated. *Decimated* is the only word that indicates that a tenth of a population has been killed. *Ravaged, diluted, weakened, thinned,* and many other words meet the needs of the sportscaster describing the injury-plagued offensive line. Why weaken *decimate* and its specific meaning by applying it to sprained ankles on a football team?

But let us grant the sportscaster his use of *decimate*. Chalk it up to figurative speech, colorful language, poetic license, even. As this kind of use proliferates and *decimate* becomes part of the vernacular, *literally* becomes ever more important. Because of the influence of multiple sportscasters and news reporters and others with dubious command of the language, *decimated* will (and perhaps has already) come to mean *riddled with injury* or *weakened*.

When an earthquake hits a small village in a country no one has heard of (as they always do), or a particularly nasty tornado visits Middle America (as it will, much to the surprise of the people who live there), or a war breaks out between ethnic groups in Europe because someone's nose is a little larger than someone else's, we might need *literally* to rescue *decimate*.

Literally is a functional word that helps us understand in what ways other words are being used, and it is especially important that we get a figurative (not a literal) grasp on its proper use. In *Merriam Webster's Tenth Edition*, *literally* is (1) "In a literal sense or manner; actually" (as in "he took the remark literally"). This seems to contradict (2) "Virtually" (as in "he will literally turn the world upside down to combat cruelty or injustice").

Webster's acknowledges that to some people uses 1 and 2 are opposites, and that many (myself among them) see the second use as a misuse. Use 2, *Webster's* points out, "is pure hyperbole to gain emphasis, but it often appears in contexts where no additional emphasis is necessary."

Use 1 is the only proper use of *literally*. If a movie is three and a half hours long, we might say "the movie was literally three and a half hours." *Literally* is appropriate here because without it some might assume we are exaggerating, that the movie merely felt that long. *Literally* allows us to establish that it actually was three and a half hours long. "I literally lost 10 pounds last week" is also appropriate, because without *literally*, it might be assumed we are exaggerating.

Abuse of use 1 is common; *literally* is thrown in with all kinds of claims that do not require it. For example, there is no need to say, "The movie was literally two hours long," because most movies are about that length. If there is no reason to think the reader or listener will doubt the literal or near-literal truth of a statement, *literally* is superfluous. For many, *literally* has taken the place of the exclamation point. It is not uncommon to hear, "That was literally the best sandwich I've ever had." In the crazy world we live in, there is something commendable about mustering up that much enthusiasm for a sandwich, but leave *literally* out of it.

Which brings us to use 2, *literally* as *virtually* for the purpose of emphasis. I can't think of a single example that validates *Webster's* use 2 for *literally*. Their example, "He literally turns the world upside down," requires no *literally* for emphasis. We know that no one can literally turn the world upside down. It is a physical impossibility. It is clear that this is a hyperbolic, figurative statement. Adding *literally* here only causes confusion—it adds no emphasis.

And using it this way destroys the ability of *literally* to serve its function in the same context. If, for example, we were discussing the plot of a Superman comic book, we might need to describe a scene in which Superman "literally turns the world upside down." The *literally* here would not be for emphasis. We would mean that Superman did indeed turn the world upside down, in a real, physical way. After performing such a feat, if you were Superman, wouldn't you be a little peeved if people, even after hearing that the story is literally true, thought it was an exaggeration? *Literally* exists precisely to make these distinctions, to make it clear that such-and-such really happened, even if it sounds fantastic.

"He wallowed in literal hell" might be appropriate if we are discussing a fictional character and want to be sure the reader understands that we are not referring to hell in any figurative sense, but that he indeed wallowed in the underworld with devils and pitchforks and all the rest. Phrases such as "It was a literal hell on earth" are not only incorrect, but cumulatively damage the English language. The literal hell is not on earth. Any description of earth as hell, no matter how horrid, is figurative. Earth is being compared to hell to give a sense of the horror. It is a metaphor to get across a point.

Literally allows us our poetry without guilt, because when we mean to indicate the literal hell, we can.

This misuse of language has moved beyond the broadcast booth at football games and to the highest levels of academia and politics. At a conference I attended, a researcher with a Ph.D. described the oratory and charismatic powers of a colleague by saying, "He had them literally eating out of the palm of his hand." Of course, all of the editors in the room held back laughter to avoid losing their jobs. In the interests of public safety and disease control, I sincerely hope that no one literally ate out of anyone's hand.

The power and beauty of the English language are due largely to metaphor and poetic use. There is no reason such necessary and valuable (not to mention entertaining) use of language needs to interfere with communication and understanding. If anything, it should enhance it.

But no language can survive an unrestrained assault on its functional words. The English language might still be figuratively breathing, but this continued figurative decimation of *literally* is leading English down a figurative road to destruction.

C.P. Kaiser
The Beeper

She felt the gentle vibration of him on the front of her hip, like she had many times before. She loved it when she felt him there; it was like a prelude to something wild, unforgiving, and deeply primordial. The gentle massage slowly sank into her bones. With a vague smile, she caressed her hip and fondled the beeper with manicured fingers. She rubbed it dreamily. It was him, she was sure of it. And it was time.

She'd have to get a sitter, or just let the oldest mind the rest. It was late and they'd sleep soon. But now, the unforgiving called. And she was a coyote under the full moon. Her insides howled at nature, called to the beginning of time, the first grunt, the first atomic moan.

She twitched as she scanned the beeper screen. She liked his choice. It was a place full of anticipation, a place that demanded the lighting of hundreds of red candles. Her thighs tightened. She imagined him there, no shirt, belt unbuckled, jeans unbuttoned, zipper casually down, dark pubic hairs springing up like hypnotic cobras. He'd be smoking—something, drinking—something, reading—something, candles casting his still shadow high on the wall.

When she reached the top of the stairs, her oldest was there agreeing to her request without it being uttered. She loved him, but she loved the night too.

"I'll be home later," she said.
"I know."
"Watch your brother and sister."
"I will."

She kissed him softly on the cheek and felt him flinch.

Her Saab screamed down the road. She thought of being tangled in the web of messy love. She thought of the alternatives. She turned up the radio.

The road was dark. The yellow lines were sharp incisors clapping at her tires. She sped on, undeterred. The bare winter birch that lined the narrow roadway beckoned her. She squirmed and could feel her red lace panties riding up her cheeks. She changed the radio station to some slashing rock. This was her time—not the priest's who swore her to empty vows, not the kids who forever needed tending, not the supervisor who ransomed her dignity. This was her time.

She pulled into the drive. A candled glow bounced off the upstairs window. Her thighs tightened. She swallowed the night, and it was good.

Alastair MacDonald Black
If It Bleeds, It Leads

As a resident of Seattle, I was disturbed when the rest of the country saw this fine city as a "Watts Jr." during the skewed television coverage of the recent turbulent World Trade Organization meeting. News directors nationwide chose to endlessly repeat some very disturbing images, such as that of Darth Vader clones stamping about the streets, beset by maddened masses surging to and fro in a fog of tear gas. If It Bleeds, It Leads is the unfortunate motto of broadcast news.

The broadcasts offered a pastiche of successive shots of the same scene from different angles, interspersed with repetitions of carefully selected dramatic moments, and thus built a picture of a city collapsing in chaos. However, as a somewhat innocent bystander, my eyes personally witnessed something entirely different, something very contained, very limited (although it is odd to describe 40,000 people sloshing about in the streets as limited—certainly it was limited in area).

Seattle citizens were no doubt distressed to see a few vandalous idiots spoil an otherwise peaceful demonstration. Sadly, there was more rock-and-bottle tossing directed toward cops than was expected in super-cool, laid-back Seattle. As one-time Atlanta Mayor Lester Maddox used to claim, "Troublemakers from out of town perpetrated much of the worst behavior." Here in Seattle, a contingent from Portland brought masks from home, but to avoid excess-baggage charges, purchased wrecking bars locally.

In the face of determined provocation, the cops showed heroic restraint. After enduring a storm of inflammatory vituperation, one or two officers could not resist meting out a head-lump here or a crotch-kick there, but no one was shot, no one was injured beyond a bruise, and though some trash carts burned merrily, no buildings went up. If there were flash grenades and tear gas, there were no attack dogs or fire hoses. I thought police behavior was reasonably satisfactory. All in all, it was a nice little dust-up as peaceably assembled citizens attempted to tell the government and corporate America that it doesn't yet have it all its own way.

Good Heads Will Roll

The investigations, reviews, and recriminations will continue as long as the media can sell ads using the demonstration story. Unfortunately, Norm Stamper, our police chief, will fall on his sword. Too bad—he's one of the best I've seen. Most complaints are ludicrous. Some of the participating youngsters have sniffled indignantly that they were arrested and jailed just for sitting in an intersection. Have they read no history, no social science? Civil disobedience has its price.

There was a lot of mumbling that the city administration didn't organize the demonstration properly. The fact is, riots are inherently unpredictable and, many times, unmanageable. A riot tends to feed on itself like a nuclear chain reaction. Damping it is delicate work. Here in Seattle, the authorities did an admirable job of cushioning, absorbing, deflecting, and dissipating the strange, inchoate fury that overtook the mob. Also, the underlying decency of Seattle-ites acted like an array of carbon rods, soaking up the worst of the heat.

There are many images that we, the people in the streets, saw that did not make your 11 o'clock news: a citizen standing with arms outspread like Jesus successfully protecting a shop window from a masked vandal; two young women righting a big concrete street planter and replanting the flowers; the cadre of private citizens with brooms, out early the next morning, to sweep up the broken glass and trash. The image you and the rest of the nation probably remember most is the close-up of the vandal swinging his new Home Depot crowbar at the window of Nike Town, dancing about gleefully in his swoosh-labeled sneaks.

More Focus Needed

Perhaps even the best news coverage could not have helped the demonstrators. Their efforts will suffer in the long run from a deplorable diffusion of goodwill interests. There were people who wanted to save sea turtles, others, laboratory mice, and still more, laboratory chickens. Some cried to save rain forests, others demanded we save American trees. Some protestors wanted the boycotting of Chiquita bananas; others said we should buy Honduran bananas; and another contingent said we should stop eating salmon. There was a demand to break up evil cartels, and another to support benevolent cartels like Microsoft. Some placards called for a boycott of Chinese steel. A scattering of signs asked that the United States make China buy Washington apples, and some others advocated keeping the Japanese from peddling Fuji apples in Washington State. One contingent wished to force the French and British to buy genetically altered beef, while another called for the government to stop the production of genetically altered beef. I think I saw a sign asking for sanctions on McDonald's to stop it from freezing out cheese blintz shops in Israel. No wonder the delegates went home confused (or perhaps why the media's coverage was so narrow—one thing TV news cannot do, in fact, does not want to do—is spur intelligent debate).

No doubt, however, the marching and yelling will have some effect, if only to force the likes of Wal-Mart and Old Navy to boost their inventory of merchandise bearing *Made in USA* tags. Of course, under current rules, that practically means that only the tag was made in the U.S.A. (For myself, I've resolved not to buy any more Boeing 747s until I'm sure that none of their engines are made in sweatshops.)

CNN's coverage (not network TV) from inside the conference chambers showed the delegates in head-on collisions over the same difficult questions being shouted outside in the streets. That both the demonstrators and the delegates perceived the same problems suggests a certain validity to the underlying issues. It also suggests that better communication between all parties could be profitable. For example, a group might be gathered to narrow the gap between commerce and human values, a group possibly named, oh, I don't know, maybe the World Trade Organization! But as long as TV news doesn't focus on anything bigger than a sound bite, we will be deprived of informative, accurate, and intelligent debate of the issues (including the peacefulness of Seattle-ites).

Scott Stein
Fluidity of Thought

July 14, 1998—The Lower East Side of Manhattan, Henry Street, walking home from work.

I watch as a Chinese boy runs across the street against the light, pumping his legs with great effort, as if to avoid being hit by approaching cars, though they are still far off. He runs right by me. He is a chubby kid—not fat, but thick in the legs and full in the face, like many children his age, maybe nine or 10 years old. His white socks with two red stripes are pulled up too high, nearly to his knees, a style apropos for the early 1980s, but not today. In this neighborhood, it is likely that he is a recent immigrant, or at least that his parents do not speak English as the primary language at home, if at all. We can forgive the boy his less than perfect knowledge of current American pre-adolescent fashion.

I chuckle at the sight of his clumsy stride, and think immediately of Lester Goran's *The Bright Streets of Surfside*, in which Goran describes his complex friendship with Nobel Prize-winning author Isaac Bashevis Singer. The scene: Goran laughs at seeing a fat kid running on the University of Miami's campus, and Singer asks what he is laughing at. Goran responds that the fat kid thinks he's athletic—that he doesn't know how silly he looks when he runs, and that it's funny. Singer answers—ridiculously, as if Goran were making some veiled insult, or challenge, against Singer—that he can run (not the fat kid, but *he*, Singer), and the elderly Nobel Laureate sprints away from Goran as proof of his own athleticism and vigor. Just one of *The Bright Streets of Surfside*'s many demonstrations of the proverbial thin line between genius and madness, and the toll age takes on even the most famous minds, and I remember how beautiful the book is.

The word *beautiful* reminds me of Goran's novel, *Mrs. Beautiful*, and I say the title to myself. The words barely aloud in my ear make me sing Harry Chapin's song, "A Better Place to Be," starting with the end of the song: "I wish that I were beautiful, or that you were halfway blind, I wish I weren't so gosh-darn fat, I wish that you were mine, and I wish that you'd come with me when I leave for home, 'cause we both know all about loneliness, and living all alone." A song like that deserves to last, and I wonder how long it will.

That leads to thoughts of the book I am reading, *Born in the USA: Bruce Springsteen and the American Tradition*. It makes the case that popular art (Springsteen's in particular) can have lasting value and real worth. I agree, but, as much as I respect Chapin's song and Springsteen's work, I know the depth and complexity of their writing—the music notwithstanding—pale next to fiction, and I think of Goran's *Tales from the Irish Club*, and that without its unexpected success he and his work might have disappeared altogether from history, and still might, a fate suffered by many a writer, I am sure. I think of what passes for art, how easily people are taken with the mediocre, or awful, of television and Broadway musicals, of Emmys and Oscars and Tonys, of the herd-like riveted and sycophantic attention society and the media pay to the insubstantial.

All of this occurs to me in the span of fifteen seconds, or twenty, in tangential leaps sparked by a running Chinese boy, and as I walk I wonder if other people think this way, with such rapid and unpredictable associations. I don't know, but am sad at the realization, not new to me but fresh nonetheless, that we live in a society at all levels increasingly less capable of recognizing, let alone appreciating, real art.

Ari McKee
We Are *Too* a Men's Magazine

Observe the human male artist—bright, creative, and yearning to express himself. He's nothing less than half the future of architecture, literature, music, design—the whole of civilization itself. Why then, does the niggling suspicion lurk that the gifted man is possibly something of a sissy boy? It lingers in our social subconscious that a fully masculine man should make a living stringing telephone cable across the western plains or beating a felon with a nightstick, not taking black and white photos of old bridges or thumbing through a thesaurus at one's ergonomically correct desk.

What a nasty little thought it is—that the neighborhood roofer earns more manliness points every day than another guy does in an entire lifetime of pot-throwing, or that the most skilled and inspired sports columnist is a big poof compared to the least talented minor leaguer.

Men's magazines like *Esquire, Maxim, GQ*, and even *Playboy* are on the frontlines of the sensitivity jihad. These pubs contain stables of brilliant men, each surely devoted to fine journalism about literature, art, music, film, and theatre for the modern reader. Those who are straight are probably married or dating bright, successful workingwomen whom they don't want to offend either overtly or irrevocably. But they need to display their balls from time to time. Big, hairy, guy balls.

Where do the balls fit in? Some work them in better than others. Nobody's doing it great all the time. Some trip over them. Some are holding on to them so hard the rest of their work comes out one-handed.

Esquire, maybe because it has some of the best writing, has the deepest, most emotional and confessional writers. Men bare their guts and spill their souls about their work, about the women they love or don't love, about their families, their kids, their fathers, their regrets and triumphs. A while back the money columnist wrote about how he and his wife struggle over spending (her spending). It ended with him squirreling money away into a secret savings fund while his wife took an impulse trip to Amsterdam.

Ouch.

A few months ago it was another married guy who was trying hard to be mature about the annual overseas camping excursion his wife takes with her old boyfriend. I haven't checked bylines, but I've offered up a little prayer that the same guy didn't write both articles. Somehow, having your wife blow the family bank account in order to pitch tents with her ex in Europe (and wanting the reading public to know about it) ... well, for God's sake, man, rent yourself a chin somewhere.

Dysfunctional or not, it's good copy. But it doesn't exactly spell B-A-L-L-Z. What's a manly editor of a manly man's magazine to do? Well, you back it up with lots of half-dressed women, what else? You do a feature on Nicole Kidman and talk about staring at her ass. You shoot Drew Carey wearing a suit with two completely naked women on either side of him like gargoyles on the Chrysler building. (Do I need to add that you don't write about staring at his ass?) You get people to write about bowling, covert wars, NASCAR, and alligator wrestling. You chase down really hot babes and write a couple thousand words about them and the length of their toes and where they shop for panties. And, to boot, it's all good writing. Problem solved. Next issue.

To be fair, it's not just men's magazines. On TV, we have *The X Show, The Man Show,* and the *Howard Stern Show.* Sometimes funny, always randy, offensive in that freshman-art-student way that's basically hostile, and always bubbling, frothing, lathering over with boobs, boobs, and more boobs. Teenage boobs, celebrity boobs, cheerleading boobs, trampoline-animated boobs, regular and new-and-improved boobs. They may be smart guys, writers, performers, filmmakers, but—dammit—they like boobs—girl boobs—and don't you forget it!

No nancy boys here. No, siree.

Of course, consciousness-raising never comes off without a hitch. Susan Faludi called it backlash. Although backlash is a real phenomenon, most of this guy stuff is a lot of noise. For all their ballsy bluster, the mags and shows are careful not to really piss anybody off in the mainstream audience. That audience may not yet include Andrea Dworkin ("when your rape is entertaining, your worthlessness is complete"), but it does include the majority of Americans who now believe things they never believed before, such as:

1. Women work and sweat and think and pay bills.

2. Rape, wife beating, and sexual harassment are real and bad things.

3. Since Ellen, everyone likes dykes.

4. Andrew Dice Clay really was a big idiot.

5. Men and women are going to hate each other's guts once in a while.

6. Women can take a joke.

7. Janeane Garafalo is far more interesting than Uma Thurman, and she makes more movies.

8. Women like sex. They really, really like it! And plenty of them, honestly, still like it with men.

9. Despite social change and contrary to all the early predictions, men are still trying—over and over, 24/7, from sea to shining sea, ad-flippin' infinitum—to sleep with women. Janeane, Uma, Alanis, Monica, Hillary, Chelsea, Tammy-Faye, Courtney, Sable, Xena, Camille—it hasn't escaped our attention that there's a sucker, maybe even fifty or a thousand suckers, for every single one of them, from the daintiest flower to the butchest she-demon. One born, as they say, every freaking minute. And so...

10. Girls rule.

Big, hairy balls or not, the boys are evolving. There's a lot of kicking and screaming and clinging to the carpet, lots of crying about their roles, lots of threats about keeping promises and promises about keeping threats, but they're getting dragged along anyway. The truly missing links, the cultural throwbacks that some modern men like to pretend to be, are inbreeding to extinction or getting shot by federal agents. The rest keep cranking out loud, cutting-edge, soft-porn clamor just to distract us away from how careful they're being, and from noticing how they really don't have an interest in turning back the clock, or in alienating the other gender. They're gamely paddling along upstream, just like they should be. Sure, they're writing crap like *Ally McBeal*, but then again they're writing crap like *Ally McBeal*. It may not be what every riot grrl is taping on her VCR, but it sure as hell isn't *Bewitched*.

Praise them, ladies, admire those hirsute and gargantuan testicles of theirs (ooh, look how BIG!), and book that trip to Amsterdam without a second thought. And if they ask you to dance naked on cable, at least get a 12-episode sitcom deal out of it.

Chuck Sheehan
Furry Doorstops and Quieter Kids

America has a drug problem. I'm not talking about pot, heroin, crack, alcohol, or cigarettes. I'm talking about a bigger drug market that's even more sinister—because it's legal: prescription drugs for kids.

It all started like this: One little kid on some playground in Middletown, USA, was a bit too hyper. Mom and Dad took him to the doctor and the Ritalin craze was born. As the years passed, the kids grew quieter and we liked that. In fact, we liked it so much that we routinely prescribed the adult drug Prozac for kids—and their pets:

"Gee, Muffy is fraught with anxiety. When she pees on the carpet, she thinks the fire hydrant will hold a grudge against her. I tell you, Doc, it's making her a wreck."

"I have just the thing. In fact, after a few doses of this, you'll have that furry doorstop you always wanted."

(By the way, a Prozac prescription for you can cost up to five times more than it does for Fido. So, yes, insurance companies aren't always the bad guys; they're getting screwed by drug companies as well.)

A recent study reported that between 1991 and 1995 there was a 50% increase in the number of Ritalin and Prozac prescriptions written for children ages 2 to 4. Wait a second—a two-year-old on Ritalin and Prozac?! Isn't a two-year-old supposed to be hyper? Isn't that his (or her) job? Has anyone ever heard of the terrible twos?

Even more disturbing is a footnote in the same study claiming that many doctors are concerned for the future of these kids since long-term effects of these drugs on young, growing bodies are not known.

We have effectively taken the effort out of raising our children. As a society, we've lost the war on drugs but have safely reduced the menace of hyperactive, anxiety-riddled kids. Do all those kids really need Ritalin? I went to school with a lot of "hyper" kids. None of them were on medicine and now they are doctors, lawyers, community leaders, unemployed, etc. They are ordinary, everyday people. Their parents disciplined them and raised them to respect others and take responsibility for their actions. They did not let the pharmacy raise their kids by turning them into zombies.

As a society, we've nearly removed the effort from being an adult as well. Just watch TV and count the number of pharmaceutical commercials in an hour. Having a bad day? Having difficulty in the bedroom? Overweight? Well, fret you not. Take a pill. Take two. No wonder our kids are over-prescribed!

Now, if there is an underlying medical condition behind your symptoms, then by all means you should do whatever is necessary to feel and get better. But I would like to talk to the doctor who can accurately diagnose a two-year-old kid with a condition that requires her to be on Prozac. Then again, maybe coloring in pre-school is more competitive than it was in my day.

Reader Comments

—Helen Cates responds to *"Furry Doorstops and Quieter Kids"* by Chuck Sheehan.
My next-door neighbor's two-year-old son is seeing a shrink. He's not speaking well and is aggressive in daycare. This kid is being prescribed Ritalin (his mother's on Prozac). What he really needs is a dose of tender loving care. He spends most of his time with babysitters—both during his mother's employment and afterwards. A typical case of lazy parents and doctors and a stagnant society!

Scott Stein
The Spice of Life ... and Death

It's happened again. Back in 1997, two teens killed two pizza deliverymen after ordering food to an abandoned house in Franklin, New Jersey. The crime was called the "pizza murders," because what is a crime without a catchy name?

This time it isn't pizza, but Chinese food. And the crime didn't take place in New Jersey, but in Queens, New York, where I was born and raised. So my interest in the case isn't a mere matter of my genetic predisposition (as a Jew) to pay attention whenever Chinese food is mentioned.

Four boys and a girl, ages 14-17, lured Jin-Sheng Liu, 44, the owner of a Chinese takeout restaurant, to an empty house. They threw a sheet over his head and beat him with fists and a brick. He died. That tends to happen when hit in the head with a brick. They're heavy.

We will hear much in the coming days about the teens and their backgrounds, to be sure. Please pay attention to how much we do *not* hear about Jin-Sheng Liu.

Charges faced by America's future include manslaughter, robbery, and gun possession. The punk who allegedly delivered the fatal blow is 14 years old, and is being charged as an adult, which means he could be sentenced to nine years to life in prison. This is sure to outrage those against charging juveniles as adults, no matter the offense. Of course, the outraged are still alive, and Jin-Sheng Liu is not.

Police in Queens say the motive for the murder was free food. But this was no Jean Valjean in *Les Misérables*, stealing a loaf of bread to feed his family in poverty-stricken France. No, apparently these teens had ordered Chinese food from a different takeout restaurant earlier the same day, but when they became hungry again they realized that they had no money left. So they used a cell phone to order $60 worth of Chinese food and had it delivered to an empty house. How poor were these kids? They had a cell phone, didn't they?

Queens District Attorney Richard Brown said, "It's a shocking crime that leaves all of us shaking our heads as to why these kids did what they did ... It's a sad commentary, it really is."

I am disappointed in the district attorney. How is he going to gain a conviction if he cannot anticipate the strategy the defense will employ? It's simple, really. If you've ever eaten Chinese food you know that a half-hour later you're hungry again. No doubt these good-hearted and peace-loving teens aren't to blame for this horrible crime. It isn't their fault they beat a man to death with fists and a brick. Probably an after-school program could have prevented the unfortunate incident.

In any case, we all know the real cause of Jin-Sheng Liu's death: Mono Sodium Glutamate, a spice used in Chinese food that makes some people feel unwell. I hear it's also the reason you're hungry again before you've even finished digesting.

Yes, ladies and gentlemen, I present to you the MSG defense.

C.P. Kaiser
The Animal Network

In a daring and bizarre crime that could affect America's worldwide domination of pop culture, the Jaded Animal Crackers Kollection of Animal Super Stars, or JACKASS, has taken credit for the kidnapping of hundreds of television executives. Among the group's demands is a call to replace said CEOs with animal stars, including Eddie from *Frasier*, Scooby-Doo, Norm McDonald's Wiener Dog, the famed Mr. Ed, Zigfried and Roy (them, not their tigers—they're so cute and cuddly), the monkey from *Friends*, and Baretta's parrot. JACKASS officials said they are tired of animals always being the butt of jokes—and poorly written ones at that, they added.

According to a JACKASS communiqué, the executives were taken to the Los Angeles zoo, where they were forced to clean up animal feces. "These so-called TV programmers will now know what it's like to *watch* their programming," claimed the missive. Zoo officials acknowledged that they had to hire extra help the day after JACKASS's stealth mission. "Apparently, these execs can't tell shit from Shinola," said Kitty Hawk, the zoo's PR spokeswoman. "There was crap all over the place. It looked liked the NBC prime-time lineup from the '80s."

The kidnapping was first discovered when executive secretary Penny Whistle thought it strange that her boss didn't answer his beepers, cell phones, car faxes, or secret hot line (only to be used if Carrot Top is in the executive suite). She called the L.A.P.D., who immediately stopped clubbing innocent black men and dispatched all available K-9 units to the scene. Within minutes of arrival, the highly trained German shepherds were shown episodes of *Cop Rock* by JACKASS infiltrators. The dogs quickly turned on their owners, forcing them to run into a nearby Dunkin' Donuts, where fresh crème-filled critters were just being loaded onto the rack. The K-9 corps was then spirited away by the JACKASS conspirators.

On *Nightline*, Ted Koppel debated with a panel of experts whether the Teletubbies should be classified as animals, humans, or gnomes. Former presidential candidate Gary Bauer said that, if nothing else, the purple one certainly should be considered an animal because of its homosexual connotations, and only animals and homosexuals engage in buggery. Chris Rock asked, "What the hell's a Teletubby anyway? Where's Bill Maher?"

It was not immediately clear which studios the detained officials were from, or how long they would be held captive. *Entertainment Weekly* and *People* magazine pleaded with the terrorists to release the television executives so that everything could return to normal. Supermarket chains expressed concern over the impending dearth of cover material for their checkout magazine section. "What will our patrons think about while standing in line for 10 minutes?" asked Tom Turkey, spokesman for the Stupor Fresh chain of stores.

In an unusual show of support, movie executives asked that all Planet Hollywoods close their doors from noon until 12:15, to show their solidarity. *The New York Times*, however, suggested that movie execs fear they may be JACKASS's next targets.

The kidnapping also threatens to further alienate masses of ordinary people from becoming Nielson families, a threat that Madison Avenue is not taking lightly. "What kind of programming can dogs and monkeys come up with?" asked advertising executive Robin Redbreast. "Monkeys might be able to type *Hamlet*, but can they direct it? We'll be ruined. There'll be nothing but nature programs on, and we all know they don't bring in the bucks."

For now, at least, it seems progress is slow. Grilling Mr. Ed for hours (without an attorney present, of course), the L.A.P.D. finally relented, releasing the famous '60s TV star on his own recognizance. "Ohh, Wilbur," was all Mr. Ed had to say.

Rev. Angeline E.M. Theisen
Fair is Better than Equal

As devoted as I am to the democratic process, I find I am not always a pure egalitarian. Sometimes I think unequal is more fair.

This week I visited an elderly man whose health in recent years has made him a near shut-in. We talked of his long life—his careers as a general practice physician and then a psychiatrist, his interest in music, and his many travels. His home attests to the last two, with its comfortable display of primitive musical instruments, and the piano and small harpsichord in the parlor.

Toward the end of the visit—much of it spiced with his lively humor—he made the first deeply serious remark. He said he'd been crying a lot lately. "And it's only for myself, nobody else," he quickly added, "Because I know I'm going to have to leave the world soon."

Throughout his long years of failing health, during each severe illness, he knew he would recover to experience more of life. After the next surgery or the next treatment, there would be a plateau of health during which there would be more—more picnics, more summer travels, more concerts, more lectures, more gatherings of friends, more life.

His friends still meet in his home once a week to play music together, but now he is too weak to join them, so he listens. His body is hooked up to machines twelve hours out of every twenty-four, just to sustain life. And suddenly, he sees no more plateaus. So he cries. "I just hate to leave," he tells me.

His wife, who has been listening to our conversation, explains, "He has always had a boyish enthusiasm for everything, like a child, so excited about it all." It is apparent to me, who knew him in no earlier period, that he still feels that way, only now his body can no longer accommodate him. So his mind races and his eyes fill with tears, as his fingers restlessly stroke the top of his cane, where his constant touch has produced the beautiful sheen. His graceful hands seem to be those of a much younger man.

I tell his wife, "It just doesn't seem fair. People with Bill's voracious appetite for life should not have to die on the same schedule as the rest of us. They should get an extra hundred years."

I really mean it. If this man were given an extra hundred years, and I, who will never achieve half of his spontaneity, die on schedule, I would never complain. It wouldn't be equal. It would be better than equal. It would be fair.

I feel the same way about my mother. My mother can tell you precisely what is going to happen to her in the moments following her death. She will be reunited with my dad and brother in a setting of white clouds, silver bells, and heavenly music. It's going to be just like those miraculous endings pictured in fantasy films of the 1940s. And I, who have a much more pragmatic view of life and death, don't think it's going to happen quite that way. But in my mother's case, I'd like to be wrong.

If, after death, she could get the heaven that she envisions, and I, who see death as the natural end of life, am stuck with oblivion, I would never grouse about it. I think my mother not only deserves her heaven, she's earned it. So if she ends up waltzing on clouds with my dad because that's what she believes, while I end up contributing to the nurture of garden flowers, because that's what I believe, that seems fair to me.

If the universe were mine to run as I like, I would give to my new friend the extra hundred years that he would use so well, and to my mother the heavenly reward that she believes in so deeply. I would no doubt keep both my limited enthusiasms and my belief in the natural order, so I would get neither.

But you wouldn't catch me complaining about it. So what if it wouldn't be equal? It would be better than equal. It would be fair.

Scott Stein
Infidel

Setting: *Small bedroom.* **STEVEN** *is sleeping in bed. An eerie red light fills the room, and a high-pitched wailing wakes him. The sound ends but the light remains.*

STEVEN: (*Sitting up quickly and looking at the light.*) What the...?

VOICE: (*Offstage, very deep*) Steven, I have come for you.

STEVEN: (*Looking around, checking under his covers, even his bed.*) Is someone there? Where are you?

VOICE: You will come with me, Steven. I command you.

STEVEN: (*Standing up*) I'm not going anywhere. Show yourself.

(*A* MAN *with horns on his head, a red, pointy tail, and carrying a pitchfork, enters.*)

DEVIL: (*Voice much less deep and intimidating once onstage.*) Here I am, Steven. You will come with me. I claim your soul in the name of evil.

STEVEN: My what?

DEVIL: (*A little annoyed that he has to repeat himself, and trying to sound as menacing as possible.*) I said, I claim your soul in the name of evil!

STEVEN: I'm sorry, sir, I didn't catch all of that. You want my what?

DEVIL: (*Shaking his head, and speaking very slowly.*) Listen carefully, mortal fool. I claim your soul. Your SOUL!

(STEVEN *says nothing, but the look on his face makes it clear that he still doesn't understand.*)

DEVIL: You have to know what a soul is!

STEVEN: It does sound familiar. Maybe if you used it in a sentence.

DEVIL: Don't play dumb with me. You can't deceive the Father of Lies.

(STEVEN *has a blank look on his face.*)

DEVIL: The Father of Lies. Perhaps you know me as Lucifer? The Prince of Darkness? I am Satan, the Serpent, the Antichrist! ... the Devil?

STEVEN: It rings a bell ... I just can't place the face with the name. But my memory isn't the greatest, you know.

DEVIL: (*Beginning to panic, showing a touch of insecurity.*) You must know me. I'm the Prince of the Underworld, the Angel of the Bottomless Pit.

STEVEN: (*Shrugging*) Sorry.

DEVIL: (*In disbelief*) What kind of moron are you?

STEVEN: Look, there's no need for insults. Not everyone has to know you. (*Aside*) What an ego!

DEVIL: Didn't you ever go to Sunday school?

STEVEN: Of course I did. What kind of person do you think I am?

DEVIL: And you never heard of me?

STEVEN: Well, I didn't go every week. My family wasn't that religious.

DEVIL: But you must have heard of the unholy alliance? Of the great uprising? Of my fall from grace? Did you learn nothing?

STEVEN: (*Dreamy look in his eyes and nodding his head.*) I remember this really cute blonde girl. She sat two seats over on my left...

DEVIL: (*Sobbing into his hands.*) It isn't fair. It just isn't fair.

STEVEN: (*Trying to comfort the* DEVIL, *pats him on the shoulder.*) It'll be OK. I've been meaning to read up on all that stuff.

DEVIL: (*Peeking through his fingers.*) Really?

STEVEN: I'm going to the bookstore first thing in the morning.

(DEVIL *looks at* STEVEN *with doubt.*)

STEVEN: I promise.

DEVIL: (*Immediately regains his composure and confidence. He pulls out a sheet of paper and a pen.*) It is of no consequence. Sign here, and your soul will be mine.

(DEVIL *lets out an evil laugh.*)

STEVEN: (*Reading the contract.*) It seems a bit complicated. Maybe I should have my attorney look at it. Do you have a number where I can reach you? I could fax it over to you in the afternoon.

DEVIL: Fax? There are no fax machines in Hell.

STEVEN: (*Scratching his head.*) Hell?

DEVIL: (*Shrieking and running from the room.*) Noooo!!!

(*The red light goes out. A soft blue light shines on* STEVEN *and violins and a harp can be heard in the background.*)

VOICE: (*Offstage, deep and pleasant*) Good work, my son. You have resisted temptation.

STEVEN: Who's there?

VOICE: It is I, King of the Universe, the Lord your God.

STEVEN: (*Slowly shaking his head.*) Who?

(*Lights out.*)

-THE END-

Bob Sullivan
Top Ten Easiest Jobs in the World

10. Robert Downey Jr.'s connection
9. Dan Quayle's acceptance speechwriter
8. Selling Girl Scout cookies to Bill Clinton
7. The guy at NASA in charge of recording signals from the Mars Polar Lander (well, it's not like they're rocket scientists!)
6. Marcel Marceau's vocal coach
5. Jesse "the Body" Ventura's ego massager
4. Soap salesperson at Parisian Bed, Bath & Beyond
3. Joe Piscopo's press agent
2. Amish television repairman

And the Number 1 Easiest Job in the World is...

1. George W. Bush's ethics adviser

Robert O'Hara
In Hitler's Defense

I was in a bookstore last week and asked a clerk where I could find *Mein Kampf*. The young woman gave me a dirty look, and said, "We don't have those types of books here."

I learned a simple truth from the young woman's reaction: it might be impossible to explore racism without being accused of it. That is the power of taboo.

Defending racists is even riskier business—just ask Marge Schott, former owner of the Cincinnati Reds. Other team owners ran Schott out of Major League Baseball, in large part because of some controversial remarks she made in an interview a few years ago, in which she heralded Hitler as an effective leader. To say Hitler was ineffective sounds absurd, but to say he was effective is somehow worse.

In November 1997, Chris Simon of the National Hockey League's Washington Capitals received a three-game suspension for calling an opposing black player a nigger. Simon, a Native-American, is no stranger to racial slurs and insists he is not a racist. In *Sports Illustrated*, Toronto Maple Leafs president Ken Dryden addressed the issue, saying that hockey players will use anything they can to rattle an opponent: "When you're mad at somebody, you pick out the most obvious thing about him and abuse him with it."

Racism—discrimination or prejudice by race—is an infection, and, like any infection, you can't find a cure until you find the cause. The cause is a lazy mind. People see patterns in society and associate them with the value of whole groups of people, such as blacks are good fighters and whites are good students. These associations hold as much merit as saying Japanese children speak Japanese the best. There is no reason to believe that a French child who grows up in Japan wouldn't speak Japanese just as well. Historical circumstance and environment breed these patterns, and nothing else. But even people who oppose racism don't want to get this deep. So the people who want to end racism the most are the furthest from the cure—hence the epidemic we have on our hands.

How many of you turned to this essay because of its title? The name *Hitler* has too much power. The swastika was a symbol of well-being and good luck for thousands of years before the rise of Nazi Germany, yet the primary definition the *American Heritage Dictionary* gives for swastika is: "The emblem of Nazi Germany, officially adopted in 1935."

Racism, nationalism, and other belief systems have us so worried about what's wrong, we can't find what's right. A book like *Mein Kampf* must remain available. You can't change the way people think if you don't know what they think and why. What's the worst that can happen—some bigot reads it and becomes even more racist than he was before? What about lost souls who may stumble upon the book for guidance? If we have to protect ourselves from that, then we may as well ban the Bible, which has fostered more discrimination throughout history than *Mein Kampf* could ever hope to. No book should be judged by what it might inspire the worst minds to do.

We should stop giving people like Schott so much attention. First, that is exactly what she wants. Second, Hitler *was* effective, and professing so does not necessarily contend that he was successful or admirable. We have to learn from him, and we can't do that if we make the mere mention of his name taboo.

And we shouldn't label these hockey players as racists—not because they deserve better, but because it is inaccurate and exacerbates the problem. You need to know what the problem is in order to solve it, and the problem in this case is a lack of discipline. Those who commit acts we have defined as racist are simply not strong or smart enough to make their point without exploiting the obvious. As Ken Dryden puts it, "The problem isn't that people don't know the words are harmful; the problem is they know they are."

Suzanne Hakanen
Recipe for Surviving Thanksgiving with Your Mother

INGREDIENTS
1 fifth of vodka that has been stored in the freezer (do not defrost)
1 six-pack of beer, separated and chilled thoroughly
1 firmly packed box of cigarettes
30 cookies (homemade)
10 cups of reflection time (separated into 60-second portions)
2 earplugs

PREPARATION
Begin preparing at least two hours before the dinner. Drink the vodka. (Vodka is a mild spirit with no discernable odor. Hopefully your mother will not notice you're totally lit).

When you get to your mother's house, grab a cold beer and your smokes and head for the backyard to "walk the dog." Remain outside as long as possible. If available, bring your spouse/significant other with you to "keep warm" in the tool shed.

When you do come in, grab the cookies and another cold beer and make a dash upstairs to your former bedroom and play some Nintendo with your siblings. Pick a game that takes two hours to play. If you don't, your cousin Robby will start whining, "I want to play the winner." Keep him out of it. Scarf the cookies down and cleanse palate with beer.

Eventually, you will have to hang out with your mother. Grab two more beers and empty them into an opaque squeeze bottle. This way, Mom can pretend she doesn't know you're drinking to ease the pain of listening to her nag and complain.

If you are an unmarried woman, your mother will probably criticize you for not being married. When this happens, take out 60 seconds of reflection time and keep your mouth shut. You DO NOT want to start the holiday festivities by telling your mother to fuck off.

If you are a married woman and have no children, your mother will probably criticize you for not having any children. When this happens, take out another 60 seconds of reflection time and keep your mouth shut. You DO NOT want to start the holiday festivities by telling your mother to fuck off.

If you are a married woman and you have children, your mother will be forced to choose from a long list of alternate nagging points, such as your hair, your weight, your complexion, your job, your husband's weight, your husband's job, your brother's girlfriend's driving record, drinking habits, hair length, job, etc. Continue to consume 60 seconds of reflection time for each point. When you run out, pop in the earplugs and smile maniacally at everything your mother says. You DO NOT want to end the holiday festivities by telling your mother to fuck off.

Scott Stein
Making Change

Danny had eight minutes. He had somehow found a spot on the Boulevard, a rare enough occurrence, and there were still eight minutes left on the parking meter. Danny took this as another sign that his luck was changing. First had come the call for a second interview with Steadfast Real Estate, then the great deal on his new suit, and now, after getting caught in traffic and worrying about being late for his appointment, he finds the perfect spot, with time on the meter no less. He smiled at his good fortune, then cursed himself for not having a quarter—he almost always had change in his pocket—and rushed from his dusty, blue Plymouth with crinkled dollar bill in hand.

The midsummer New York sun broke through the clouds, and Danny squinted and shaded his eyes with the manila folder containing his letters of reference. He adjusted his tie and walked with forced confidence as he mentally prepared for the interview: firm handshake, maintain eye contact, nod agreement, remember to smile. Eight minutes were plenty to make change, and he would actually be on time for his appointment. He stopped outside the video arcade where he'd played Pac Man as a boy and admired his reflection in the plate glass window. Neat hair, shoes shined, gold watch he'd received a year prior from his parents for graduation—all hinted at success. Still, his new navy blue suit was fraying slightly at the sleeves, and Danny resolved not to shop at discount outlets in the future.

The arcade was dark and crowded with children and teenagers; Danny felt old as he weaved his way to the change machine. A freckled girl in denim overalls with red ribbons in her blond hair scooped her quarters from the machine and moved off. Danny inserted his dollar and awaited the clank of coins as they hit the tray, but heard only a dull hum as his money was returned to him, rejected. He flattened and rubbed the dollar against the metal surface of the machine and tried again, releasing the bill into the slot with a restrained flourish, as if to influence the outcome. For a second he was sure it had worked but was disappointed when it was again rejected. He searched in vain his pockets and wallet, knowing before he looked that this was his only dollar.

Danny glanced at his watch—he still had six minutes. He briefly considered leaving his car in the spot without feeding the meter, but knew that there was time enough to both get a quarter and make his appointment. Danny had parked illegally for his last job interview, with a telemarketing firm nearly two months earlier, and remembered now how this had rattled him. The memory of the spectacle he had made, sweating through his shirt and hiccuping sharply for twenty minutes as the Personnel Manager explained that a calm, smooth phone manner was the main requirement for the position, brought a burn to the back of his throat as his stomach tightened. His mother had told him that one day he would laugh at this experience, that at least he had a story to tell from it, but amusement was far from his mind now as his breathing quickened and the dollar bill grew moist in his hand. He couldn't afford a parking ticket, less still another failed interview. No, there was plenty of time.

"Excuse me," Danny said in a soft voice to a cluster of teenage boys. "Does anyone have change of a dollar?" The boys just laughed and hooted as they watched the onscreen digital champion gleefully decapitate his vanquished opponent. Danny thought it would be best to ask someone else.

A large man, even fatter than he was tall, in faded blue slacks, like the kind janitors sometimes wear, was leaning against a pinball machine. With every ring and buzz his enormity jiggled as he shoved, pulled, and nearly lifted the machine in an attempt to move the silver ball closer to one of the flippers. His yellowing T-shirt didn't quite cover his torso, and he pushed his black-rimmed glasses higher on his nose in a well-practiced motion every few seconds, his hand darting back each time to its station at the machine's side.

Danny stopped next to him and waited a moment for the man to acknowledge his presence. The large man took no notice, and paused between turns to light a long brown cigarette, apparently unaware of the No Smoking sign on the wall to his right.

"Excuse me," Danny stammered. "Do you have four quarters for a dollar?"

"Machine's over there," he answered, gripping the cigarette in his teeth and not looking away from the ricocheting ball.

"I know, but, you see, it won't take my dollar." Danny wiped his forehead with the back of his hand.

"Shit," the man said as his turn came to an end. He looked Danny in the eye. "You broke my concentration."

Danny swallowed hard. "I didn't mean to. I mean, I'm sorry. I really just need change for the meter."

"Don't have any change," he said, turning back to his machine.

There were two rows of quarters resting on the glass in front of the man, but Danny asked, "How about a dollar? The machine won't take this one."

The man turned to Danny. "You're not gonna leave, are you?"

Danny smiled nervously, thinking he should leave.

"Gimme that then." The man snatched the dollar from Danny's hand. He pulled a billfold from his shirt pocket, removed a single, and handed it to Danny. "Can I play in peace now?"

Danny took the crisp bill and thanked the man, who shook his head in disgust. There was no line for the change machine and Danny nodded in triumph as he worked the pristine dollar between his thumb and forefinger. As he was reaching to insert his money he saw a small flashing red light next to three simple words: Not In Service. Danny halfheartedly kicked the machine, careful not to draw too much attention. Ridiculous, he thought, how could a video arcade be out of change?

The little blond girl with red ribbons was standing on a plastic milk crate at a machine, firing the brightly painted gun at several video bank robbers who each died with more blood and commotion than the last. Danny heard pained grunts and explosions as she shot cars, windows, bystanders and their pets, along with the criminals, who succeeded in ending the girl's game with the toss of a grenade. The girl stamped her foot on the crate—it swayed—and dug into the pocket of her overalls for change to play another game. The screen lit up and assured her in writing, beneath the seal of the FBI, that Winners Don't Use Drugs.

Danny had four minutes. "Little girl, do you have any quarters?"

The blond girl turned halfway and stared at him, but said nothing.

"Do you have any quarters?" he asked again.

"I don't talk to strangers" was all she said before stepping down from her crate and walking to another game, on which was mounted a larger gun. Danny followed her.

"I'm not a stranger," he said, breathing harder now, "I just need a quarter. Do you have any?" —*hiccup*.

The girl giggled. "That's funny. Do it again."

"No. It's not funny. I only have three minutes" —*hiccup*.

She sort of cackled, pointing at him and doubling over, and said through her laughter, "I'll give you a quarter to do it again."

Danny's face reddened and he grabbed her arm. "It isn't funny."

She stopped laughing, her eyes watered over, and Danny let go.

"I'm sorry," he said, "Don't cry. I barely touched you" —*hiccup*.

The girl didn't laugh this time but only looked at him, tears beginning to trickle down her face.

Danny ran outside, his head throbbing, sweat dripping from his upper lip. He dashed up the block and into a 51 Flavors Ice Cream shop. The window's flickering neon ice cream cone reflected palely in the display case glass. Chocolate and vanilla giraffe-shaped cakes with rainbow sprinkles lined one shelf, assorted candles and plastic decorations, the other. The recently mopped tile floor smelled faintly of ammonia and two small, round tables with three wood chairs each were against the wall opposite the cash register. Danny stood beneath a ceiling fan.

The coolness calmed him a bit, and he ran a finger around the inside of his shirt collar to let in some air. He breathed deeply and fanned himself with his folder. He hadn't really done anything wrong. Take it easy, he told himself, don't blow things out of proportion. He still had an interview, there was still time to get change.

"Excuse me," Danny said, offering his dollar to the teenage boy behind the counter. "Can I have some change please?"

"I can't give change unless you buy something," the boy told him as he wiped his hands on his maroon apron.

"I just need a quarter for the meter," Danny assured him.

"I'm sorry, sir, but I'm not allowed to open the register without ringing up a purchase."

Danny thought about looking elsewhere, shrugged his shoulders, and said, "Fine. What can I get for a dollar?"

"One of these," he answered, pointing to a birthday candle with a smiling clown's face just below the wick.

"Great," Danny said, "just what I need. I'll take one."

"That'll be eighty cents."

"Eighty cents?"

"Yep."

"You don't have anything cheaper? I need a quarter for the meter."

"Oh," the boy said, "this is the cheapest thing we have."

"I don't believe this," Danny muttered.

"You don't want the candle then?"

"No, I don't." Danny could barely get the words out.

The boy shook a confused look from his face and walked into the back storeroom.

On the counter, next to the register, was a large plastic jug filled halfway with change. Meals for the Blind was written in large letters across its side, and Danny smiled. He leaned across the counter to be sure that the boy wasn't coming out of the storeroom and, with trembling fingers, quietly unscrewed the cover. The coins warmed his fingers as he picked out four quarters. It was funny, he thought, how things work out, and for the first time today knew in his heart he was going to win.

"What do you think you're doing?" a deep voice asked from the shop entrance. A police officer, a young man with broad shoulders and dark sunglasses, stood in the doorway with his hands on his hips.

"Oh, officer, I was just getting change." Danny held his dollar in the air as proof.

"You were?" the policeman asked.

"Yes, I have an interview for a job and I needed change for the meter."

"I don't have time for this anyway," the cop said. "Did you see anyone run by this store? A large man, with a scar across his cheek and a gun?"

"No, sir." Danny was relieved that he wasn't in trouble for his small indiscretion with the donation jug.

"Some bastard just assaulted a little girl in the arcade down the block. You sure you haven't seen anyone?"

"Yes, sir. No, I mean, I haven't seen anybody at all." Danny felt a lump in the back of his throat.

"OK, then." The officer turned to leave.

–hiccup.

"What was that?" He turned around and rested a hand on his nightstick.

"What?" Danny asked.

"That sound, you didn't hear it?"

Danny shook his head. "No, sir."

"You're sure?" He stepped closer.

Danny nodded. *–hiccup.*

"So you think you can slap little girls around, do you?" The cop grabbed Danny's arm and twisted it behind his back. Danny didn't resist as the folder with his letters of reference fluttered to the floor.

"You make me sick," the officer said, throwing Danny up against the wall. "What kind of person attacks an innocent girl? And stealing from the blind, you piece of garbage." He handcuffed Danny and shoved him through the doorway, making sure to bang him up against the door as they exited the shop.

C.P. Kaiser
If Boys Will Be Boys, Why Can't Girls Be Girls?

Did you see the commercial where former Senator Bob Dole touts the benefits of Viagra, admitting proudly, "It works well." We could all read between the lines: Good ole Bob was fucking Liddy like he hadn't in 40 years (and certainly not for reproductive purposes).

In addition to the communal psychic disturbance of the image of that so-called conservative Republican smirking with sexual satisfaction, there were some serious social ramifications, namely, the ever-widening gap between what men are allowed to do with their reproductive instincts and what women are not allowed to do with theirs.

Maybe I wasn't listening too closely, but I heard no protest from the conservative white male hierarchy who routinely assault female sexuality as if it were a spreading cancer in need of control and cure. Did anyone on the right complain about this abuse of sexual power? No, because we respond differently to men's sexual escapades than we do to women's.

How about some equality? In order to make the use of Viagra and a man's control of his sexuality meet the same anti-choice restrictions as women's birth control and abortion in the United States, the following standards ought to be established and enforced:

- You must be married to obtain a prescription for Viagra.

- You must get spousal consent to obtain Viagra.

- Use of Viagra for masturbation is illegal, unless sperm is collected in a sterile container and donated to infertile couples trying to conceive.

- Military personnel may not access Viagra at overseas military facilities, even if they use their own funds.

- If you work for the government, your doctor may not prescribe, refer, or even discuss Viagra with you. If your physician does so, he will no longer be permitted to participate in a government-subsidized medical care program.

- If a patient is over the age of 65, before he can obtain Viagra he must appear before a judge to demonstrate that he is in command of his faculties and understands fully the impact and responsibility of inducing an erection.

- Viagra shall only be used for the purpose of procreation.

- The FDA shall receive no tax dollars for research for any drugs (including further research on Viagra) that promote sexual promiscuity.

- Medicaid recipients shall not receive Viagra, as one must be financially established in order to accept the responsibility of an erection.

- If a pregnancy results from the use of Viagra and that pregnancy ends in an abortion, the physician who prescribed the Viagra will be punished to the fullest extent of the law.

- Pharmacies should be routinely besieged by religious protestors belligerently trying to persuade Viagra customers to go home and think about their decision to have an erection.

In an equal world, not only would we watch and accept Bob Dole's advice on achieving the ultimate boner, but we'd eagerly watch Liddy Dole's endorsement of the female condom.

Jeffrey Scheuer
Hooked: A Journal of Addiction and Malediction

For years, I've wanted to tell General Barry McCaffrey, the Clinton drug czar, about my Coke addiction. I have been a Coke addict for approximately the last fifteen years. Not regular Coke, but Diet Coke. Now, you may think this doesn't concern you or the good General. But it does. First, a bit more autobiography.

I guess I have a somewhat addictive personality, but I don't go into withdrawal when deprived of Diet Coke or commit crimes to support my habit. I enjoy beer and wine, in moderation. And I've never been a hard drug user—only a soft-drink abuser. I do enjoy marijuana, and it's never done me anything but good. I'm not addicted to it and never have been, and I doubt it's an addictive substance. It's got none of the strangely mesmeric properties as does Diet Coke.

In fact, my only addictive experience outside of Diet Coke has been with pipe tobacco. I've never been a cigarette smoker. I puff an occasional cigarette as a pipe substitute. And when I say puff, I mean it: like our President, I never inhale. I used to be a hardened pipe smoker, and that's a difficult habit to break. Mine is probably, in clinical terms, an addiction. I smoked a pipe from my late teens until my early thirties, for one and only one reason: it was immensely pleasurable. It also helped me focus when working, inducing a trancelike state of heightened concentration. After more than a decade, I quit cold turkey, for medical reasons (which, as it turned out, quitting the pipe failed to alleviate). In a symbolic gesture, like Ahab in *Moby Dick*, I threw my lit pipe sizzling into the ocean, hoping the literary bond would steel me for withdrawal. I missed the thing for months, but I got over it.

A decade later—which is now about five years ago—I started pipe smoking again. Once more I found the habit pleasurable and a boost to my concentration. Maybe I was addicted (or re-addicted) to nicotine, maybe not, despite never inhaling. I never experienced the desire to smoke as a physical craving; it always seemed more like a wish for pleasure, or at worst, an emotional tool. Call it what you will.

A year or so ago, I gave up the pipe once again, this time at the strong suggestion of my dentist, who worried that I might get cancer of the mouth.

"How soon?" I rather stupidly asked him.

"Tomorrow would be soon enough," my dentist replied.

I didn't wait until tomorrow; I quit that day.

There have been a few occasional relapses, but by and large I think I'm finished with the pipe (at this writing I haven't touched it in more than three months). The thing of it is, quitting is not hard. And there, as Captain Ahab said, is the most diabolical difference, a weird, nasty paradox: giving up pipe smoking is never a question of can or can't—I always can. It's a question of the deprivation I'm willing to withstand. And the more often I *occasionally* smoke, the harder it is to withstand the craving. If I stop for a few weeks or a few months, the craving usually abates or disappears entirely. (Right now, however, I'd love to light up; I've thought about it every day for the past week. Only my self-esteem prevents me.) It's a craving I seldom give in to, but it's a big nuisance.

As for marijuana, I enjoy smoking it; under the right circumstances I enjoy it a lot. I don't smoke dope often—seldom more than a few times a year—and I'm certainly not addicted to it, and I doubt it's addictive at all.

Again, some personal history: I first smoked pot in high school, on a very limited basis, then in college, on a less limited basis, but still only occasionally. For years after college, I smoked very infrequently—maybe once a year or less. It wasn't a conscious choice, more a matter of lifestyle and with whom I hung out. When around pot smokers, I'd have the occasional toke and enjoy it; when not, I didn't miss it. I still don't.

Then, a decade or so ago, I started having severe back pain caused by a herniated disc. On many occasions, my condition has been so debilitating—my back being in a state of spasm—that I have barely been able to walk for days or weeks at a time. I found that marijuana eased the pain far more effectively than painkillers or muscle relaxants, with none of the side effects—the grogginess or lethargy, even depression, that can accompany heavy pain medication. So, after years of virtual abstinence, I began smoking marijuana again, every once in a while. In my entire life, I probably have smoked fewer than a hundred joints. But I enjoyed every one of them.

Except during those periods of back pain (which have abated somewhat in recent years), smoking has been a purely social event for me; only once or twice have I ever smoked a joint alone. And I've never felt a compulsion to smoke it. It has not been a "gateway" to anything but a good time or pain-reduction. Tobacco is a far more difficult substance to disengage with.

Now here's the tough part: We Americans have a deep, neurotic fear in our national psyche. It's not about hard drugs, which we are sensible to shun. It's about pleasure and consciousness and guilt. And I think this is why we still classify marijuana as a drug while treating nicotine and alcohol as some sort of adult candy. This is why we tolerate draconian laws that not only punish harmless people to an outlandish extent for possession or use of marijuana, but even worse, deprive sick people of its medical benefits. It's a national disgrace.

And another disgrace is the dangerously stupid talk about the dangers of marijuana. All this propaganda is a disservice to our citizens who need to understand the real dangers of substance abuse. Hard drugs, alcohol, and nicotine kill hundreds of thousands of people annually, ruin lives on a daily basis, and misguide children. I have kids of my own and I want to protect them from such things. I certainly wouldn't encourage them to use marijuana—but I won't lie to them about it either. (Diet Coke? Well, we can take that up another time.)

The frailty of our democracy is its vulnerability to systematic folly when fools are looking for votes. It's easier to demonize marijuana and enact tough laws against it than to explain why it should be legalized. Coming out against anything makes politicians look tough and resolute. No one, certainly not in the media, demands that our politicos engage in critical thinking and discriminate between harmless and harmful psychoactive substances. To a politician, one substance is pretty much like another. Nuances only count for political posturing. If our candidates had any courage, they would debate the legalization of marijuana (what the heck, one of them has to lose anyway). Just once I'd like to see a furious debate about marijuana where no one comes up for air until all is said and done (literally, a debate where no one inhales).

A recent study by NORML (National Organization to Reform Marijuana Laws) titled "Still Crazy After All These Years," states, "Marijuana prohibition is a misapplication of the criminal sanction which undermines respect for the law in general and extends the government into inappropriate areas of private lives." With that in mind, our courageous presidential candidates, in preparing for their lively debate over decriminalization of marijuana, might start by putting a few facts before the American people. For example:

- As many as a quarter of all Americans have smoked marijuana at some point in the last decade, with few or no ill-effects.

- The National Commission on Marijuana and Drug Abuse recommended to Congress in 1972 that marijuana be decriminalized, finding that the prohibition of it is significantly more harmful to the user than is marijuana itself. Subsequent studies have come to the same conclusion.

- Since that recommendation to decriminalize marijuana was made nearly thirty years ago, some ten million Americans have been arrested on marijuana charges, at enormous public and personal cost.

- American taxpayers are spending about $7 to $10 billion per year, conservatively estimated, on marijuana enforcement alone—not counting the costs of prosecution and incarceration. (It costs about $23,000 per year to incarcerate someone, not counting the external social and economic costs of their incarceration.) And get this: marijuana arrests in the Clinton administration are up 30% over the Bush administration. So, Mr. Clinton, who never inhaled, has gotten really tough on those miscreants who do. Our prisons are overflowing with harmless, low-level "drug abusers."

- According to NORML, "Nonviolent marijuana offenders often receive longer prison sentences than those allotted to violent offenders." This is both morally and fiscally appalling. Talk about a cause for disrespecting the law and the criminal justice system! Police and prosecutors should be on the front line for legalization.

- Marijuana is known to have therapeutic value for alleviating the symptoms of cancer, glaucoma (the leading cause of blindness in America), and multiple sclerosis. Marijuana is most often used medically as an anti-nauseant for cancer chemotherapy patients. It is also a successful therapy for symptoms (such as nausea, vomiting, and loss of appetite) experienced by AIDS patients.

- Criminalizing marijuana has not stemmed its use or had any positive effects on American society. By any reasonable measure, social, scientific or otherwise, alcohol and tobacco are far more dangerous than marijuana.

- Yes, there is some evidence that continuous heavy use of marijuana is unhealthy—for example, that it damages memory. It is likewise dangerous to drink or smoke heavily, or to eat too many Mars bars.

- There is evidence suggesting that marijuana, if used to excess, is as bad for you as tobacco. If that is the case, we should treat it like tobacco and educate people about its harmful effects—not throw them in jail. I would indeed be worried about the health risks of marijuana, if I smoked regularly. "[A]side from its psychoactive ingredients," states the NORML report, "marijuana smoke contains virtually the same toxic gases and carcinogenic tars as tobacco." Good reason to take it easy on marijuana smoking—which I do. The only difference is that tobacco is much more addictive, and pipe smoking tobacco even more so (even though I don't inhale—really). "Fortunately," NORML reports, "the hazards of marijuana smoking can be reduced by various strategies," including using more potent cannabis because it can be smoked in smaller quantities; using water pipes and other smoke-reduction techniques; and taking marijuana orally instead of smoking it.

General McCaffrey, tell the truth to the American people. Marijuana, in the general scheme of things, is fairly harmless, and what harm it does is almost exclusively to the user, and not (as with alcohol) also to society. It's certainly less harmful than other substances that are legal for adults and readily available to our children, such as alcohol and nicotine. Don't be a dope, General. Relax, tell the truth, and have a Diet Coke. I'll join you.

Scott Stein

Alzheimer's, Max and Flo

Where are my shoes? The stupid rascals.
Who are you? What is this place? Where's my car?
is my name and I was born in Poland but that was back in
I can still walk but they make me use this chair—I was a butcher

Bronx but my
You look familiar
leave me alone
I don't need any pill

have you seen my pill?
them talking about me
I don't know you at all
when I shot Arafat and
there was singing and
I bought that mountain
they stole my car from
my son, his name is
Give me a minute, if only
Why are you bothering me?
I push but the door is locked
they're after me but I'll get them
eight silver dollars up in the closet
call my son, he'll know what to
do, in the crawl space
in a cigar box under
a sheet. Why do you
look at me like that?
Don't touch those
silver dollars, they're
from my wife, God
rest her soul. Go
away. Please. Go.

I'm
your
wife and
my name
is Flo and there
are no silver dollars.
But I'm still here and
will not leave until
you're sleeping.
Dream well,
Max.

www.WFtheColiseum.com

Jeff Podell
A Choice? Maybe. But Whose?

"A woman's right to choose"—a very interesting phrase. The ability to make choices for oneself is inseparable from freedom. In fact, to many it is synonymous with freedom. Our country is based on freedom. The freedom to associate with whom we desire, to say what we please, and to worship as we see fit; the freedom to enter into contracts without coercion or duress and to defend our lives and the lives of our family; and the freedom to travel as we please and for our private property to be used as we determine.

In order to maintain these freedoms and human rights, which broadly speaking are life, liberty, and property, we have empowered ourselves through our government to protect such rights. We have done so by punishing crimes against life and other forms of bodily harm (murder, rape, assault, etc.), against liberty (kidnapping, slavery, false imprisonment, etc.), and against property (larceny, fraud, unlawful search and seizure, etc.).

Now let us return to the curious phrase "a woman's right to choose." To choose what? Obviously, an abortion, but what is an abortion? An abortion is the purposeful termination of a pregnancy through the destruction of the fetus. A fetus, of course, is a pre-born human. Once conception occurs it is an inescapable fact that if allowed to develop, a pre-born human is born, becoming a post-born human. Every single one of us was at one time a pre-born human, and never has a pre-born human developed into another creature, like, say, a frog. It just doesn't happen. What then really is the difference between a pre-born human and a post-born human? At times along development, a pre-born human is closer developmentally to a newborn than a newborn is to a 35-year-old adult human. The only substantial difference between a pre-born human and post-born human is their place of residence.

So a woman's right to choose is actually the right to destroy or kill a pre-born human. A legal right to abortion is in fact a legal right to kill. And since there is no example of a guilty pre-born human, abortion is the killing of an innocent human and, therefore, homicide. Now, in our society, we have rightly put degrees of criminality on homicide or, in some cases, declared some forms of homicide, such as killing in self-defense, to be justified. In our society, we have made decisions on these gradations by democratic means. However, in this one case, without a constitutional amendment, the Supreme Court has determined for all of us that as a result of a "right to privacy," which is nowhere in our Constitution, a mother has the right to kill her child as long as it is pre-born.

This decision, *Roe v. Wade*, has destroyed the democratic process. Much like the infamous Dred Scott case in the 1850s, which gave Constitutional protection to slavery, *Roe v. Wade* has removed the ability of citizens, through the democratic process of electing state representatives and/or petitioning their state government, to determine the law when it comes to the availability of abortion. If not for this decision, different states, through democratic means, would rightfully determine which forms of this type of homicide would be criminalized and which types would be justifiable and, therefore, legal. Some states may decide that all abortions with the exception of the protection of the mother's life should be illegal. Others may justify the homicide in cases of rape or incest or of a pre-born human having serious deformities, while still others may keep abortion completely legal. This is how our system of government is supposed to work.

Because the democratic process is no longer an option, some are turning to other means (civil disobedience in the same vein as the Underground Railroad), such as setting up "rescue movements" to picket clinics, while some extremists are turning to terrorism (some extreme pro-lifers make the comparison to John Brown) by assassinating doctors performing abortions and bombing the facilities in which they take place. This radicalization will only get worse and turn more deadly, unless and until *Roe v. Wade* is reversed and the power to determine this issue is returned to its rightful place, the people through their state legislatures.

So in one breath on a fateful day in 1973, nine men in black robes determined that the people in this country may *not* under any circumstances decide to protect the lives of pre-born human beings. Using the starkest of examples, a child born three months premature is considered a baby and afforded all protections under the law, while citizens of this country may not interfere with a woman and doctor conspiring to partially deliver a pre-born human, leaving only its head in the birth canal and killing it by sticking a scissors through its skull and sucking out its brain. What a shame—all this in a country we call civilized. By hiding behind phrases like "a woman's right to choose" and "reproductive rights," we change the meaning of words in an Orwellian manner to anesthetize ourselves to the homicide of thirty million babies and close our eyes, ears, and hearts to their silent screams.

Reader Comments

—*Cathy responds to "A Choice? Maybe. But Whose?" by Jeff Podell.*
Your view that states' rights are any more sacred than the right of nine men in black robes to legalize medical killing is terribly flawed. Let's say that the decision to legalize killing unborn babies is reverted back to the states. Will it be any more right that a majority of apathetic, glued-to-their-beer-and-TV-programs people say it is OK to kill an innocent person? Whether a majority on the Supreme Court or a majority of citizens in a state make such a ruling, that ruling is wrong.

—*Matthew responds to "A Choice? Maybe. But Whose?" by Jeff Podell.*
Thank you, Mr. Podell, for a well-thought and written essay on the inconsistency of the so-called pro-choicers, who, in trying to defend the indefensible, must resort to a fraud that resonates with a democratic society. The question should never have been who chooses but rather what elements of murder and torture may be chosen to inflict on another living human being?

Choice is the ideal of the pro-aborts, but they lie; the unborn child never is allowed to choose. For the babies, I am very pro-choice. Let's let them choose. Please write another piece about the hundreds of women who have been killed since 1973 as a direct result of the abortion that also killed their baby. Write another exposé about the women who because of their abortions can never conceive another baby.

—Don Shannon responds to "A Choice? Maybe. But Whose?" by Jeff Podell.

Mr. Podell, I would have to disagree with you, to an extent, and the rest of the pro-life individuals out there. I would like to call attention to the fact that you are a man, and that you cannot give birth nor do you have the physical capacity to provide for a newborn baby. Who are you, or any man for that matter, to dictate to women how they are allowed or not allowed to control their bodies? What if the woman had an abortion to protect that unborn child from a life of neglect, very little food, and/or a lack of proper shelter? The pro-life stance would say give the baby up for adoption. If you did that and stopped abortion, do you truly believe that thirty million babies would have been adopted?

Take a good look at the true workings of this country and where a large majority of these abortions take place. Would you not agree that they take place in the inner cities where it is well known that people are poorly educated, if they are at all, and there is a much higher rate of drug use and alcoholism? Is that an ideal environment in which to have a child born? Instead of reversing the Court's decision, why not educate people on the practice of safe sex as well as proper forms of birth control? But I do not condone the choice of an abortion as a form of birth control; for that I believe punishment is warranted.

—David "Preacher" Slocum responds to "A Choice? Maybe. But Whose?" by Jeff Podell.

I disagree with much in Jeff Podell's column about abortion. Probably the most annoying is the semantically misleading statements and gaping holes in his logic. He states, "An abortion is the purposeful termination of a pregnancy through the destruction of the fetus. A fetus, of course, is a pre-born human." Of course? That statement presupposes that everyone in the world agrees with the nonsensical "pre-born human." Why not say "pre-dead human" since we are all going to die at some point? Why not take it a step further and call apes and chimpanzees "pre-evolved humans" and call goldfish "pre-evolutionary-aquatic humans"? (Forest Gump was right.)

Podell goes on to say, "What then really is the difference between a pre-born human and a post-born human?" and, "A legal right to abortion is in fact a legal right to kill." These statements are pure solipsism and emotional garbage. The author tries to get the reader to link himself emotionally with a hypothetical fetus and then uses our social bias against killing people to make the destruction of that fetus despicable. He is using emotion as a bludgeon to force his viewpoint where logic fails.

Another phrase that leapt out at me (figuratively speaking) was, "So in one breath on a fateful day in 1973, nine men in black robes determined that the people in this country may *not* under any circumstances decide to protect the lives of pre-born human beings." This phrase is nonsense. The author's attempt to re-word the decision of the Supreme Court is ineffective at best, slanderous at worst. The Court decided that the decision to have an abortion rests with the mother, not with the Court. They could not and did not attempt to define when sentience began, and that definition is at the root of this entire debate. When does the cluster of cells that may or may not become a living human gain consciousness? On this point, unlike the author, I profess ignorance. There has never been a scientific study that proves incontrovertibly either way.

The part of this entire debate that puzzles me is not whether it is right to abort a pregnancy, but why it is an issue at all. Realizing that I am in the minority, I feel that the human race would have benefited immensely from the abortion of a significant portion of the current population. The question, in my mind, is not why we allow abortions, but rather why do we allow unrestricted breeding among the general population?

—Angela responds to "A Choice? Maybe. But Whose?" by Jeff Podell.

Jeff Podell raises complex issues in his essay on a woman's right to have control over her body and to choose to have her pregnancy terminated, yet he stirs it all up and boils it all down to the very simplistic argument of killing a "pre-born infant," equating it to the killing of human beings in the process.

A baby is not just for Christmas, Mr. Podell, a baby is for life. The fears of not being able to cope with raising a child are real fears and a woman who has decided on abortion, rarely a decision lightly taken, has gone through a complex process of having to come to terms with that decision. I believe that this goes above and beyond any governmental law and is about human rights. As long as the fetus is joined to its mother by an umbilical chord, it is not a separate human being.

Wouldn't it be marvelous to live in a society where every child was a wanted child that would be guaranteed a loving and supportive environment? Even with abortion as a last-ditch, desperate means of contraception, that clearly does not happen. The irony is that pro-lifers are often very squeamish about every aspect of human sexuality and are the very same people who kill open debate and discussion on the difficult aspects of human existence and fight the dissemination of knowledge about birth control. Indeed, when looked at in this vein, I find the term *pro-life* totally inappropriate. Call them *anti-abortionists* or *pro-reality distorters*. The fantasy world that they inhabit is obviously an altogether different place from the world that I inhabit. Still, despite its dark side and its difficulties, I would not want to exchange, for my world is an altogether more tolerant place, which understands human frailties.

Bob Sullivan
Top Ten Thoughts That Make Your Dog Smile

10. *No fingers* means *No need to become computer literate.*
9. And to think—*doggie style* was named after ME!
8. Gee, only half a year until I can hear those dogs sing *Jingle Bells* again.
7. I'm *so* glad Michael Dukakis is out of the race! Who wants a First Lady named *Kitty*?
6. I'd like to see *humans* lick themselves like this!
5. The world is *so* much brighter since the advent of Snausages.
4. At last! *Cats* is *finally* closing on Broadway!
3. That neutering bastard Bob Barker's getting kinda old.
2. At least *I* don't have to choose between Gore and Bush!

And the Number 1 Thought That Makes Your Dog Smile is...

1. Another dog's butt!

Scott Stein
40,000 Lies About the Culture of Violence

With the investigation into the "culture of violence" in full swing following the Columbine High School massacre in April 1999, it was reported by various news agencies on June 8, 1999, that President Clinton said the typical American will see 40,000 dramatized murders by the age of 18.

That's 2,222 murders each year, starting from birth, or six every day, for 18 straight years. Six murders a day! What a ridiculous number. If we make the common sense assumption that the typical American is not watching such provocative programming or playing video games with such violent content until at least the age of 5 or 6, a very conservative guess, then the murders the typical American needs to see each day to reach 40,000 by the age of 18 jumps to about eight. Surely over a span of about 12 or 13 years, there are many non-fatal days even in the most media-saturated home, which means the typical American child must see well more than 10 murders most days to stay on pace for 40,000.

Does anyone really believe this? One would have to tape and watch every show on primetime television and see every violent movie released during the year to even come close. Even if video games are considered, it is unlikely that even a single person will have seen 40,000 dramatized murders by the time he reaches 18. Much video game violence is cartoonish, and hardly qualifies as "dramatized murder." And most boys play these games during a small window of the 18-year period, certainly not enough to bring the number to 40,000 in most cases. Girls, generally, do not play these games at all, throwing the numbers way off.

And Clinton was talking about the typical American, which means that many will have seen substantially fewer murders and many will have seen substantially more. Substantially more than 40,000 dramatized murders? Absurd.

There are many American kids without computers, without cable television, thousands of poor kids who see movies sparingly, lots of parents who actually are aware of what their children see and do. These kids are not seeing even half of 40,000 dramatized murders by the time they're 18. If we are to believe what we are told, the "bad" kids with less parental supervision and more access must be seeing far more than 10 murders a day.

They are seeing dozens, or hundreds. Maybe even thousands. They would have to be, to make up for all the kids who aren't holding up their end of the bargain. There would have to be thousands of kids dropping out of school and devoting their lives to finding murders to see in order for 40,000 to be close to being accurate as an average number.

Of course, no kid is seeing thousands of murders day in and day out, because 40,000 is a fake number. It cannot be accurate, and is inflated to such a degree it is unlikely to be based on any scientific approach.

If violence on television and in movies and video games really makes children violent, if there is truly an epidemic as some would claim, if steps could be taken by the entertainment industry to improve the situation, then isn't a reasoned approach required? Exaggeration of this kind makes the enterprise of examining the culture of violence seem a sham, as perhaps it is.

Is it any wonder people don't trust the media or politicians? Why do politicians present such blatantly exaggerated and falsified information as fact, and why do reporters repeat the bogus claims without ever questioning them?

Isn't it obvious that the so-called culture of violence stems not from television car chases or gory video games or rap music? The culture of violence wasn't mentioned as the cause of the July 1999 killing spree in Atlanta by a day-trader. The media found a different culprit for the adult's murderous rampage—day-trading and economic trouble. So kids kill because of movies and adults kill because of money. Just get rid of both and violence will disappear.

Lots of adults have lost more money than that lowlife without ever killing anyone, just as lots of kids see violent movies and play video games without ever hurting anyone. Only when people face the ugly truth—that some humans, if given a chance, will kill other humans no matter what the culture or circumstances, and society is not to blame for the actions of any individual—will there be hope for addressing the real issue. How do you keep a killer from killing?

Alex Joseph
Fatness

My sister is fat (5'7", 300 pounds). This is the singular fact of her life, by which I mean, she may go on to do remarkable things: fall in love, get married, have children; write a book, or several books; participate in remarkable court cases (she's currently in law school); or become a doctor. She may do all of these things, or some of them, or none of them, and still have a remarkable life of some kind, but she will always be fat, and that will always be the one thing that everyone she meets will notice about her instantly, and what she will feel most profoundly about herself, her *fat identity*.

She will never be thin. She will probably never be thinner than she is now, even if she has the operation she says she wants to have, which would staple her stomach in half so that she will not be hungry. Maybe she'd be somewhat thinner than she is now, but she will always be fat.

My sister "talks" about her fat. It's probably the most painful thing she ever has to discuss, but she does find ways to talk about it. Once, when we were driving through Baltimore—she was giving my boyfriend and me a ride around town—and she was pointing out buildings, she said, "There's the courthouse, there's the library, there's the public housing, there's the gym I haven't been to in over three months, there's City Hall...." She didn't simply say, "I have not been to the gym in over three months," because then we would be able to talk about it.

Another way my sister talks about her fat is to say that it depresses her. "I don't have any sex life because I'm fat." "No one is friendly with me because I'm fat." "Yes, it looks like my hair is thinning, but my hair is not thinning—the follicles have spread out because I'm fat." We cannot comment on her fat in that context because it would be like punching her after she has already fallen to the ground. So she puts us into a double bind—of inviting discussion and then blocking it at the same time.

My sister has always been heavy. Pictures of her in the scrapbook show that she's always been big—bigger than other girls of her age. There is a picture of her at around 16, standing in the doorway of our kitchen, wearing a pink velour pullover. She has a sheepish smile. Underneath this picture, my mother has written the caption "I didn't eat your Sugar Corn Pops!" in her elegant cursive. The picture and caption are supposed to be funny, a charming rebuke.

I remember my parents had my sister on a grapefruit diet, the Weight Watchers diet, and the NutriSystems diet. My mother went on this last diet with her, and I remember the two of them had little scales and charts and plastic baggies to keep track of all their food. My parents did not allow us unrestricted access to sweets. If my parents had cookies in the house, they hid them in cabinets, behind dishes, in little cubbies. I remember searching for sweets with my sister in the kitchen. My parents, at one point, even kept the cookies in a little strongbox, with a lock on it, that my sister and I quickly learned how to jimmy.

My sister became seriously fat when she went to college, an all-women's college. I sometimes think she chose an all-women's college so she could be left alone to get fat. When I was 17 and she was 20, she came home from school for a break, and I remember her throwing her arms around me the minute I came in the door. My sister has always done this—attacked with affection—but this time I think she did so specifically because she did not want me to see immediately that she had gained nearly 40 pounds.

My sister is 33 years old. After her adolescence, after college, after the diets and the hiding of the sweets, my sister tried other methods to lose her fat. She tried psychotherapy, she tried a drug (Zoloft), she tried rooming at an extremely expensive weight loss center, she tried exercise, and she tried more diets. My sister does not like to exercise and she is not a healthy eater. I have never once seen her willingly eat fruits or vegetables, except for one time when I saw her eat a banana. She says that citrus fruits make her mouth itch. Vegetables "don't taste good." If she gets a sandwich with lettuce, tomato or onion, she takes them off. My sister likes to eat potato chips and chocolate and chicken salad sandwiches and Chinese food without the vegetables. She likes pancakes and bagels with cream cheese and Diet Coke. There is no diet in the world that will allow her to eat this way.

There are certain people who would like my sister to believe that she could certainly lose weight if she just tried, if only she really applied herself. They do not understand my sister. They are blithely ignorant. In one diet book, for example, the author writes, "For the first week of the diet, all I want you to do is to give up soda. That's it!" This person cannot possibly understand 33 years of getting up with the painful and necessary identity of *I am fat.*

Then there are other people—"fat advocates"—who say that fat is entirely genetic, and there is no connection between it and being unhealthy. My sister has sleep apnea. My sister has trouble walking long distances. My sister has bouts of exhaustion—pulling over to the side of the road during her one-hour commute so that she can take a two-hour nap. My sister has had episodes of paralysis—what she calls "brain farts"—and I believe that all these health problems are in some way related to her fat.

I have known women who are fat, but they are also active, and social, and sexual. My sister is none of these. She had a boyfriend once, but he disappeared suddenly, "probably because I am fat," she told me. My sister's fat is like a second person trying to share her skin. It is as if she were fighting this person. It is as if she has lost the fight, and the person still has not left.

My sister has great empathy for her legal clients—poor people, sometimes with AIDS—and sometimes she calls me up and cries because their lives are so unfair, because they are stuck on the wrong end of a bad deal they have made (sometimes unwittingly) with a mate, or with the state welfare agencies, or with themselves. But when my sister called me a few weeks ago, she was crying because her Pap smear results were irregular, because she needed to have a biopsy taken of her uterus.

My mother died of ovarian cancer. My sister knows that obesity is linked to cancer. And yet I do not believe that my sister will ever lose weight. I sat on the phone, and I listened to her crying, and I had absolutely no idea what to feel.

Jody Lane
Everything a Really Big F**king Idiot Needs to Know About Drugs and Alcohol

"The first installment in the Everything a Really Big F**king Idiot Needs to Know *series is sure to be an instant bestseller! This book is literally packed from cover to cover with profound wisdom and practical advice for addicts, social users, and politicians alike!"* –The User's Review

*"Defies the generation gap! A book for the whole family! We are already Really Big F**king Fans!"* –Marijuana Monthly

Editor's note: And now, exclusively for the readers of *When Falls the Coliseum*, a sneak preview into the drug-free (but warped, nevertheless) mind of author Jody Lane as she relates the contents of her latest accomplishment.

Table of Contents

Chapter 1: The Big Bong Theory

Chapter 2: Quaalude 7:14 and Other Missing Bible Verses

Chapter 3: The Fourth Wise Man Offered Hops

Chapter 4: Turning Water into Wine–The Complete Christian Home Brew Source

Chapter 5: "Before There Was Crack" and Other Great Tales for the Kids

Chapter 6: Dry? Top 10 Places Your Kids Hide Their Drugs

Chapter 7: Ritalin–A Family-Friendly Drug

Chapter 8: Acid for the Color Blind: Overcoming Handicaps

Chapter 9: Legends I: "I Didn't Inhale"

Chapter 10: Legends II: Drunks Don't Swallow

Chapter 11: Blackouts and Solar Eclipses: Is There a Connection?

Chapter 12: Spanish Flies, Bar Flies, and Tsetse Flies: A Scientific Study from the USDA

Chapter 13: Your Level of Tolerance and the Bigot Myth

Chapter 14: Paraphernalia or Paranormal: How to Describe Your Alien Encounter

Chapter 15: Head Shops: What Are They Really Selling?

Chapter 16: When the Lab Rat Dies: 101 Things That Pharmaceutical Companies Don't Want You to Know

Chapter 17: How to Start Your Own Tax-Free Business: The Dos and Don'ts of Pushing

Chapter 18: The IRS and Drug Money: You Don't Have to Report It

Chapter 19: Co-Dependents: Take That Exemption!

Chapter 20: Addiction and Subtraction: How to Deduct Your Nasty Habit

Chapter 21: The Frat Diaries—Make Big Money from Future Politicians

Chapter 22: Diuretics! A Practical Guide for Passing the Piss Test

Chapter 23: You Know You Are in Trouble When You Can't Spell DUI

Chapter 24: Is It Bad to Puke on the Judge? FAQ on Courtroom Etiquette

Chapter 25: Allergic Reaction: It Could Happen to You! *One woman's horrifying story of falling down, losing her purse, and waking up pregnant in Toledo.*

Bob Sullivan
The Matrix and the Culture of Violence

Just before the worst school shooting in American history (Columbine High School, Littleton, Colorado, April 1999), Al and Tipper Gore went to see *The Matrix*, starring Keanu Reeves as Neo. After the film, Al said he and Tipper just loved it—words that came back to haunt him following Littleton, as both the Clintons and the Gores tried to present a united front condemning the "culture of violence." With news stories about shooters Harris and Klebold and the Trench Coat Mafia fresh in their minds, audiences suddenly found *The Matrix* disturbing, especially scenes in which Neo pulls automatic weapons from beneath his long black coat and graphically guns down various people in his way.

The culture of violence is an easy scapegoat, but it raises the chicken-or-egg question: Do violent movies and television shows and music and video games and even professional wrestling cause violence in society, or do they merely reflect and occasionally comment on the violence that is already there? Humans have always demonstrated outbursts of violence, while the various media—including plays, poetry, and the Bible—are comparatively recent developments. There is little evidence media violence has any effect on the serious crime rate.

When Arthur Penn directed the classic *Bonnie and Clyde*, he was most interested in depicting the inevitable result once people jump on the merry-go-round of crime and escalating violence and then find themselves unable to jump back off. The film was brilliantly written, directed, and acted, it did particularly well in the inner cities and, where it was most heavily watched, there were indications that the crime rate actually went down.

Of course, a million viewers could realize the futility of a life of crime and, as a result, put down their weapons, and not a single one of those million stories would make it onto the evening news. Yet let two jerks dressed like Bonnie and Clyde pick up weapons and the story makes national headlines. No matter how much good a film may do—whether teaching life lessons or making a political point or providing a release valve, or simply providing a much-needed diversion—usually only the bad that a film does is visible and deemed newsworthy. It would be disastrous if the content of movies were dictated by the actions of the most irresponsible, worse if dictated by some government or industry board trying to second-guess what the most irresponsible might do.

Some of the best movies ever made—including *Bonnie and Clyde*, *Goodfellas*, *The Godfather*, *Raging Bull*, and *Taxi Driver*—are violent, and all of the violence in them is an essential part of their greatness. One female acquaintance of mine said she wouldn't see *Saving Private Ryan* because she didn't want to see a film that "glorified violence." My response: "Boy, have you got the wrong idea about that film!" The grueling opening half hour of

Ryan—which I still believe to be the best film of 1998—is perhaps the most moving antiwar message ever committed to celluloid. It is the antithesis of glorifying war, and any viewer (except the most bizarre) is going to come away with a greatly heightened antiwar sentiment.

One reason *Shakespeare in Love* may have won the 1998 Oscar for Best Picture (along with its wit, costumes, and year-end release) is that many female Academy members felt that they shouldn't vote for a film they refused to see. And they were probably right not to go see *Ryan*; it was almost too much for me and I'm a guy! But then there's no compelling reason for most women to go see it, since, unlike men, most women already have the sense to know that war is bad.

But it's one thing to deliver a message well, to have sympathetic characters whose pain is felt by audience members, and another thing to have endless waves of stick-figure bad guys being blown away or blown up, followed by some witty remark by the superhero.

I loved *The Matrix*, but then I've always had a particular weakness for any work that suggests that this world daily entering our eyes and ears and other senses is, in fact, an illusion. After all, life is but a dream. *The Matrix* is also a digital-age retelling of *The Greatest Story Ever Told*, complete with a black John the Baptist, a Mary Magdalene, and a Judas. At the beginning of the film, some of Neo's acolytes tell him that he is their Jesus Christ; when Neo is told that he is the chosen one destined to save humanity, he at first has serious doubts; at one point he dies and comes back to life; and the last shot shows him ascending heavenward.

But I found the violence-glamorizing aspects of the film—the thousands of bullets, the cascade of gleaming shell casings falling from the helicopter—both troubling and unnecessary. The martial arts and dodging of single bullets showed some imagination and demonstrated Neo's growing supernatural abilities, but the only motivation I could find for the endless rounds of automatic gunfire is to transform a blockbuster into a megablockbuster by alienating some female viewers while attracting droves of teenage male repeat viewers. It's in this area that *The Matrix* must take some of the blame for contributing to the culture of violence, even if Harris and Klebold were making their plans long before the film ever came out.

It's a shame, because the film is so good otherwise. Right after Littleton, when I took my beloved (who I've been trying to convince of the illusory nature of reality) to see *The Matrix*, not only did the violence cause the message to be lost on her, it attached a huge psychological negative to the message, making it all the more difficult to convince her. One can only hope that the inevitable sequel to *The Matrix* will replace the excessive violence with the ample imagination so ably demonstrated elsewhere throughout the film.

Scott Stein
In the Morning, After Breakfast

"Not everybody eats breakfast," he said. "You can't title a story 'In the Morning, After Breakfast.' You've excluded whole portions of the human race with your title alone."

"What people don't eat breakfast?" she asked.

He shook his head. She was so naïve.

"Don't shake your head at me," she said, "like I'm a child unable to understand an explanation. If I want my story to take place in the morning, after breakfast, what's wrong with that?"

"It's your story," he said.

"Philip!" Her indignation manifested in a slight growl.

"Suzanne, don't get mad at me. I'm trying to help you."

"What's wrong with breakfast?" she asked.

"Nothing," Philip said. "Some think it's the most important meal of the day."

Suzanne didn't laugh.

"It's just a joke," Philip said. "Lighten up."

Suzanne didn't laugh.

Philip put down his coffee mug. "Are you trying to limit your audience? Do you want people to look back a hundred or a thousand years from now at your story and say, 'Isn't that quaint' or 'What's breakfast?' Or do you want your story to reach out to all people, everywhere, across time and space, and give you life beyond your life?"

"Life beyond my life? Philip, you draw cartoons of cats and dogs in tuxedos attending the opera, with captions saying things like, 'It isn't over till the fat cat sings.'"

"This isn't about me. And what you mock has been called incisive social commentary. Those cartoons, as you call them, are paying for your writing workshop."

"That's not fair. You know I'm going to pay you back when I publish my first book."

"I don't care about the money. Suzanne, you're a writer. You have the opportunity—no, the obligation—to reach beyond the parochial and say something truly universal. If you make the right choices, you have immortality. It is an option I with my cartoons don't have."

"Maybe my stories are social commentary, like your cartoons," Suzanne said.

"No," Philip said. "They're more than that. They matter."

"They can't matter around the breakfast table?"

"I suppose they can, in a limited way," he said. "But will the starving African know what you mean by *breakfast?* Will people even be eating breakfast a few decades from now?"

"So I'll change the title," Suzanne said.

"You need to do more than that." Philip smeared low-fat cream cheese onto his poppy seed bagel. "Your two main characters have a heterosexual relationship."

"They are married," Suzanne said.

"Be that as it may, 10% of the population is homosexual. A full tenth of humanity cannot relate to your characters. In the future more and more of them will be out of the closet, and your work will be remembered like *Ozzie and Harriet*, as a quaint irrelevancy, not connected to the reality of its own time, let alone ours."

"But if I make my characters homosexual, doesn't that exclude the other 90% of humanity?"

"Yes, you can't do that either," Philip agreed. "Your best bet is to be vague regarding their sexuality."

"Philip, it's a story about adultery and betrayal. How can I be vague about their sexuality?"

"That's another thing," he said. "You assume that marriage is something with which all people can identify. Many people are not married. Half who were once married are divorced or widowed. A hundred years from now marriage will probably be a ritual observed only by religious fundamentalists. It isn't natural."

"Philip, no one put a gun to your head. You proposed."

"Suzanne, don't take criticism personally. This is about your story, not our wedding."

"You've eliminated sex and betrayal. What's left to write about?"

"Sex and betrayal aren't good subjects for a story. Not everyone can relate. How about the longing for freedom? That's universal. Maybe a story about a caged animal, say an abused dog or cat, that slips away one night from captivity and runs through the forest, rediscovering its wild spirit as it gets further from its cage."

"You'd like that, wouldn't you?" Suzanne's hands quivered and she cried, muffled, into her clenched fist.

Philip stared for a second, looked away, then back again. As if further proof were required, he thought. There was just no understanding women.

Robert L. Hall
The Two Religions

"Beware lest any man spoil you through philosophy and vain deceit, after the tradition of men, after the rudiments of the world." – Colossians 2:8

It always pains me when I see or hear derogatory comments in the media about matters of faith and the people of God. The main reason is that usually the things of God are not afforded the same degree of circumspection that other areas of the human experience are afforded.

For instance, if one wanted to know how to go about solving a difficult mathematical equation, one would naturally approach a mathematician. If one wanted to know about a scientific phenomenon, then a knowledgeable scientist would certainly be consulted.

But if anything concerning religion or faith is up for discussion, it seems that only those self-appointed rulers of the media have access to the masses. And their viewpoint is, generally speaking, the only one ever heard.

Let me lay it out for you. There are only two types of worship on this small planet we call earth: worship of men and worship of God.

The worship of men is called humanism. It consists of the adoration of one or more of men's attributes, whether it be character, beauty, power, possessions, or money, to name a few. Humanism holds that we are all cosmic accidents conceived in error in the back seat of our parents' Chevrolet in a weak moment when they weren't practicing birth control (which would explain why most parents nowadays don't raise their kids properly, spending just enough time and energy on them to keep the social workers and law enforcement officials from arresting them for child abuse).

There's just one major problem with humanism. The person most humanists worship is themselves; and when you worship yourself, anything is justified and justifiable—morals, or the lack of, especially. After all, why obey the laws of God (or even the law of the land) if you *are* God?

I'll let you in on a little secret: I used to be like that. And it nearly ruined my life. I learned a few lessons the hard way before graduating *magna cum lousy* from the school of hard knocks. I found out that I couldn't be trusted to make all the right decisions about my life. Wanna know why? Because I'm not perfect. And I'm not God. And neither are you.

I want you to know I'm happy now. I'm making a good living with a wonderful wife by my side and living in a fine house. And on Sunday ... well, on Sunday, I go to the house of God and I cry out, "Why did it take me so long to find you, Lord? Why?"

As the saying goes, "I was blind but now I see."

Reader Comments

—Scott Stein responds to "The Two Religions" by Robert L. Hall.
Robert L. Hall makes several assertions that require examination:

1. He implies that the media has been unfair in its coverage of religion. In my opinion, the news, local and national, is generally respectful of stories regarding religion. How can he claim that the Establishment is anti-religious, when religion is the Establishment? Anyone listening to a presidential speech knows how they all end ("God bless America"), just as anyone who watches a post-game interview with an athlete knows who is responsible for scoring the winning touchdown—God. And candidates can't get to enough churches and synagogues during political campaigns.

2. He compares religion to mathematics or science, arguing that those who are not religious should not be the people we ask when we have a question or concern about religion, since we would not ask a non-scientist a science question. What he fails to point out is that, unlike science or math, religion is something many, if not most, people have direct experience and training in. Many of us attended Sunday school, for years perhaps, and have been to countless holiday dinners, weddings, christenings, bar mitzvahs, and the like. Some non-believers come from very religious families, and have extensive knowledge on which to base their opinions. The same cannot be said for non-scientists and science.

3. There are only two types of worship, and the worship of God is one of them? It is quite a stretch to lump the many religions, some polytheistic, others monotheistic, some accepting Jesus as savior, others not, into the same boat. If these different religions are so alike, what have people been killing each other over for the last few thousand years?

4. He assumes that if one does not worship God, one must worship humanity. For people that have been conditioned since in utero to worship, I put forth a radical concept: It is possible not to worship anything. One can admire the accomplishments of some people, and the positive traits some people exhibit, without shutting one's eyes to the reality that human beings are far from perfect.

5. What he calls a "cosmic accident in the back seat" might be called a triumph against exceptionally long odds. A Darwinian view of life need not diminish the value of life. Accident or no, intelligent life just existing is quite a triumph, and ought to be considered precious on that account alone.

6. I really am happy for Mr. Hall, and if religion has helped him, or if he thinks it has, good for him. But he is projecting his own tough life and poor decisions on the rest of us. Perhaps he needed the crutch of religion. That doesn't mean everyone does. There are also stories of religion causing harm to one's psyche, breaking up families, fostering prejudice, and so on. Personal anecdotes are no substitute for reason and evidence. Even if we agree that religion is good for people and society, that would have no bearing on the truth of the beliefs. And, of course, even were Mr. Hall to acknowledge this and attempt to argue that God does exist (no easy matter), he would be faced with the far more daunting task of giving reasons for believing in a particular religion, in having a belief in a specific god.

7. Now that Mr. Hall has found God, does he no longer take responsibility for his own actions? He writes, "I found out that I couldn't be trusted to make all the right decisions about my life." So is he no longer making decisions? Is he no longer making mistakes? How exactly is God telling him how to behave from moment to moment? As the philosopher Jean-Paul Sartre pointed out, the belief in God is really beside the point in determining our behavior. He gave the example of a young French man during the Nazi occupation who was faced with a difficult decision: stay home to comfort and help his mother, or go off to fight in the resistance for freedom, for his country, and to avenge his father's death. This young man might or might not have been religious, or of a particular faith, but isn't the final decision his? Can't we find strong support in any religious book for either course of action? Aren't they both honorable paths? This boy will find reasons in whatever source he consults to do that which he wants to do. He might attribute his decision to God's will, or quote scripture, but does that mean he didn't decide his own fate?

—Lila Guzman responds to "The Two Religions" by Robert L. Hall.
Mr. Hall had it right. There is a definite anti-Christian bias in this country.

You will say the following is anecdotal, but it's typical of what is happening every day in this formerly Christian country. In the second grade, my daughter studied Hanukkah, including its religious implications. She studied Kwanzaa and what it meant. For Christmas, did she study about the birth of Jesus (the true meaning of the holiday)? No. Christmas was Santa Claus and Christmas trees. This is just one example of the many, many times when Christians are treated like second-class citizens in this country.

And, Mr. Stein, you totally miss the point in all your numerous examples trying to prove Mr. Hall wrong.

When God is in control of your life, everything changes. Your priorities change. The way you treat others changes. The way you make decisions changes. Non-Christians don't understand this because their hearts have not been changed.

There are only two religions on the face of the earth: the religion of God and the religion of man. Whether you wish to admit it or not, the only true worship is the worship of God. Whether you worship Vishnu or a two-headed goat, if you do not venerate the one true God, then you are worshipping man.

Before you say I am intolerant, I am not. Anyone may worship the way he or she wishes. However, don't ask me to put my approval on any religion except Christianity.

Your vicious attack on Christianity and Mr. Hall has turned me off to *When Falls the Coliseum*. You owe Mr. Hall an apology. He wrote an essay from the heart.

Face it. He is right. You are wrong. You are clearly not a Christian and cannot understand that we know we are right. There is no room for argument. Either you worship God or you are wrong.

This weekend, a woman sat down next to me at a writing conference and said she was "sort of" a Christian. If she's not sure, 100% sure, then she's not a Christian. It's like saying "I'm kind of married" or "I'm a little bit pregnant."

Either you are or you aren't.

I am certain that there is only one true God. Mr. Hall knows this too. We both pray that you will discover the truth and will experience the inner peace we have. We don't have to worry about making the right decisions. We have already made the most important decision. We worship God and only Him.

—Scott Stein responds to "The Two Religions" by Robert L. Hall.

Lila Guzman just doesn't get *When Falls the Coliseum*. To say that there is "no room for argument" is to miss the whole point. An exchange of ideas, even those we disagree with, is part of why the Web site exists. Every group seems to be in sole possession of the truth, and the Internet, like other media that came before it, is as fragmented as the rest of the country. There are Christian sites and liberal sites, conservative sites and atheist sites, and every variation in-between, with people of different beliefs badmouthing each other without ever talking face to face, so to speak.

Although it is clear I do not share the religious perspective of Christians, *When Falls the Coliseum* continues to seek out diverse viewpoints and writers who can express them well.

I cannot assume that Ms. Guzman speaks for Mr. Hall, but I would like to address the accusations above:

At no time in my first comment on Mr. Hall's essay did I attack Christianity. In fact, Mr. Hall's essay did not even mention a particular religion, and neither did my comment. Although I know he is a Christian, I focused my response on the content of his essay. I do not have a bias against Christianity relative to other religions. My essay "A Talking Ass, or a Braying Mule?" (p. 152) happens to be about Judaism and a bat mitzvah, and takes issue with a rabbi.

Mr. Hall presented us with a rational argument for why he thinks worshipping God is important. I challenged some of his points. Where my critique is valid is up to each reader to decide for him- or herself. If Mr. Hall disagrees with every point, that is his prerogative.

While Ms. Guzman is certain of the truth and is sure the only reason I could not grasp it is my failure to already be a Christian, Mr. Hall must have thought an argument on rational grounds was worth making, or he wouldn't have written "The Two Religions."

At no time did I attack him personally. By his own admission, he needed religion because he made bad decisions without God's help. So my calling religion *a crutch* is a paraphrase of his stated position, not an insult, since a crutch is something people use to help them because they are not capable without it. That is exactly what Mr. Hall's essay is about.

I will not apologize for holding an argument, no matter what about, to the same standards I hold all arguments. There are questions raised in my first comment above, and I think they are valid.

—Jody Lane responds to "The Two Religions" by Robert L. Hall.

Robert L. Hall wrote, "Usually the things of God are not afforded the same degree of circumspection that other areas of the human experience are afforded." Assuming that the author is defining *circumspection* as forethought, as opposed to caution or wariness, the statement implies that if a person makes a derogatory comment about matters of "faith, people or things of God," then they have clearly not afforded those subjects the proper amount of thought, which in turn implies that derogatory comments are *usually* made out of ignorance. And thus, only those who do not make derogatory comments on these matters have given the required degree of circumspection to the subjects and have become more knowledgeable (thus less ignorant) and have formed the same, right conclusions, which are above reproach.

Sound familiar? The Church, i.e., the People of God, used the same logic during the Inquisition. The only difference is that the Church labeled derogatory comments as heresy and burned the offenders at the stake instead of shaking their sanctimonious heads and accusing them of ignorance.

Christians are not born knowing that they should be Christians. Yes, even Christians are born without knowledge of faith or matters of God. Everything a Christian, or anyone else, knows, he was either taught and accepts blindly, or found through a personal quest for knowledge that delivered him to his present convictions. The latter warrants a little respect regardless of what conclusions a person's soul-searching and researching leads to.

The key word here is *taught*. It is very easy to be taught. It is easy for one to congregate with the flock on Sunday and listen to someone else read the Bible, tell you the difference between right and wrong, how to raise your children, what to believe and not believe, and where to drop off your cash tithe. The hard part is to learn: to question the conflicts (if you have them) with what you have been taught and to search out answers for yourself—to find your own truths and base your convictions on what you learn, whether that be with or without God.

I suppose it may happen, but I do not believe that people just wake up and convert to an alternative faith or way of life. "Good Morning, Honey! Today, I will forget everything that I have ever been taught about God and ostracize myself from my family, friends, and polite society because I want to be different! Today, I will be a Jew, a Muslim, a Christian, an Atheist!" A certain degree of circumspection is required of any person who desires an honest faith, or lack thereof.

You can choose to think me misguided or led astray, believe that I will burn in Satan's hellfire for my beliefs. These are the rights you have in practicing your own faith. But, please, do not suggest that I have not afforded the same degree of circumspection to the "things of God" (because I have spent a lifetime doing just that), and I won't presume to label seventy million Christians as ignorant.

—Alex Harman responds to "The Two Religions" by Robert L. Hall.

Mr. Hall may be an expert on Christianity, but he's a complete ignoramus when it comes to humanism. Whatever Mr. Hall may have been before he became a Christian, he was certainly never a humanist. Humanists do not worship themselves—indeed, we do not worship at all—and we have a better track record than Christians when it comes to obeying the laws of the land. (It is not true that there are no atheists in a foxhole, but it is very nearly true that there are no atheists in a penitentiary—and those that are there generally do not belong to that sub-set of atheists who identify themselves as humanists.) We subscribe to the following set of principles and values known as The Affirmations of Humanism (www.campusfreethought.org):

1. We are committed to the application of reason and science to the understanding of the universe and to the solving of human problems.

2. We deplore efforts to denigrate human intelligence, to seek to explain the world in supernatural terms, and to look outside nature for salvation.

3. We believe that scientific discovery and technology can contribute to the betterment of human life.

4. We believe in an open and pluralistic society and that democracy is the best guarantee of protecting human rights from authoritarian elites and repressive majorities.

5. We are committed to the principle of the separation of church and state.

6. We attempt to transcend divisive parochial loyalties based on race, religion, gender, nationality, creed, class, sexual orientation, or ethnicity, and strive to work together for the common good of humanity.

7. We want to protect and enhance the earth, to preserve it for future generations, and to avoid inflicting needless suffering on other species.

8. We believe in enjoying life here and now and in developing our creative talents to their fullest.

9. We believe in the cultivation of moral excellence.

10. We respect the right to privacy. Mature adults should be allowed to fulfill their aspirations, to express their sexual preferences, to exercise reproductive freedom, to have access to comprehensive and informed health care, and to die with dignity.

11. We believe in the common moral decencies: altruism, integrity, honesty, truthfulness, and responsibility. Humanist ethics is amenable to critical, rational guidance. There are normative standards that we discover together. Moral principles are tested by their consequence.

12. We are deeply concerned with the moral education of our children. We want to nourish reason and compassion.

13. We are engaged by the arts no less than by the sciences.

14. We are citizens of the universe and are excited by discoveries still to be made in the cosmos.

15. We are skeptical of untested claims to knowledge, and we are open to novel ideas and seek new departures in our thinking.

16. We affirm humanism as a realistic alternative to theologies of despair and ideologies of violence and as a source of rich personal significance and genuine satisfaction in the service to others.

17. We believe in optimism rather than pessimism, hope rather than despair, learning in the place of dogma, truth instead of ignorance, joy rather than guilt or sin, tolerance in the place of fear, love instead of hatred, compassion over selfishness, beauty instead of ugliness, and reason rather than blind faith or irrationality.

18. We believe in the fullest realization of the best and noblest that we are capable of as human beings.

Forget the Ten Commandments—if you want a better, happier nation, let's post the Affirmations of Humanism on every classroom wall in America!

—Damon Vix responds to "The Two Religions" by Robert L. Hall.

Although I disagreed with most of the points raised, I will limit my comment to one point, namely, Mr. Hall's contention about the lack of moral character inherent in humanists. Moral character is not defined by belief in God. Not only are morals subjective in nature, but being religious has no causal effect upon one's morality as evidenced by countless atrocities made by religious persons throughout human history.

The framework for morality instead lies in our emotions. Complex feelings such as love and compassion are instinctive and help hold humanity together in all of its complex social structures and institutions. With or without religion, mankind will have morals, for without them, humans could not be social creatures. One could argue further that faith and spirituality are simply emotions that serve to bind larger groups of people together in times of social upheaval. One need only examine emotions for a short while to see the similarities between the common emotions and moments of extreme spiritual fulfillment. Spirituality can actually overcome racial discrimination in some instances and has no doubt played a major role in the formation of our modern societies. Quite a powerful emotion indeed!

Finding God is nothing more than finding an emotion and not knowing what it is. The feeling is real, but it should not be attributed to an outside source when its cause is internal. For more information on the subject try reading Barbara Thiering.

And if the blind want to see, they are better off trying something like LASIX surgery than a communal meal.

Jason Stein
Gang Bang, Anyone?

When I hear stories of slashing another person as initiation into a gang, it's almost too ridiculous to be believed. Is this what kids in public school have to look forward to? How are children supposed to learn anything when they're always looking over their shoulders?

Instead of slashing someone for initiation, how about doing some homework—now there's an idea. How about this for the initiation process: long division or a spelling bee. Spell three out of three words correctly and you're a new member. Congratulations! It's scary to think that you have nine-year-old boys sexually attacking eight-year-old girls in the bathroom of their school. When I was nine years old, I remember sliding across my parents' kitchen floor in closed-feet pajamas. That was my thrill. Boy, have times changed!

The news showed a meeting at the local high school about gangs and gang-related anything. The auditorium was filled up with mostly mothers. Here's a brilliant question for anyone who's listening: Where are the fathers? If you're around, please make your presence felt, or is everyone off on another crusade or march somewhere? The question we have to ask every gang member is "Where are your parents?" Gang members have no problem abiding by the rules of the gang, why can't they abide by the rules of the family as well?

When you get right down to it, a family is nothing more than a nonviolent gang (for the most part), with a leader and some soldiers. When one comes from a family structure with rules and some kind of value system, society has a way of functioning better. It's not that I'm an expert on this. I just call it common sense. Unfortunately, many parents are lacking in this area.

We have had gangs in the past, so what makes today's gangs any different? The acts committed by gangs are much more violent, daring, apathetic, and consequence-free than anything we've seen on television. Did I say television? I meant real life. How did society get this way?

It's scary to think that most gang members, who by the way at one point were not gang members, will have a criminal record by the time they are eleven years old—or younger. I say cut out the juvenile justice system. A hard line must be taken.

The problem is that we live in a compassionate society. A fifteen-year-old will slash someone or shoot someone and then weeks later appear in court all nice and clean and sorry and innocent-like, and this is bullshit. Kids are very smart—I should know; I was once a kid—I'm still a kid, just bigger. Here's a secret: Kids will push the button, so to speak, as long as they can, without getting caught. Believe me, they do know right from wrong—they choose to ignore it. They don't see any consequences for their actions.

They play the system. If they did it and got caught, they're sorry. If they did it and don't get caught, they're not sorry. It's that simple. Are there any judges out there reading this?

I think we all need to arm ourselves. Let's surprise them. Form your own gang, have your own initiation, but don't tell anyone. Gang members and potential gang members will think twice about physically and emotionally hurting a citizen (of this great country) when there is the possibility of getting hurt themselves. Rubber bullets, anyone? It's not fatal, but they will live to feel the pain. Hey, anyone out there want to join my gang?

C.P. Kaiser
Deciphering Dot-com Ad Speak

There's a lot of loot to be made in Silicon Valley. Even Stanford M.B.A.s are quitting school early to found Internet start-ups and cash in on the IPO (initial public offering) boom.

You can't turn a page today without coming across a comparison of dot-com mania with the California Gold Rush of 1849. In fact, the people who leave six-figure jobs for the promise of a rewarding IPO are affectionately called "e-49ers."

And everything in the Valley is happening at light speed. Companies start and fail at a dizzying rate: Only 1 in 30 that receive venture capital funding ultimately goes public. Yet, employers can't find enough employees.

As with anything happening at such a quick pace, the buyer must beware. The spate of dot-com startups has created a whole new language for job seekers to decipher. I've compiled a list of actual ad language and the real meaning behind it.

What the ad says: Excellent opportunity to get in on the ground floor of a leading edge Internet startup. **What it means:** We are crammed into an office the size of a dorm room.

What the ad says: Experience working with creative teams. **What it means:** Familiarity with beanbag furniture.

What the ad says: Excellent organizational talent. **What it means:** Must be able to fit entire bedroom into cubicle.

What the ad says: Must be self-directed. **What it means:** You will work 18 hours a day because it's fun.

What the ad says: A willingness to learn more. **What it means:** Must memorize the Tony Robbins motivational sayings on the walls.

What the ad says: We need a well-organized individual with solid office and computer skills who can solve problems and communicate effectively with our internal staff. **What it means:** You will have no social life.

What the ad says: Potential for work-at-home. **What it means:** We don't want to deal with OSHA or unions.

What the ad says: No technical background required. **What it means:** You have to order the Chinese takeout.

What the ad says: The ability to perform effectively and maintain a positive attitude under pressure. **What it means:** Willing to eat a Milky Way bar when your Moo Goo Gai Pan doesn't arrive.

What the ad says: This individual may also be managing the work of outside vendors. **What it means:** You must tip the Chinese deliveryman.

What the ad says: Transition to full-time position if desired. **What it means:** You'll still work 80 hours a week but now get paid for 30.

What the ad says: Pay includes equity participation. **What it means:** The employee health plan is to be married to someone who has a health plan.

What the ad says: Are you a smart, driven, dynamic team player in search of a hot pre-IPO opportunity? **What it means:** Free Happy Hour every Friday.

What the ad says: A fast-paced environment with tremendous learning opportunities and great career growth potential. **What it means:** Foldout desks and below-average salaries.

What the ad says: Must have a strong portfolio of existing work. **What it means:** We're fresh out of ideas.

What the ad says: We are devoted to helping people achieve long-term financial freedom. **What it means:** Recent college grads don't know any better.

What the ad says: We're not myopically market-focused. **What it means:** You'll have no social life.

What the ad says: We value imagination and humor. **What it means:** We expect you to laugh at the long hours and imagine a future payoff.

What the ad says: We offer competitive salaries and pre-IPO stock options. **What it means:** We're moving from my home into office space soon.

What the ad says: Work in a collaborative environment. **What it means:** You will have no say.

What the ad says: Must be able to focus completely on subject matter. **What it means:** You can't play Nerf ball with the rest of the staff.

What the ad says: You are the experienced, professional presentation rainmaker of our dreams! You've got oodles of experience in PowerPoint, Illustrator, Photoshop, and GIF builder! You scoff at clip art! **What it means:** Be wary of ads that are just too hip and overuse exclamation points! They want million-dollar talent for under $15,000!

What the ad says: Can juggle various projects at once. **What it means:** You'll have no social life.

What the ad says: Odd, last minute deadlines are cake for you. **What it means:** We have no business plan.

What the ad says: We are pioneers... **What it means:** This is our twelfth startup attempt.

What the ad says: Come show us your stuff and join our skyrocketing company. **What it means:** We're still desperately seeking venture capital.

What the ad says: Work with a team of established veterans of the industry. **What it means:** Gray-haired burnouts from Xerox.

What the ad says: We are growing feverously and have positions opening daily. **What it means:** Terminations occur more frequently than Joan Rivers' face-lifts.

What the ad says: Relaxed, fun environment. **What it means:** Free coffee and a basketball hoop over the trashcan.

Scott Stein
Bruce Springsteen's "The Ghost of Tom Joad" and the Problem of Barbra Streisand

In 1995, Bruce Springsteen released "The Ghost of Tom Joad," a CD perhaps notable to non-Bruce fans for receiving the Grammy for "Best Contemporary Folk Album." It is a remarkable work, coming closer to meeting the potential of good fiction than any other album I can name.

Taking the title of his album and one of its catchiest songs from a character in John Steinbeck's *The Grapes of Wrath*, Springsteen explores the poverty, drama, and desperation of, among others, immigrants, legal and otherwise, in the southwestern United States in the 1990s. As a chronicler of human frailties, Springsteen makes the listener walk in someone else's shoes for a while. A fiction writer is supposed to create drama, make us care about characters we might not otherwise have understood, and lead us to some conclusion about being human. A good fiction writer will do it without preaching or lapsing into didacticism. On this album, Bruce never does. The events of his songs carry their own weight.

There is the lonely INS border patrol officer who is faced with a tough choice when he falls in love with a Mexican woman desperate to get into the United States in "The Line." In "The New Timer," a man leaves his home in Pennsylvania looking for work, and rides freight trains like the hobos of days gone by. His desire for revenge when his friend and train riding mentor, Frank, is killed, is tinged with a sincere poignancy that many fiction writers would do well to study. We care about the characters in these songs, but the lessons we draw from the moving stories on "The Ghost of Tom Joad" come from our experience of its art, not from any overt statement of the songwriter's political stance.

Springsteen had never been very political. Yes, at concerts he often told young people that they should know what is going on in the world and shouldn't follow leaders blindly, before his blistering rendition of "War"—sensible advice. And yes, he urged fans to donate to food banks and help support veterans groups, which he himself did generously—also sensible, and even admirable.

But when it came to supporting specific policies, Bruce was mostly silent. He did make it clear that he did not endorse Ronald Reagan when the President mentioned Springsteen in a reelection campaign speech during the "Born in the USA" era, but he left his response to his music. Springsteen felt that "The River" said it better than he could. He sang about the down-on-their-luck and made his audience understand the experiences of others instead of preaching. It was a decision I always admired.

His policy of letting his art do the talking changed after "The Ghost of Tom Joad," when Springsteen publicly came out against California's Proposition 209, which sought to reduce affirmative action programs across the state. Bruce appeared onstage with Jesse Jackson and others, and the

New York Times Magazine's January 1997 cover story called him "The Pop Populist."

The writer of that article never questioned the health of a society that relies on popular artists to tell it what to think and feel about public policy. I am not concerned here with affirmative action or providing benefits for illegal immigrants, or any other issue Springsteen might have been stumping for in California. The question at hand is what role artists—popular artists especially—should play in the democratic process. My critique is aimed not at the artists so much as the society that has given them their disproportionate influence over public opinion and, as a result, public policy.

Politically active diva Barbra Streisand maintains that as an artist and a citizen (a "citizen-artist" is what she calls herself), she has the right to support causes she believes in. Of course, I agree—free speech is my lifeblood. If Barbra or others want to walk the picket line or raise awareness about issues or help the Clintons pay for legal bills, they have the right to do so. But Babs is not the only citizen-artist afflicted with Streisanditis and intent on using fame to further a political agenda.

Rosie O'Donnell, a mediocre comedian and talk show host famous for singing off-key show tunes and throwing Twinkies at her audience, is now an advocate for banning guns, using her daytime talk show as a bully pulpit. In 1999, her impromptu debate with show guest Tom Selleck about the National Rifle Association made national news. Selleck is famous for looking good and driving a red Ferrari. Intellectual Howard Stern, famous for Fartman, used his radio show to chastise Rosie for her misguided do-goodism. Are these the people we want leading the national debate?

And do we really need Alec Baldwin to tell us what to think? As a political activist and a Democrat, his hosting of the first annual Seconding the First, which I attended, in support of the First Amendment, was unnecessarily partisan. It was made clear by Baldwin and other celebrities in attendance that Democrats care about free speech and Republicans do not. If any event ought to have been nonpartisan, a celebration of the First Amendment was it. Was it Baldwin's influence that made the show close with the image of a burning American flag? Or, as an actor, used to reading lines written by someone else, did he not realize that one can support the right to free speech and even the right to burn the flag without glorifying flag burning?

Television's *Politically Incorrect* is perhaps the apex—or is it the nadir—of this trend. Hosted by Bill Maher, *PI* nightly brings together four unqualified celebrity guests to argue about the issues of the day. No one is given more than a few seconds to make a point, just as well since most of the guests don't know what they are talking about.

On one episode, "Downtown" Julie Brown, half-famous for being a VJ during the early days of MTV, actually argued that Mark Twain's *Huckleberry Finn* should be banned from schools because it contains the offensive word *nigger* (in writing this essay I have discovered that Microsoft Word doesn't recognize the word). When told that not only wasn't Twain racist but that the book accurately represented the way people talked back then and was conveying the racial attitudes of the time, Brown repeated that the word was offensive and should not be in schools.

Remove *Huckleberry Finn* from schools? Why not remove all reference to slavery in history books as well? It is an offensive world—we can't delete everything, can we? Pretending horrors of the past did not exist is doing a disservice to the truth and to those who need to learn from it. Maher took Brown to task for her ridiculous opinion, but night after night people who haven't read a book or had an original thought in years, famous only for a sultry gaze or a raspy voice, debate the issues while America drifts off to sleep.

Perhaps I am overreacting. Maybe all of this is just entertainment, and no one bases voting decisions on the opinions of celebrities. Yeah, and the millions buying WWF and WCW merchandise and watching wrestling matches know it's fake, but elect Jesse "the Body" Ventura governor anyway. OK, maybe the public is influenced, you say, but our elected officials aren't that stupid—they do what is right, regardless of what the celebrities advocate. I take comfort in your words and breathe a sigh.

Then comes word that pop-music sensation Ricky Martin has a meeting scheduled with President Clinton. Among the topics Martin says he will address in his summit with the Commander-in-Chief of the world's most powerful military is the use of a Puerto-Rican island for missile tests. Clinton's wife is running for office in New York, home to a large Puerto-Rican population, and they will be paying close attention to the Clinton-Martin summit. It is no exaggeration to say that Ricky Martin has the power to influence policies directly connected to the national security of the United States of America.

Living La Vida Loca?
Indeed.

Cassendre Xavier
Who Is God?

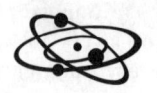

Contrary to popular belief, God is not a longhaired, old, white guy sitting up there on a throne.

Sometimes God is a dredlucked goddess who grants your wish for a parking space.

Sometimes God is what happens when Patti LaBelle opens her mouth to sing.

But most of the time, God is a figment of our imagination—an imaginary friend, created by us and for us. That is why one person can believe God loves her, while another knows God wants all queers stoned; and why one person can say God is gentle and loving and accepts every kind of good-hearted person, while another can call blacks subhuman and say God meant them to be segregated; and why one person can find the words in the Bible to declare God's love for all living things, while another can find the same words to declare God's hatred of homosexuals, abortion, and women's suffrage.

Did you ever wonder why some people say it's their job to help everyone love God, while others think it's their job to help God kill as many faggots as possible?

The gods we invent are our allies. They do what we want. I like to change my gods on a regular basis. Sort of like my Brita water filter.

David "Preacher" Slocum
Shotguns and Rifles and Pistols, Oh My!

The fight over interpretation of the Second Amendment to the Constitution has raged for more than 60 years. The amendment reads: "A well-regulated militia, being necessary to the security of a free State, the right of the people to keep and bear arms, shall not be infringed."

The battle seems to revolve around the exact definition of the word *militia* and how it applies to modern society. Supporters of the amendment argue that a militia consists of all able-bodied men between 18 and 35 years of age that can be called on in time of need to defend the country against its enemies. Opponents feel that the militia is nothing more than the National Guard and that only these military units should have firearms.

The intent of the framers of the Constitution is very clear:

"No man shall ever be debarred the use of arms. The strongest reason for the people to retain the right to keep and bear arms is, as a last resort, to protect themselves against tyranny in government." —Thomas Jefferson

"Arms, like laws, discourage and keep the invader and plunderer in awe and preserve order...." —Thomas Paine

"Firearms stand next in importance to the Constitution itself. They are the American people's liberty teeth and keystone under independence. The very atmosphere of firearms everywhere restrains evil interference." —George Washington

"Besides the advantage of being armed, which the Americans possess over the people of almost every other nation, the existence of subordinate governments, to which the people are attached and by which the militia officers are appointed, forms a barrier against the enterprises of ambition, more insurmountable than any which a simple government of any form can admit of." —James Madison

Can there be any doubt what these men thought about Americans owning and keeping arms? They had just rebelled against their government—a government they felt was oppressive and unfair, a government against whom they and fellow patriots, through strength of arms, defeated.

Even later in American history, presidential hopefuls recognized the need for personal arms:

"Certainly one of the chief guarantees of freedom under any government, no matter how popular and respected, is the right of citizens to keep and bear arms... The right of citizens to bear arms is just one guarantee against arbitrary government, one more safeguard against tyranny." —Hubert Humphrey, (liberal) Vice President

Intent of the Constitution aside, the issue remains one of personal freedom: The freedom to take up arms and defend yourself, your family, and your community against predators. The police departments cannot, and will not, protect you against attack. Not only do they not have the manpower and

When Falls the Coliseum

funds, but for them to make this nation truly safe would necessitate creating a tyranny unlike anything we, as Americans, have ever seen.

Let's clear up a common misconception, that of police protection. The courts have ruled, no less than 23 times, that the police have no responsibility to protect a citizen against violent crime. Sound unbelievable?

Riss v. New York decision: The government is not liable even for a grossly negligent failure to protect a crime victim (*Riss v. New York*, 22 N.Y.2d 579,293 N.Y.S.2d 897, 240 N.E.2d 806, 1958). In the *Riss* case, a young woman telephoned the police and begged for help because her ex-boyfriend had repeatedly threatened, "If I can't have you, no one else will have you, and when I get through with you, no one else will want you." The day after she had pleaded for police protection and been refused, the ex-boyfriend threw lye in her face, blinding her in one eye, severely damaging the other, and permanently scarring her features.

Hartzler v. City of San Jose decision: The court held that the San Jose police were not liable for ignoring Mrs. Brunell's pleas for help (*Hartzler v. City of San Jose*, 46 Cal. App. 3d 6, 1975). Ruth Brunell called the police on 20 different occasions to beg for protection from her physically abusive husband. He was arrested only one time. One evening Mr. Brunell telephoned his estranged wife and told her he was coming over to kill her. When she called police, they refused her request that they come to protect her. They told her to call back when he got there. Mr. Brunell stabbed his wife to death before she could call the police to tell them that he was there.

(Important note: It is illegal in both New York and California for an ordinary citizen to carry a firearm for personal protection.)

As evidenced above, the police cannot and will not protect you against crime. Are you willing to stand idly by while your wife, your children, or even your neighbor is victimized? If so, then I submit that the problem is not one of gun ownership, but one of backbone.

Scott Stein
Conspiracy

Setting: *A basement: Three people, two men and a woman, are sitting around a table.* **JOHN** *is wearing army fatigues and is smoking a cigarette;* **ANN** *is provocatively dressed and sipping a glass of wine; and* **HENRY** *is wearing glasses and a bow tie, and is writing in a notepad.*

JOHN: (*Banging a gavel on the table.*) Attention, attention. This meeting of the Soldiers of Truth is hereby called to order. Henry, please read the minutes from last week's meeting.

HENRY: (*Clears his throat and reads from his notepad.*) First, old business: It was determined last week that Ted Harris is losing his hair and has been using spray paint to hide the bald spot on the back of his head. Also, Coach Johnson has been having an affair with the school crossing guard for the past three months.

ANN: (*Excited and impatient*) And what about new business?

HENRY: (*Irritated*) I was just getting to that. (*Clears his throat.*) New business?

JOHN: Well, soldiers, did we uncover any diabolical schemes this week?

ANN: (*Raising her hand enthusiastically.*) I've got one.

JOHN: Ann, please give us your report.

ANN: Well, I did some snooping, and I have discovered that gases from automobiles and factories are damaging the environment.

JOHN: Really?

ANN: Yes. These gases are making it hotter every year. Eventually it will get so hot, the polar ice caps will melt.

JOHN: My God! What do you call these gases?

ANN: (*Sipping her wine.*) I call them greenhouse gases.

JOHN: Brilliant!

HENRY: Hold on a second. You didn't discover greenhouse gases. Everyone knows about them.

(ANN *gives him a look, then turns to* JOHN.)

ANN: And I call the resulting increase in temperature global warming.

JOHN: Fascinating!

HENRY: I know all about global warming.

JOHN: (*Taking a drag from his cigarette.*) Of course you do. Ann just reported on it for us. Pay attention, Henry.

ANN: That isn't all.

JOHN: (*Smiling at* ANN.) Please go on.

ANN: (*Returning the smile.*) Thank you. I also learned that the sun is going to explode.

JOHN: (*Ducking under the table and covering his head with his arms.*) Get down! Get down! The sun's going to explode!

ANN: Oh, not yet, maybe not for another billion years. But our sun will one day die.

JOHN: (*Sitting up again.*) Incredible! And what is the government doing about this?

ANN: Not a thing.

ANN and JOHN: (*In unison*) Conspiracy!

HENRY: Look guys, everyone knows about the sun exploding. It's a star. They all do that eventually.

JOHN: (*Suspiciously*) You seem to know an awful lot about this, Henry. Maybe there's something you're not telling us.

HENRY: What do you mean?

ANN: Just when did you know about this exploding sun thing, anyway?

JOHN: And why haven't you reported it to us earlier?

ANN: What are you trying to hide?

HENRY: Wait a minute. You're not accusing me of trying to...

JOHN: (*Taking a drag from his cigarette.*) Guilty conscience, Henry?

HENRY: Slow down. I'm not part of any conspiracy. Seriously.

(ANN *and* JOHN *look at him for a moment, then* ANN *breaks the tension by asking* JOHN–)

ANN: (*Taking a sip of wine.*) Well, John, what did you find out?

JOHN: You're not going to believe this. I discovered that long ago, before there were any people, giant reptiles roamed the earth. I call them dinosaurs. They had tremendous teeth and could eat a person in a single bite.

ANN: How horrid!

JOHN: That's not all. The government keeps the skeletons of these dinosaurs in giant vaults.

ANN and JOHN: (*In unison*) Conspiracy!

HENRY: (*Exasperated*) Are you people insane? The government isn't hiding dinosaur skeletons from us. Those giant vaults are called museums. And everyone is free to go and see them.

ANN: (*Suspiciously*) And how many of these so-called museums have you been to?

HENRY: I don't know ... two or three.

JOHN: (*Standing and shouting, accusingly.*) Well, which is it–two or three?

HENRY: (*Stammering*) Three, I guess. No, two. Definitely two.

JOHN: Henry, there's no room for liars in the Soldiers of Truth. Maybe it would be best if you left us.

ANN: I agree.

HENRY: (*Relieved, then has an idea for revenge.*) Maybe you're right. Can I make my report before I go?

JOHN: (*Looks at* ANN, *who nods her approval.*) Well, Henry, did you uncover anything?

HENRY: (*With a hint of a smile.*) Actually, I did. It is a conspiracy so terrible ... well, I hesitate to even tell you.

(JOHN *and* ANN *huddle together in fear;* JOHN *takes a drag and* ANN *takes a sip.*)

JOHN: You must tell us.

HENRY: (*Looking around, then speaking just louder than a whisper.*) I have discovered ... that smoking cigarettes causes lung cancer. And drinking wine causes liver cancer ... but this is our secret. Well, see you around.

(HENRY *leaves.*)

(ANN *waits a second, then runs to the door and looks out.*)

JOHN: Is he gone?

ANN: (*Sitting back down next to* JOHN.) Yes. I thought we'd never get rid of him.

JOHN: (*Pulling* ANN *closer.*) You know what else I learned this week?

ANN: (*Rubbing his shoulder.*) What's that?

JOHN: It seems that the government has been hiding medical information from us all along. There's a cure for cancer.

ANN: Really? What is it?

JOHN: (*Looking around to make sure no one is listening in.*) Sex.

ANN: (*Smiling and sitting on his lap.*) You don't say!

(*Lights out*)

-THE END-

C.P. Kaiser
(un)-Sound Bytes

Gullible.com
Gerald Levin and Steve Case, the two high priests of the new AOL/Time Warner temple, claim that global media is more important than educational institutions and nonprofits. They want to *redefine* global media corporations as *instruments of public service*. As MediaBeat columnist Norman Solomon told Jim Lehrer, "By happy coincidence, the media course that would make them the richest was the same one that apparently held the most fulfilling promise for everyone on the planet." Believers of such, please send $10.00 to Gullible.com, a new Internet company whose altruistic mission is to save the sea gulls.

With Friends Like These...
On average, nearly four American women are killed each day by a husband, ex-husband, or boyfriend, according to the Bureau of Justice Statistics.

Where's the Justice?
A nursing home aide was found guilty of raping a comatose patient and sentenced to prison. OK, that's justice. However, the comatose woman was allowed to give birth to the baby who now suffers from severe brain damage and needs round-the-clock care, as does her mother. What kind of justice is that? Who made that decision: the family or the medical establishment? Whatever, that baby should have been aborted.

Changing Calendars
It's hard when it's the year of the dragon and you keep signing "year of the rabbit" on your checks.

If I Don't Wake Up, Kill Me
A public-access cable station in Oregon caught flack for airing "Final Exit," a how-to video on assisted suicide for the terminally ill. Critics claimed it would encourage the desperate to act on their impulses. Why don't I hear these same critics decrying the normal network television programming, especially the local news? Are we so warped that we'll show all kinds of murder but won't show compassionate suicide? Local police and a crisis hotline reported no increase in the number of people trying to kill themselves the morning after the broadcast.

We Complain about Work, But What If...?
If money were no object, what would you do? Well, according to a poll by Roper Starch Worldwide, 63% of college-educated adults *would work fewer or more flexible hours*. That's right—better than half of those surveyed would actually still work! And a whopping 18% would *work the same number of hours*! Why are we so connected to our jobs? Can't we find worth outside of

a paycheck? The smartest of those queried (14%) said they would quit working altogether, while 4% were not sure. OK, since those queried were college-educated adults, my question is: What the hell are we teaching them?

Ari McKee
Scared Straight (Well, Mostly)

The first time I smoked pot was in seventh grade. I attended a prestigious prep school where we all had time on our hands and money in our pockets. So not only were there plenty of drugs, there were plenty of good drugs. After school at a friend's house, someone pulled out a bag of Mexican marijuana and a small wooden pipe, and the four of us smoked it, bowls and bowls of it. I have never, before or since, been so completely wasted.

I was a smallish 13-year-old with corduroys and a not-very-bouncy Dorothy Hamill haircut. The dope inspired me to write out a thesis explaining my new realization of the "seven levels of awareness." I spent most of the trip smoking and coughing and bent over my Earth Sciences notebook furiously recording the details of this monumental theory of consciousness. There were even bar graphs. My best friend found the way my handwriting gradually deteriorated to be the most interesting part of my thesis. And so it went for an hour, perhaps, until, finally, there was popcorn.

This experience taught me two things: that the human mind is a fascinating mechanism, and that I should never do hard drugs. I was not an overly sophisticated seventh grader, but I didn't need to be Keith Richards to figure out that if a pot trip was that mind-altering, anything stronger might take me to a place from which I could not find my way home. It was the best of all possible deterrents: experienced fear.

Twenty years later, there's a battle raging right now in my town over whether parents should be called if an underage college student is caught drinking by school authorities. Most parents love the idea, but school authorities aren't too crazy about it, wishing, I'm sure, to avoid contact with irate parents whenever possible. The argument for it seems sensible—bring in Mom and Dad and put some hurtin' on the little ingrates. There's just one sticking point: consistency. For example, parents would not be called about an 18-year-old's parking ticket or a 19-year-old's marriage license application. They would not be called if their 20-year-old made an appointment for a Pap smear and they would not be notified of the abortion of their potential grandchild. Parents don't sign leases, they don't sign report cards, they don't sign draft notices, and they don't sign ballots. Parents aren't needed to purchase cigarettes, peepshows, or three-speed vibrators with attachments. Except for this lone fermented facet of American culture, college students are officially no longer children.

Whether you agree with that or not, it is so in the eyes of the law. Now, I won't try to argue that 21-year-olds aren't smarter than 18-year-olds, which may very well be true. Personally, I had myself together much better at 16 than I did in my 20s for a while, but maybe that's the exception. Operating under the assumption that we get more mature with age, will someone tell me why we're allowed to drive for five years before we can buy a beer? Why is it OK to have children, even presumably stone cold sober children, behind the wheel of a car day after day, but even four years later they're not allowed to sit in their dorm room and play quarters? Where is the greater potential for harm?

OK, drinking–bad, driving–good. I can get that. Personally, I like both, but I understand the reasoning. When you think about it, though, which is more likely–that I'll kill someone drunk in my apartment or sober in a Buick? Will I ever get drunk enough to walk outside and kill a family of four with my bare hands? Or, contrary to that, will I ever achieve such celestial heights of sobriety that there's absolutely no way I could make a split-second bad decision and cause a fatal accident? Why do children have the right to drive and not the right to do so many other, less life-threatening things like voting for city council members and watching bad porno movies?

What I am advocating is an across-the-board standardization. When an American citizen reaches our ONE hopelessly frivolously chosen age, be it 16 or 18 or 37, that's the day we let them:

- Drive
- Drink alcohol
- Get married
- Die for their country
- Vote
- Own a gun
- Get a lap dance

The thing is, parents have eighteen years to get it all right. It doesn't seem nearly long enough to screw kids' heads on straight, but it will have to do. Some kids will break our hearts, temporarily or permanently, and all the tattling in the world won't stop them. Some of them will make mistakes and learn from them; they'll acquire experienced fear. Some of them will make mistakes that can't be undone. Some of them won't make many mistakes and we'll lose them anyway. It's no goddamn fair, that's for sure, but handing out adult responsibilities in this arbitrary, piecemeal way isn't fair either.

I'll tell you what else isn't fair–having this crackerjack "seven levels of awareness" idea rattling around in my head in one form or another for twenty-some years and not acting on it. I'm sure it's a pioneering new insight into the chemically-altered mind, with bestseller written all over it, and a forward by Stephen Hawking or Paddy Chayefsky. Then there's thirty-something me ... too freaked out to go do the fieldwork. Oh, well, it's another tragedy of the middle-aged middle class; the anguish of the hopelessly alert and reality-based. Hey, is the popcorn ready?

Scott Stein
Absolute Denial

Imagine this scenario: You're an electrician preparing to work on high-voltage wires. You ask your assistant if the power supply to the wires has been turned off. He replies, "I'm fairly certain." Do you start working on the wires, risking death by electrocution?

Or: You're a skydiver, and before you leap from 10,000 feet out of a perfectly good airplane, you ask a fellow diver if your parachute backpack is properly fastened. "I'm fairly certain," she answers. Do you jump?

What you want to hear before touching high-voltage wires or jumping from an airplane is "I am certain." Unlike so much of the information transmitted by language, *certain* leaves no room for doubt. But "I am certain" is a phrase being uttered more reluctantly than ever. Afraid of being blamed for wrongdoing or just not convinced of the possibility of really knowing anything, people have fallen back to modifying absolute words like *certain* with *fairly, mostly, almost,* and others. *Fairly certain* allows for the defense "I didn't say I was certain."

The problem is that *fairly certain* doesn't express what people using it mean to express. They mean that they are certain, that it is OK to touch the wires or jump from the plane. The electrician's assistant turned off the power with his own hands, and the skydiver can see with her own eyes that the backpack is properly fastened.

"I am certain" is an absolute expression and anything less than an absolute is its opposite. "I'm fairly certain" means "I am not certain." One cannot be mostly certain any more than one can be mostly dead.

Despite the humor of Billy Crystal's wisdom in *The Princess Bride,* there is no such thing as being "mostly dead." As close to death as one might be, there is a point when a person is alive and a point when dead. *Dead* and *alive* are not gray terms, with shades of meaning. If one is dead, one is not alive, and vice-versa.

What about those who have had near-death experiences, you ask? A near-death experience is not death. Even if doctors thought someone was dead, and that person exhibited symptoms of deadness, the person was not dead if he or she ended up alive at the end of the experience. Death doesn't allow for second chances. Finality is built into the meaning of the word. It is an absolute term.

While we're at it, nothing can be "very unique." *Unique* is an absolute term. A unique item is one that has no double. What would a very unique item be? One that really has no double? Adding *very* to *unique* is a pointless enterprise. Yet people say it anyway. "He has a very unique point-of-view." What does *very* add to this sentence? Nothing.

In life there are few absolutes. We face uncertainty every day. Perhaps the continuing erosion of confidence in social institutions has contributed to this sense that we cannot be sure of anything. But science's acknowledgment on the quantum level, for the moment, that there are some things we cannot know does not mean that we cannot be certain of anything.

Language, the tool that makes understanding possible, has absolutes that correspond to reality. Certainty is possible, so say "I think" and "I believe" when appropriate, but don't be afraid to know things as well. And banish *fairly certain* and *very unique* from your vocabulary. There is enough confusion in the world without people meaning one thing and saying another.

Rev. Angeline E.M. Theisen
The Weekly Challenge

"*Dear God: I pray that when the time comes, and all eyes and ears turn my way, that somehow–despite my shortcomings–I become an instrument of grace. Let light flow through me. Amen.*" —Rev. Daniel Simer O'Connell, *The Secret Life of Preachers*

At one time or another, students for the ministry ask themselves and each other: Where in the world will we find enough sermon ideas to fill the pulpit 40 or more times each year, year after year, without repeating? Veteran ministers usually respond that you'll have more ideas for sermons than you will ever have Sundays to preach them. Now that I'm a veteran, I find that I agree.

Sometimes it is hard to tell when exactly the germ of an idea for a sermon first appears. With last Sunday's, I can cite the specific moment–it came from a conversation with a board member. I had telephoned to speak to her husband, Ron, about some church matter, and before Mona called him to the phone, she asked if I had a minute to discuss something else, and I did.

I was astonished when she told me that some members of the congregation were nervous about hearing that I work on my sermons Saturday night. Instantly, I was angry. Who are these malcontents, and let me at 'em! Whose business is it when I write my sermons, as long as they are done on time and they're good? I checked this latter point by asking her: "Are they saying they don't like the sermons?"

"No, no," she insisted. "The sermons are fine. They just worry that you write them on Saturday night."

"How do they know I work on them Saturday night?"

"Because you so often say that while you were writing on Saturday night, this or that happened."

"Well, I also work on them Wednesday or Friday nights."

"But you don't refer to working on them those nights."

Finally, I said in exasperation, "Look, I've been working to deadline through 20 years of school and 18 years of sermon writing. I'm not going to change."

Mona patiently explained, "You don't have to change the way you write them, just don't say you write them Saturday night."

After I completed my business with Ron, I hung up the phone, still steaming. How can a problem be solved by not talking about it? And besides, as an interim minister–one who helps a church get ready to call its next settled minister–I have an obligation to my successor to straighten this out before the new minister arrives. Supposing Dr. Beloved–the pet name by which our Search Committee refers to its unknown future minister–is one of those rare birds who gets up early Sunday morning to compose the sermon? What kind of John the Baptist would I be if I let the Messiah walk into this mess?

Right along with my angry musings, however, I was simultaneously aware that Mona stayed perfectly calm in all her responses to me. I had gotten irritated. She had not. This puzzled and intrigued me. If she could continue to so patiently explain to me how people were feeling and what might make them feel better, then it must at least make some sense to her. Even though I didn't get the impression that she shared their concerns, she seemed at least to understand them. I didn't. That gave me something to think about.

I've spent enough effort in the ministry trying to correct people I thought were wrong—which I've come to see is about as practical as trying to straighten out the tar baby. In both cases, you end up stuck with three limbs and hopping on the fourth. Now, I pay attention to what other people think I should pay attention to, and Mona obviously thought I should accommodate folks on this issue.

Saturday of that week, I was invited to one of our dinner discussion groups in a member's home, and although I rarely attend—Saturday nights being, as you've just heard, somewhat busy for me—this time I accepted the special invitation and I went. The company was great, the food was the stuff of legend, and I was having a wonderful time. However, just before dessert, I caught a glance at my watch. It was 9 p.m. I wanted to go home to work on my sermon, only I had just been asked to seriously consider never saying that.

I handled the situation in typical Angie fashion. During a break when there were just three of us sitting at a porch table, I piped up: "It's 9 p.m. and I want to go work on my sermon, but I have been advised not to say that because it makes people tense to hear I'm still working on it this late." The first person at the table immediately began to commiserate, telling me how, as a professor, he has to constantly deal with how others tell him how to teach. The other, who happened to be our host, just listened. He was looking down at the table, maybe a small smile on his face, saying nothing. That seemed almost Zen-Mona-like, and it made me curious. So I asked him: "What do you think?"

He said, "Why don't you say you want to go put the finishing touches on your sermon?" And the skies opened up and the angels sang and I thought: "That's it!" I don't know exactly why, but I knew that approach would work. And besides, it was true. By Saturday night, my sermon is always fundamentally finished. I usually just have to give it one last readthrough, type in a few changes, maybe switch to a larger type for these aging eyes, put it through spellchecker and print it out. I decided to test out the advice immediately and went into the dining room where the largest gathering was getting ready for dessert, made my apologies, and boldly excused myself to go "put the finishing touches on my sermon for tomorrow." Nobody got tense. Everybody just beamed. It worked like a charm.

Everyone seemed more relieved than I that the sermon was actually done—after all, I always know the sermon is going to get done. If something happened to disrupt my Saturday schedule, some church or family emergency that took all day, I know I would simply work into the night until my sermon was complete, and no doubt poignantly illustrated by the crisis of the very day on which I wrote it. This has never happened—I mean an up-all-Saturday-night writing session—although once I did write my sermon on notepaper over several hours while sitting with a family in the intensive care waiting room after a member's mother had suffered a stroke. For the most part, sermon writing is much less stressful than that.

Sermon ideas can come from anywhere. They come from things in the news that catch your eye; trends in the culture some researcher reports; something someone says that surprises you, drawing your attention to preconceptions you didn't even know you had; or a comment someone makes at a meeting sounds just like what someone else said last week, and you wonder what's on people's minds. Ideas come from your areas of passionate interest, which are never far from your awareness, and occasionally gel into sermons that must be written. Writing styles and timings and locations can be anywhere. Some fine preachers have a complete manuscript polished and printed by Thursday. Some fine preachers step into the pulpit on Sunday morning with just a few notes scrawled on three-by-five cards. Some meet with lay readers during the week and rehearse them and other parts of the service until they are perfect. Some hand a printed sheet to a congregant on Sunday and say, "Want to be a reader this morning?"

Some ministers are only completely happy with a service when everything comes off exactly as planned, without a hitch. Some take even a huge faux pas in stride, sharing the mirth of the congregation, or its delight that something far more creative than anything we could have planned serendipitously happened.

The most important thing is that the congregation and minister is a good match. Churches that conduct the Sunday worship in non-variable multiple parts carried off in lockstep precision require a minister who values and works well with that style. Such a congregation would not appreciate the minister who suggests we push all the furniture against the walls and sit in a circle on the floor just this once. At the opposite extreme, congregants who routinely attend church in shorts in order to be ready for their after service tennis matches, who set their tennis rackets beneath their seats in order to have both hands free for the coffee they sip during the minister's remarks and the talk-back that follows immediately—in case you are wondering, I do in fact have a particular church in mind with that description—will not be happy with the minister who follows rigidly the standard order of worship and wears a robe to preach.

And, of course, congregations come in a thousand variations in between.

It is important that churches understand how ministers create sermons, each in their individual ways. It is important that clergy be sensitive to congregants' concerns. I know I'll continue to "put the finishing touches" on my sermons on Saturday nights, and, along with struggling, celebrating, laughing, weeping colleagues all over the world, pray that when the time comes for all eyes and all ears to turn my way, somehow—despite my shortcomings—I can become an instrument of grace, and let the light flow through me.

Robert O'Hara
Where my Marsupials at?

Turn on MTV, ESPN, or BET and you might think you're watching *Animal Planet*, the way animal nicknames are used. But it's not just on TV. When you go out to shoot some hoops, or have a beer with friends, you very well might see your "dog," Gator, talking to some hot chick. Now more than ever, it's a sign of identity and accomplishment to garnish your name with a zoological epithet.

In Rap, you have Tim Dog, Nate Dogg, Snoop Doggy Dogg, and even the Dog Pound! The realm of sports covers a broader range of genera with monikers like The Big Cat (Andres Galarraga), The Hit Dog (Mo Vaughn), The Shark (Greg Norman), and Jake "the Snake" Plummer. What's more, the presence of animal nicknames among the not so famous has intensified, including my cousin John, who is The Jaybird.

On the streets, everyone is your Dog: "My dog this" and "my dog that!" This can be confusing, because of the recent popularity of pit bulls in the ghetto. When a guy refers to his dog, I don't know whether he's talking about his two-legged friend or his four-legged friend.

I once heard my grandmother refer to some lady from her youth as a "strange bird," and there are countless movies and cartoons from the fifties and sixties identifying someone as a "cool cat." I guess allusions to members of the animal kingdom have always been popular when addressing others, but there weren't as many canine names, and they were much less personal. I am not a zoologist, so I can't pinpoint the exact time or reason "cats" became "dogs." But I do know something is missing: Where are all the other animals?

There are thousands of species of animals on this planet; consequently, I am surprised that no one has taken advantage of the giraffe, the hippo, or the monkey in dawning a moniker. Tall basketball players, especially, could take advantage of the giraffe's reach. But I guess pro athletes like the ferocity of their chosen animal, and musicians favor the creature's keen characteristics.

Whatever it is, it's obvious they believe that the beast says something about the man. But in many cases, a different beast may say it better. For instance, wouldn't The Blue Whale describe the physical prowess of home-run hitter Andres Galarraga better than The Big Cat? OK, so The Blue Whale isn't vicious enough—but neither is the alternative. I have a big cat, and all she does is sleep on the porch and wait for food.

Some bypass the chance that the formal animal title might not say enough, and adopt a popular animal's common name or quality. I know a guy we called Tweety from high school. Former Eagles quarterback Ron Jaworski was always known as Jaws, and almost everyone has heard of Sting, who takes his tag from a bee's natural defense reaction. I even include baseball star Mark McGwire in this group. After all, a Big Mac is really just chopped up cow.

It seems athletes like Tiger Woods and Larry Bird have the least to worry about. Their zoological epithets are built right into their real names. It would be confusing if they added to them. Imagine Tiger "Dog" Woods, or Larry "the Shark" Bird.

What's so disappointing is that zoological epithets have not been adopted by more conservative genres such as the literary world, academia, and politics. I have always thought they should call Steven Hawking the NightHawk, Hillary Clinton the Llama, and Bill Gates the Wasp.

I shall not disappoint, however. I will assume a nickname that epitomizes my animal-like virtue. Just call me the Possum. I am wily, nocturnal, and often feign death when threatened.

C.P. Kaiser
Vaginal Ghosts

At a recent christening, I expected to help my brother-in-law's family welcome their newborn baby boy into the community. Instead, I was exhorted to help exorcise the supreme spirit of evil from his diapered "soul."

The Catholic priest began the ceremony by telling the congregation that exorcisms are alive and well. "This," he said, referring to the baptism and pointing to a row of proud parents holding their spawn, "is an exorcism." Those six uninitiated babies had barely crapped themselves and already they had to be cleansed of the devil's presence. I looked at the six young pairs of yearning eyes and felt sick at their condemnation. I needed air.

Outside the church, a headstone on the lawn read Shrine to the Unborn. I asked myself, Why is it that before babies are born, they're fetal deities, but once born, they're the devil's own kin? Based on the Vatican's misogynist bent, one might surmise the tyke's taint comes from its passage through the vaginal canal. Apparently, only virgins are prized, only women who will not (barring divine intervention) bring children into the world are valued. All other women, in the Church's eyes, are inferior and contaminated, because of the very sexual nature of pregnancy and birth, the two processes that lead directly to life, life being the Church's supposed top concern. In effect, the Church elevates the fetus in the womb but condemns the mother for having sex to fill her womb. It's a no-win situation for women. The Church's real concern is for power, not the sanctity of life.

Back at the baptism, the priest warned his flock about the month-long heat wave and drought choking most of the East Coast. He didn't need any Doppler radar to explain the deadly weather pattern. He said that it was a chastisement from his Catholic god.

I would have liked to ask this representative of the mainstream Catholic church, Who is god punishing? You? Me? I don't think so, because we can both stay locked away in our air-conditioned splendor and buy fresh fruit and vegetables year-round, no matter the local weather. The ones being "punished" were the farmers. They lost millions of dollars in spoiled crops.

The priest might be onto something, though. Perhaps the farmers were being punished for poisoning our immune systems with pesticides, or feeding us meat from hormone-injected animals, or keeping chickens in claustrophobic cages under 23 hours of light, or selling genetically altered fruits and vegetables without any labels that say so.

The fiery preacher had none of these "sins" in mind. He said our punishment from his Christian god comes from our collective sins, from having abortions, from not praying, from using birth control, from experiencing pleasure, especially sexual pleasure.

Catholics have no choice but to believe in vaginal ghosts, otherwise their entire house of dogmatic cards will crumble and fall. In order for

Catholic doctrine to remain so inflexible, it must submit that Jesus' mother Mary didn't taint herself with Joseph's penis or sperm. According to fourth century Pope Siricius, "Jesus would not have chosen birth from a virgin, had he been forced to look upon her as so unrestrained as to let that womb ... be stained by the presence of male seed" (*Eunuchs for the Kingdom of Heaven*, Ute Ranke-Heinemann, Doubleday, 1990, p. 5).

The Vatican must also routinely fight off speculation that Jesus had several brothers and sisters. According to the teaching of the Church in Ranke-Heinemann's book, "Jesus would have looked for another mother if Mary *had taken pleasure* in bearing more children besides himself" (emphasis mine).

So, back to the unborn memorial on the church lawn. Why enshrine the unborn when every process leading to their viability is supposedly contaminated? Sexual pleasure is wrong, conception except via divine providence is defilement, sperm fouls a woman's womb, and as babies are born, they assume the sin of the tainted vaginal canal (hence, the need for baptism). The Church, it seems, wants to hold life sacred yet deny us our very life, our humanity, which includes our sexual nature.

I think the Vatican needs to exorcise its own archaic doctrinaire demons. When it does so, the baptismal ceremony, a so-called rite of passage for the newborn, will be exposed for what it is—a ritualistic oppression of women, in particular, of women's sexuality. Then, in this new world, all women will be respected, regardless of what happens between their legs.

Reader Comments

—*Jody Lane responds to "Vaginal Ghosts" by C.P. Kaiser.*

Bravo! I attended a funeral not long ago where I overheard my aunt speaking of my atheism and that she was keeping her children away from me because their souls were too new. Apparently she thinks the babes will be tainted by my presence. If only I had read this essay earlier I could have explained to her that in fact it is I who am in danger from her sinful little beasts!

Scott Stein
Garghibition

The pill didn't make one taller. That wasn't the issue. It wasn't a case of medical science tampering with God's design, or biological engineering in an effort to transform the human race into a different, better species—a taller one. No, all the oblong, indigo "Gargantuanx" did, miracle of miracles, was create the illusion in the mind of the consumer that he was taller. That's all.

The pill didn't take immediate effect. For about 10 minutes you felt nothing. Then you were taller. That is, you believed you were. The drug convinced its user, whatever his height, that he was three inches taller. It was a new technology, and its power was limited, if perfect in its simplicity and specificity. Three inches was all it added. Gargantuanx could not alter the physical world—boxes of pasta on supermarket shelves that were out of reach before taking the pill did not get any closer after a dose. But under its influence, one was certain that the shelf of pasta was three inches higher than it had been, so the illusion that one was three inches taller was intact. Other people remained the same height, of course. Gargantuanx was not sophisticated enough to create visual illusions, and shrink everyone to make the user seem taller by comparison. So it did the next best thing. It convinced the user that everyone else had also grown three inches. Insurance companies refused to cover the new drug, and retailers charged ten dollars a pill to those willing to pay anything for a couple of hours of believing, despite all evidence to the contrary, that one was three inches taller.

Gargantuanx aggressively suspended disbelief. If a basketball rim seemed no closer to a consumer of the pill, he had to believe it wasn't regulation height—"off by three inches," he would say. When a tape measure was brought out and the hoop was measured from the ground up, to demonstrate that it was indeed the proper 10 feet high, the Gargantuanxer had no choice but to believe that the tape measure was incorrect. Errors in production were made all the time—why should tape measure manufacturers be exempt? They were busy trying to meet deadlines, and it was certainly reasonable, if disappointing, that a few of their tape measures might be missing an inch or three. If it were pointed out that without exception all the numbers were there on the tape measure, the Gargantuanxer suspected that the size of each inch on the device was mistaken, so that an indicated total of 10 feet was in actuality 10 feet and 3 inches. It didn't help to bring 20 tape measures, or 50, or 1,000. If shown a million the Gargantuanxer would give no ground. He was forced to believe in a massive conspiracy among manufacturers of tape measures—and anyone who defended them—to convince people that they were three inches shorter than in fact they were.

What was unsettling to those not lured by Gargantuanx's promise of three inches and the accompanying boost in self-esteem was that taking the drug was a voluntary act. This wasn't a science fiction movie or a clever book about alien or government control. People chose the pill, and consumed it, with full knowledge of its effects. They wanted to be taller. Failing that, they wanted to think they were taller. Whatever their motives, they knew going in that the pill would create the illusion of additional height. The implications of a drug so powerful it could fool those who knew it was going to fool them worried lawmakers and concerned citizens. What would be next? A pill to make one think he was a spy or assassin for another country? Clearly, legislation was required.

Short people were divided. Speaking to the panel investigating Gargantuanx, the President of the Undersized Persons Society (Ups) made a passionate plea for a permanent and unequivocal ban on "this bane to the existence of undersized persons." For years undersized persons had been fighting for equality. They had only recently won a major court battle, resulting in a federal mandate requiring shoe retailers to carry larger supplies of women's sizes 4 and 5 and men's size 6. Plans were already underway to sue the Motion Picture Academy for the under-representation of undersized persons as leading men and women in American film, and the theater owners were on the list too, for deliberately designing audience seats so that anyone under the height of five feet six inches would be unable to see the screen when an overheighted person sat in the row in front of them. With all the progress made by undersized persons in this country, it was embarrassing, no, humiliating, that the government allowed this pill to be sold as a legitimate medication. Was the government implying that undersizeness was an ailment that required a cure?

After a quick sidebar discussion with her public relations advisor, the presiding senator assured the President of Ups that, of course, undersizeness was not an ailment, and she would personally sponsor legislation to ban Gargantuanx forever from this land of purple mountains majesty. This created an uproar. Other short people demanded to be heard. If they wanted to be deluded into thinking they were three inches taller, what business was this of the government, or anyone else? Gargantuanx was a victimless drug, if ever there was one. The proposed legislation was the subject of serious discussion on television and at water coolers around the nation. Small people, pretty much every man under five-foot-eight and woman under five-foot-five, couldn't come to an agreement—Gargantuanx was too popular, and the inflated sense of non-earned pride it provided was too tempting. Tall people, even those of average height who dabbled in Gargantuanx, by and large stayed out of the debate. Short, that is, undersized people dominated the discussion with a passion all out of proportion to their own dimensions.

That the nation was divided was indisputable. But Ups had powerful friends and deep pockets, and the legislation passed by a considerable margin, making it a felony—a federal offense—to even possess Gargantuanx on American soil. Ups claimed a victory for all undersizekind, but many people were distraught at the news. Not only was this an assault on the principle of self-determination and individual freedom, but also many of them wanted desperately to be able to think they were taller. A black market developed overnight. The people wanted their Gargantuanx and they were willing to pay for it. Pills went for twenty dollars, sometimes thirty, apiece. Rival dealers used intimidation and even murder to corner the local market. It wasn't long before gangs had infiltrated the schools, hooking kids, who were the only ones after all who didn't need the drug, since greater height was to them still attainable. But it nonetheless became fashionable to get hopped up on double and triple doses of Garg and go to the mall, where innocent clerks struggled in vain to convince strung-out shoppers that the jeans they were trying on were just too long and that the label was not mistaken.

The violence associated with the illegality of Gargantuanx led some to call for decriminalization, but the Ups lobby would not give in. Instead they declared a war on Garg, and local governments set up task forces to sweep the malls and raid the schools. If there were kids out there trying to be taller by any but the means provided by nature, they were going to suffer the consequences. Lockers were searched, athletes were banned, bus drivers were randomly tested, short parents were turned in by their short children, the very fabric of our society began to unravel. The corruption and terrorism of Al Capone's Chicago paled next to the nationwide frenzy caused by Garghibition.

Finally, even the zealots from Ups had to relent. If they couldn't squash Gargantuanx outright, then they would control it. Garg was legalized, and regulated, and taxed. Strict guidelines were developed for its production and distribution and the government banned forever any changes to its formula, to prevent an escalation in offending the sensibilities of certain influential short people. They had, they thought, won a limited victory.

But I'm a short person as well—I hate the undersize euphemism—and I've been in my lab for nine straight weeks now. After four failed tests of my new pill, Tremendocyclin, I finally have success. Oh, sweet bliss of greater height. I am five inches taller than I was just a moment ago. And nothing you say or do will convince me otherwise.

Bob Sullivan
All Hail the New Quayle!

While we all need a good laugh and like to share the latest joke, this doesn't mean we should elect one for President. The future of the Free World is too important to jeopardize just to make Jay Leno's and David Letterman's jobs easier.

It was worrisome enough knowing that Vice President Dan Quayle, with his notorious malapropisms and garbled speech (such as his famous paraphrasing of the motto of the United Negro College Fund: "What a terrible thing to have lost one's mind. Or not to have a mind at all. How true that is"), was a heartbeat away from the presidency. If anything had happened to George Herbert Bush, the consequences would have been disastrous.

But in 2000, one of our two choices in the voting booth will be Texas Governor George W. Bush, whose own continuing bouts of foot-in-mouth disease make one suspect that either a cocaine-booze mix is particularly injurious to mental synapses, or (my preferred theory) that President Bush and Vice President Quayle had a son together who grew up to be governor of the Lone Star State. I'm not suggesting anything sexual between Bush Sr. and Quayle, but many have long suspected that, for decades, government scientists have been conducting cloning and gene splicing experiments in our nation's capital.

How better to explain his statement to audiences, while touting his education policy, that the most important question to ask is, "Is your children learning?"

Or his statement: "Some say give [the federal budget surplus] to the taxpayers who pay the bills. That some is George W. Bush."

Or his claim to have "learned from mistakes I may or may not have made."

Or his statement, while discussing the need for a strong defense, "There is madmen in the world, and there are terror."

We're not talking about getting the names of world leaders wrong, just mastering basic first-grade English.

Elucidating on his world terror theme, he said, "When I was coming up, it was a dangerous world and you knew exactly who they were. It was us versus them and it was clear who them was. Today we are not so sure who the *they* are, but we know they're there."

He has also tackled domestic topics, as when he said, "What I'm against is quotas. I'm against hard quotas, quotas that basically delineate based upon whatever. However they delineate, quotas, I think, vulcanize society."

His simple solution for parents concerned about all the violence and profanity on television? "Put the off button on."

Favoring arbitration for disputes between patients and health maintenance organizations, Bush suggested the creation of an "arbitrary panel."

While campaigning, Bush reacted to McCain's pledge to end negative advertising with the words: "This is a man who says he's going to do one thing and does another. You can't have it both ways in the political process. You can't take the high horse and then claim the low road." He further asserted, "I've got a record, a record that is conservative and compassionated."

Bush may also have had a spotty career as a Texas oilman. His Bush Exploration never turned a profit and was continually being bailed out by his father, his uncle, his father's friends, and by acquaintances currying favors—such as James Bath, a front man for such shady Saudi investors as the father of Osama Bin Laden. Bush Exploration was eventually rescued by Harken Energy, which was then awarded special drilling rights (over such established firms as Amoco) off the coast of Bahrain, even though it had neither international experience nor experience drilling under water. When Bush dumped two-thirds of his Harken stock on the eve of the company's announcement of a huge quarterly loss, the Securities and Exchange Commission launched an insider-trading investigation, but eventually chose not to file charges. Despite this, Bush has pointed to his oilman days in his attempt to show solidarity with entrepreneurs, adding, "I understand small business growth. I was one."

In January 2000, meaning to say "missile launches," he spoke of "a world of madmen and uncertainty and potential mental losses." He also said, "We must all hear the universal call to like your neighbor just like you like to be liked yourself."

On January 26, 2000, Bush spoke of the need for "tackular" nuclear weapons. During a breakfast speech the following morning, he expressed admiration for single mothers who work hard "to put food on your family." That afternoon, after watching a local elementary school perform songs and skits centering on that month's theme of Perseverance, Bush praised them by saying, "This is preservation month. I appreciate preservation. It's what you do when you run for President. You've got to preserve."

When asked what he was not good at, Bush replied, "Sitting down and reading a 500-page book on public policy or philosophy or something." This is obviously an understatement. While humorous, we must keep in mind that, not only is the President the most powerful man on earth, whoever is elected next will most likely be selecting several Supreme Court judges, who will shape the course of our legal system well into the 21st century. Even though the extra effort to come up with monologues may put additional strain on Letterman's heart, putting a boob in power is not worth the laughs.

Perhaps Bush acquaintance Edward Flaherty put it best when he said, "George Bush couldn't get a clue if he was in a field full of horny clues during the clue-mating season and he smeared his body with clue musk and did the clue-mating dance."

David "Preacher" Slocum
Recipe for Brewing the Perfect Liberal

INGREDIENTS*
Rose-colored glasses
Detachment from reality
Social guilt
Environmental consciousness
Overindulged childhood
Lack of self-esteem
Unrealistic expectations
Sense of entitlement
Illogical arguments learned by rote
Well-heeled parents or third-generation welfare parent
(**NOTE:** If you use the optional third-generation welfare parent instead of the well-heeled parents, you must replace overindulged childhood with undisciplined childhood. You should also add a pinch of institutional anger.)

PREPARATION
Take a clean slate and using 2 well-heeled parents as a base, add 2 portions of overindulged childhood, 3 scoops of a sense of entitlement, a pinch of social guilt, and a dollop of a lack of self-esteem.

Allow this mixture to rise in an unstable household for 12 to 13 years. (The addition of an alcoholic or drug abuser to the home adds color to the final product. Some experts assert that a dash of infidelity will liven up the flavor, but that's optional.)

Mix in 3 cups of unrealistic expectations and sprinkle liberally with detachment from reality. Set this mixture aside for four to five years and allow it to ferment. Through a chemical process called liberalization, anger becomes infused into the mixture without having to induce it artificially. During this time, you can also add in 25 arguments learned by rote, as they will be useful in the lifetime of this product.

Decant the mixture into a college setting for the finishing touches. Here you will add a teaspoon of environmental consciousness as well as the rose-colored glasses as a garnish.

*Some ingredients are expensive. If you cannot afford them, you might try several gallons of excessive taxation.

C.P. Kaiser
Legislators with Gonadal Dysfunction

It's heartening that Jeff Podell in his anti-abortion diatribe ("A Choice? Maybe. But Whose?" p. 89) is so concerned about women bringing their fetuses to full term. Some might consider his position noble. In fact, entire armies of retired white males routinely spend their waning years harassing women going into and coming out of reproductive health clinics. A noble crusade, they say.

I suggest an even nobler crusade for Mr. Podell and his ilk—harassing the corporate chemical and agrarian conglomerates that routinely spray harmful pesticides on our food, dump toxic waste into our streams, and spew poisonous particulates into our atmosphere. These chemicals, in turn, are ingested by us all, but especially by pregnant women who pass them on to developing fetuses. Poisoned fetuses brought to full term have permanent neurological and physiological damage. Apparently—and it doesn't take a quantum physicist to figure this out—toxic chemicals disrupt the "exquisitely calibrated biological dance" needed for a developing organism ("System Failure," *Mother Jones*, July/August 1999).

Just as Rachel Carson was denounced by powerful corporate interests for her 1962 book, *Silent Spring*, which warned of the dangers of the pesticide DDT, Dr. Theo Colborn has been similarly discounted for her 1996 book, *Our Stolen Future*, which warns of the dangers of exposure to many of the man-made chemicals found in common plastics, cleaning compounds, and cosmetics. Even though 15,000 synthesized compounds are currently under investigation as potential endocrine disrupters (EDs), a panel of so-called experts recently concluded that there is insufficient evidence to say that EDs are causing human cancers and other problems like infertility. And though past studies have routinely linked toxic chemicals with neurological problems in test *animal* embryos, this expert panel called for *proof* that EDs are actually harming *human* fetuses as well.

Scientists dismayed by the panel's conclusion felt that more research will not help people who need to know NOW whether the food, water, and air they ingest and the plastics they use will be harmful to them and their progeny. But Capitol Hill is a carefully parceled piece of real estate, owned largely by corporate conglomerates including the powerful chemical and farming industries. Therefore, meaningful legislation against toxic substances such as EDs has little chance of making it past committee.

The endocrine, or hormone secreting, system is critical for the development of a growing fetus' organs, including the brain, kidneys, liver, thyroid, and reproductive organs. According to *Mother Jones*, research began to emerge in the 1980s showing that mothers who were heavy eaters of polychlorinated biphenyl- (PCB) contaminated fish had heavy amounts of PCBs in their umbilical-cord blood. Testing done at birth, age 4, and age 11 indicated that the children born to these mothers suffered from sub-par memory function, responded poorly to standard motor and cognitive tests, demonstrated poor reflexes, trembled in response to stress, and were easily startled.

An alarming increase in male reproductive abnormalities, including testicular cancer, low sperm counts, and gonadal dysfunction, has been linked to fetal endocrine system poisoning. Why critics find this hard to believe is beyond me, especially in light of the devastation caused by diethylstilbestrol (DES), an estrogen-mimicking compound given to women in the 1950s to prevent miscarriage. Daughters of those women have had many reproductive problems including cervical cancers and implantation problems.

The Environmental Protection Agency is in the middle of a multiyear review of allowable pesticide levels, a survey mandated by a 1996 law. Apparently, levels of allowable toxicity are based on the adult body and children may be at greater risk than supposed. Some researchers are linking a rise in hypospadias, a condition in newborns of incomplete sexual differentiation, to EPA findings of male rat reproductive system dysfunction. For boys born with hypospadias, the placement of their urethra opening is uncertain, appearing somewhere on the genitals other than at the tip of the penis—in the worst case, as far away as the scrotum. How deformed must our babies be before lawmakers take action? Perhaps legislators themselves are victims of gonadal dysfunction and lack the balls to enact legislation that will stop corporations from poisoning our land, water, and air.

Despite the declaration by our panel of so-called experts that there is insufficient evidence to say that EDs are causing human cancers, the federal government recently set new restrictions on methyl parathion (also known as Penncap-M) and azinphos-methyl, two chemicals used on a variety of crops, including apples, peaches, wheat, rice, pears, sugar beets, and cotton. The two are among some 40 pesticides classified as organophosphates, which account for most pesticides used by U.S. farmers. The restrictions stem from fears that the pesticides can cause damage to the brain and nervous system, especially in young children.

Environmentalists claim that this move by the EPA proves that farm groups and chemical companies who have said there is no problem are wrong. But industry personnel maintain a stoic optimism. "It's nothing to worry about," Allan Jennings, the director of the Agriculture Department's Office of Pest Management Policy, told CNN. "I still plan on feeding my kids as many [apples] as they will eat."

I guess Mr. Jennings isn't looking forward to having any healthy grandchildren.

Scott Stein
Let Them Eat (Their Own) Cake

Just last week I discussed fair and unfair methods of argumentation with my Humanities 101 students, freshmen at Drexel University. Politicians and others trying to persuade readers often use what is called *the false analogy*. A *false analogy*, as defined by *The Brief Holt Handbook* textbook we're using, is "Assuming that because things are similar in some ways they are similar in other ways." The book gave a lame example. A better one did not occur to me while I lectured, and I fear that my students did not get a clear understanding of why the false analogy is a misleading and poor method of argumentation.

(Un)Fortunately, the American people never fail to bail me out, and I can now direct my students to this essay, which contains a horribly effective but dishonest false analogy. David Mitsuo Nixon, of Seattle, had his letter to the editor published in *USA Today* on October 24, 2000. I have reproduced it here in full, and will make clear just how misleading his argument is at its conclusion:

Tax plan not fair
"GOP candidate George W. Bush says his tax plan is fair because it gives all taxpayers a tax cut ('Bush shifts gears and sharpens attack,' News, Friday).

"I teach practical reasoning at the University of Washington, and have to say that Bush makes a really awful argument.

"If I have to divide up a birthday cake among 10 children, and I decide to give one of the kids half the cake, and the others the remaining cake slivers, then all 10 kids will have received some of the cake.

"Does that make the distribution of it fair? Obviously not.

"There are a number of tax plans that would give tax cuts to all taxpayers—if that is all Bush is worried about.

"But not all of these plans are equally fair. Bush chose a plan that gives—according to the Citizens for Tax Justice, a Democrat-leaning group—about $560 billion to the richest people in America.

"He could have, for instance, proposed giving those people a mere $1 billion and given the rest of that money to education or the military or health care.

"But Bush decided that it was more important to give the money to the rich. I don't know whether his plan is fair, but it certainly paints a clear picture of his priorities."
- David Mitsuo Nixon, Seattle, Washington

Mr. Nixon should be ashamed of himself. This is a teacher of practical reasoning? His reasoning is practical indeed—so practical, that maybe we shouldn't call it reasoning at all.

Let's examine the false analogy:

If I invite children to a party and serve them cake, it is fair to assume that I would try to give somewhat equal portions. After all, they are at the party by my invitation. They are my guests. And they are children, easily upset if they do not get the cake they think they have coming to them.

But what if it isn't a birthday party? What if the cake is a reward for raking leaves? What if eight of the 10 children didn't rake the leaves, but chose to watch cartoons instead? Would it be unfair in this scenario for me to give larger portions of the cake to the two children whose hard work deserved rewarding?

Let's make the analogy fit the reality even more closely: What if two of the children saved up for and purchased the sugar and frosting and other ingredients needed to make the cake? And what if the same two children mixed the ingredients and preheated the oven and watched over the cake while the remaining eight children played outside? Would it be unfair to allow the two children who made the cake's very existence possible to have most of the cake? What claim do the other children even have to the cake that the two paid for and worked to create?

Is the cake even ours to give? If the two children bought ingredients and prepared the cake, what right do we have to confiscate it from them to give it out to the other eight as we see fit? Because we are adults and they are children, one might say. In other words, because we are big and strong and they are weak. Because we have the power to do so and how can they stop us? Because their money and effort are not theirs, but ours. Because we are bullies. Because children are our slaves, until they become adults.

Analogies only take us so far, and can be used to confuse the real issues. Of course, we are not really talking about cake; we are talking about money. And we are not talking about children; we are talking about adults. Whose money is it? Mr. Nixon pretends that it is America's money, or the government's money. But the money in question was not earned by *America*, which is after all just a concept, just a word used to describe a nation made up of millions of persons. And it wasn't earned by the government. The government does not—and isn't supposed to—create products or services that generate a profit. There really is no such thing as national wealth. What we call *national wealth* is just the total wealth of people in a nation. But people talk about the surplus tax money as if it belonged to all of us.

The surplus was earned by individual people, much of it by the very richest people in the country. The federal government taxed them at too high a rate and ended up having more money than it needed for its budget. It already used much of the budgeted money to provide services for people who did not pay for those services. The taxes from families earning $30,000 per year do not cover the services they use. So lots of extra money was taken from those who earn more, to provide police, firefighters, military, and many other essential services for those who do not pay for it. Lots of other non-essential services are also provided to those who do not pay for them, courtesy of the richest. *Courtesy* is not the right word. The richest have no choice, and must pay for others or face prison.

The wealthy and the very wealthy are not getting government services that equal the taxes they pay. Bill Gates earns much more than I do. He pays much more in taxes than I do. While he might own more land and require more police to protect his property, the amount he pays in taxes is still obscenely high. He might need 10 or even 100 times the services I need (probably not), but he is paying thousands of times more in taxes than I am. It is likely that Bill Gates and his family are not using public transportation, needle-exchange programs, public schools, and a host of other services either paid for or subsidized by his tax money. He pays for services for himself and thousands of other people who do not pay their own way. Mr. Nixon should thank Bill Gates for paying for services for all those who do not pay for them. Of course, no one thanks Gates or any other rich person. Instead, the wealthy are called greedy by the very people eating the cake the rich made.

When it became clear that the federal government had confiscated through taxes far more money than it needed for its already bloated budget, some of our leaders insisted that the extra money be redistributed *fairly* to everyone, in the form of many more, even less essential, services. Others have suggested that returning some of that money to the people who earned it is appropriate.

It is time people understood that *fair* and *equal* mean different things. In economic terms, *fair* means that you get as much or as little as you have earned. *Equal* means that money is taken from those who have earned it and given to those who have not. Mr. Nixon wants everyone to have an equal piece of the cake, no matter what the bakers think.

Bob Sullivan
Top Ten Signs You're Getting Old

10. The regulars on *60 Minutes* refer to you as "That Old Geezer."
9. Williard Scott's office just called to see if you have a photo.
8. Couldn't wait to see *The Crew* and *Space Cowboys* just to watch those hunky lead actors.
7. When you try to straighten the wrinkles in your pantyhose, you realize you're not wearing any.
6. When you wake up in the middle of the night thirsting for a glass of water, you have to go into the bathroom to find one *without* teeth in it.
5. You recently broke a hip opening a pull tab.
4. You can't have major dental work performed without express written permission from the American Historical Society.
3. You start repeating yourself and don't even realize it.
2. All the numbers on your speed dial are doctors.

And the Number 1 Sign You're Getting Old is...

1. You start repeating yourself and don't even realize it.

Ari McKee
Can't We Wait Until His Head's a Little Bigger?

Once in a while my all-girl side gets a hold of me and I wander over to the Lifetime Channel and get stuck there. Today, it was "A Baby" that snared me, a story of an American birth. As is typical of this program, it featured some nice youngish couple earnestly preparing for their firstborn-to-be, shopping for the layette, picking a pram, unrolling adorable wallpaper borders. Their excitement is contagious, their complete cluelessness is endearing, right up to the point when the expectant mom inevitably chirps, "We're planning on having the baby naturally!" The viewers saw the same young woman march happily to her ultrasound; we have no reason to believe she's dealt with her cavities, hemorrhoids, or hayfever *naturally*—but, for some reason she's decided that the only way to get an eight pound being out of her belly is to listen to a John Lennon CD and breathe funny.

Great figures in modern psychology like Freud and Skinner have theorized that human beings are designed to seek pleasure and avoid pain. That must be some kind of guy thing. Women are way into pain—and they're getting better at it all the time.

What did they come up with in the old days? Bound feet? Corsets? Stiletto heels? Big *deal.* Twenty-five pound wigs? Garter belts? Sleeping in rollers? Boo-*hoo*.

Women today have reached a whole new level of suffering. Sure, they've thrown out the girdles, but only because they're busy weaving their own out of Abs of Steel. We used to just shave—now we pay to have those tender hairs ripped out with strips of hot wax, or better yet, to have tiny electrified needles poked into each follicle. Each follicle! Over and over again! It takes weeks! Getting gorgeous these days is more than the occasional tweezing—true beauty requires changing the dressings and watching for red streaks. Don't even get me started on piercing.

Foremost in the new pain culture is the retro-delivery trend. It's hot now for babies to be delivered commando-style, in the manner of our pioneer foremothers—without doctors, delivery rooms, I.V.s, or even a bullet to bite on. The better the pain technology, the more it's rejected. For example, there's medication now that lets the mother move around and push, that doesn't enter the baby's bloodstream, and takes the pain down to a barely perceptible level. Mom stays awake and alert. "What the hell for?" you might ask. "To coast through this like it's just a kidney stone?" After all, this isn't about comfort—it's about everybody and their mother (especially their mother) listing natural childbirth as well as the Los Angeles Triathalon on their personal goal spreadsheet. Spinal blocks and narcotics are rejected out of hand, of course, though I should note that nobody asks the baby if maybe *she'd* like a hit of Nubain to take the edge off of being squeezed like a grape for seven to twelve hours. She's too little to understand that the most important thing about this event is not the outcome (a healthy mom and infant); it's about feeling, feeling, *feeling*—being deeply, Zen-ly aware of the whole horrific—uh, I mean *beautiful*—thing from start to finish.

Why? I dunno. One school of thought says that the retro-delivery movement is about "authenticity" or being "present in the moment." I hear some women in California are specifically seeking out sanitary rice paddies in which to squat when their time comes. Others are opting for an at-home birth, otherwise known as the no-oxygen-tank Everest expedition of childbirth. All the pain, all the worry, and at least *twice* the danger of a hospital delivery—plus, you get to wash your own sheets! There are no doctors or ICUs cluttering up the place, no pediatric surgeons or ER nurses, none of that unattractive emergency equipment interfering with the *feng shui*. The mom can rely on her flawless, documented prenatal ESP (the same mom whose personal astrologer is on stand-by alert to whip up little Leo's chart at the moment of his entrance into the cosmos) to guarantee that there will be no problems that require rapid medical intervention. What can go wrong? It's all *natural*. Women have been doing it for centuries—and, OK, dropping like flies, some detractors might claim. But, don't you see? That only makes it more challenging.

And of course, if something does go wrong, well, you can just imagine the suffering then. Something like that could wipe foot-binding clean off the books.

Ron Schorr
Circus Crap

Is it me or does the circus smell like shit? You take your kids out for a fun day and all you smell is shit. Forget the fat four-year-old with sticky, blue and pink hands from pounds of cotton candy, or the 100 midgets trundling out of a VW bug (now there's some funny shit!). The pervasive smell of animal dung makes this supposedly enjoyable outing a very unpleasant adventure.

You sit in the bleachers watching trained and highly skilled acrobats performing death-defying feats, and every five seconds this shitty smell wafts up and smacks you like a two-by-four across the face. The baby next to you may have a load in his diaper, but that pales in comparison to an 11-pound elephant dump. (I wonder if the humans living with these animals have had smell-reduction surgery?)

Of course, you're never told the price of admission includes the gangrenous aroma of shit. It's not part of the marquee. I've never noticed "Ringling Brothers presents the Human Torch, the Flying Tortellinis, and Lots o' Shit."

Did you ever go to a concert or a sporting event while the circus is in town at the same arena? Shit, shit, and more shit! First you blame the people you came with, until you realize it's those damn circus animals. You can't avoid the stench. It's as if a layer of feces has replaced the asphalt in the parking lot. Not even loud, raucous music can soothe your battered olfactory glands.

Oh, sure, it's funny watching a man in a red suit and top hat step into a huge pile of shit left behind by a mammoth animal, but do I need to smell it throughout? And what's with the guy sticking his head inside a lion's mouth? If successfully done, you think, Wow, he put his head in the mouth of a trained, toothless, overfed lion who needs Ex-Lax every five minutes just to begin to feel normal. If by chance he's unsuccessful, he dies, the circus is cancelled, and you're out $150 and the opportunity to smell more shit.

Scott Stein
A Talking Ass, or a Braying Mule?

In the early summer of 1998, I attended a cousin's bat mitzvah in Maine (yes, there are Jews in Maine—not many, but apparently I am related to all of them). To conclude the bat mitzvah ceremony, as is the custom, the audience was treated to a 12-year-old girl's interpretation of a portion of the Torah and to her reflections on the Torah's connection to modern life. Let's call my cousin "Sharon."

The Torah portion Sharon read concerned an abused donkey that surprised its human owner by speaking—in a comprehensible human tongue—its objection to the beating it was receiving. I was impressed by my young cousin's ability to express her concerns and examine the issues raised by the Torah's story.

Sharon had questions about the veracity of the story—it seemed to contradict what she knew about the real world, and part of her speech discussed the answers her rabbi had offered during Sharon's preparation for the ceremony. Sharon didn't believe that a donkey could talk. She wasn't being rebellious—she was simply pointing out what we all know and accept: Donkeys cannot speak in an articulate human language. No one denies this. Yet there it is in the Torah.

A bat mitzvah (or bar mitzvah for a boy) ceremony symbolizes the beginning of adulthood, yet that day it was the child's voice and honesty that was admirable. The rabbi—instead of presenting Sharon with evidence and various interpretations, both supporting and disputing the truth of the Torah, as intellectual integrity demands—had done what many religionists do when confronted with the obvious logical contradictions of their holy book: evaded and gave a vague explanation.

She had told Sharon that the Torah could be true without being literally true. That is, this rabbi didn't believe that a donkey could talk any more than Sharon did. Her answer to Sharon, that something could be true without being literally true, sounds wise at first, but what does it mean to say that something is true but not literally true? Can something be red but not literally red? Good but not literally good? Dead but not literally dead?

Sharon assumed it meant that the story of the talking donkey was true because it taught us an important moral lesson, that these stories are metaphors that convey some truth. No one agreed with her more than I did about the importance of and possible "truth" of a story. As a fiction writer who takes his work seriously (even when I am writing comic scenes), I believe that literature and art can convey the truth, but that the truth conveyed is not always the literal truth.

What I mean is that characters and events in a fiction can probe morals, convey the essence of an era, capture the human experience and the dilemma of being an intelligent living creature on our planet. Fiction can leave a reader shaking his or her head, as I often do when I read Kafka or James, stunned by the author's insight into the nature of the human mind or the human condition.

As a work of fiction, historical fiction, or poetry, or any kind of art, the Torah, or the Bible for that matter, has a claim to conveying metaphoric truth. But, while the story of a talking donkey or Moses communicating with a burning bush might tell us symbolically how to behave, or how hard it is to be a leader or a good person, or perhaps provide insights into what being human means or ought to mean, that is the limit of its truth-giving capacity (I am clearly using *truth* in its most inclusive sense). Art can make no supportable claim to providing objective knowledge of metaphysical reality.

Whereas other works of art seek to help us understand things, the Torah is treated as a source of knowledge. About an afterlife or the existence of a god, or *the* God, or an absolute system of morality or the origin of the world or living things, the Torah can tell us nothing by way of metaphor. Literal truth is being asserted, or interpreted by many readers, and literal truth, no matter the source, must meet the standards to which we hold all knowledge.

The questions raised by the talking donkey cannot be brushed aside. If the story of the donkey is not literally true (for experience teaches us that donkeys do not talk), what are we to think of the story of Adam and Eve (for we know that serpents do not talk), or the parting of the Red Sea, or the slaying of the first born in Egypt, or changing water into wine, or walking on water? If a part of the Torah or the Bible is not literally true, is any of it? How about the part where God created the earth and all living things? How about God's very existence?

Are religious people willing to admit that God is just a metaphor, that there is no literal truth to his existence? Probably not. So they believe that part of the Torah is literally true. A specific god's existence is as supported by evidence as a donkey talking in Hebrew or Latin. Why believe one and not the other?

If parts of the Torah are not literally true and others are, who gets to decide which parts are which? The answer, of course, is people: fallible, power-hungry, weak people, with all their foibles, mental illnesses, and ulterior motivations. Unless religionists want to believe that their all-knowing and good God wrote an imperfect book full of untruths, exaggerations, and convoluted metaphors, they are left with a book written by primitive, superstitious people, being translated and interpreted by still other superstitious people over thousands of years, as the basis for their lives.

The other choice is for religionists to believe that the Torah was written by God and is literally true. This choice requires them to accept talking donkeys. I am not prepared to accept talking donkeys. If they are, I can be tolerant, but how can one who values reason respect the opinion that donkeys, under the right conditions, speak fluent Hebrew, Latin, or English, just because an old book says so?

Sharon values reason. She doesn't believe in talking donkeys, doesn't believe in miracles, and in her speech wondered if miracles today aren't subtle, like peacemaking efforts in the Middle East. Here an adult's honesty might have helped her: There is no such thing as everyday miracles. Miracles defy logic and reason—they are contradictions. By definition, a miracle is something that cannot be explained. Peacemaking is not a miracle. Neither is modern medicine, or surviving an illness against the odds. A talking donkey is. But we don't believe in talking donkeys, do we?

Sharon is a reasonable, rational person, with a curious, open mind. At the end of her bat mitzvah service, the rabbi, like an obstinate mule wearing blinders, said that she hoped Sharon would get over her problems with Judaism and religion. It didn't seem to bother the rabbi that the problems are real. I only hope that Sharon remains committed to the integrity of her own thoughts and the honest evaluation of the evidence, and that societal and familial pressures don't force her to accept that which her intellectual instincts have already told her is false.

Reader Comments

—*Edmund Weinmann responds to "A Talking Ass, or a Braying Mule?" by Scott Stein.*
This is not what theists mean when they speak of miracles. They mean a divine intervention into the natural order, producing a result that would not otherwise have occurred. For believers—at least in the Abrahamic religions—a miracle is not simply a phenomenon for which we do not yet have an explanation, but which may, with the progress of science, one day be explained. It is evidence of their God acting in the world.

A lot of believers will also justify calling something like peacemaking an everyday miracle by saying that it can only take place by and through the grace of God, that if God were not willing, the attitudes of the warring parties would have been such that the peace could not have been achieved, just as the hearts of various rulers in the tales of the Bible were often either hardened against some ideas, or made more receptive to them, by divine grace.

We all have models, according to which we attempt our explanations of things. Some of these models include a personal god, but others do not. These models are never themselves proven to be right, or to be wrong, regardless of whether particular explanations, made within them, are eventually shown to be correct, or not. They are only found, over time, to be of greater or lesser utility to those employing them, and accordingly are retained, or abandoned. But keep in mind that *utility*, here, includes the comfort afforded by being able to consider the fortunate events in life the result of the benevolent intentions of an all-powerful supreme being, rather than just pieces of good luck, which might as easily have been bad luck, instead.

—*Scott Stein responds to Edmund Weinmann's comments on his "A Talking Ass, or a Braying Mule?"*
Webster's primary definition of *miracle* is "an event or action that apparently contradicts known scientific laws and is hence thought to be due to supernatural causes, esp. to an act of God." I think most people, when reading the Torah or the Bible, would define a miracle even more strictly: A miracle is not just an event that cannot be explained with known scientific laws, but is unable, in principle and in the future, to be explained except by God's

intervention.

In order for an event to be evidence, as Mr. Weinmann says, of a god acting in the world, it needs to be something that cannot be explained any other way. Otherwise why bring God into it in the first place? It is possible to conceive of peacemaking or modern medicine taking place without God's intervention, so these events are not evidence of God.

The above essay challenges the literal truth of religious books, and claims that if portions of the books are not true, believing in anything asserted by the books not supported by evidence is an arbitrary exercise. In order to believe in the literal truth of a religious book, one must believe in miracles, not of the peacemaking variety, but of the talking donkey variety. If there is a scientific explanation for a talking donkey, or if an explanation is discovered a thousand years from now, then that talking donkey is not evidence of God. One must believe either that a donkey could talk without God's intervention or that God did intervene to make one talk in order to believe in the literal truth of the Torah.

Individuals can believe what they want, of course. If they want to attribute peacemaking or a flu shot to divine intervention, I cannot stop them. But aren't they then treading very close to the worldview of ancient pagans and primitives, believing that every natural event is a deliberate act of God? They might as well dance in a circle or sacrifice the nearest virgin to make it rain. If they want to dismiss the notion of cause and effect in favor of unsupported superstition that is their business.

Mr. Weinmann has the view that we should judge beliefs only on their utility. If the utility we value is the ability to make accurate predictions about the world and give us verifiable explanations, the scientific method and rational inquiry are superior to religious teachings by a magnitude that makes comparison unfair. Mr. Weinmann suggests that the emotional and comforting utility of a method is also important. My essay is about the truth, not about feeling good. I have no quarrel with Mr. Weinmann's assertion that some people find religion to be useful because it comforts them. Many, however, claim that it does not make them feel good. None of this has any bearing on whether or not it is true.

Finally, giving credit to God for smiling on us with good luck and not blaming God when we experience bad luck is arbitrary and irrational, comforting or not.

—Merilyn Brunner responds to "A Talking Ass, or a Braying Mule?" by Scott Stein.

Mr. Weinmann's suggestion that peace in the Middle East is possible because God softened peoples' hearts is absurd. If everything depended on that kind of intervention, then God is responsible for world war. That lets a lot of villains off the hook, doesn't it?

Robert L. Hall
Blame Game Justice

I'm waiting for some nincompoop to jump up on a national news program and proclaim, "There is evidence today of a gene, just discovered, that is responsible for no self-control in the human behavior pattern."

Then, of course, what will follow will be the test cases in court, with lawyers offering not guilty by reason of the "no-self-control-gene defense." Judges will be letting the most heinous criminals off scot-free because they just couldn't help sawing an old lady in half with a blunt knife, or just had to strangle their girlfriend because the no-self-control gene made them do it.

The O.J. Simpson trial will pale in comparison.

Think it far-fetched? Not at all!

We already have criminals getting off on defenses based on their growing up as a battered child or in a dysfunctional family or due to their socially malnourished backgrounds. I recently heard of a teacher who had 10 dollars stolen out of her purse, and the educational superintendent said it was the teacher's fault—not the child's—because one had to expect that type of behavior from a person from a deprived background.

Even our politicians are all marching against gun rights because they consider people too stupid to act in their own best interests. They think people don't know that shooting each other is a bad thing, that they commit violent crimes only because they can, not because they choose to. Changing the laws is not going to stop people from committing crimes.

Mr. President, how about we have a national campaign for Child Control instead of Gun Control? Instead of asking "Parents, do you know where your children are?" perhaps we might try "Children, do you know where your parents are?"

Judging from what I've seen of juveniles in the schools, streets, stores, restaurants, and even churches, parents need to do one of two things: either stop disciplining their kids, or start disciplining their kids.

Everyone complains about people who abuse their children, but what they don't say is that neglect in the form of gross permissiveness is just as abusive. If you don't give a damn about your kid, go ahead and let him or her grow up to be a selfish, overindulgent monster; we still have plenty of room in our jails.

How about a Self-Control campaign for the supposedly grown-up segment of the populace? I am reminded of the incident recently where a motorist, in his blind fury, reached into a lady's car, grabbed her pet dog, and flung it under the wheels of oncoming traffic, just because the poor woman accidentally happened to bump the guy's rear fender.

Get a grip, people! C'mon, grow up!

What this country needs is a little old-fashioned justice. We no longer have a criminal *justice* system; instead we have a criminal *rights* system, because everything is tilted in the criminal's favor. We've mollycoddled hardened felons so long that we actually encourage them to pursue lives of crime. Why shouldn't they? They can't lose.

We can't catch them, we can't arrest them, we can't convict them, and they get off with plea bargains and backroom deals. Judges with no social conscience let them out of jail, or stay executions of those who richly deserve that penalty. What ever happened to due process and a speedy trial? Instead, we have convicted killers making endless petitions and inmates who have been on death row for ten and twenty years.

And please, somebody tell me what gives a judge the right to step in and change the sentence (or worse yet—the conviction) of a killer who has been convicted of a crime and found guilty and sentenced by a jury of his peers? What is a judge like that doing living among foolish mortals like us? Why doesn't he just ascend straight to the Godhead, where he evidently thinks he belongs anyway?

Judges, like the rest of our society, accept the most ridiculous explanations from criminals: I shot the old lady for her cookies; I was hungry; my mommy didn't feed me; my dad doesn't love me; my girlfriend dumped me; I was in a piss-poor mood; I was out of money.

Let's stop blaming societal injustices and mood swings for every criminal act that is committed in this country. I don't know about you, but I have crappy days sometimes, and I don't go out and shoot people or boost their cars. If some poor schmuck gets caught with his hand in the cookie jar, it would be refreshing to just once hear him stand up and proclaim, "It's true. I made a terrible mistake and I sincerely regret having done it. I accept the punishment I have earned."

C.P. Kaiser
Alcohol Problem? Break Out the Leeches and the Bible

I've been an atheist for most of my adult life. More than a few times, however, due to a then-undiagnosed chemical disorder that caused severe mood swings, I ventured into several cult-like self-help groups and god-based religiosity groups to "get back on the right track." One of those groups—that fits both categories—was Alcoholics Anonymous.

I entered into the Fellowship, as it is known, dragging a battered suitcase full of unrealized dreams, miserable relationships, and unfulfilling jobs. I was to self-actualization as my ass was to Uranus: not even on the same planet. I suspected AA had some kind of power because my dad got sober in AA and dramatically changed his life (he too suffered from undiagnosed depression categorized as alcoholism). Little did I know, however, that the power of Alcoholics Anonymous was insidiously ascribed to the all-American Judeo-Christian god.

The complaints of a newcomer in the rooms of AA are met with a lot of skepticism. Everyone just thinks you're trying to weasel out of staying sober. Hence, my complaints about the god-based elements of AA recovery were met with stern reproach from old-timers who supposedly knew better because they had seen scores of eager men and women stumble through the AA doors only to waltz out a few short months, or even years, later thinking—albeit wrongfully, according to the AA Gestapo—that they had recovered.

At first the god-based theory of staying sober is cleverly disguised. You are told to believe in a higher power, but they say that higher power can be anything, including the group of drunks that surrounds you or the radiator against the wall of the church basement where you're meeting. Nobody forces you to go to church, but all meetings end with either The Lord's Prayer or the so-called Serenity Prayer, or both. I never saw anyone kneeling in front of the radiator asking for serenity.

As a newcomer in AA, you're pretty much a sack of shit, having experienced any number of the five Ds: DUI, detention, detox, divorce, or death. The beginning of AA sobriety is basically like boot camp. The old-timers—more zealous than televangelists at a leper colony—constantly remind you of your boot-lickin' status, except they call it humility. You're basically asked to give up your identity, your free will, and your decision-making powers and do exactly as they say. After all, they say, it was those things that took you down; or as Bill Wilson, the founder of AA, said, "It was your self-will run riot that made you a drunk."

All of Wilson's philosophy can be found in the "Big Book," a large, blue tome written in 1939 by Wilson. I found much of it dated, poorly written, full of clichés, and with as many mentions of god as a *Sports Illustrated* awards banquet *and* the Oscars ceremony combined. My complaints about the stodgy philosophy were treated as heresy. Like most cult leaders, the old guard stood by its bible as if Moses's god had inspired every word (which, of course, is what they think).

"He'll come around," the old-timers would mutter to each other whenever I protested about the god thing, as if my disbelief in god took me down while their belief in god had nothing to do with their 3 a.m. Sterno binges.

Nevertheless, I stayed active in AA for three years, creating a safe community for myself. I enjoyed weddings, births, funerals, picnics, ball games, golfing weekends, hiking trips, and boating jaunts. I had some really good times with some really good people from all professions, careers, and segments of society. No matter how hard I tried, however, I couldn't separate god from the drunks. I tolerated them as much as they tolerated me.

Despite the American Medical Association's contention that alcoholism is a disease, AA still treats it as if one is possessed by the devil and in need of an exorcism. In fact, Bill Wilson said the key to sobriety is a "change of heart" (try getting your HMO to pay for that!). The 12 suggested steps (the "suggestion" aspect is as suspect as AA being a nonsecular organization) of the program include an admission of powerlessness, a moral inventory, and surrender to the biblical god (when was the last time your cardiologist suggested any of those for angina?). Wilson just missed the mark, however, when he wrote that alcoholism is a symptom of a deeper malady. If he had meant a chemical or hormonal imbalance, or some other organic brain disorder, then I'd say he was on to something. But, alas, he simply meant a deeper, *spiritual* malady that could only be fixed by one's increased reliance on a god.

It's hard to believe that a group as large and influential as AA (indeed, Aldous Huxley called Wilson "the greatest social architect of our century") basically relies on exorcism to curb and cure an AMA-sanctioned disease. We may as well leech blood and turn to phrenology for answers. I can remember sponsors (old-timer mentors) refusing to let their pigeons (barely sober protégés) take psychotropic drugs because they believed getting better was in some god's hands. I also remember those same sponsors furiously popping Tums or downing Pepto Bismal after a particularly spicy pasta night. Beelzebub, apparently, doesn't cause acid reflux.

Wilson's AA philosophy has its roots in the Oxford Group, a strict, proselytizing religious sect that has its roots in the Bible. AA's debt to the Oxford Group lies in a number of areas, including special focus on the need for a god and his guidance, the importance of fellowship, the importance of witnessing, and the necessity for practicing Christian principles as a way of life. AA bought these ideas whole hog, whatever they call them.

Wilson's own words tell the story more succinctly:

> It was only a matter of being willing to believe in a Power greater than myself.... There I humbly offered myself to God, as I then understood Him, to do with me as He would. I placed myself unreservedly under His care and direction. I admitted for the first time that of myself I was nothing; that without Him I was lost. I ruthlessly faced my sins and became willing to have my newfound Friend take them away, root and branch. I have not had a drink since.

No matter how AA disguises its Christian bent, no matter how much it pretends to be a secular organization, the truth is plain: Wilson's belief that the Christian god of the Bible had saved him from alcoholism is the crux of his AA philosophy, and it is that philosophy which must be adopted by all who enter the organization's doors. Actually, this setup is fine for common schmoes who come into AA of their own volition; they're free to walk out as well. Problems begin when U.S. courts of law sentence drug- and alcohol-related lawbreakers to serve time in Alcoholics Anonymous. These courts are, in effect, saying, "Go and turn your will and life over to Jesus Christ and we will not incarcerate you." This is a flagrant violation of the separation of church and state.

After a decade of not drinking, interspersed with bouts of psychological counseling and binge memberships in other cult-like self-actualizing groups, I was still suffering terrible mood swings. I felt as if I was passing all my subjects and still being left behind a grade each year. Finally, a psychologist recommended I read *Listening to Prozac* by Peter D. Kramer. I had come home. I recognized myself on every page. I got the drug and have been on a steady incline in health ever since. And, if I want, I can drink responsibly. My brain's chemistry no longer forces me to put out the fire of depression with more alcohol.

Of course, the world's history is rife with blurred distinctions between biology and metaphysics. For example, in Leviticus 15:19-31, menstruating women are considered unclean, impure, and untouchable and must therefore sacrifice two turtledoves before the Lord "lest they defile his tabernacle." In the nineteenth century, tuberculosis was considered a disease of sensitive, poetic, soul-sick people until scientists discovered it was caused by a bacterium. Even today, many people believe AIDS to be a holy scourge sent from on high to teach homosexual "sinners" a lesson (witness Ronald Reagan's do-nothing approach to the burgeoning AIDS epidemic throughout the 1980s).

As unique as everyone's situation is, I still think our culture places an undue responsibility on those suffering from organic brain disorders, otherwise known as mental illnesses. If we're not expected to "will" away our hypothyroidism or have the gods take away our liver cancer, then why do we expect our alcoholics and drug addicts to pray themselves into health? The body is a finely tuned running machine, and the brain, its engine. My engine's synapses have problems with serotonin, a neurotransmitter that helps the brain function. Just as you wouldn't stand over your car's seized engine praying for the deliverance of oil into its crankshaft, you shouldn't be expected to pray for serotonin, dopamine, acetylcholine, or any other neurotransmitter to suddenly appear in your brain.

As a society, we don't believe mental illness is caused by demonic possession. Yet, if we look closely, we still treat the mentally ill as if their disease were their fault, as if they are weak-willed or unclean. Neurotransmitters such as serotonin and hormones like insulin are chemicals produced in the body. When the body stops producing them, they need to be supplied from the outside. Let's take seriously the AMA's contention that addiction is a disease and treat it as such, instead of asking our addicts to walk on water, raise the dead, and feed the multitude with two fishes and a loaf of bread.

Alex Joseph
Sheep

My father comes home from work early. He enters the kitchen and sets his brown briefcase on the glass-topped table. I'm leaning on my elbow, six inches away from the small black-and-white TV, watching *The News Hour with Jim Lehrer*. Behind me, on the stove, three pots with copper lids are rattling and belching steam. The kitchen smells like burned rice.

"Hello, son," my father says.

"Hello."

He keeps standing there. "Did you make dinner?"

"Yep. I reheated that pork and made some broccoli. I had to make two pots of rice because the first one got overcooked. Mom never showed me how to make it." I say this into the television. On screen, a woman in a lab coat speaks into a microphone. A pair of identical sheep stands in a small pen behind her. My father reaches past my shoulder to turn off the set. I sit up, blinking as though awakened from a dream.

"Mr. Settle called me at work." My father is still standing there in his beige London Fog overcoat; that's how I suddenly know it's an emergency.

"Brian got hit by a car on his way home from soccer practice."

"Is he all right?"

"No. He's not all right." I can't look at my father's face. It's like it's all his fault. Instead, I look at his briefcase, hating the color. My father tugs on the belt of his coat, rearranges the salt and peppershakers on the glass-topped table.

I go up to my room without eating and crawl into bed with my clothes on. From downstairs, I can hear my father removing lids from the pots, making a plate for himself. Outside, it is already dark. It gets dark around six now, and usually around five, since my mother died, I start to get a sick feeling.

Brian and I played soccer together when we were little. We were best friends. The summer we were 10, we built a tree house and lit bonfires in his backyard. I still remember the sharp outline of his shadow flickering against the garage. When the fire had burned down to its embers, we whooped and galloped down to a shimmering creek that ran in a tiny ravine behind his house. At dinnertime, Mrs. Settle clanged an enormous, brass bell. We came inside, still muddy, and Mrs. Settle sat us down by ourselves at the round table in the kitchen, and brought us trays of things my mother would never make—nachos; homemade doughnuts and fresh cider; something called Weenie Winks, which were hot dogs split open and filled with cheddar cheese and draped with tendrils of fatty bacon. Then Brian started Varsity, and I don't play any sports, and we weren't such good friends any more.

I wander over to the window and gaze down the street toward his house, but it's at the end of the block and I can't quite see it.

The phone rings. After a moment, my father calls out to me. I retrieve the upstairs hall extension.

"Hello," I say.

"Barry." It is Mr. Settle. "How are things?"

"Fine. Well, not fine, but..."

"I know what you mean."

After a second, I say, "Do you want me to..."

"Well, actually, yes. Mrs. Settle and I ... we were wondering if you wanted to come over."

"Right now?"

"Oh, if you'd like to," he says quickly. "Only if you'd like."

I walk over without a coat. It is cold. Orange leaves skitter around my feet. Next to Brian's place, the rest of the neighborhood feels dark. Yellow light streams from every window.

After my mother died last spring, I started to go over to the Settle's house again, to see Mrs. Settle. We sat in the kitchen, talking, on the afternoons when Brian played soccer. Mrs. Settle wore dark-colored sweaters that crept up her neck and faded blue jeans on her slim legs. Her fingers were red. The skin on her hands looked nearly translucent. She told me she wanted to start painting again. When Brian came home from soccer practice, I snuck out the back door.

I walk slowly down the block, but the moment my foot hits the bottom step of Brian's porch, Mr. Settle throws open the front door.

"Barry," he cries, as if we hadn't just spoken. He's wearing wool pants and a blue oxford shirt with the top three buttons undone. Ice cubes are tinkling in his drink. "Please, come on up." Then he disappears inside his house.

I open the screen door. Inside, the TV plays the second broadcast of the *Lehrer* show for the empty living room. It's the woman with the sheep again. She says, "Of course, this discovery raises the potential for numerous ethical dilemmas."

The house is very warm. I close the door.

"C'mon up!" Mr. Settle yells again.

I follow the sound of his voice up the stairs. The hallway jogs to the left, and then I'm standing in the doorway of Brian's room. Mr. Settle is sitting at Brian's desk, turning his tumbler of brown liquid around in slow circles. Mrs. Settle is filling up a cardboard box with the soccer trophies on Brian's bureau. She's wearing a pair of dark blue jeans with the cuffs turned up, and her hair is pulled away from her face by a red bandana. She stops when she sees me. Her face is bright red, maybe from exertion, her bright eyes embedded in her head like two red coals.

"There you are," she says. She blows a wisp of gray hair out of her face. "We've been waiting for you."

"I'm sorry," I say.

"Don't be. You're here." She puts the last of Brian's trophies into the box. "There," she says, and sneezes. "Whoo, the dust. I know you wouldn't let your things get so dusty."

"Ah," says Mr. Settle, "but he's not a ballplayer either, Marge."

She stalks over to him, bends down until her forehead is nearly touching his. "Roger. Barry reads. He reads books."

"Oh, I know. I know, don't get me wrong," Mr. Settle says.

Mrs. Settle turns and takes a few pictures off the wall. "Now, I don't know what you're going to do about the posters." She drops the pictures in the box, beside the trophies. "I mean, you don't like race cars, I assume. Or those Olympic ones." These posters are old. Brian had them up when we were 12. I still like the one of the man balancing himself on the rings, the tendons on his arms standing out.

"We'll see," I say.

"OK," says Mrs. Settle. "Now, dinner's gonna take about twenty minutes. Simple stir-fry. Obviously, I'm not prepared, but everything's fresh, at least."

"Sounds great."

"Let me get this stuff out of your way then." She puts the box under her arm, and heads past me. "I'll call you when dinner's ready." Mr. Settle nods at me, and follows her out.

I hear them descend the stairs, talking to each other, and then they're in the kitchen. I switch off the light and lie on Brian's pillow, my arms crossed under my head. Something's not right. Then I realize it's just the conversation, the overheard sound of two voices, one male, one female.

I lie there, not sleeping, feeling this way, until I hear Mrs. Settle call my name.

Scott Stein
If At First You Don't Succeed...

Second chances are the American way. If you fall off a horse, get back on. Everyone loves a comeback. If at first you don't succeed, try, try again.

I hope I am not being un-American and that the FBI will not open a file on me when I suggest that there are some second chances we should not grant.

In March of 1999, 42-year-old Georgette Smith was paralyzed from the neck down when her mother shot her in the spine.* Shirley Egan, 68, shot her daughter when she heard that Ms. Smith wanted to place her in a nursing home. The legal controversy began when Ms. Smith won the right to have her life support disconnected in May of 1999. She was aware that the decision to be removed from life support would result not only in her death but probably in murder charges against her mother as well. In the twisted tale of this sad family, it is the legal question that has taken center stage.

As the Associated Press reported, this might be a case without precedent. Many criminals have been charged with murder, and convicted, after the lingering effects of their actions resulted in the death of their victims. But Georgette Smith was of sound mind when she chose to be unhooked from life support, and understood that her decision would end her life.

Who is responsible for her death? Ms. Smith, for her decision to not go on living? Or Ms. Egan, for leaving her daughter dependent on machines and irreversibly paralyzed, with only the ability to wiggle her nose and tongue and blink her eyes, unable to control bodily functions and at risk for pneumonia, ulcers, and bed sores?

Prosecutors are eager to charge Ms. Egan with murder instead of attempted murder, now that her daughter is dead. According to David Orentlicher, a professor of law at Indiana University, a murder prosecution could succeed: "The question is, are they doing something that is so unreasonable that it's not fair to blame the shooter.... In this case we have a well-recognized reason for refusing treatment."

Of course, some legal experts disagree. Peter Arenella, a professor of criminal law at the University of California at Los Angeles, said, "You can't be held responsible for someone else's death unless you cause that death. The daughter made a conscious decision to end her life, and should be held to be the actual cause of death."

Legal scholars, judges, and lawyers, as is the proud adversarial tradition of the American judicial system, are bound to look for precedents and to argue about what is legal. This case, however it concludes, will set a new precedent, and future lawyers and judges will look to it for guidance when another twisted tale of a sad family comes across their desks. But what about what is right? Isn't this case the perfect illustration of the absurdity of America's distinction between murder and attempted murder?

If Ms. Egan had shot her daughter in the head, killing her immediately, she would have been charged with murder. Since her shot did not kill Ms. Smith instantly, but merely paralyzed her for life, Ms. Egan was initially charged with attempted murder.

Why should there be a lesser penalty for failing to kill? Don't we want our murderers to be successful achievers? Why reward failure? If America is going to have the best murderers in the world, coddling the incompetent is no answer. Ms. Egan is being rewarded for being a bad shot.

Seriously, attempted murderers get out of prison sooner than successful murderers, and have a second chance, maybe to get it right the next time. Does this make sense? Ms. Egan's intent was the same no matter where the bullet landed. The threat she poses to society doesn't change if the daughter died right away or made a full recovery. Ms. Egan's actions are equally deplorable no matter the consequences.

Some might argue that the distinction is important because in hostage situations, negotiators are able to say to attempted murderers, "You haven't killed anyone yet," thereby saving the day when the bad guy realizes that he will not be convicted of murder if he doesn't kill anyone. I don't know how often this comes up outside of movies and TV police dramas, but the *Hawaii Five-O*-type negotiating tactics aside, I think abolishing the distinction would be in the best interest of our society.

The rationale is simple. You may not kill someone, and you may not try to kill someone. You may not shoot or stab or hit people over the head with a large brick. Whether or not they survive, that behavior is unacceptable. Maybe I am a radical when it comes to violent crime. Maybe you see me as a fascist because I am not full of forgiveness for people who intentionally injure and maim and kill, or try to kill, other people.

Second chances might be the American way, but maybe it is time to change that American way, and draw a line (if not in the sand, somewhere) and say no, we will not allow those who try to kill people to improve their aim and succeed the next time. Murder and attempted murder are the same—once is more than enough.

---

*The details of this case and the quotes from legal experts are drawn from an Associated Press article written by Rick Bragg on May 19, 1999.

David "Preacher" Slocum
Insert Foot

Sometimes it doesn't pay to open your mouth.

Just the other day at the office I was confronted by a group of coworkers. In an intervention-esque manner, they surrounded me and demanded to know why I never attended company or employee functions.

The company that employs me holds monthly "Associate Recreation" events, from tickets to the local B-league hockey team and the professional basketball team to bowling to Habitat for Humanity PR stunts.

The employees, in addition to the company-sponsored events, often hold promotion parties, retirement parties, baby showers, housewarmings, and any other reason to get drunk. I don't go. Not once. Not ever.

When the insistent group would not take the standard brush-offs (projects around the house, after-school activities for the kids, etc.), I was forced to do something I find distasteful: discuss my true feelings. After assuring myself that they did, indeed, want the truth, the whole truth, and nothing but the truth, I bared all.

"I don't like you."

Needless to say, this did not go over well. After giving them time to vocalize their dislike of my statement, I tried to explain.

I get along with people. I could probably get along with Hitler on a daily basis if I had to. While I thought that, for the most part, they were nice people, I didn't want to hang out with them at a bar, I didn't want to go over to their houses for a barbecue, and I sure wasn't going to invite them to my house. I didn't want to go to sporting events and I could really not care less about the many and varied social causes that my employer tried to involve us in. It did not concern me if someone got promoted or retired and I didn't care that someone had whelped another brat.

After work, one of the last things in the world I want to do is spend hours rehashing the day's events with the same people I just spent 10 hours with. I want to go to my beautiful home, and just relax in the company of my gorgeous wife who, incidentally, has her own set of coworkers that she avoids.

You would have thought that I had murdered the Pope right there in the office break room. How dare I not like them? How dare I not be concerned with their petty causes, or be fascinated by their latest addition to overpopulation? How dare I not spend my every waking moment basking in the glory that was their presence?

Well, I have to say that since this little conversation took place, I no longer have to lie to my coworkers about why I am not going to "___." On the other hand, I found out that a couple of my coworkers have started a pool ... $1 per slot on "When Slocum will go POSTAL."

Katherine Hauswirth
Punch Drunk

Turning sixteen meant I was finally allowed to date. I made sure I swaggered (in a feminine way) on the way to class. I tottered ever so slightly on my heels to allow my hips more obvious sway. I wore tight jeans and heels, not tight or high enough to be slutty, but enough to sell my availability. I elongated my lashes with mascara and made sure my hair swung when I walked by the corner where the senior boys convened to check out girls. I tried to own the runway. I was ready.

Or so I thought. A bona fide football team member asked me out. Paul was sweet, gentle, and oversexed. He ambitiously juggled a 4:40 a.m. paper route, the late shift at McDonald's, and football practice. His upper lip smelled vaguely of McDonald's, as if his job had somehow been absorbed there. He cruised up to my house in his classic Cutlass, the car pulsating with coolness and *Synchronicity* by The Police. I was prim and unattainable on our dates. My naïveté had not yet caught up with my sex drive. I wasn't quite sure what I was doing, but I sure liked being wanted. I was smug about myself in a way that only an adolescent can be. My looks, my power, my invincibility were unquestionable.

All fits of grandiosity call for a humbling experience. Mine was memorable. Paul invited me to the McDonald's holiday party. This was to include a lot of actual adults, and I knew I had to shine. I wore my angora Christmas sweater and *Charlie* perfume, and made sure my mascara was thick. I should have known when the evening started that the humiliation was just beginning. I greeted Paul, then glanced down at my blue-jeaned thigh to spot a tumor-like lump pressing the denim outward. I had slipped my jeans on in haste from their spot on the floor, and realized in horror that a discarded pair of balled-up panties had become incorporated into my ensemble. I remedied the problem upstairs and thanked God I had not made it out the door with the underwear soft sculpture attached. If only that had been the end of the embarrassment.

I arrived feeling inferior from the near-fatal wardrobe faux pas. While the stereo droned *Culture Club* tunes, it occurred to me that Paul and I had very little in common. He and his McDonald's cohorts knew sports, sang drinking songs, and got paychecks. I knew nothing. I was mousy and prim and wordless. I smiled a lot and tried to look desirable. I felt my lipstick caking and my high heels starting to sweat. I felt like a kid wearing Tinkerbell makeup and a grown-up costume. The other females there were *women*; I was a girl. Paul wandered off to socialize.

The Kool Aid with sherbet punch was my friend. That and 9 varieties of Boone's Farm, Malt Liquor, and probably rubbing alcohol. All I knew was that it went down easy and kept me occupied.

I remember feeling very sophisticated, then a big black space of nothing until I woke up on my bathroom floor, surrounded by regurgitated remnants of McDonald's hash browns. My self-image was shattered. I couldn't conceive of feeling even remotely OK again. I didn't feel unattainable anymore.

Unattainable—*oh no*. Had I finally allowed my sex drive to escape? I had kept it so in line, but that punch had made me feel very sexy. I remembered that much. I realized this sickness-coated amnesia must be what they call a *blackout*. I longed for the simple embarrassment of an insufficient wardrobe. The hangover of destruction was forever emblazoned on my pounding brain. I felt like a Greek tragedy. I prayed I was still a virgin.

I moaned and crawled for the phone. I dialed and redialed. My hands were dirty, nails broken, right index finger inexplicably scabbed with a jagged laceration. My hair was sticky. I couldn't recall the last digit of Paul's number. I dragged myself to my bed and sat upright. As I sighed and burped my older sister Linda appeared with my high-heeled pumps in hand. She had found them in a pile of leaves while walking our dachshund. She yelled; I cried harder. I sobbed that I couldn't remember what had happened—if I had gotten sick on Paul, if I had ruined his McDonald's career, how on earth I got out of my clothing.

The phone call was the height of humiliation, but I ascertained that Paul had remained his usual nice guy self. I hadn't jumped him nor vice versa. Besides, I was too out of control to catch. I learned that I had nearly suffered head trauma climbing up onto his car roof, and then spat at strangers from my perch. I had then declared in a loud voice that I had to pee and insisted I needed a particular brand of chocolate donut. When we finally arrived home, I wandered away from the house toward a distant fire hydrant, and fell against the curb. My sister had appeared sleepily at the door and for six seconds I looked completely sober. Paul left as I got sick, after making sure I was sitting up and near some running water. True love certainly didn't blossom after my "episode." Paul broke up with me by attrition, avoiding me in increasingly larger circles.

The lessons here: priceless. I learned not to drink so fast, even if the punch tastes like ice cream. If you're planning on embarrassing yourself, do it with a nice, reliable person around. Someone who'll buy you chocolate donuts, get you to a bathroom fast, and limit the number of horrified onlookers. But more importantly, I learned that feeling together doesn't mean you actually are. To this day, my aversion to smugness and self-inflation is second only to my distaste for hash browns. Like the scar on my right index finger, this lesson has left a permanent impression.

Scott Stein
Thoughts on the Death of Nafés Johnson

Nafés Johnson was killed last month in Philadelphia. He was struck in the head by a stray bullet while sitting in a church van. Nafés had just been ordained as a Baptist minister and had, shortly before his death, given his first sermon. His death was the lead story on all of the local news stations and in newspapers. You can guess the headlines. It wasn't bad enough that this man had been killed for no reason; this was a minister, committed to improving life for people in his neighborhood, and he was so young, barely in his early twenties. And he was a father.

There are perhaps some in the "atheist community" who might have seized on this horror to show that God either does not exist or is malevolent. How could this young man be allowed to die so senselessly, just as he was devoting his life to helping others and spreading God's word? Though, to my knowledge, no one actually used his death to support a philosophical position, I was angry at the possibility and at the thought crossing my mind. I like to think that even at my most annoyed with organized religion, even in the heat of my most passionate diatribe against blind faith and close-mindedness, I wouldn't have exploited his death for such purposes, even if I didn't know him.

I did know him. I knew Nafés. When I heard the name I recognized it immediately. Last year, I had a student named Nafés Johnson when I taught at Cheyney University of Pennsylvania, a historically black college with an almost entirely black student body and an open-enrollment policy. He had taken two courses with me: Grammar Review and Freshman Composition. I remembered him well. But I wasn't sure my student was the same Nafés Johnson.

In retrospect, it is silly, I guess. How many Nafés Johnsons could there be in the Philadelphia area? I didn't think it was a common name, but before I taught at Cheyney, all sorts of names I wouldn't have guessed were common turned out to be not so rare. So I held out hope that some stranger had been killed, as if that made the facts of the case any less heinous.

In the paper the next day there was no mention of Cheyney, but the photo resembled my Nafés. It was more than a strong resemblance. Still, it was a dark picture, reproduced in a newspaper, so I wasn't certain. The man in the photo had a beard, looked a little different than I remembered. It had been a year since I'd seen him, so maybe he had grown up a bit. Maybe I just wanted it to be someone else. I decided that it was probably him. What were the odds that the name would be identical and the photo would resemble a person in the same geographic area and turn out to be someone else?

Pretty long odds. That night on the news they showed a perfectly clear photo. It was the same Nafés Johnson who sat on my left during my trying first semester teaching in college. It was the same Nafés Johnson who, in frustration, told me that Grammar Review was boring. I had agreed. Of course it was boring. It *was* Grammar Review. This was something students were supposed to know already. They had been let down by every school they'd ever attended, I guess, by their parents, by society, by themselves—whomever we want to blame for their lack of skill in writing standard English.

At some point Nafés became less bored with me—he signed up for my Freshman Composition course the following semester. I conducted that class much the way I conduct *When Falls the Coliseum*—lots of debate, passion, disagreement, laughing, skipping from topic to topic when it interested me or my students to do so. I learned a lot from them, and not all of it was pleasant or politically correct.

Some of my students had such poorly developed writing and study skills, I was sure that they were never going to amount to much, academically and perhaps professionally. A few could not read well, and two could not write a single correct sentence in an entire essay. I am not talking about using too much slang or not conforming to "white" English—I mean that they did not know to put a subject and verb in a sentence, that punctuation is required. Many of my students had acquired poor social in addition to academic habits—they talked while I lectured; they came into class late and made as much noise as possible dragging a desk or eating their lunch; they didn't attend class or prepare for class or know that it was not polite to answer a cell phone while the teacher lectured.

In fairness, when I moved to Drexel University and had mostly students from wealthier backgrounds with far better academic preparation, I encountered some of the same bad habits. True, it was a much smaller percentage of the students, but one day—this is no exaggeration—in all four of my classes a cell phone rang. Two of the students actually answered the call. And a few of my current students have an embarrassing lack of writing ability and basic understanding of their native language (not on the same scale as my Cheyney students, but enough to make me feel old and shake my head as I say, "Kids these days").

Despite the absence of hope I had for some of my Cheyney students, there were bright spots. Nafés Johnson was one of them. I don't know if he was ever going to be a technically sound writer, but he was a good critical thinker and enjoyed a spirited argument, as did many of my students. Sometimes they surprised me. I learned from them that white people and black people who have appointed themselves the voice of the "inner-city" black community do not always accurately represent their views. Many of my students, for example, hated welfare, and launched into attacks on the people in their neighborhoods they saw abusing it while they were working to make something better of themselves. Some of them wanted harsher punishments for violent criminals, having seen firsthand the results of violent crimes. And I had no experience that could make me understand how too many of them felt about the police.

I tried, as hard as I could, not to treat them any differently just because I was the only white person in the room (sometimes in the building), just because we came from different worlds. This meant not holding back on sarcasm and humor, and not avoiding sensitive issues even if my views were not expected or popular. Some of my students didn't really notice anyway, and stared off into space or doodled to kill the time. But some laughed and argued back and even learned a few things about writing and arguing. A fortunate few (I count myself among them) were able to understand, if just a little, the views and experiences of another. It was an education.

I am glad not to be teaching at Cheyney University anymore. It was a long commute. The facilities were in bad shape. The students were ill prepared. The curriculum was uninspiring. But the death of Nafés Johnson reminded me of what I took away from that place, of the potential some of those students had. I admired the ones who refused to be limited by their backgrounds, who wanted to be more than they were told they could be, who didn't believe there was no hope, and who were willing to work for the life they desired.

Nafés Johnson was more than a symbol, though. He was a person, cut down before he had the chance to even really live. I will remember him.

C.P. Kaiser
Just Another Bloody Mess

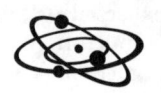

Now that we're in the 21st century, we can look back and arrogantly scoff at the unenlightened rabble of the past millennium. From our special and unique position in the "modern" world, it's easy to dismiss historical folly as superstitious nonsense. And nowhere is the ignorance of those who came before us more evident than in the treatment of women experiencing their monthly cycle.

For instance, the Bible, a major force of Western thought (not to mention the tome on which we still swear in court), calls menstruating women "polluted and dangerous to men." Fortunately, this tome is no longer opened and used as courtroom evidence in most states; Salem's witch trials were enough—what would women convicted on evidence of PMS be called—victims of a bitch hunt?

Modern religion is not the only guilty party—ancient philosophers and politicians share the blame as well. Pliny, a heavy in the think tanks of ancient Rome, claimed menstruating women "cause wine to sour, vines to wither, grass to die and fruit to fall." East of Pliny, in the cradle of Western democratic theory, ancient Greek intelligentsia taught that menstrual blood harbored a *materia prima* where a man's sperm was shaped into an embryo; the woman, apparently, was merely a vessel for the man's magic. (It seems the negation of women is embedded in the very genetic code of democracy *and* piety.)

But that was then, in the old, primitive days. Today, we're comfortably astride a gleaming escalator gliding toward the top floor of a new millennial mall, full of wit, wisdom, and Madison Avenue savvy, right? Not so fast, shoppers. I suggest we check our baggage before going any further.

Paleontologists have an evolutionary term, *punctuated equilibrium*, which describes long periods of slow or no change, followed by the sudden appearance of a very different beast. Unfortunately, in terms of male acceptance and bravado regarding the female periodic flow, no such beast has yet appeared.

In this century alone, in various parts of the world (including America—land of the panty shield with wings, home of the super-absorbent tampon with applicator), menstruating women are still much maligned. In certain orthodox sects, even in America, menstruating women are sometimes forced to sleep in special quarters or forbidden to cook for their husbands or even prohibited from having sex.

Not along ago, the Catholic intelligentsia (the ultimate oxymoron) forbade menstruating women to swallow the sacred communion wafer. And as recently as 1974, editors at *The Lancet*, a well-regarded medical journal, were wondering why flowers wilt if held by menstruating women. That's 1974—just five years after Neil Armstrong shook moon dust from his boots!

Remember, we're talking about a simple biological process of shedding the uterine lining via vaginal bleeding. (What would men think if the female intelligentsia through time had assigned some mystical, satanic rationale to the male proclivity for methane expulsion—an activity far more frequent, and certainly more offensive, than the lunar cycle—and followed that up with similar restrictions? To this day men might still be imprisoned round-the-clock in not-so-well-ventilated rooms.)

Several years ago, Harry Finley opened the Museum of Menstruation in the basement of his New Carrolton, Maryland, home. He boasts displays of sanitary napkins from ancient Egypt to the present, among other items. He says his reason for opening the place is, in part, to demystify the phenomenon of menstruation.

"What's to demystify?" asks a friend of mine. "Once you start menstruating, there's no mystery. It's just another bloody mess."

"In truth," writes John Travis in *Science News*, "there are few mysteries left about menstruation." The one puzzle that remains, he admits, is menstruation's biological significance—why did evolution select this phenomenon? Theories he cites include: to cleanse pathogens brought in by sperm; to conserve energy rather than keep the tissue ever-ready for implantation; and to differentiate the endometrium cells for oxygen- and glucose-hungry embryos.

So, although we don't quite understand the cosmic significance of menstruation, we are, at least, now studying the subject with scientific acumen and not Dark Ages superstition. We've come a long way from blaming a natural monthly process for souring wine and wilting flowers.

The trick, now, is to disseminate the American Medical Association's contention that PMS is a valid biological phenomenon—a real condition—not something "all in your head."

As that piece of knowledge reaches the unenlightened rabble of the new millennium, the women among them may breathe a collective sigh, and then explain, with science on their side, "Not tonight, honey. According to the Surgeon General, I really do have a headache."

Suzanne Hakanen
A Kill-Halloween Party

Remember when Howard Stern ran for governor of New York? He had an agenda. He said, "Elect me. I'll reinstate the death penalty and restrict road construction to evenings and weekends. Then I'll step down."

A great man, Howard Stern. He understands how the morning commute affects your day.

I propose the same arrangement: Elect me for president. And I'll fulfill my agenda of eliminating unnecessary holidays. Then I'll step down.

The first year in office, I'll kill Halloween.

That's right. I'm down on Halloween. And before you call me a Scary Scrooge, hear my side.

First, some history: As you may know, the name *Halloween* is derived from *All Hallow's Eve*, the day before the "holy" celebration of All Saints' Day. (Evidently, many Christian faiths celebrate the lives of saints on November 1, a saint being a person who lives a miserable life in hopes that people will speak well of him after he is dead.)

Many interpretations of All Hallow's Eve abound, including a pagan celebration of Satan. Apparently, these "primitive" people offered animal and human sacrifices to His Holy Hellness in hopes of appeasing his anger. Satan hated all living people but liked dead ones (don't ask me to provide a logical explanation of Satan's prejudices).

The Druids, on the other hand, celebrated October 31 as the eve of the New Year. The Druids observed a strict diet during religious holidays, and on that night they traveled among the villagers requesting special foods. If the food was provided, the beggars left in peace; if the *treats* were not offered, the Druids laid curses over villagers and their homes. In an attempt to protect themselves from the evil spirits, the villagers cloaked themselves in masks and costumes. (Obviously, we're talking about some pretty stupid spirits here if they can't identify John Smith once he puts a corn stalk over his head.)

This pagan ritual has evolved into our modern day trick-or-treat ritual: Suburban parents dress their kids in brightly colored, highly flammable trash bags and send them to strangers' houses to ask for candy. (In *Suzanne's Thesaurus*, the synonym for *trick-or-treating* is *panhandling*.) The implications for homeowners such as myself are twofold: (1) you have to keep answering the door and (2) you have to buy frightfully expensive candy.

And what's with the so-called fun size candy bar scam? That's what really gets me pissed about Halloween (and I know Nestle, M&M, Mars, and Hershey know what I'm talking about). Did you ever check out the prices on those bite-sized beauts? It rounds out to about $12 a pound just for a two-inch Almond Joy.

How do the manufacturers get away with charging a higher unit price per fun-size bar? I don't know, harder to wrap them, perhaps? Can you imagine factory workers slipping those tiny logs into little blue-and-white sleeves all day? It must kill their eyes.

But why the hell are they called fun size to begin with? I mean, what is so freaking fun about them? These candy bars are one-sixth the size of a regular bar. My definition of *fun* is something that provides amusement or enjoyment. Seems to me that the king-size candy bar would provide more enjoyment and, hence, be more fun.

It seems the only people deriving any amusement from the small candy bars are the CFOs, who, of course, guffaw behind our backs as we fork out five bucks for a sack of twenty tiny yellow boxes, each containing exactly three Milk Duds.

And we have no choice but to buy the small candy bars for trick-or-treat. What else are we going to do—buy the regular-size candy bars and cut them up into squares and wrap the squares in plastic? That would at least bring the unit cost down about forty cents per bar, but no sane yuppie is going to let their kid eat a square of Hershey bar that came in a piece of Saran Wrap. I can see and hear it now. Crazed super moms in Range Rovers clutching at their cell phones: "There's this strange woman living in the white house at the end of the road," they'll whisper to the 911 operator. "She didn't give my little Freddy the fun-size candy bar. It's just a piece of regular Hershey bar wrapped up in cellophane." Pause. "Poison? I don't think so. But I'm telling you, she's dangerous."

Was the fun-size label created by the advertising industry to lure consumers into purchasing these items by promising some higher-than-average sensory reward? If so, that's just plain false advertising. If anything, you're more likely to get pissed off eating the fun size because you need to eat 10 of them to get any satisfaction.

Now, we all know that the extra-large candy bars are called king size. I don't have a problem with that, since *king size* means to be longer than regular size or unusually large, and, as far as I'm concerned, that's an accurate description of the king-size bar (and besides, who doesn't feel like "royalty" when clutching five ounces of solid chocolate?).

Scott Stein
The Same River Twice

I didn't always dream or think or do anything remarkable. I was a fish, like the rest of them, and not a particularly noble one at that. It is true that I swam and ate and slept, and on that level, at least, I was exemplary. I spent most of my waking hours, though, hiding from one thing or another, but mainly from Indigo, a swift and brutal bully nearly twice my size. Without provocation, as if I had cause or courage enough to provide any, she would launch at me, nipping at my tail or ramming my side, for no other reason, I presumed, than to watch me flee in terror. Fortunately, I wasn't exactly slow, and panic has a way of making one quicker. I always managed to make it under a rock or behind a plant, and usually she tired soon after the chase had begun. I'd often thought about challenging her, but thoughts can only take one so far.

It's not that I was Indigo's only target, just her favorite. Sometimes I was granted a respite, and she would torment Red or Yellow for a while. I was fond of them, but was always relieved at the diversion they provided her, and used these opportunities to swim as fast as I could. I knew that I was born to swim, and in those days all I thought about was cutting through the water. I could only travel for a few seconds until the world came to an end before me, and it seemed a shame, that I should have such talent and energy for swimming and nowhere to go.

"The world is perfect," Yellow said once, before everything started changing forever.

Red was a bright fish with a prominent dorsal fin and a black-speckled tail. Yellow's dorsal was also substantial, though less pronounced, and her tail was equally sprinkled. How proud we all were of our color! After a feeding we would be brighter and after a good swim, which was rare in our confinement, we were brighter still. When Indigo bullied us our colors would fade somewhat, but she would almost glow with her power. Though we despised her and her cruel ways, we all agreed that her color was consistent and true.

One day, while chewing on the thick, green softness extending from the world's border, I thought I saw movement on the other side. My eyes almost didn't catch it, and even when they did I couldn't quite believe them. It lasted for the briefest moment and when it was over I wasn't sure that I had seen anything at all. We'd never even tried to penetrate the boundaries before. I guess we'd always figured that we wouldn't be able to see anything, but maybe it just never occurred to us that there might be something to look for.

"Did you see that?" I asked Red.

"See what?" His bloated cheeks undulated as he talked around a wad of greenness he had pulled from the wall and was trying to swallow.

"Nothing." I was sure that something outside had moved, but I also knew that our world was all there was. I looked hard at the green wall, trying to see past it, but it was too thick, and I doubted that I had ever seen beyond it. Besides, if Red hadn't seen anything, what made me think that I had?

Indigo was in one of her moods and, as my snout pressed up against the wall, she whipped by me. It was a warning and I would not get another. I whirled to face her, waited for her to make her move, then darted past her once she'd committed. Three times we raced the length of the world before I squeezed through a hole in the corner rock.

There wasn't room for me to turn around, and the high pile of white gravel under the rock nearly forced me to swim out to her. I scooped some in my mouth and, turning carefully, spit it through the rock's hole, a mere fish length from a waiting Indigo. I repeated this shoveling until there was enough room. I sat, nestled in the hard gravel, with rock above me, a narrow hole the only source for light. My tail brushed up against the spongy green wall and I shook involuntarily. When Indigo finally left I emerged and went back to chewing on the green, still not sure what I'd seen, but not caring very much anymore.

It didn't take me long to forget the movement I'd seen on the other side. The constant swimming with nowhere to go made one dull. The perpetual hiding and the digging and the green void that looked into me as I looked into it made me forget, had me longing only to sleep. I was relieved when the sun finally clicked to black.

That night, for the first time that I could remember, I didn't fall immediately asleep when the light went out. The darkness was strangely liberating. The slumbering fish around me didn't know I was awake, couldn't know, I supposed. We always slept easily and deeply, and when night came we slept, always without hesitation. I looked around, still coming to terms with my surroundings. So this was darkness. It was odd, that I could see more clearly now than when the sun glared from above.

What mysteries revealed themselves to me in the night! I was scared to keep my eyes open, scared that I wouldn't like what I found, still more afraid that I might. There was a light breaking through the darkness from outside, from beyond the green void. The softness was gone. I must have been dreaming or insane, to think not only that the green abyss had opened up for me alone but that I could see past the end of the world. I was not dreaming and was no less sane than I had been earlier that day. I saw everything simultaneously and understood nothing, and it is with great difficulty that I recall what I witnessed as distinct observations.

The fish were not bright or full of color at all, but pasty and pale and horrible to view. Every nick and scratch they had ever suffered was visible. Red had a long scar along his back and Yellow had a series of small branchlike marks on her side. Or maybe Yellow was Red, and had the long scar. They were both so faint I might have mistaken each for the other.

There was no trace of the green veil that eternally blocked our view. There was definitely a faraway light somewhere out there, and something was indeed moving, but I couldn't make out any details. I stared long into the void with no further results, and finally slipped into an uneasy sleep.

I awoke with the sun, at first not remembering the night. The wall was still clear and it came back to me. The darkness, the distant light, the movement. It not only wasn't a dream, I could still see it all. I turned to Red, then to Yellow, hoping to see in their eyes the excitement I was feeling. Their faces were blank, as usual, and I knew that they didn't see a thing. I wanted to shout, to announce my discovery to them, but I just swam to the wall and looked out. How could I explain it to them when I scarcely understood it myself? Already the veil was returning; already my vision was being obscured.

Why should I alone see this, why did I have no one to share it with? My memory would soon fade, was already evaporating with each moment I didn't speak these thoughts. Perhaps everything would have returned to normal if only the day had passed without incident. A new fish was among us before night.

Our first real knowledge of the outside world came with the arrival of Gold, a lean and muscular fish with large, deep eyes. Positioned wide and high on his head, they moved slowly, but constantly. There were years in those eyes. I tried to read all they had to tell, but I sensed that they saw things I would never really understand. Despite their power, his eyes weren't the first things I noticed that day.

Gold's color overwhelmed not only his other features, but the surrounding environment as well. It was difficult to look at him directly without being blinded, and he reflected white off every horizon, refracting through the wall and back again, encompassing the spectrum as he turned the plants red and yellow and blue, in turn, before he settled down to a very intense orange, and the plants returned to green and the world was the same as before but not the same ever again.

He came from above, and we hid for a while as he explored our world with abandon. Even Indigo retreated behind a plant, her face contorted with confusion. He swam with power and she made no move to challenge him. Not an inch was spared his inspection. A sadness came to his eyes as he concluded his tour.

None of us had seen this before, having been brought into the world young and without memory. I guess none of us remembered the past with significance because, until then, nothing significant had ever happened. But we remembered this. A fish, like us, but different, because he came from out there. Who was he? Where was he from? What secrets did he know? And why were we suddenly asking such questions?

Gold hesitated, then quietly said, "It is better that you do not know."

"You must tell us," I said. "I need to know."

"I suppose it doesn't matter," Gold said. "I had hoped that this world would be different, but they're all the same. The truth is, I come from the river."

Now, as I have said, we were just fish, stuck all our lives in this tiny world, and were unprepared to receive him. Red looked at me, then at Yellow, but we offered no answers.

"I understand your confusion," Gold continued. "I have been in a world like this once before, and I know how easy it is to accept it as the way things really are, as they are supposed to be."

Red shook his head, an impossibility given our physiology, and his whole body quavered as he objected. "World like this? There is only one. Tell us, where did you come from? Who sent you?"

Gold laughed. "You don't understand, do you? I will try to make it simple. We are fish, slaves to those who build these worlds, subject to their whims. Look at these plants; they're fake, you can't eat them. And that harsh light above. If only you could see the sun as it sets over the water, you wouldn't believe it. But you never have seen a sunset, have you? Here there is only day and night. You've been in this world for your whole lives, for as long as you can remember, haven't you?"

I understood him. Not his words, perhaps, but the meaning behind them. I felt as I had in the darkness. Everything around me looked as it had during the night, when the glare no longer blinded me and the truth flowed freely.

Red and Yellow, distracted by a string of green protruding from the far wall, swam away.

"What about these other worlds?" I asked Gold.

"The other worlds are unimportant. Some are smaller than this one, some larger, but they are all the same. All are false."

"And what are these sunsets?" I asked.

"You see, I wasn't born in confinement like the rest of you. I come from the river, not this puddle," Gold said, almost ecstatically. "The river is always in flux, never the same from one moment to the next. The plants do not look alike. The water is constantly flowing over them, fish are eating them. They aren't at all the same, some aren't even green. The colors you see in the river, the endless swimming, the speed. The fish, all free and different."

He indicated the tiny bubbles dribbling sluggishly from the green tube that was stuck to the wall just above the gravel. "We got our air from a sky so clear and blue..." His voice wavered, and he continued, more reserved, "The sunset is what I miss most. All the colors you could ever and never imagine come fleetingly together, then are gone... The trick is to see the movement. If you can see it, it's there. They can't force you to live in stagnation if you see it flowing. That's the only way to win."

If Gold believed this, whether or not he was really able to fool himself into seeing the river, I don't know. His color faded steadily and when I awoke the next day, Gold wasn't quite glowing. He actually seemed pale and somehow we all knew he wouldn't live. I don't know if it was age or something in the water, or if he just couldn't convince himself that he had brought the river with him. Maybe he had special words of wisdom to impart before his death, but I couldn't bring myself to get close enough to him to find out.

We had never beheld death before, but somehow we all knew how to act. Everyone stayed as far from Gold as possible when his body began to twitch, and we hid behind plants as he was helplessly propelled from one end of the world to the other. Next he moved hardly at all, and several times I was certain he had died, only to see him jerk again in agony. He struggled to stay close to the gravel but couldn't, and slowly fluttered toward the sun until, finally, he floated to the surface.

Moments later, it seemed, a colossal shadow stretched across the world and Gold was gone. A new fish was in his place.

The end began with the arrival of Green, an old and bloated fish whose movements were exceeded in slowness only by his speech. Every word he spoke was chosen with deliberate care, and his eyes, set high and forward on his wrinkled head, never moved. The other fish were curious about our new cohabitant, as was I, but I was still more interested in something else. I had seen our master.

"My fellow fish," Green said, "I am here to speak the truth."

A giant being, very unlike a fish, was watching us from outside. I'm sure what follows will sound fictive, and if I hadn't seen it myself I wouldn't have believed it either. Our master was larger than the world itself, and was of such a strange shape and appearance that our words could not describe It. (I don't know if He or She applies). There were the strangest pink protrusions and black, gaping caverns, all connected in so huge a form, I couldn't make heads or tails of It. The only feature that was at all familiar was Its eyes, which were rather like larger versions of our own. The rest was completely foreign. There was no water or fins or plants, and everything was enormous.

No one else saw It. Red and Yellow and even Indigo were waiting for Green to continue, and I too turned to hear what he had to say.

"I bring perfection to your world." Green told us of the Lake. He came from a world, he claimed, where fish shared their color, where no fish did anything without consulting all others, where only happiness mattered and no fish ever died.

I had my doubts. "What about sunsets? Does the Lake have those?"

"The sun doesn't set, my foolish guppy," Green said. "The sun is on and then it is off. There is no setting."

I had seen things during the night and learned enough from Gold before he died to know that it wasn't as simple as on and off. I wondered how Green knew what he claimed to know, what made his opinion more right than mine. "There is no Lake," I said. "Only the river."

"We will never achieve the Lake with this dissension," Green said. His promise of happiness enticed my fellow fish. A lifetime of cramped frustration suddenly made sense to them, and their sacrifices for the first time had purpose. Their recent experience with death had not left their minds, and Green's warning was a powerful one. "All must agree or all is lost," he said.

Indigo wasted no time, and tried to bite my left fin. If not for my reflexes she would surely have taken a piece of me with her. I swam straight to my rock and hid. Red and Yellow seemed very afraid, and looked menacingly in my direction. Green told them of the Lake, of how they would never again have to think about anything, how they would have peace and quiet and stability forever.

The idea was appealing to me, I must admit, but to accept it I had to reject everything I'd seen and felt. Red, Yellow, and Indigo had never seen or felt anything, and were able to picture themselves in eternal stasis without the slightest conflict. About Green I couldn't know. Maybe he was from one of those other worlds that Gold had told me about. He wasn't from the river, had never seen the sun set, and was unable to look beyond our world to see what I had seen.

During the days following Green's arrival I was harassed constantly.

Indigo's attacks were more vicious than ever, and I was barely allowed to eat each day. I expected as much from her. What I didn't expect was that Red and Yellow would join in the persecution. I couldn't swim for more than a few seconds without at least one fish chasing me. I stayed under my rock most of the time.

Green lectured the other fish and they listened intently, remaining still for hours. It was pointless taking pride in their color, trying to swim fast and eat through the mush on the world's border. Green's lectures did have one positive result: Indigo no longer attacked Red or Yellow. In order to reach the Lake they needed uniformity, and activities that enhanced one's color at the expense of another were not allowed. If they swam with too much enthusiasm or bragged about their color they were immediately chastised by the other fish with gentle bites and condescending stares. Soon they no longer swam fast or chased each other or did any of the things fish were apt to do. They were like the world we lived in.

Something else changed during those first few days, but at such a gradual rate that I didn't notice until the transformation was complete. Red and Yellow were no longer red or yellow. They were both a hideous, dull gray. I didn't know them anymore. Indigo still maintained a degree of her color, though lacking her usual sheen, and somehow she seemed smaller. Green, however, was brighter than ever, with hints of other colors peeking from behind his native green.

I had a lot of time to think while under my rock, too much time, and in my isolation I began to believe that if this was what the Lake was like, without color and with only slow, equal fish, then I would take my chances with the river. Rejecting Green became a matter of principle. Accepting his ideas would be admitting that I was like him, like them. I would not be colorless, unable to think for myself. I was a fish, which meant that I lived to swim and to flash the brilliance of my color for all who would look. That is what my life had always been about, would always be about, and I refused to give it up for the promise of some Lake.

One day, as Green spoke to the fish about the beauty of the Lake, I watched our master as *It* dropped some pellets for our sustenance. The other fish rushed to gobble them up and, as had become my habit, I waited for them to finish before venturing from my cave to eat the remaining scraps. It is difficult to explain what I saw, because my vision was always distorted by the thick translucence between us, but after our feeding that day I watched as our master began to shake, and *It* twitched as Gold had. Long streaks of pink crashed into the side of our world and screeched sharply, sending a chill along the length of my back and prompting the other fish to seek refuge behind plants and rocks. A horrible, muffled howl echoed throughout the world, and *It* fell from sight. Our world quaked violently. I waited and waited but didn't see *It* return.

We were all tired and ready for sleep, but the sun remained bright. This disruption of their customary schedule disturbed the fish, and they asked Green to tell them what was wrong, but he was as confused as they were. They swam in circles and bumped into the walls in their terror.

I came out of hiding and announced in my strongest voice, "It is over— we will soon join Gold in the river," and felt at once both relieved and the unbearable weight of a new burden.

This claim was bold enough to stop them, and I was suddenly the focus of their very strong emotions. Indigo and the gray fish lunged at me with a fury unnatural for fish, and I barely made it to my rock in time. Fortunately, Indigo was still too large and the gray fish were now too feeble to come in after me.

There was no more darkness and the sun continually blazed from above. None of us knew how much time had passed, but it felt like several days. It was difficult to sleep without night, and we were all exhausted and hungry and weak, but at least nobody attacked me anymore. The bubbles emanating from the tube at the bottom of the world became less plentiful, sometimes seeming to have stopped altogether until, at last, they did stop. The water was slowly disappearing; we tried to ignore it, but we were soon too cramped to pretend any longer. There was no room to swim, breathing required an exceptional effort, and I knew that the end was near.

The gray fish suffered worse than I did. They were too weak, too stupid really, to know what was happening. They were afraid but they didn't know why. Green was scared, but was trying to be brave for them; his color was fading too, and his age was beginning to win this race. He had turned my friends against me, had corrupted them and stolen their color, had destroyed the glory of being a fish, and I hated him. But I couldn't be angry with my friends, even if their grayness was repulsive to me, even if they had rejected everything I knew to be true.

The gray fish were the first to go, and they did so without much fuss, except for a piercing scream in the final moment, a scream I still sometimes hear. Green was next; his pilfered color could not protect him. His death gave me no satisfaction, for I knew my own was not far behind. Indigo held on longer, two days I guess, and I thought perhaps she was too mean to even die; but eventually she gave in too, though not without a good deal of thrashing about first.

I've lasted too long. I estimate three days since Indigo died. I speak these words to no one, and no thing. They are all dead, but I am alive. Even though I hate Green and what he did to my fellow fish, I think that, in the end, they had it better than I do now. I don't think fish were meant to see such things as I have seen. I sometimes wish that Green had convinced me, that I hadn't met Gold or stayed awake when I should have been sleeping. Maybe they were living a lie, but at least it was a lie they could live with. More importantly, it was a lie they could die with.

The movement is hurting my eyes; I can't look away; the wall almost shakes; the rock seems to swirl in the strangest way; I am dizzy. I want to turn away, free myself, but the rock is pulsating, and I swim closer. I understand, I see everything. Even in this foul puddle I see the movement. How I wish I couldn't see it. Gold would say that I have won, but is there a fate worse than dying alone? Stagnation is appealing now. Wouldn't I give all my color just to die among friends?

I searched this out. If I had closed my eyes in the darkness, if only I'd left the void alone. If Gold had remained silent, if I had paid him no mind like my fellow fish. But once you swim in the river the river forever swims in you.

The water level is down to my back, and I feel the cool rush of air on my dorsal. The queerest sensation, this air. I wonder what it will taste like.

C.P. Kaiser
Homeless, Not Heartless

It's very easy to pass homeless people with nary a nod in their direction. After all, to linger on their plight would signal either our own powerlessness or our indifference, neither of which are acceptable emotions on a daily basis. I contend, however, that we don't have to be afraid to look the destitute in their rheumy eyes and give them, if nothing else, a kind look, a hand on the shoulder, a few words of encouragement, or even a coin or two. In return, you'll get more than a copy of *Street Spirit* or whatever publication they're handing out for a donation.

In all major cities, the homeless population is increasing steadily. According to St. Anthony's Foundation in San Francisco, that city has the highest rental rates in the country. The average studio costs $1,000 per month, and the average one-bedroom unit costs $1,500 a month, requiring a salary of close to $17 per hour just to get by, yet, minimum wage is $5.75 per hour. San Francisco has almost 15,000 people on the waiting list for public housing and nearly 10,000 on the list for rental vouchers.

The federal definition of affordable housing, according to the National Coalition for the Homeless, is 30% of your income. In the median state, a minimum-wage worker would have to work 87 hours each week to afford a two-bedroom apartment at 30% of his or her income.

The American myth is that anyone can make it if they apply themselves. And it is that myth which allows a lot of us to separate ourselves from feeling any responsibility to help the homeless. I see a myriad of dot-comers passing the homeless each day on their way to pre-IPO madness, agitated that homeless people block their walking path and force them to see them. What does it take to give them a few bucks or even a kind look? They are, after all, fellow humans.

"Each person that is homeless needs to be seen as an individual," says a homeless San Franciscan woman who fled an abusive husband and was subsequently raped in a shelter. "Each of us is a different person."

It is truths like hers that we fear we'll come to know when forced to look into the eyes of the homeless and see them as people.

A major contributing factor to female homelessness is male violence: battering and sexual assault. The most common reason for women to enter a shelter (when there is room) in the United States is domestic violence. Women, especially with young children, are often faced with the impossible choice between staying home where their lives and their children are threatened, or fleeing and exposing themselves and their dependents to the sexual and economic dangers that can result from being tossed on the streets. Women face a decline in physical living standards for themselves and their children when they leave a violent partner.

In the Bay Area particularly, the fantastic rise in the cost of housing as well as the decline in jobs that pay enough to afford rent have contributed to the rise in homeless women. No minimum-wage job enables a single mother to house herself and her family. Being poor means being an illness, an accident, or a paycheck away from living on the streets.

In the absence of a consistent, comprehensive, flexible, and compassionate national policy, it has been an insurmountable challenge for cities to address the challenging, complicated, and multi-layered needs of the homeless community, including those with severe disabilities and victims of domestic violence. We need to work on a personal as well as a governmental level to alleviate the terrible plight of homeless men, women, and children.

Ari McKee
Why Vote? That's What Electors Are For

The main gripes about the electoral college system are all the *"what ifs."* What if one loses the popular vote but wins the electoral vote? What if one of those electors decided to defect and vote against the popular vote? What if there was a true tie? While these are all frightening possibilities inherent in the system, the rhetorical quibbling overlooks the college's real and present unfairness—do non-voters deserve to have an electoral vote?

States are allotted electoral votes based on their representation in Congress, which is based on the census. Therefore, it can change every ten years, as the census changes. Representation based on population—fair, right?

There are two reasons why it's not fair. First, voting is not an act that requires representation. *You* go out and vote, submit your two-cents worth, and have your say. Your Senators and Congress members don't vote for you, because though we may, as a majority, trust them to push bills and sign laws and the like, we don't exactly want a bunch of people who've been holed up in D.C. for years to decide who's going to be the next President, for God's sake. Our right to choose who sits in the Oval Office is sacrosanct. Otherwise, we may as well have a monarchy.

The second reason why it's not fair is not a "what if." It's because the premise—that a population deserves a vote *even if they don't vote*—is screwed. The electoral college system is untrustworthy because it assumes that a region will vote based on how many warm bodies it contains. It assumes that the actual turnout is less important than the potential turnout. It's "vote welfare."

Everyone's appalled that national voter turnout is only 38%. Except for a few of us, those of us in less than a dozen states who went out and *voted*, baby. I'm a proud Minnesotan when I report that 71% of us ventured into the driving sleet the other day and filled in our little black boxes. Seventy-one percent! Aside from a pat on the back, what does that earn, on a national level?

After a couple of painful hours crunching numbers, here's what I realized: Representative voting by population can only be wrong and unfair and undemocratic, because it counts *uncast* votes. I dug around the election results figures and came up with examples like this: Tennessee cast eleven electoral votes and 2,072,200 actual votes. Minnesota, on the other hand, contributed only ten electoral votes even though 2,439,101 people actually showed up at the polls. So, even though almost 367,000 more voters participated in Minnesota, they actually got one less electoral vote to show for it. What's so representative about that? The same thing happened between New York and Texas. Texas, with 32 electoral votes, came up short against New York's 33—even though about 150,000 more people voted in Texas.

Some more examples: Colorado, Arizona, Connecticut, Oklahoma, and

Kansas each have eight electoral votes. Actual popular votes cast in these states varied from a low of 1,234,277 to a high of 1,744,088, but the electoral votes stayed at eight. Half a million citizens' votes *didn't* matter. California should have had *more* than twice as many voters as Florida to justify its 54 electoral votes to Florida's 25. Instead the popular count was only up by 3.8 million, a little more than one and a half times Florida's turnout. Almost twice as many Nevada folks voted as Hawaiian residents, yet each state contributed four electoral votes.

So, whether or not the electoral process usually reflects the popular vote, it is a system that not only fails to represent real voters, but actually discourages real voting. More than twice as many people voted in Montana as in the District of Columbia. Two hundred and fifteen thousand Montana voters did nothing to change the three-electoral-vote allotment to each state. Why should they have bothered?

I wanted to believe the punchy news crews falling over each other Wednesday morning trying to be the first to say, "Look! Look how tight this race is! Don't let anybody tell you your vote doesn't matter!" I was brought up to believe that voting is a duty, an ethical obligation. It made sense to be a part of the process. It wasn't until I began thinking about the turnout that I lost interest in this race. We know it really isn't a matter of a couple of hundred votes, but somehow we accept that all that hand-counting in Florida will really tell us whom we elected.

How about assigning the next election's electoral votes based on the previous election's turnout performance? If your state clears 40% you get an extra vote, 50% earns two, and so on. So if your state comes up with a standout turnout, you'll have more electoral clout in 2004. And if, like California, you're consistently ballot slackers, you lose influence. Unfortunately, that suggestion satisfies my spiteful nature, but it is unfair to those voting for the first time, and it still punishes voters for their nonvoting neighbors.

Another tantalizing idea is to wait for an actual popular count and *then* assign electoral votes based on those numbers. One vote per quarter-million voters or something like that. The more voters, the more electoral votes, which would all be awarded to the majority winner of the state. The best part of this plan is that it would make the whole process much less predictable to the media because even if the election in a particular state were obviously leaning a certain way, the real impact of that leaning would not be known until the turnout tally decided the variable electoral votes. Less predictability, more suspense, more voting excitement, more state pride—how can this lose? We'd have something new to fight about with Wisconsin. Go Vike votes!

There is a case for scrapping the whole stupid electoral process with all its "certificates of ascertainment" and reams of correspondence from the "Archivist," and God knows how many forms and copies and orgies of bureaucratic i-dotting and t-crossing. This isn't a democratic function, it's some sort of goofy Masonic ritual, and it's way overdue for a good hard once-over.

It's time to take back the vote, a vote based on each act of every thinking participant, not our demographics or our density or our district. Let's *vote*. Are you with me?

Scott Stein
Prideless, and Proud of It

Pride is one of the seven deadly sins, if you believe in that sort of thing. And if you paid attention when reading Homer in high school English you know that in classic literature hubris often leads to the downfall of great men. And somewhat more recently, *The Pride of the Yankees* centered on a player known for being humble. Lou Gehrig didn't swagger. He didn't need to. He was Lou Gehrig.

Yet, pride is all we hear about these days. Yes, some of the talk about pride is understandable. A society cannot enslave a race of people and tell them that they are worthless for centuries and then complain when some members of that race find it necessary to campaign for black pride. And when people are taught that they are an abomination, that they will wallow eternally in hell for acting on their sexuality with consenting adults, should anyone be surprised that there are gay pride parades? And when women are not allowed to vote, told that they belong in the kitchen, and for centuries prior used as a sort of currency in forging family alliances, should there be shock at the hard line some feminists have taken?

Given the history of oppression that indeed took place, only the ignorant or politically motivated would pretend not to understand why pride movements exist. Yet, despite the historical underpinnings of such movements and the past wrongs often committed by members of one group against members of another, pride remains shameful. I am not talking about having pride in a job well done or a hard-earned achievement. Self-esteem is important. Unfortunately, what passes for self-esteem usually has nothing to do with the self.

We see it everywhere, and among members of every group.

There are Jews proud of the accomplishments of other Jews, pointing to Einstein's genius as evidence of their own value, bragging about how many doctors and lawyers their people have produced, claiming with pride that their ancestors were more successful than other ethnic groups in becoming Americans.

There are African-Americans talking of black pride, focusing on the contributions of their race to civilization, fighting for representation of their people on television and in movies, some so insistent on ethnic loyalty, they are willing to defend the actions of murderers and thugs like O.J. Simpson and Mike Tyson.

There are Americans from all backgrounds proud to be Americans, holding their heads up high whenever World War II is mentioned, whenever they are reminded that they put a man on the moon, that they saved Western civilization.

There are proud Christians. And Muslims. And women. And Italians. And Irish. And gay men. And union members. And lesbians. And white people whose ancestors came over on the Mayflower. People are proud of the city they live in, or the one they come from. They are proud of being a fan of a certain football team, of having seen a certain band in concert eight times, of how tall they are. Of how tall their kid is.

I guess what I am most proud of is not having that kind of pride, of not identifying too much with any *they* or *we*. If I am American, it is because I was born here. If I am Jewish, it is because my parents are. If I am from New York, it is because my parents lived there. If I am white, it is because of an accident of pigmentation.

I did not put a man on the moon, just because a few people from the country I reside in were able to. And I did not come up with the theory of relativity, just because a genius who happened to be Jewish did. And I did not fight to win World War II, just because some people from the country I reside in did. I would no more take pride in the achievements of others than I would take responsibility for the atrocities of others.

I am not against pride, though. My ego is more than healthy. But I am proud of *my* accomplishments and traits, not those of people with coincidentally similar backgrounds. I am proud of *When Falls the Coliseum,* of a few sentences I have written here and there, of my first novel. I am proud of my Ping-Pong game, of my sense of humor, of my skill in arguing, of my not-so-famous baked ziti. Mostly, though, with summer on the way, I am proud of my fade-away no-look hook shot (legendary to myself and maybe to a few basketball buddies) that has a way of going in when it shouldn't. Not bad for a white-American-vertically-challenged Jew from New York.

Amy Boshnack
Recipe for Getting to Work by Public Transportation

INGREDIENTS
1 bus or train schedule
1 hour traveling time
30 minutes waiting time
1 umbrella
1 cellular phone
2 magazines
1 book
1 Walkman (with tape or CD player); extra batteries recommended
1 ass, no more than 1½ feet wide
Many evil thoughts (amount may vary)
5 doses of patience (some suggest vodka in a flask, others prefer little yellow pills—consider motion sickness and local intoxication laws when making your selection)
Deodorant—please, I beg you, lots of deodorant
NOTE: Minimum preparation and travel time: 1 hour and 30 minutes. Minimum time you will be annoyed: 1 hour and 30 minutes

PREPARATION
You will always arrive at the train station or bus stop just after the train or bus has departed. Blend the Walkman here with 1 dose of patience, and use your 30 minutes of waiting time. Think evil thoughts.

As usual, you forgot your umbrella, guaranteeing that it will rain. Now you will be wet and uncomfortable all day. You should have paid more attention to the ingredients for this recipe.

Every 5 minutes take a look at the schedule you brought along and wonder why the train or bus has not arrived yet. Notice with a feeling of superiority how your fellow commuters neurotically need to check the schedule every 3 minutes. Some people!

After you get on the train or bus, take your ass (making sure it is no wider than 1½ feet) and squeeze it in between the two people on either side who did not make sure their asses were not wider than 1½ feet. Think evil thoughts.

Now you will need to mix in another dose of patience, as the two people you are sitting between will continue to give you dirty looks for infringing on their sitting space the rest of the trip.

Delicately pull out 1 of the 2 magazines (your preference; pornography is not recommended).

When you realize there is an overturned car or jackknifed tractor-trailer holding up the bus or some technical problem with the train, vigorously mix the cell phone to let your boss know that you will be late to work once again. Your obnoxious fellow travelers will use their own cell phones to loudly do the same. Think evil thoughts.

At this time you might want to mix in 2 full doses of patience—this will alleviate the intense desire to smack the person next to you for constantly leaning over you to get a look at what is causing the delay.

Now would be a good time to pull out that book. This could take a while. The 4 doses of patience you've indulged in might make for slow reading, but you're not going anywhere anyway.

You might have noticed that this recipe forgot all about the deodorant. Unfortunately, so did your fellow passengers. All of them. Every day.

Consume final dose of patience and think evil thoughts. Very evil thoughts.

SERVES: Too many damn people.

David "Preacher" Slocum
Affirmative Action: Is It Working If I'm Not?

Two things happened in the summer of 1994 that changed my life. First, the California Equal Opportunity Commission reviewed my county's sheriff's department for complaints it was discriminating against minority applicants. The second was that I, being ignorant of the impending political battle, decided that civilian life was boring me to tears and I wanted to be a cop.

As concerns the first event, the NAACP was pushing the EOC for a judgment because the sheriff's department was set to hire five new deputies before Christmas. Despite having only one black employee, the sheriff's department claimed it was in compliance with state quota regulations because it employed seven women and 23 Hispanics. When the EOC did rule, it determined that the county was not in compliance and ordered that four of the five new hires be African-Americans.

As pertains my quest for copdom, I made the final cut after months of physical and psychological testing, as well as a battery of written and oral tests. All that stood between me and that blue uniform was a final interview and the selection board (so I thought). My scores were good, perhaps not the best, but I was satisfied that I had done well. Then the list came out and I wasn't on it. Saying that I was disappointed would not begin to explain how I felt.

A couple weeks later, the newspapers broke the story about the EOC review. I admit, I was curious and more than a little upset. After some snooping and calling in every favor I had, I was able to con and connive my way to see the combined test scores of all 63 applicants. I checked the names of those hired against the scores on the list and found that three of the new deputies had lower scores than I did. Not just lower by a point or two, but lower in most categories. This left me with the inescapable conclusion that I had been left off the list not because my scores weren't good enough but because of the color of my skin.

That's when I got angry. I called the sheriff's department and voiced my complaint. They quickly referred me to the EOC in Sacramento. Three phone calls, five hours, and about a bazillion flunkies later, I was told that there was nothing I could do. It's at this point in my life that I became anti-affirmative action. Until then, I had been ambivalent, at best, toward the whole concept, since it had never impacted me personally. But if the system that may have started with noble intentions had become so warped that it allowed less qualified applicants to be hired in crucial, public-safety positions purely to satisfy racial quotas, something was very wrong. Knowing that those less qualified applicants were going to be running around protecting my family left me cold.

But I had a larger objection, one based on a principle that some of you might remember from the '60s: Giving preference to one race at the expense of another is wrong. Isn't that what the fight for civil rights, which led to affirmative action, was all about? To paraphrase Martin Luther King Jr., Let's not judge people by the color of their skin, but rather by the content of their character (and their well-earned test scores).

Jody Lane
The Mechanics of Humility

(Excerpted from the diary of a single woman who just wants a little freakin' help!)

As if planned by an unknown power, the toilet backed up, a vicious rodent got trapped in the crawl space, and my car broke down at the exact same moment that I signed my divorce papers.

What was I to do? I was alone. There was no one to watch over my shoulder and hold my super pneumatic plunger while I rescued a Ninja Turtle action figure from the horrors of the real-life sewer. No one to comfort and hold the children safely on top of the picnic table while I ventured under the house—outfitted in my protective oven mitts—in hot pursuit of a potentially rabid rodent. And, alas, there was no one to offer me a refreshing cold drink while I beat my car with a tire iron. Some things changed on that fateful day, but most did not. I was used to doing things for myself, by myself. Life was good! Almost.

The first two incidents were well within my areas of expertise. I have successfully fished more toys, aquatic toddlers, and small household appliances out of the toilet than an avid angler ever dreamed of catching blue gill. And the heinous rodent? Well, he didn't stand a chance against the power of my children's persuasion. Once they convinced me that he was really just an ugly, hairless, but otherwise harmless dog, they chained him to the side of the house and he now cowers from them in the crawl space day and night.

If my marriage taught me anything, it taught me to be self-reliant. I can manage to get up from the couch and change the channel manually (without help) if the baby flushes the remote. I can shoot my underwear at the hamper like an overpaid, green-haired basketball star and then actually pick them up and put them inside with minimal cursing when I invariably miss. I can take a 9-volt battery from a Barbie Convertible and make the microwave work with only minor violations of local ordinances and EPA regulations.

Damn it! I can separate the whites! Eggs ... laundry ... it doesn't matter, if there are whites, I can separate them!

However, the third incident was an entirely different matter. Sadly, I am not the slightest bit knowledgeable about the mechanical wonder formerly known as my trendy foreign import—presently referred to as my foreign piece of crap. As a newly single parent, I had not had a chance to work out the budgetary details. A budget, even the proverbial shoestring budget, requires having some money to earmark for life's little necessities and emergency roadside service. In a state of absolute denial, I refused to believe that my car was broken. Ignoring the clunking noises and the black sooty emissions, I drove 10 miles before the smoke forced me to roll down the windows or asphyxiate the kids. I think I could have made it another 10 if it hadn't been for the state trooper.

Weighing my options carefully, it was obvious to me that the best solution to my financial and automotive predicament was to follow my mother's sound advice and find a man willing to barter monthly maintenance for meaningless sex—but I wasn't ready to get married again. I needed a mechanic!

One pathetically tearful and cajoling phone call later, I found the man I was looking for. He was a good mechanic, but more importantly he was sympathetic and therefore willing to forego the hourly labor charge. He kindly explained the effects of continuing to drive a burning vehicle and why the repair time had been significantly increased when I neglected to turn off the engine at the first sight of the open flames. He was a good man. He became the new man in my life and by the end of the month I became his worst nightmare.

After two weeks, I began calling every day for an update on my car's prognosis and the daily escalating cost of repairs. He was patient and informed me of the price of every part, as well as explaining why I actually needed a transmission. Ever mindful of my dire financial situation, I soon became quite skillful at converting the price of auto parts into diaper equivalents. For the cost of a new hydraulic clutch, I estimated that I could buy approximately 3,762 ultra-absorbent, cloth-like diapers in patented "wetness indicator" prints for boys or girls.

The daily phone calls graduated into occasional unannounced visits. The visits progressed to constant lurking behind the hydraulic lift. His goodhearted patience wore thin. Before I knew it, he was also giving me a detailed opinion of the emotional and psychological problems I was suffering from in addition to my mechanical maladies. I stalked him. I harassed his wife. Being stranded without a vehicle for over a month had become an inconvenience when we needed little things like, well, food, for instance.

Ironically, five weeks after it moved into the shop, my car was paid off—it belonged to me. With a fully packed bag of beer and diapers, I buckled the baby into the stroller and boldly walked right over to my mechanic's garage for an anticlimactic celebration.

When I arrived, I stood in the doorway for a long teary-eyed moment staring at my car. It looked the same as it had the day before. I choked up. No, I am not a sentimental fool over my foreign piece of crap. I was on the verge of hysterical tears because my car literally looked exactly the same as it had the day before! Same steering column on the back seat, same gooey black stuff oozing into a pan under the front end, and the same assortment of extra parts and miscellaneous tools scattered on the floorboard. In fact, the same little tiny hammer in my mechanic's hand was still beating the hell out of what I assumed was the same stubborn part that he'd been beating the hell out of the day before!

I could tell by the irritated expression on his face that he was less than pleased by my appearance.

"Can I get you anything? A metric wrench, maybe? A bigger freakin' hammer? A beer? I brought beer!"

Although he still looked somewhat less than pleased, he no longer looked murderously intent. The little hammer wavered for a split second in a mid-air salutation. I handed him a cold one.

"So ... Rex ... hmm ... what are you beatin' the hell out of ... I mean ...

what are you working on there?"

The hammer paused in mid-air again, this time it wavered menacingly about my right ear. I took a step back and maneuvered the stroller between us. I opened a cold one for myself and spent the next spellbinding hour listening to the most stimulating lecture on torque converters that I have ever heard.

Three beers—mine, not his—and one crash course in clutch assembly later, I had sufficient courage to ask the question of the day.

"Uh ... Rex ... I hate to ask ... but ... well ... do you think my car might be done soon?"

Big mistake! I knew I should have waited until his third beer. But I'd had enough! Before I chickened out, or he formulated the strangled grunts issuing from between his clenched teeth into whole sentences, I took a deep breath and plunged on.

"Rex, you have had my car for over a month! It was just a little fire! My kids need to see the doctor, I have a parent-teacher on Thursday, and I haven't been to the grocery in I don't know how long! We are living on creamed corn for Christ's sake! I'm just gonna have to pay somebody else."

"Paaaaay!!!! You ... never ... what?"

I turned and stomped out before he could finish.

Walking home I could not stop thinking about the look on his face after my outburst. Maybe I had been too hasty. After all, he was a good mechanic. No. He was the best mechanic and he worked for practically nothing! He was billing me at cost. No charge for labor! I made up my mind to call him as soon as I got home.

Rinnggg.

"Hello ... Can I talk to Rex? ... Oh, he is? ... Well, it's his sister. Tell him I'll be right back to get the baby."

Jason Stein
The Temp

Temping is like Special Forces—I go in, get the job done, and I'm out. No prisoners, no worries ... oh yeah, and no health benefits either.

Temping is also the highest form of on-the-job training. Last week alone I earned a Masters in Photocopying, a Doctorate in Filing, and a First Aid Certificate in how to prevent paper cuts. It's not often one has the opportunity to receive these rare, sought-after degrees. Who knows what I'll learn next week, or where I'll be?

How do I survive the daunting task of starting a new job every week, sometimes several in a week? Simple. I have mastered my own customized Jerry Lewis impersonation, and have used it to ward off all stress and responsibility on the job. Fellow temps and co-workers might think I am not well in the head, but they also tend to leave me alone. Feigning incompetence and speaking with just the right high pitch keeps supervisors from asking me to do anything too difficult. A useful tool, that Jerry Lewis.

Why not just get a permanent job, you ask? Because temping has its advantages. Temping is great for people who are pursuing their dreams, or finding their passion, or in the midst of a career change and need the flexibility for their schedule. If you don't like the place where you're temping, you can discontinue your service there and wait for something else to pop up. Please keep in mind that your paychecks will be discontinued as well. The trick to temping successfully is consistency and the trick to paying all your bills is temping consistently. Sounds like an oxymoron, doesn't it?

One day I was called away from my current temping position to go on a special assignment: gift wrapping! It was holiday time, and they needed a true professional to handle anything at any time, anywhere. This isn't work—I like wrapping gifts. If I didn't like wrapping gifts, then it would be work.

It's the same thing with lovemaking: If you like lovemaking, it's not work; if you don't like lovemaking, oh, it's work all right. And if you have to work overtime during lovemaking, it's hard work—real hard work, sometimes without compensation (that depends on you).

You ask what wrapping gifts and lovemaking have in common? Just one thing: There's a deep sense of satisfaction upon completing the wrapping session. When you place that bow on top of the gift, you're done. There's nothing left to do. But there are differences as well—lovemaking generally requires a partner, whereas temping is the gift you can give yourself.

Temping is very popular these days. It's an integral part of society. Freelance workers are widely accepted. Are these temporary employees doing more harm than good? Are they accountable for their work, and how has the temp trend changed the American office? Well, even people working for many years at one place no longer want to be accountable for anything. Maybe they fear the axe if they make the wrong decision—they feel underpaid, so why stick their neck out just to get it chopped? As a temporary employee, with no stock options or pension plan to worry about, my response to customers with attitudes or tough questions on the other end of the phone is, "Sorry, I'm just a temp. Please call back later." I bet that if you had the chance you'd use this method too. If not, act like Jerry Lewis. Trust me. It works.

Temping is the American way. Accountability? Who needs it? Heck, even the President of the United States is temping—only four years, maybe eight. With all the temps in the House of Representatives, it's amazing any of them can find the bathroom without asking where it is.

Well, my lunch hour is almost over. Time to get back to the office. When I sign back in from lunch, I must put down the exact time to the second or else they freak on me. Let's see, is it 1:56? or 1:58? or 2:00? or 2:02? or 2:03?

Ah, who cares? I'll have a new job tomorrow.

Reader Comments

—C.P. Kaiser responds to "The Temp" by Jason Stein.

I love Jason Stein's piece about temping. As one who has pursued art as opposed to "a career," I laughed all the way through because of the truth of it. However, I must disagree with him when he lumps the President and the Congress in with temps. Even though their positions are somewhat temporary, they do not suffer from a lack of pension, a lack of perks, or a lack of health insurance. And one might even say that their temporary employment as servants of the people is an apprenticeship for becoming corporate lobbyists. The real temps out there only wish they had it so good.

Scott Stein
Recipe for Exhibition in the Museum of Modern Art

Bob Sullivan
Scam the Sham and the Pharaohs

In terms of ostentatious excess and big-money overkill, the 2000 Presidential campaign promises to put the Pharaohs of Egypt to shame. And most of the blame can be laid at the feet of the American people, who are either too stupid, too indifferent, too distracted, or all three to take our lawmakers to task for failing to pass meaningful campaign finance reform legislation. Lots of voters rant and rave about gun control or environmental issues or workplace safety or higher taxes, but unless and until something is done to rectify campaign financing, they might as well save their collective breath; all of those other issues will continue to be decided by Big Money.

In 1992, Bill Clinton said George Bush, Sr. "won't break the stranglehold that the lobbyists have on our government, but I will." At the time he said that, there were about 7,500 registered lobbyists in Washington (with far more unregistered ones). Today, there are more than 15,000 registered lobbyists and, according to Washington's number one lobbyist, Thomas Hale Boggs Jr. (brother of Cokie Roberts), the amount lobbyists now spend in our nation's capital is at least one hundred times as much as it was in 1992. Also according to Boggs, the latest round of window-dressing reform legislation had absolutely no effect on Big Money's control over Congress.

Actually, *control* might be too strong a word, since a congressman is now just as likely to ask for a contribution as Big Money is to ask for legislation. In a recent letter to business leaders requesting donations, Senate Majority Leader Trent Lott wrote, "By failing to act today, you could lose a unique chance to be included in current legislative policy debates that will affect your business for many years to come." It's becoming increasingly difficult to tell where Big Money ends and Congress begins.

Lobbyists always favor incumbents since incumbents already have the power and are more likely to be elected, so incumbents have a vested interest in keeping things exactly as they are. Television commercials cost so much that many congressmen have to raise as much as $25,000 per week (or $5,000 a day, or $10 a minute) just to stay competitive. For every congressman, there are more than 38 registered lobbyists spending $2.7 million a year—and at least twice that many unregistered lobbyists spending God knows how much. They have little time to legislate (though of course they have to make sure to do the lobbyists' bidding), and why should they bother when they can buy their way into office and then pal around with their rich buddies? (It's such an "Old Boys" network that I am excluding from this discussion the few congresswomen we have, especially since the worst abusers are men.)

Under current law, lobbying is a fantastic deal for the lobbyists, who wouldn't be spending all that money and time unless they were getting paid back many times over. This undoubtedly leads to higher taxes. Before the last presidential campaign, computer firms and drug companies contributed $9.8 million to candidates and in return got a reduction of the tax on overseas earnings; automakers and dealers contributed $4.2 million and got a phase-out of the automobile luxury tax; and restaurant and pizza delivery companies contributed $2.5 million and got a huge tax credit. Those changes will cost the American taxpayer $590 million over 10 years—so in effect, politicians took out a $16.5 million loan in order to get elected, agreeing to pay it back with interest totaling 3,500% of the borrowed amount using *our money*. It is hard to imagine a more convolutedly inefficient system. Politicians claim that the money only buys access, not votes, but they and the lobbyists are well aware that unless they deliver, the well will run dry and they will not be reelected.

A decade ago, contributions to the Keating Five and the resultant savings-and-loan debacle wound up costing American taxpayers $2.6 billion, but that amount didn't just vanish into thin air; a lot of bankers got very rich very fast. In 1996, the Senate delayed adjournment by two days just to pass a law giving lavish contributor Federal Express a special exemption from a 1923 law regulating railway express companies, thereby helping FedEx resist efforts by its employees to unionize. As with all industries, less unionization means lower wages and more profits, benefiting management and stockholders at the expense of the workers, so the rich get richer and the poor get comparatively poorer. Is it any wonder that the top 1% of people in this country have more combined wealth than the bottom 95%, with an ever-increasing number of children growing up in poverty?

And it's not just money that's affected. Corporate interests ensure the election of legislators who then hammer out legislation on everything from public health to workplace safety to genetically altered food to clean air and clean water. And why should corporate heads, lobbyists, and legislators worry about clean water as they sit around sipping their Perrier? Why should they worry about workplace safety when the worst workplace injury they face is a paper cut from handling all that cash?

The NRA contributes tons of money to congressional campaigns, so we end up with the tragedy at Columbine, while the congressmen sit safely in their gated communities. Gun deaths undoubtedly most affect the poorer classes, and even though the consequences of the proliferation of guns are slowly creeping into more affluent communities, it's all worthwhile as long as each politician, his children, his wife and his eventual newer younger wife are all well provided for.

Some may point out that the money is earmarked for congressional campaigns. But with all that money floating around and all those rich cronies, the wealth is guaranteed to rub off, especially since, upon retirement or defeat, one-fourth of all congressmen then become lobbyists. Dole, who said in '96 he could only go one of two places, the White House or home, is now working for one of the top lobbying firms in Washington. In the Big Money network, even reputation doesn't matter—only wealth and connections—as lobbyist Bob Packwood is proving every day.

And how is Campaign 2000 shaping up? As of September 1999, George W. Bush had already raised $50 million, with at least another $5 million expected next month. Four years ago at this time, Clinton and Dole had raised less than $40 million combined. Bush has announced he will not be participating in the presidential public finance system, the main post-Watergate reform law intended to curtail the blatant selling of the White House. This means he won't get matching funds—though at the rate he's raising money he won't need them—but it also means he won't be subjected to spending limits or certain disclosure requirements. His lack of spending limits may force Gore and others to opt out of public financing in order to stay competitive, and the resultant financial arms race would undoubtedly increase lobbying and spending from their current incredible levels to levels that are truly grotesque.

The most promising suggestions for reform include free television airtime and a shorter campaign season (as in Britain), the elimination of soft money or at least soft money loopholes, more stringent contribution limits, and enforcement of those limits. To curry public favor and to look better in the television ads they spend so much on, some congressmen are offering up promising legislation, knowing full well that their colleagues will never pass it. The House Republican leadership, led by Majority Whip Tom Delay (R-TX), is proposing legislation that would actually make things much worse. Reps. Delay and John Doolittle (R-CA) introduced a campaign finance bill that would repeal all existing federal limits on campaign contributions, claiming that the bill's requirement of full contributor disclosure will provide the necessary checks and balances. The idea that lackadaisical American voters will bother to research who is contributing and then vote against any candidate who seems overly influenced by his contributors is ludicrous on its face.

Will Rogers once observed that the United States Congress was "the best that money can buy." That may have been true fifty years ago when he said it, but at the doorstep of the new millennium, our campaign finance laws continue to ensure that the United States Congress is at best mediocre and at worst catastrophic.

Cassendre Xavier
I'm Not Seeking a Husband, Just a Well-Trained Boyfriend

A few years ago, a very controversial book about dating and romance between men and women was published. *The Rules: Time-Tested Secrets for Capturing the Heart of Mr. Right* by Ellen Fein and Sherrie Schneider preached to husband-huntin' women the virtues of playing the game of old-fashioned hard-to-get.

Among the rules are: Never call a man or return his phone calls, and set a timer to end every phone conversation in ten minutes. We are also supposed to be very happy, very busy, and mostly inaccessible, seemingly prematurely ending dates and conversations with a cheerful, "I've got a million things to do!"

Women are instructed not to discuss anything "heavy," and to answer questions as briefly as possible, giving little or no information at all. The idea is that the less we give, the more the men will want us.

At first, I (and most of my feminist women friends) scoffed at this book, claiming that it set liberated women back years. What happened to the honesty, we wondered? What happened to just being yourself, no matter what? Didn't men want us to be honest? I did notice, though, that the women who wrote this book were married, and that my friends and I were not. Granted, most of us did not want to be married right then, and certainly not in the conventional sense. But we did want more commitment than the casual dating and, well, boffing that we were doing.

I'd been dating a series of jokers who were incredibly hot in the beginning and total assholes later on. As we are taught not to do, I told each of them about *The Rules*, because I was really excited about it. All of them, without exception, said the book was stupid and that men didn't want women to be that way, and that I should just be myself.

Well, after each and every one of those relationships failed, I decided to examine my behavior. I noticed that in each instance, I was very friendly, open, and accessible with these men. I was not a challenge. They dug me and I dug them back. They wanted my time, my attention, my affection, and I said yes.

Well, according to *The Rules*, the answer shouldn't be *yes*, but it shouldn't be *no*, either. The trick is to learn the art of maybe. Men absolutely adore challenge, say authors Fein and Schneider. They are equipped to work and love to work for what they have, and, of course, after they've worked so hard for it, they value it more.

Since I'm the experimental type, I decided to go against everything in my nature and play by *The Rules*. Partly it was out of curiosity, but mostly it was out of frustration. So, I decided to reserve my "chum" act, which incidentally was never an act at all, for my chums.

Recently, I met a cute guy, who expressed interest right away, and we went on a date (he asked). At first I'd forgotten about *The Rules* and stayed with him too long. Our conversations were incredible and before we knew it, we had spent six hours together at two different venues. Luckily, at the last minute, I remembered that I was the one who was supposed to end all dates. So I did. He seemed a little surprised, and when we went to part, I could tell he wanted to hug me, but I quickly walked away, waving cheerfully at him from across the street.

In the olden days, I would've hugged him and called him the next day "just to chat." We would've dated hot and heavy for exactly four weeks, and then he would've moved on to some chyk he had to work for. This time I didn't call him, ever. He ended up calling me, e-mailing me, and even dropping by my job to see me. Each time, I spoke with him for only five minutes or less. I have to admit that while at first it was difficult holding myself back, pretty soon being on the receiving end of that kind of attention from someone I was diggin' was pretty sweet!

I also have to admit that at first I resented not being able to be my usually assertive, demonstrative self with men. It was such an effort holding back that energy, like holding back the flow of urine when giving a sample at the doctor's office. But now I've reframed it for myself. I'm not holding back my energy; I'm simply allowing myself the (sadly new) experience of being pursued by someone I'm attracted to. And I'm giving my suitor his rightful pleasure of pursuing me in the most correct and natural way. We are animals, after all. That's what *The Rules* boils down to: letting a man do his (natural) thing. And for giving him that gift, we women are then rewarded with devotion. Whether or not this devotion is sincere is not a concern of mine right now. I'm not seeking a husband, just a well-trained boyfriend.

And so far, it's working.

Last night I was speaking to one of my best friends. He said (of course) that *The Rules* was bullshit. "That works if the kind of guy you want wears Dockers and votes Republican."

I said, "Well, if a guy doesn't talk to me first, it means he didn't notice me or find me attractive. Or he didn't like me enough to muster up the gumption to talk to me. And I don't want that guy. I deserve to be sought. Why should I talk to him first?"

He said, "Because the kind of guy you want is an interesting freak who was probably unpopular in high school. Maybe he's shy."

And I thought about that. I really did. Then I read one more chapter of *The Rules* and went to sleep happy, wondering what sweet thing my new guy was going to do for me next.

Scott Stein
The Politics of Star Trek: Peace on Earth, Klingon Racism, and Bleeding-Heart Vulcans

In March 1996, Barbara Adams, an alternate juror in the Arkansas Whitewater trial, was dismissed from the case for talking to the press. *American Journal* had interviewed Ms. Adams on camera because she had worn a *Star Trek: The Next Generation* red and black commander's uniform to each of the case's eight court sessions, complete with a Federation of Planets badge, communicator, and phaser weapon. Her nontraditional outfit was not the reason for her removal from the case, but it was what drew the press to her.

That Adams was dismissed from the case or even selected in the first place is less relevant than her reason for wearing the uniform to court each day. According to CNN, she told *American Journal* she believes in the ideals expressed in *Star Trek*. She said she found *Star Trek* an alternative to "mindless television" because it promotes inclusion, tolerance, peace, and faith in humankind. The uniform was the message. If only we could learn the lessons of *Star Trek*, was the implication, what a wonderful galaxy—that is, world—it would be.

I should note that at one time I watched *Star Trek: The Next Generation* regularly, and must confess affection for it. For a television show, it was generally well written, with acting and character-driven plot lines as its greatest strengths. It was usually a pleasant hour with a few laughs. The show's profusion of primary colors and strong production values didn't hurt. A child of the *Star Wars* generation, I liked a good laser—I mean phaser—shootout as much as the next guy, but I have to take issue with the multitudes who insist on seeing *Star Trek* as a blueprint for the future. Upon closer examination, *Star Trek* turns out to be decidedly political, simplistic, and chock full of contradictions and inconsistencies.

In the vision of the future that is *Star Trek*, many life-spawning planets have formed a Federation of Planets, a sort of United Nations of different sentient species. The show's characters trekking about the galaxy work for and owe allegiance to this Federation, not any individual planet. No planet is permitted to join the Federation unless its peoples have achieved peace and partnership—a planet must speak with one voice.

Some might consider this approach a noble one—loyalty to concepts and principles instead of nations or planets. Others are sure to see the similarity to the subordination of national sovereignty to the "will of the international community" in our own time. Whatever your political orientation or agenda, there are questions that need to be asked if we are to consider claims that *Star Trek* presents a future worth emulating.

Are we expected to believe that this joining of all nations into a united earth, a prerequisite for Federation membership, involved no bloodshed? Can we accept that despite the thousands of years of war and conflict and power plays, the Russians, the Chinese, the various European nations, the Americans, the whoevers, and the everybodies simply came to some understanding of the mutual benefit of peace on earth and one-world government? Even were we to grant this as a laudable goal, does anyone believe that a few hundred years from now it will happen? If so, can anyone believe it will happen peacefully?

Ancient prejudices, human flaws, economic pressures, and genuine disputes that lead to war time and again are not going to simply disappear. The end of the twentieth century, with its many armed conflicts and massacres despite the "resolve of the international community" offers ample evidence that world peace is not going to come. In *Star Trek,* governments and people somehow came to the realization that peace is important as a result of the "evolution of ideas" (apologies to Darwin).

No such evolution is forthcoming. If world peace as *Star Trek* sees it is to come, many will have to kill and die to establish it. Not acknowledging this is naïveté. The course to peace our world leaders have set us on involves bombing those nations that don't do what "the world" wants them to do. In *Star Trek* terms, peace is enforced with the business end of a phaser.

Star Trek also fails to live up to its own agenda of diversity. If the Federation of Planets is made up of many worlds and species, why do humans dominate the crews of the starships? If harmony and equality have been reached on earth, why do white people still far outnumber other ethnic groups on the Starship Enterprise? Where are all the Chinese and Indians? And why is everybody speaking English?

In *Star Trek* there are two minority actors represented in the crew, both black. Of those two, one is a black actor playing a Klingon, and does not represent a human minority. The other, played by Levar Burton, is blind. *Star Trek* manages to get credit for being inclusive of minorities and the physically disabled with the same character. This is efficient planning on the part of the show's creators, not diversity.

Those who praise the show as a model of racial tolerance might be asked why it is that the members of the violent Klingon race are dark-skinned. In the original series, the Klingons had an Asian appearance, complete with Fu-Manchu mustaches. In *The Next Generation,* special makeup effects and sensitivity to that portrayal have resulted in less overt Klingon racism.

Say what you want about the politics of the show's creator, Gene Roddenbury, and point out if you like that the first interracial television kiss was on the original *Star Trek*. The fact remains that dark skin was his selection for the appearance of a savage race of violent warriors. That was his decision to make, and depicting a specific ethnic group as violent might not have been his intent. But, considering the insistent multicultural (to the point of multi-planetary) message of the show, shouldn't we ask just what this visionary of equality was thinking when he chose minority features for his savage race of Klingons?

Inclusion isn't the word I would use to describe this vision of the future. There are no fat people, no short people, no frighteningly ugly people, no gay people, no religious people, and certainly no dumb people on the Starship Enterprise. In summary, there are no people on the ship, just well proportioned actors in bright uniforms saying amusing things or defending themselves with judo flips or phasers set to stun. Dare we ask what happened to the fat, the depressed, the short, and the ugly? Maybe technology allowed people to avert these fates for their children. If not, where are they all?

It is as if people with no access to knowledge of the real world created *Star Trek*. We learn that crime came to an end on earth because technology was able to meet people's material needs. Money was no longer necessary. This assumption that money is the only cause of crime is reassuring. It's a good thing no one ever got killed over religion, abortion, politics, or racism. How fortunate for the human race that people with material goods never hurt anyone, that there has never been a crime of passion or jealousy, that kids with two attentive parents with stable finances never opened fire in a school lunchroom.

And of course, it is never explained how all this technology came to be in a world without money. With no profit incentive, with no need to work to put food on the table and nothing to be gained by working hard, the people of the future didn't do what most people of our time would do—spend all day on the Internet looking for free porn. No, they advanced the cause of science and learned languages and practiced playing the trombone. How noble these people are not to cheapen themselves with the pursuit of money. But, since they don't need money, can anyone explain why the crewmembers in this future are endlessly playing poker? What are they betting and why? What do they buy with their winnings?

Perhaps most contradictory is *Star Trek*'s assault on logic and reason. In the original series, Mr. Spock, a Vulcan, was frequently the object of satire for his people's commitment to logic and their suppression of all things emotional. In *The Next Generation*, there is Data, an android, who wants nothing more than to be human. The Enterprise also has a counselor, a therapist with racially bestowed powers of empathy. Even the captain of the ship is required to see her and talk about his emotional life. Feeling, in the *Star Trek* world, is very important. Art, music, role-playing, and acting are among the hobbies of the ship's crew. Being human, with all it entails, seems to be the highest value.

Yet the whole history of the ideal *Star Trek* future is based on a rejection of humanity's passionate history, on a negation of all human feeling. *Star Trek* disputes the anger and violence of humanity, blaming it on material want. It discounts laziness and the necessity of motivation for hard work and innovation. It also preaches diversity and self-righteous equality without demonstrating it.

For those who enjoy the show for what it is—bright colors, character stories, and cleverness—*Star Trek* is harmless, I suppose. But the Internet's swarming, faithful, convention-attending fans that base their political philosophies on a television program have some questions to answer.

Jody Lane
The Committee (A Fairy Tale)

Once upon a time, in a decade not too long ago, on a newspaper where I was employed, a committee was organized to investigate complaints made by non-smoking employees against smoking employees. The committee, made up of non-smoking employees, unanimously agreed that the smoking employees were an abomination and advocated their immediate extermination.

The smoking employees were outraged by the severity of the non-smoking committee's recommendations and sought clemency from the publisher. The non-smoking publisher agreed that the smokers were offensive, but he thought the death penalty for the entire sales department might be detrimental to the budget and have adverse effects on projected advertising revenue. The benevolent publisher intervened on the smokers' behalf and sentenced them to the more humane, eternal banishment. The smokers accepted the verdict with only a small amount of grumbling because the newspaper was located in Florida and other than a few tropical depressions, periodic tornadoes, water spouts, and level-five hurricanes, the weather usually permitted tar and nicotine intake in the great outdoors with minimal cruel or unusual discomfort.

Time passed (about three days) with only minor incidents between the two factions.

Then, on the fourth day, a smoking employee and his soggy cigar were unfortunately drowned by being sucked down a storm drain in the great flash flood of '92. This caused the non-smoking employees to become concerned and they commenced complaining anew. "Smokers are endangering themselves!" they cried.

Another non-smoking employee committee was duly formed and, after fully investigating the newest complaints and allegations for nearly twenty minutes, determined that the smokers were indeed a danger unto themselves. Citing statistics from the American Lung Association, the American Cancer Society, and a state-sponsored study that conclusively proved smokers were 83% more likely to be sucked into storm drains than non-smokers, a report to the benevolent, non-smoking publisher was published. The Non-Smoking Employee Committee (NSEC), still firmly advocating capital punishment, had by now assumed capital proportions and capital letters. The official report stated, "Due to the evidenced self-destructive nature of the addict by his or her complete and total disregard for the opinions of special interest groups, the politically correct, non-profit organizations, and tax-free foundations, and by negligently smoking too close to storm drains during flash flood conditions, this committee recommends that all smoking employees be required to attend AA meetings."

Again the smokers were outraged! The Concerned Smoking Employees of a Florida Newspaper Against Coerced Rehabilitation Committee

(C.S.E.F.N.A.C.R.C.) was summarily formed one smoky night in a local church basement—after the Serenity Prayer, of course.

Rapidly growing into a formidable force, the first official act of the C.S.E.F.N.A.C.R.C. was to commission an even more scientific study than the initial NSEC study. The findings of said report proved conclusively that 3 out of 4 dentists found non-smokers were 83% more likely to be anal retentive than smokers. In a report addressed to the publisher, the new pro-smoking committee stated, "Although the participating dentists evaluated several corrective measures for the malady, extensive probing with an electric cattle prod proved to be the most effective therapy."

In time, the benevolent, non-smoking publisher, shocked by the prod and, of course, by the entire proceedings, suggested that perhaps a committee should be organized to monitor the actions, opinions, and personal freedoms of the members of the original committees. Yes! That was the answer! A bigger, better committee to determine how best everyone can live happily ever after!

C.P. Kaiser
When Murder Becomes a Footnote

Why do we persistently romanticize historical explorers when in reality they were little more than raping, pillaging, and murdering thugs?

Take *Time* magazine's May 8, 2000, cover story, titled "The Amazing Vikings." The title itself indicates the story's bias, which is that these "explorers" are to be hailed in some way as exceptional because of their economic exploits. The story says that "for hundreds of years, these ruthless raiders would kill, plunder, and destroy, essentially at will," and that "terrified Anglo-Saxons composed special prayers customized for protection against the mighty Norse invaders." Yet, *Time* also says the Vikings were *amazing*, calling them democrats, master metal workers, and intrepid explorers.

Though admittedly considered brutes by all their victims, *Time* says, the Vikings were *more* than that (emphasis mine). Recent archeological finds apparently tell historians that the brute view of Vikings is wildly skewed. They were indeed raiders, says *Time,* but they were also traders whose economic network stretched from today's Iraq all the way to the Canadian Arctic. I don't know about you, but I have a *huge* problem with dismissing raping, pillaging, and murdering because of the subsequent establishment of excellent economic advantages. Imagine this history lesson: "Yes, the Iraqis under Saddam Hussein were brutal to the Kuwaitis, but they did more than rape and plunder; they opened new trade routes to the West and established a record number of oil wells. The price of crude decreased significantly for two hundred years. They were great explorers."

Of course, multinational corporations, including Time, Inc., have a vested interest in romanticizing this worldview. After all, they regularly take their businesses out of the United States to economically rape and pillage foreign workers. It's only natural, then, that *Time*'s writers, Michael D. Lemonick and Andrea Dorfman, conclude that certain historical dictators-murderers-plunderers were actually a boon to society as long as the traffic in money was impressive.

As a matter of fact, these sentiments sound very much like the rallying cry the United States still selectively uses when deciding whether to "help" or "not help" a Third World country. For example: the CIA destroyed Salvador Allende in 1973 because he wanted U.S. corporations out of his country and profits in the pockets of the Chileans; and Reagan's reason for supporting Central American governments embroiled in civil wars was only to destroy peasant organizing, which inevitably interferes with corporate profits; and today's debate to grant China most favorable nation status really only hinges on its economic power, not human rights abuses. Let's face it: if the Vikings were a nation today, several of them would have already sipped morning coffee in the White House after a good night's sleep in the Lincoln bedroom.

How much time has to elapse before we forget the carnage and only see the economics? In a thousand years, will *Time* be telling my progeny about "The Amazing Nazis" and their V2 rockets, their genetic research, and their "exploration" of Poland, Czechoslovakia, France, Belgium, England, Italy, and North Africa? If the Nazi carnage is horrendous after 50 years, even 100 years, what will make it not so in 1,000 years? After all, the mainstream press feels safe romanticizing 11th-century Vikings: "Without their superbly designed ships," *Time* writes, "the Vikings' *achievements* [emphasis mine] in exploration, trade and *conquest* [emphasis mine] across enormous stretches of Europe and the North Atlantic would never have been possible." I don't recall *Time* glowing about Saddam Hussein's conquest achievements in Kuwait.

Time's article coincides with the opening of "a wonderfully rich exhibition" (*Time*'s words) at the National Museum of Natural History titled "Vikings: The North Atlantic Saga" (note the word *saga* and its romantic connotations). Haven't we learned anything from our reevaluation of Columbus' exploits, or the mistaken "policy" of Manifest Destiny, which essentially called for the killing of any Indian standing west of Trenton, New Jersey? We may as well open "a wonderfully rich exhibition" of the Serbian saga, which also began over a millennium ago: "The Amazing Serbians: For two decades, these ruthless people killed, plundered, and destroyed, essentially at will, and the terrified Bosnians, Croats, and Kosovars composed special prayers customized for protection against Milosovic's invaders. Yet, they were more than brutes. Starting in the 11th century, they built beautiful churches, minted exquisite coins, and established trade routes throughout Eastern Europe." The only difference between the Vikings of yore and modern-day marauders is time, and Time, Inc. doesn't seem to get that (and this fault is not limited to *Time*'s coverage of so-called mythic explorers; PBS regularly flaunts the "greatness" of historical murderers).

Authors Lemonick and Dorfman actually write: "And while rape and pillage were part of the agenda, they were a small part of Norse life." Rape as a *small* part of the agenda!? Certainly not a small part of the victims' agenda! What nation would we lionize today that had rape built into its constitution? If we had allowed the Third Reich to live out its intended thousand years, the 20th century extermination of Jews, homosexuals, Gypsies and other undesirables by the Nazi "explorers" might have shown up as a footnote in *Time* magazine's May 8, 3000, edition. After all, with the above criteria, 50 years of killing followed by 950 years of economic expansion deserves to be looked at in a favorable light.

Within the last couple of decades, there seems to have been a slight shift in public opinion regarding so-called historical heroes, including the backlash against Columbus and the interest in telling the truth about the African diaspora. It's unfortunate that a magazine like *Time* can so coldbloodedly dismiss raping, pillaging, and murdering because said brutes left the spread-eagle legs of terrified female captives long enough to establish excellent trade routes.

Just because we're the rightful heirs of the Vikings (*Wednesday, Thursday,* and *Friday* come from the Norse gods Odin, Thor, and Freya) doesn't mean we have to idolize their exploits and romanticize their crimes. Just as we don't accept the murderous exploits of the 20th century (on paper, anyway), neither should we accept those of the 11th century. Presenting these historic "sagas" through rose-colored prose is the perfect multinational propaganda; instead of feeling righteous outrage, we accept historical and modern-day exploits-for-profits as harmless exercises in global trading.

Helen Cates
Blame It on Uncle Sam

How many times have we heard the saying: If you're old enough to serve your country, you're old enough to drink? Well, that little ditty was music to my ears when, as a 17-year-old, I was thrust into the ranks of the adult military world.

My first experience with "legal" drinking happened right after basic training. After weeks of grueling push-ups, insults, a screaming CC, kissing brass on the ass, endless inspections, and shaking in my cotton panties, I was ready to get POLLUTED!

Uncle Sam was very obliging and sympathetic. The enlisted club on base was conveniently within walking distance. And even though I'm sure I looked 12 in my uniform, the bartender didn't bat an eye. No I.D. checks. No questions. Just booze.

When asked what I wanted to drink, I was actually at a loss for words. My only experience with boozing had been sneaking cheap wine and beer on vacant dirt roads. Heck, babysitting money can only be stretched so far. I decided to order a Budweiser.

As the evening progressed, I became pleasantly and blearily sloshed. I was a bona fide sailor doing what sailors do best. Now all I needed was a tattoo. (I probably would have gotten one if Uncle Sam had subsidized that as well.)

My fellow underage comrades and I decided to try out the cocktails. We conversed with our heads close together on what to order. We decided on a round of screwdrivers. The next round became martinis. As our vision began to double, we started to get silly. Not one to pass up a dare, I approached the bartender, feeling all grown up.

"Could I please have a *slooooowwww*, comfortable *screeeeeewwww* (pausing to hear the giggling coming from my table) and make it on the rocks!"

So anyway, that was my welcome mat from Uncle Sam. I became a regular contributor to the pockets of our government. Sea pay, scraped pennies, and chow money all were put toward our diminishing brain cells.

After I was introduced to the Fleet, I was sent to Hawaii. Fortunately, the drinking age was 18. How lucky can a person get? So with my all-expense-paid trip to a tropical island, I was ready to party!

Gracing the bars on the shores of Oahu, I was living up my bright-eyed youth. Long Island iced teas, bourbon and Cokes, rum and Seven-Up. It can get expensive for a minimum wage enlistee. A sailor draining his entire pay allotment in one sitting was not unheard of.

Uncle Sam was a real hero, though, and no party pooper! He liked to keep the parties going until the flag went up. He somehow convinced the taxpayers to install affordable beer vending machines inside our barracks. We showed our appreciation by chunking loose change all night long and hugging the toilet seat.

Finally, Uncle Sam decided that the navy was getting fat. We all eyed one another as word got around that the fatties were going to get booted. I figured that the Department of Defense would have to call in the Boy Scouts of America for support because half the Navy was sporting a gut. Instead of confiscating our beer machines and taking away our reduced-priced cocktails, however, Uncle Sam pointed his finger at everyone but himself. Nothing changed.

And Canada was no different. They pulled their fancy ships into our ports and lulled us onto their gangplanks by serving twenty-five-cent shots of whiskey. Who can turn down a drink for that price? Yes, shame on Uncle Sam for allowing the Canadians to seduce us into sheer oblivion.

Now some idiot is wrenching the blame from Uncle Sam and calling our drinking a disease. OK, well, I have some questions: Can I be cured? Is it contagious? And if so, did I contract it from the local 7-11? Can I turn this disease down by just saying no to alcohol? Give me a break! And another thing: Uncle Sam is taxing this disease!

OK, so if it's not Uncle Sam's fault that half the military is pickling their insides, then whose fault is it? Maybe it's the breweries' fault. Maybe we should blame the farming industry for growing hops. Or maybe we should blame our genetically inferior ancestors. What about blaming God? After all, he created everything. Or did the devil make us do it?

But let's be honest. Really, the only person I have left to blame for my drinking is myself.

Scott Stein
And the Loser Is...

Everyone's a critic. This is America, and everyone is not only entitled to an opinion, but wants to be sure everyone else knows what it is. It's a free country, after all, and we were all created equal. We all, for example, have thumbs. And we all can turn a thumb up or a thumb down.

But some thumbs are more sensitive than others. Some thumbs are capable of seeing complexity. Some thumbs understand things. And some thumbs do not.

There is an overabundance of thick thumbs in this country, unable to appreciate dramatic art, or to even understand its purpose beyond providing entertainment. Witness the following letter to the editor, written by Arleen P. Mercorella of North Bellmore, N.Y., and published in *New York Newsday* on March 4, 2000:

"Regarding the Oscar Nominations: Has Hollywood really gone mad? If *American Beauty* is the best that our filmmakers can create, then this country is really in trouble. *American Beauty* portrays suburban life as the most dysfunctional society imaginable. This story is pure garbage and certainly does not reflect the typical American suburb.

"Perhaps the writer should visit Long Island and other suburban communities. What a poor example this shows to our youngsters. *American Beauty* does a terrible injustice to so many hardworking people trying to raise their families in an honest and caring way. How are we ever to teach our youngsters that there still are good, normal and hardworking people in this country if trash such as this is deemed the best?

"If this film should get the award for best picture, an honor that has been given to many truly great motion pictures before it, I will lose all respect for the Academy Awards."

Ms. Mercorella's letter belies a thorough misunderstanding of the dramatic arts, shared by many and sometimes leading to protest and bizarre rating systems and even calls for restrictions on freedom. Where to begin? I am dizzy with possibility.

The filmmakers did not portray suburban life as the "most dysfunctional society imaginable." *American Beauty* did not address other kinds of life in America. For all we know, urban life and rural life might be even less appealing than suburbia if treated by the filmmakers.

Movies have a long history of exploring the desperation and misery of the poor, of inner-city life. Where was Ms. Mercorella's letter protesting the critical acclaim of *Boys N the Hood?* Oh, I see. She doesn't live in a black ghetto, so showing those people as living in an unimaginably dysfunctional society was acceptable. It probably was acceptable as well to show the dysfunction of a small town, as portrayed in *Footloose*. Only when her own backyard is defamed should Hollywood be chastised.

Calling the film a "terrible injustice" is itself a terrible injustice to those who have actually been the victims of terrible injustices. But hyperbole and her emotional need to defend her territory aside, she is right when she writes that *American Beauty* "certainly does not reflect the typical American suburb."

Who said it did, or was supposed to? Did *Jaws* reflect the typical shark? No, it was about an exceptional shark, and sharks the world over should not file a class-action lawsuit against the filmmaker for defamation. Most sharks are not ravenous man-eaters, we know that. Even sharks knew it was a movie, a work of fiction, and that a two-hour depiction of a typical shark's day would be pretty boring. Who wants to watch two hours of swimming and eating small fish?

Is *Taxi Driver* about the typical cabbie? I hope not. Imagine that movie if it was. I don't want to sit in a cab for two hours, and I don't want to pay nine dollars to watch someone else sit in a cab for two hours. Even DeNiro couldn't pull that off. Something interesting has to happen for it to qualify as drama. Driving in circles is not interesting, and that is what the typical taxi driver does. Drama has nothing to do with the typical anything.

Hamlet isn't about the typical prince. The typical prince is boring. *Hamlet* is about a deceitful, murderous, borderline incestuous royal family. Should royal families the world over protest the acclaim Shakespeare's play has garnered? No. They understand that *Hamlet* is about a character named Hamlet, and, by extension, humanity. Its setting is part of the illusion that all dramatic art employs. If a less royal setting had served the story of *Hamlet*, Shakespeare would have used one. Hamlet said, "The play's the thing," and he was right. The story was the point, and any comment made about a specific portion of society was secondary. In good drama it always is.

American Beauty is not the first drama to tackle the American suburbs. John Cheever and John Updike, two great American authors, and many others have used this setting to probe fear, mortality, faith, violence, desire, and greed, and every other human challenge or failing the perceptive writer's eye can find. Were they condemning the American suburb, relative to other human societies? No more than Dostoevsky was condemning the Russian city when he set his fiction there. By necessity, writers use settings they know, but the story is not necessarily about those settings.

Of course there are happy families in the suburbs, like anywhere else. But I don't want to see a movie about them. As Tolstoy said in the famous opening to *Anna Karenina:* "Happy families are all alike; every unhappy family is unhappy in its own way." Maybe there are people who are interested in only the happy families. Maybe they desire the Brady Bunchification of the dramatic arts, with smiling siblings and every dilemma solved in neat fashion (except on those occasions when the solution to a problem is to be continued the following week). I don't want to have dinner conversation with those people. Life is too short.

What about the children? Ms. Mercorella wonders, "How are we ever to teach our youngsters that there still are good, normal and hardworking people in this country if this film is deemed the best?" What young people (writer's tip: *youngsters* should be discarded from your vocabulary, unless you are over the age of 80) are even seeing *American Beauty?* It is a serious film, intended for adults. Yes, an R rating will not prevent children from seeing it, but the children who do sneak into R movies are not doing it to see this film. This is *American Beauty*, not *American Pie.*

If as a parent your biggest worry is that the Academy Awards' decision is a bad influence on your child, count yourself lucky. Children don't need an awards show to teach them to value hard work and honesty, or to give them a sense of the value of their community. That is why they have parents. And if their parents and their community do not teach them to value and aspire to embody these traits, does anyone really think a little gold statue given to any movie is going to help, or hurt?

Contrary to Ms. Mercorella's selective memory, Oscars and critical acclaim have gone to controversial movies before. *Midnight Cowboy,* at the time X-rated, won Best Picture in 1969. No role models there. Widely admired, *The Graduate* is about a young man having an affair with an older married woman until he falls in love with her daughter. That's family values for you. Film schools teach that *Citizen Kane* is the greatest movie ever made, but I don't think Charles Foster Kane is the ideal role model, unless greed, loneliness, manipulation, and bitterness are the highest values.

The arts are not here to give us role models. They are here to entertain us, to give us drama. At their best, they entertain and mean something, and help us to better understand others and maybe ourselves, but they are not how-to videos or instruction books.

Stop looking for someone to follow. It's time to lead yourself. Losing respect for the Academy Awards is the best thing that could happen to Ms. Mercorella. Maybe then she would be able to think for herself, determine for herself what she should value, be her own role model, and be one to the children around her.

Awards ceremonies are for the insecure, and mean nothing. Watch them if you like to critique the latest fashions, or because your brain needs a rest from a hard day. But don't take them seriously. You don't need others to tell you what to value.

On Oscar night, no matter what wins Best Picture, the losers will continue to be those who really care.

David "Preacher" Slocum
The Confederate Flag Debate in South Carolina: Heritage or Hate?

Let's take this debate one side at a time.
Those For
Those for the removal of the Confederate flag from the South Carolina statehouse believe it stands for all that is racist. They point out that the skinheads and other Nazi groups use the Confederate battle flag, or some variation, as their own flag. They also point out that the KKK, the epitome of racism against blacks, uses the flag as a constant reminder to blacks of their slave heritage. They believe that no healing can be complete while the government is flying such a standard and that the government of South Carolina is deliberately showing its racial prejudice by refusing to give in to their demands. The NAACP (The National Association for the Advancement of Colored People) has urged a boycott of South Carolina businesses until such time as the flag is removed from the statehouse by law. They hold Abraham Lincoln up as the Great Emancipator for his part in abolishing slavery after the Civil War. They see the Civil War as all about slavery.

Those Against
Those against the removal of the Confederate battle flag believe it is a memorial to those who fought and died for what they believed. They believe it stands for states' rights and is a constant reminder to the people of the United States that the government can and will usurp the sovereign powers of the states by force. They hold Abraham Lincoln up as a traitor and a lying politician who went back on his word to the nation and used the military to enforce his vision of the future. They see the Civil War as all about states' rights.

The Facts
- The northern states enacted tax and tariff laws that placed an undue burden on the slave-owning states of the South in the hope that these taxes would force an economic end to slavery.
- Slaves were initially owned in every state in the Union, but highest concentrations were in the southern states. Yet, less than 10% of the population of the southern states owned slaves.
- South Carolina is the only state with the Confederate battle flag flying above its Capitol. It was raised at the statehouse in 1962 to commemorate the Civil War's centennial (although Georgia and Mississippi incorporate the Confederate symbols in their state flags).
- Jefferson Davis, the president of the Confederacy, considered blacks subhuman. In his speeches, however, he stressed the sovereign rights of each state as the cause for the war and said that the slave issue was secondary.
- President Lincoln, in his first inaugural address, said, "I have no purpose, directly or indirectly, to interfere with the institution of slavery in the States where it exists. I believe I have no lawful right to do so, and I have

no inclination to do so.... Resolved: that the maintenance inviolate of the rights of the States, and especially the right of each State to order and control its own domestic institutions according to its own judgment exclusively, is essential to that balance of power on which the perfection and endurance of our political fabric depend, and we denounce the lawless invasion by armed force of the soil of any State or Territory, no matter under what pretext, as among the gravest of crimes." He also pointed out that the law was very specific and that any elected politician who did not live up to his oath and support that law was without honor.

History is history and despite the revisionist texts of both sides, we will never know the true thoughts and inspirations of these historical figures.

What we do know is that this all comes down to heritage. Do the blacks in this country have a monopoly on heritage? Some have embraced their African roots and made them an inseparable part of their identity. They have adopted the name African-American, making that heritage an indelible part of who they are.

At the same time that African-Americans are embracing their heritage, they want to deny the white southerners their right to claim their own personal heritage. The white people of the southern states have strong ties to the Confederacy, and the beliefs and passions that ignited a war. Are they not allowed to honor their past in the same way?

True equality cannot exist if one segment of the population insists on preferential treatment.

Fair is fair, right?

Reader Comments

—C.P. Kaiser responds to "The Confederate Flag Debate in South Carolina: Heritage or Hate?" by David "Preacher" Slocum.

The Confederate flag represented a conglomeration of states whose economy depended on the continuance of slavery. The states' rights that David "Preacher" Slocum writes about is none other than the right to own slaves for the profitable cultivation of agriculture. He says that less than 10% of the population of the southern states owned slaves. Of course! That was the percentage of plantation owners.

Preacher also tells us that the Confederacy's president, Jefferson Davis, considered the subhumanness of blacks (hence their "enlistment" into slavery) to be secondary to states' rights as the cause of the Civil War. Is he saying then that we should overlook this "secondary" cause and cheer on Davis and his ilk because of their commitment to states' rights, and celebrate this commitment by flying the Confederate flag over government buildings? One might also overlook Hitler's "secondary" extermination of Gypsies and homosexuals, because his primary Final Solution focused on the eradication of the Jews. I find Preacher's myopic vision hinders his powers of persuasion. Following his logic, why don't we just fly the KKK banner on statehouses, because, after all, the Klan says their primary concern is free speech and Euro centric ethnic awareness.

TJ Walker, an Internet pundit, commented how this whole flag controversy has enhanced the self-esteem of citizens in Alabama and Mississippi because "now, even they have a state to look down upon."

But Harry Shearer, host of the weekly *Le Show* on PBS, says it best: "The losers of war don't get to fly their flag. That's the difference between winning and losing."

—Sam Harmon responds to "The Confederate Flag Debate in South Carolina: Heritage or Hate?" by David "Preacher" Slocum.

As a migrant from the deep South many years past, I must say that I never could understand why President Ulysses Grant and the Supreme Court of that period did not enact laws to prevent flying the Confederate flag anywhere in the U.S.A. as one of their first acts after the assassination of President Lincoln and the complete and utter defeat of the Confederacy. The Confederate flag, especially today, has little to do with Southern heritage. The flying of the Confederate flag by the Southern white majority is used basically as a symbol of defiance in the face of total defeat for supporting a system of human slavery, sexism, racism, class consciousness, homophobia, and countless segments of religious animosity beyond world acceptability. The constant blast of War Cries and the waving of Confederate flags at public functions is a recipe for continued racial hatred. The German Nazi flag is not flown in Germany as a symbol of heritage and neither should the Confederate flag be flown from public buildings in this country.

—Bernd D. Ratsch responds to "The Confederate Flag Debate in South Carolina: Heritage or Hate?" by David "Preacher" Slocum.

Very good essay. I wholeheartedly enjoyed reading about the fact that some misguided people in this nation actually associate these Southern inbred idiots, calling themselves "neo Nazis," with the flag. Not to forget the KKK who have a rather boring wardrobe and have to hide their faces underneath what looks like a dunce cap. Getting back to the whole Confederate flag debate: It's a flag people! Every state flies its own identifying flag either below or above the U.S. flag—what's the problem? Hatred is in the hearts of people, not the color of our skin, religious beliefs, or especially in the cloth or stitching of a piece of linen!

—Scott Stein responds to "The Confederate Flag Debate in South Carolina: Heritage or Hate?" by David "Preacher" Slocum.

I am usually among the first to point out double standards, hypocrisy, and misguided political correctness, but I think Preacher is missing an important distinction in his discussion of the Confederate flag. Public property and private property are very different things. Everyone who pays taxes pays for public property. Public property therefore has an obligation to be inclusive of all taxpayers, to the extent reasonably possible. Of course, it is not possible to accommodate every single person's tastes and biases when decorating a public building, so there will be times when we might dismiss a complaint as being overly sensitive or nitpicking. The objection to the Confederate flag is not such a case.

A significant portion of South Carolina's taxpaying population not only objects to the flag, they consider it to be an attack on their very existence. Citizens should not be made to feel like outsiders and the enemy in their own state. I do not think this is an issue for the rest of the country to decide, but leaving the decision to South Carolinians means *all* South Carolinians. Express your heritage, particularly if it is offensive and intimidating to whole groups of people who happen to be taxpaying citizens of your state, in your own home and on your own property.

—Anonymous responds to "The Confederate Flag Debate in South Carolina: Heritage or Hate?" by David "Preacher" Slocum.

I did not realize there are still people out there that will stand up for our rights. I believe we need to not give in anymore. When they cry out they always receive. We need to take a stand and stop letting them get everything they want. They have their heritage and we have ours and the flag is one of ours. If we do not fight and if South Carolina takes down that flag, they will know they have won everything. So, please, fight for the flag to stay flying! The federal government gives them everything; the state government gives them everything. Recently my husband went for a job and lost it because the African-American got the job. We don't have a fighting chance anymore. Our government and everyone are scared of them because the African-Americans are a very strong organization. Thank you and may God bless America.

—sthnldy responds to "The Confederate Flag Debate in South Carolina: Heritage or Hate?" by David "Preacher" Slocum.

We loosely throw around the terms *racism* and *discrimination,* but rarely do we ever dissect them in a more productive way. Racism and discrimination are two of the same. They state that services or products are not issued to people due to the fact that they are a minority group. Their skin, color, age, sex—all of those biological aspects—set them apart from receiving what they deem necessary.

Now, let's look at those terms in regards to the Confederate flag. Is it not racist and discriminatory to say that we can't fly the Confederate flag because it is a symbol of slavery and racism to a minority group? When will the taking over of our heritage ever stop? Why must we censor a part of history? If a simple minority group can raise so much stink over the removal of the Confederate flag, then I *demand* the removal of the American flag. Under the American flag, my Native American ancestors were marched onto reservations, where they did not have enough food to feed the hungry—children were killed and the white solders raped women.

You see the childishness in this? The Confederate flag stands for a lot more than racism and oppression of people. It stands for states' rights and people who loved and believed in their country and nation enough to die for it. What's wrong with America today is we forgot we are a melting pot of cultures. If we throw out every little thing that has to do with slavery and injustice then *nobody* would have any history or heritage left. Spain, Britain, France, Africa, America, the Confederacy, and so many other nations have owned slaves at one time in their history. If one flag is removed for this simple issue, then let's make it fair and remove all of them!

Bob Sullivan
Top Ten Signs Your Favorite Presidential Candidate is on Drugs

10. Can't stop giggling whenever an announcer says he and someone else are making a "joint appearance."
9. Maintains that if his father was allowed to be king, he should be allowed to be, too.
8. Is secretly convinced the moon is trying to kill us.
7. Doesn't accept matching funds so an unlimited amount of cash can flow through his coffers, making it easier to skim funds for his insatiable desire for Fritos.
6. Keeps taking fact-finding junkets to Columbia.
5. Calls himself a Christian while installing electric bleachers on Death Row.
4. His running mate: Robert Downey Jr.
3. Can't wipe that smirk off his face.
2. Keeps referring to his mother as "that Quaker Oats guy."

And the Number 1 Sign Your Favorite Presidential Candidate is on Drugs...

1. There's a four-minute pause between "My fellow" and "Americans."

C.P. Kaiser
Getting Laid Was Never So Easy

English is a dynamic language, constantly changing. Read the Middle-Age poem *Beowulf* or any original Shakespeare manuscript and you'll discover an English language far different from the one you speak daily.

In the twentieth century alone, every new fad has brought its own argot, from the Roaring Twenties (flappers, jazz) to the gangsters (moll, lam) to the beatniks (cool, hip, vibe) to the hippies (groovy, flower child) to the gangstas (chill, illin).

Not just words are changing and evolving, but grammar is as well. How long ago could you absolutely not end a sentence with a preposition? Even the prestigious *New York Times* breaks that traditional taboo.

I love the changing English language. Evolving slang is music to my ears. My problem is with the strong minority power base of mainstream pundits, academics, and journalists who seek to stop English's dynamism by forcing certain usages on the public when the common vernacular overwhelmingly favors another. These people are either afraid to think out of the box or they consider any deviation from the supposed norm to be an assault on their heritage. To those people, I propose some changes:

None are: According to *Webster's Seventh New Collegiate Dictionary*, the pronoun *none* is singular or plural in construction, with singular being the preferred listing. But you will never hear the mainstream media use *none* with a plural verb, and I say it's about time we did. For example, the preferred usage is: None of the passengers is hurt. It's clear we're talking about more than one passenger here, so why not say (or write): None of the passengers are hurt. Every time I hear *none* taking a singular verb, my ears feel as if they heard an A flat when they were expecting a C sharp.

Data is: Again, my dictionary allows for the singular *or* plural usage of *data*, with plural being the preferred listing. It even lists *datums* as an acceptable plural (*datum* being the original Latin singular form of *data*). I propose that mainstream broadcasters come up for air in the 21st century and use *data* as a singular, collective noun. To say "the data are here" just doesn't cut it for me. We don't say "the information are here." *Data* came into popular use this century with the advent of the computer. I can understand linguists' initial desire to remain true to its Latin origins, but *data* basically means a collection of information, and both collection and information act as singular nouns encompassing more than one in their body. The data is in and it's a collective, singular noun.

Attorney Generals: There are several compound words whose plural seems awkward to me. Whenever I hear the pundits on TV or radio talking about the *attorneys general*, my skin crawls. Why can't they just say *attorney generals*, pluralizing the *general* instead of the *attorney?* Again, the dictionary lists both variations as correct, but the preferred usage pluralizes *attor-*

neys. As a writer, when I deliberately use *data* as singular or *attorney generals* as plural, some might think me unschooled. According to the dictionary, my usage is correct, just not common. That's why I propose that the pundits and academics lighten up and accept these variations as correct, or at least correct enough for print.

Passer-bys: Another compound word whose plural needs some tweaking. I know the protagonist of the phrase is the passer, but because of the usual structure of the English language, putting the *s* on the first part of the compound sounds weird to my ears. Although my dictionary doesn't list any plural variations of *passer-by*, I propose we use *passer-bys* as the plural, putting the *s* on the by.

Lay, Lie: These two verbs are big problems. *Lay, laid, laid* (to put, place or prepare) always take a direct object. Examples are: I will lay Hilary on the table (meaning to put or place her there, not to have sexual intercourse—unless that's part of the plan, in which case, it'd be better to say: I will fuck Hilary on the table.) I laid Hilary on the table yesterday (again, meaning to place her there). I had laid Hilary on the table.

Lie, lay, lain (to recline or be situated) never take a direct object. Examples are: Hilary lies on the table. Hilary lay on the table yesterday. Hilary had lain on the table. Confusion occurs because the meanings are complementary, in part because of the overlapping of principal parts (*lay* being present tense with a direct object and past tense without).

We're accustomed to using *lay* in the present tense and *laid* in the past tense (as should be in one type of construction), but hardly any commoner uses *lay* as the past tense or *lain* as the past participle of *lie*, mainly because they sound awkward. More often *laid* is used, such as I will lie down; I laid down yesterday; I had laid down to rest. *Laid* is grammatically incorrect here. But I say get rid of *lay* as past tense and just use *laid* and then we can lay this matter to rest.

Quickies:
Why is a picture hung but a person hanged?
Can't we simply order an ice tea instead of an iced tea?
Do you have a mid-size car or a mid-sized car?

Scott Stein
Kangaroo Court

"Don't give us that cock-and-bull story," the prosecutor said. "We can wait till the cows come home. Let's talk turkey."

"You're trying to throw me to the lions," the accused said.

"You're in the doghouse all right, but I'm giving you a chance to keep the wolf from your door."

"It's a fine kettle of fish I'm in."

The prosecutor was impatient. "Just grab the bull by the horns."

The accused had to tell the truth. "That night it was raining cats and dogs, so I stopped in for some Wild Turkey—"

"You were at that bar at 6:15 p.m.," the prosecutor interrupted, "but I guess the early bird catches the worm."

The accused continued. "I ruled the roost ... I was the cat's meow, and there were plenty of fish in the sea. Besides, though my wife watched me like a hawk, when the cat's away, the mice will play.

"But I guess birds of a feather flock together, because my wife was there too, with him. And that was a horse of a different color. Though he was strong as an ox, I didn't play possum. He was a bee in my bonnet, and she had really gotten my goat. Maybe it was like closing the barn door after the horse had run away, but I'd have been a monkey's uncle if I had let sleeping dogs lie. So, like a bat out of hell and in two shakes of a lamb's tail I was next to them.

"'Every dog has his day,' I said to him. I waited for her to eat crow.

"But she said, 'What's good for the goose is good for the gander.' And then, adding insult, 'Monkey see, monkey do.'

"He waved his hand at my breath and offered, 'Hair of the dog that bit you?'

"'It's for the birds!' I told him. Right then I'd quit cold turkey.

"'Get off your high horse,' my wife said.

"But he assured her, 'His bark is worse than his bite. Besides, you can catch more flies with honey than with vinegar,' and he hugged her.

"He had been my best friend, but I guess only a dog is man's best friend. I saw that he was really a wolf in sheep's clothing. So was she. He'd been to my home countless times, like a fox in a henhouse.

"I wanted another chance, but my wife said, 'You can't teach an old dog new tricks, and a leopard can't change its spots.'

"So I flipped them the bird and left the bar."

The prosecutor was silent as a mouse, but then he asked, "Like water off a duck's back, is that what you're saying?"

The accused nodded. "It's a dog-eat-dog world."

"Don't look a gift horse in the mouth. I'm giving you a chance to feather your own nest."

"You can lead a horse to water, but you can't make it drink ... but I miss my wife and wish she were alive. Him too."

"Spare me the crocodile tears. You know what I think? I think you felt like a black sheep, that this was the straw that broke the camel's back. And I also think your wife was a white elephant, that you wanted the lion's share of what you'd squirreled away for yourself. It's sad, because she was a real warhorse, the goose that laid the golden egg. But to you she was just a fly in the ointment, wasn't she?"

The accused cleared the frog from his throat, and asked, "You really think that I would kill her?"

"Does a bear shit in the woods?"

"But my marriage was a sacred cow."

"What kind of snake oil are you trying to sell? You knew that there was more than one way to skin a cat, didn't you? You decided to kill two birds with one stone, didn't you? Didn't you? We want to know."

"Curiosity killed the cat," the accused answered.

"That might be, but the best laid plans of mice and men often go awry."

"Don't put the cart before the horse—I don't see any witnesses. They're both food for worms, sleeping with the fishes, gone the way of the Dodo."

"A bird in the hand is worth two in the bush. The chickens sure have come home to roost. And an elephant never forgets."

The accused shifted uneasily. "I thought I smelled a rat. What stool pigeon turned me in? Where's the snake in the grass?"

"You're a sitting duck," the prosecutor said.

"Don't count your chickens before they hatch. I believe you like I trust the boy who cried wolf. Your threats are a paper tiger."

"This is more fun than a barrel of monkeys," the prosecutor said, laughing like a hyena. "Let me introduce to you a canary that can sing, a woman with more lives than a cat—your wife."

She walked into the courtroom and sat in the back row.

The accused said nothing.

"What's the matter, cat got your tongue?" the prosecutor asked.

The accused was a deer caught in the headlights, and decided to cooperate. "You've been a busy beaver, and I see that my goose is cooked. I guess there's no choice but to fish or cut bait."

But the judge had heard enough, and said to the prosecutor, "It looks like you have all your ducks in a row."

And the accused howled in horror and was taken away in chains, to spend the dog days of every summer after in a cage not fit for an animal.

Ari McKee
The Slow Food Movement

"I believe very strongly that if we have lost our sense of family in this country, it's because we no longer sit down and eat together," says Minneapolis chef Ronald L. Huff. Huff is a leader in the eleven-year-old Slow Food Movement (www.slowfood.com) started by columnist Carlo Petrini.

It is the movement's assertion that the fast-paced lifestyle (" ... juggling a Big Mac in one hand and a cell phone in another ...") is the cause of much of our society's social ills, and that if we could just all sit down and eat together, s-l-o-w-l-y, we could regain our golden past.

The Slow Food Movement is unique in that it unites both liberals ("corporate food is a plague on the land") and conservatives ("life would be better if everyone would just act exactly like my family did in 1956"). And it's hard to logically refute their premise, that " ... a firm defense of quiet material pleasure is the only way to oppose the universal folly of Fast Life." While most social movements are sure that they have found a clear path to righteousness as yet undiscovered by their neighbors, the Slow Movement not only believes it but went ahead and wrote it into their mission statement: "May the [Slow Food movement] ... preserve us from the contagion of the multitude who mistake frenzy for efficiency." They are the Way.

And they are *serious* food people.

I am reminded of an article I read about an ordinary man, a businessman, who suffered a mild stroke. There were no lasting detrimental effects of the electrical storm his brain experienced, other than an awakening of a passion for food, for taste. He lived out the remaining years of his life as a brilliant food and restaurant critic. Food became much more to him than sustenance—it was his calling.

He is not alone in his enthusiasm—60,000 members in Slow Food attest to its appeal to foodies. Like Huff and Petrini, they are chefs and critics, hobbyists and zealots, folks for whom food carries powerful sensual, emotional, and psychological import. The smell of bread baking, the taste of a Madeleine cookie, the toasty, cozy, sweet and sour memories of our childhood are often couched in food. It's primal, intensely personal, even prenatal.

And, frankly, it bores the crap out of me.

I do have food memories. My uncle Jimmy lived in Indiana for a long time, and the first thing he'd do when he hit our town was to get a big sack of White Castles, something he couldn't get back home. I have warm, cozy memories about stacking the empty white hamburger boxes—I can envision the plate of discarded pickle slices. Pathetic? Maybe. There are other food memories in my life, like the big bowl of popcorn and tall glass of chocolate milk I had every day after school in junior high. I had an amazing grilled ham & cheese sandwich in London once.

My mother cooked and she was a good cook. It just never planted a big food-freak seed in my soul. I prefer to eat alone, with a newspaper. I enjoy a good diner breakfast. Medium-rare prime rib can just about make my day. But, that's about it. I eat because I'm hungry or because something somebody else is eating smells good.

We have an enormously overweight society that doesn't need any more reasons to eat. Instead of adding new rivets to the food-love bond, we should be loosening the grip. Food won't solve boredom, loneliness, anger, or teen pregnancy. Eating slowly and ritualistically will not help Dad and Johnny get along if Dad won't listen and Johnny won't talk. The health clubs and Weight Watchers' clubs are filled with people for whom food has overly intense, even crippling importance in their life. Do we really want to increase that number? A crappy family is just as crappy when they're at the table eating homemade lasagna.

Discussion of the superiority of raw-milk cheeses or the Zen of bread-baking should be left to people who are into it—as we do with any other passionate enthusiasm, from quilt-making to coin-collecting to antique refinishing. Just because it's your thing, or the thing of 60,000 foodies like you, doesn't mean the rest of us are doomed to a life of poor family relations and unsatisfying victuals.

Time with each other *is* vital. The Slow Food Movement is right on target when it points to the importance of getting to know each other as families, of talking and discussing and enjoying each other's company. The food thing is secondary or lower—and I'll go so far as to say that to irretrievably bind the two is a kind of fast-paced American way of killing two birds with one stone. To suggest that every family should make mealtime the primary time-consuming activity of its day—or suffer dysfunction—is irresponsible and insular.

But don't be completely discouraged. Call me when the Slow *Life* Movement starts; I'll be first on board. Just don't ask me to cook.

Helen Cates
How about Keeping the Sex in Sexual Harassment?

I just read that sexual harassment is not about sex. OK, so what is it about then? Well, according to recent surveys, sexual harassment is about power. Men do it to control and humiliate women.

My dictionary defines sexual harassment as *unwanted, repeated sexual attention*. According to this definition, the following are examples of sexual harassment (drawn from literature by *9to5, National Association of Working Women*):

- Repeated offensive sexual flirtations, advances, or propositions

- Continued or repeated verbal abuse or innuendo of a sexual nature

- Uninvited physical contact such as touching, hugging, patting or pinching

- Comments of a sexual nature about an individual's body

- Display of sexually suggestive objects or pictures

- Jokes or remarks of a sexual nature in front of people who find them offensive

- Prolonged staring or leering at a person

- Making obscene gestures or suggestive insulting sounds.

Well, according to the above, I've been sexually harassed—or to be politically correct, humiliated and controlled—my entire life.

Kindergarten
I remember the first time I was sexually harassed: A boy in my kindergarten class slipped me a crumpled piece of paper with a crudely drawn naked man and woman. I remember blushing and giggling when all of a sudden the teacher's arm shot out and snatched the incriminating evidence. The two of us were forced to sit in the hallway facing the wall.

Adolescence
As puberty took hold, the sexual harassment intensified. I heard every comment imaginable about my bust size. Boys would peek over my head at my cleavage or drop their pencils at my feet and glance up my hem. If that wasn't enough, the chorus of jeers and catcalls coming from the school bleachers signified not appreciation for my athleticism and skill but only that my cheerleading uniform was way, way too short.

To be honest, most of the time I liked the attention. It had never crossed my mind that these guys were trying to humiliate or control me.

Sure there were a few incidents when things got out of hand, the "accidental" brush against my boob, or the "friendly" pat against my backside. But those were rare. And usually with a scathing look or a biting remark, the boys' antics would wind down for a while.

Sure we knew what went on in the boys' locker room, the dirty jokes and the bragging about sexual conquests. But boys will be boys and, might I add, girls will be girls as well!

In the Military

I can remember taking smoke breaks during basic training. We women would cram as many cigarettes that ten minutes would allow, groaning over our aches and pains and joking among ourselves. What did we talk about? Sex—the same as the men in the other barracks. Now, I've heard men talk and they can get downright filthy, but I must admit, I've heard women talk worse than guys.

Lately it seems as if the military is fighting a losing war, the battle of the sexes. I hear a lot about sexual harassment in the military. My question to these women is, "What did you expect?" The military is predominantly male—not that outnumbering women is a license to act like animals—and men are going to look at women. It's a fact of life. I learned this when I was taught about the birds and the bees. I'm not condoning sexual harassment, but I think, for the most part, we're dealing with overly sensitive women— the kind who tend to regard all male attention as a threat.

Even more ridiculous are the women claiming to be traumatized by sexual harassment. A study conducted by Yale University School of Medical researchers found that sexual harassment was four times more likely than active military duty to cause post-traumatic stress disorder (PTSD) among female military veterans. According to the study, PTSD symptoms include nightmares or flashbacks, avoidance of places where stress occurred or things that remind the individual about the stressful incidents, emotional detachment from loved ones, unwarranted suspicion of others, and nervousness and anxiety. Some PTSD patients experience these symptoms for years after the stressful event occurred.

On the Job

Sexual harassment charges and violations are epidemic in the civilian world as well. Recently, my husband was forced to attend another meeting dealing with sexual harassment on the job. Of course, his company is afraid of getting sued, but I think it's ironic how some working women are dressing. My husband's company does not enforce a dress code and I've seen plenty of mini skirts and spiked heels sauntering through those offices. (According to tales from the guys, plenty more has been seen under the skirts as well.) It could all be a case of giving and getting mixed signals.

I'm sure there are genuine cases of sexual harassment. My husband's is a classic case. A woman in upper management, ahead of him in the chain of command, has been e-mailing him sexual propositions. She's been pestering him for weeks to take her to lunch. She even mentioned a one-night stand, saying, "We can keep it a secret from your wife." I didn't believe my husband at first, but then he forwarded me her e-mails.

My immediate response was to e-mail her and call her a slut. I wanted to tell her everything my grandmother would have said if she were still alive.

I mean, what kind of a woman talks and acts like that? But I seriously doubt she wants to humiliate and control my husband. She just wants sex.

Finally, something else dawned on me. How was my husband reacting to her? He said he'd shrugged off her remarks, turned down her offers, but was polite about it. Upon further probing, he admitted that he was flattered by all the attention. Now, how can I blame him for that? What person wouldn't be flattered by the attention? We all like to be considered attractive.

I never did e-mail her. Not only do I trust my husband, but, I had to admit, maybe she was getting mixed signals from his lack of intervention.

This brings to mind another incident. A coworker approached me and confided that she was going to report a man for sexual harassment. I asked her why.

"Because he keeps touching my arm and making sexual suggestions."

"Did you tell him to stop?"

"Yes, and he knows that I'm married."

"What does he do?"

"He keeps coming back."

I suggested that maybe he kept coming back because of how she was handling the situation. Each time I saw them together, she was smiling at him. I told her that she doesn't need to be so nice about it, but to give the guy a chance before running to the office.

Maybe that's what we all need to do, give one another a chance. It could be a simple case of men are from Mars and women are from Venus—giving and getting the wrong impressions.

And for those women who just plain don't appreciate a man's whistle or a compliment—I can only suggest two things: Get a life or take a job in a morgue.

Scott Stein
I Passed on Passover, But Happy Easter

I don't do Passover. This should come as no surprise to readers of *When Falls the Coliseum* who are familiar with my writing about religion. I don't like it. Religion, that is. Passover either. Somehow, although my parents, family, and friends are generally aware of my views about religion, my mother never fails to be shocked—no, hurt—when I choose to skip Passover. So, for all the mothers and future mothers out there, and all the people who just don't understand their anti-religious family member or friend, let me offer an apology.

I am sorry that I do not believe what you believe.

It would be easier, I know. But I don't. So, no Passover for me.

In college, a young woman, a fellow Jew, chastised me for ordering a sandwich in the school cafeteria, violating the prohibition against eating bread during Passover week. She had on her plate ham and cheese between two slabs of matzo. I exaggerate not. Of course, ham is prohibited by Jewish law, as is mixing dairy with meat, but my friend didn't care. She was following the rules of Passover, not the rules of Judaism. I was baffled that it was I being accused of being a bad Jew. Perhaps I was and am, but integrity and reason are pillars in my life, and hypocrisy is the enemy. So, no Passover for me.

But do not misinterpret my seder boycott as an attack on the importance of family. I do not skip Thanksgiving or Rosh Hashanah dinner or any other chance to see my family and break bread with them. We are close, and I look forward to festive meals and laughing at the dining room table. In my family, these other holidays do not involve ritual or prayer of any kind, so I gladly attend. At all dinners except Passover no one is expected to read from a book that I do not believe, praise God for freeing slaves I do not believe he freed, and dip fingers in wine symbolic of plagues I do not believe were sent.

So I am faced with a choice: Attend the seder and participate fully, reciting words I do not believe and embracing superstition I abhor; or do not attend, and suffer the wrath of mothers and mothers-in-law who just do not understand my reason for not attending a "simple family dinner." Of course, a third choice is to attend and refuse to participate, but that's plain rude.

You see, I have a young nephew and a younger niece, and they are just now becoming interested in their Judaism. They are not my children, so their religious upbringing is not my concern, or at least not my decision. I accept that. The kids are learning religion for the same reasons many of us did: tradition, or they happen to attend a Jewish daycare facility, or to their parents it seems like the thing to do.

It is not my place to tell these kids what to believe, but if I were to sit there staring dumbly into space while everyone else recited nonsense without reason, the kids just might (as kids often do) ask why I am not also reading and dipping and singing. Picture the scene: Me, sitting next to their parents, insanely explaining to a five- and eight-year-old why their religious beliefs are false and that they should disregard all they have been taught, on Passover no less.

OK, I probably would be able to exercise restraint. I really have no wish to impose my views on anyone else. I have said elsewhere that people can believe whatever they want. I will continue to argue and make my case using logic and reason and humor, trying to persuade those with open and critical minds, but not during Passover seder at someone else's house and with someone else's kids.

I respect parents trying to do their best with their children. And I respect people who are authentic, who practice what they preach. I even respect hypocrites who eat ham and cheese on matzo. I respect all people who exhibit kindness and do not impose through legislation their beliefs or pretend-beliefs on others, religious or otherwise.

So, though my assault on irrational beliefs unsupported by reason or evidence will continue, and while I will resume my probing of hypocrisy and inconsistency, whether it be in politics, religion, the arts, or everyday life, for now I'd like to wish a belated happy Passover to our Jewish readers who believe, and a happy pretend-Passover to our Jewish readers who pretend-believe. And, to all our gentile readers, believers and pretend-believers alike, happy Easter.

Robert L. Hall
One Word: Responsibility

The first job I ever had was working at a state-run alcohol and drug rehabilitation unit for three years.

While there, I saw it all: the voluntarily and involuntarily committed, the washouts, the drunks, the pill heads, the severely mentally handicapped, and the criminals. It wasn't very pretty and I don't tend to linger on those memories for long.

Although not always a good experience, it certainly was a learning experience, because I saw what addicts do, how they think, and why. And I'll tell you, the number one thing I learned from working there is that the choice an individual makes about whether to use drugs or not boils down to a single word: responsibility.

There, I said it.

Now, I'm sitting here waiting for the backlash from all of you who are thinking, He doesn't know what he's talking about! Addiction is a disease, isn't it? This guy is gonna start blaming those poor people for their addictions. What a bully he is to do such a thing—how politically incorrect, how insensitive!

Silence (as I sit here waiting for you to get over your tantrum).

More silence. Now, are you ready to hear the truth?

We were not allowed to call a spade a spade or a drunk a weak-willed person at the place I worked because the people could not be responsible enough to face up to what they had become.

I heard it all at the Center, as they called it (apparently, the word *hospital* sounded too cruel for the "inmates," another so-called cruel term we were instructed to replace with *residents*). Anyway, the residents spent the day wandering back and forth between talk therapy, music therapy, art therapy, AA meetings, biofeedback sessions, and rap sessions with their "counselors," who in fact were licensed mental health workers (*shrink* was also considered too uncool a term).

In the evenings, the residents were free to mingle and even visit each other in different block buildings, which they often did, having sex freely, shooting dope, smoking weed, and generally behaving as physically violent and personally irresponsible as they did on the streets.

All in all, they had it made. I mean, they could sit there and waste untold amounts of their parents' or relatives' money (or the state's money, if they were involuntary patients, I mean, *residents*). Then when they got out, they could get all the sympathy in the world from their *enabler* (a term for all those people who encourage their habit either willingly or unwillingly by monetary and moral support). Then it would be back to the Center for another year after a crash and burn overdose.

The possibilities for self-pity were endless. In the meanwhile, they didn't have to hold down a job, act responsibly, or contribute to society in any way whatsoever.

Here are some examples of the beauts I dealt with while at the Center.

One time I saw a patient being admitted who was just grouchy, not too much wrong with him. On his second admission, however, all he could do was walk in small circles incessantly, moaning over and over again. He didn't even know his name. No amount of medication could stop him from circling without the possibility of it killing him.

Then there was the man who spent his evenings recruiting followers, going from building to building having sex with all the female addicts. Even though he was very young, overdosing had blown out his mind. He wore a Confederate cap all the time. He got on the wrong side of the officials at the compound when he took a knife and etched an X in the forehead of one young girl. I saw the X myself with the dried blood on it.

Or the pièce de résistance: One evening I was called in by the nursing staff to help wrap up the body of a Demerol addict so we could get him to the morgue. When the curtains were moved aside and I came in to help, I could see the guy was laying on the gurney naked, his body covered from head to toe with huge knots and missing hunks of skin where he had been shooting up the drug for his entire life. He looked like a monster! To this day I cannot get the picture of that terrible waste out of my mind.

So go ahead and use drugs. Use them till they kill you!

But for me, I choose to live responsibly. I've seen enough irresponsibility.

Want some drugs?
No thanks!

C.P. Kaiser
Enough Male Bashing

I often receive e-mail from a female friend whose relationship history can be delicately described as disastrous. Most of her correspondences are sexist, male-bashing jokes that say more about her than any one man. Following is her latest contribution, which, to me, explains why she continually spends Saturday evenings alone.

Top 10 Things That Men Understand About Women
10.
9.
8.
7.
6.
5.
4.
3.
2.
1.
Just smile and pass it on!

This joke contains the right elements of humor: the setup and the twist. It takes the Top Ten list, a familiar source of comedy thanks to David Letterman, and turns it on its head; it leaves it blank.

The joke might be funnier to me if I didn't feel so much sympathy for my friend's pain. After hundreds of jokes about male insensitivity, small penises, and large egos, each joke she sends is like a bottle of scotch in a depressed, angry alcoholic's hand. She's just feeding her addiction to her pain. And she needs to gather as many converts as necessary (hence, the admonition at the end to "Just smile and pass it on!") so that she doesn't have to look at her own part in the myriad of failed relationships that litter her subconscious.

I decided my friend needed an intervention and turned her joke on its head to accentuate some of the more positive attributes gained by men from living with and loving women.

Top 10 Things That Men Understand Because of Women
10. Changing diapers
9. Conflict resolution
8. World peace
7. Facial blotters
6. Compassion for life
5. Separating the whites
4. Walking through a mist of perfume

3. Gentle wash cycle
2. Toilet seat down

And the Number 1 Thing That Men Understand Because of Women is...

1. PMS
Just smile and pass it on!

Scott Stein
A Second Chance

Roberto mumbled at himself for oversleeping as he applied a base of thick, white makeup to his face. The bathroom's tiled floor was cold despite the radiator's knocking rattle, and Roberto, leaning close to the mirror and balancing on his toes, painted a red smile around his lips and high onto his cheeks with broad strokes. With the phone mounted above his kitchenette's pygmy refrigerator, he tried to call Mrs. Johnston to let her know he might be late for Timothy's party, but there was no dial tone. Had he paid the phone bill? Yes. Maybe his check had bounced. Why did they have to shut off his phone every time he missed a couple of payments?

Buttoning a multicolor striped vest over his bright green shirt and grabbing a black bag like the kind doctors used to carry, Roberto ran from his studio apartment down four flights of cracking, marble stairs as fast as his oversized, purple, floppy shoes would let him, and headed for the subway station. If his timing were just right, he could make the party.

Roberto wasn't of Spanish descent, and could claim no ancestry from anywhere more exotic than the Bronx. His real name was Robert Feldbaum and his parents had called him Bob, but he always introduced himself as Roberto. His black hair and olive complexion didn't contradict the name, and he thought, without much evidence to support his theory, that women would be more interested in *Roberto*. Besides, who would hire boring Bob the Clown when they could have Roberto the Clown or, as he sometimes called himself, The Magnificent Roberto?

He was an accountant during the week, but hated working with numbers and couldn't seem to pass the CPA exam though he'd tried for four years running. Roberto would have liked to be a better accountant, and worked hard most of the time, but he secretly desired something more dramatic for his life. He sometimes wished that he had been born to an earlier time, in a different place, when bravery was still tested, where he might have had a chance to be a hero, to do something, anything, exciting. He read World War II spy novels and knew that he would have made a great double agent had he been alive back then. His recurrent dream was of Camelot—riding alongside Arthur into battle on a galloping, armored horse, leading his men to victory over evil. But there were no heroes today, and instead he clowned on weekends for extra money, mostly for birthdays, though he picked up the occasional bar mitzvah and, once, quite by accident, a bachelorette party. His popularity that night had faded rapidly when it was discovered that not only wasn't he happy to see anyone, but it *was* a bicycle horn in his pocket.

Roberto continued to pull items from the black bag and dress himself as he half ran, half shuffled five blocks to the subway, and by the time he reached the station he was done: red wig and nose, water-squirting plastic flower on his lapel, and gray hobo's hat with white plume reaching toward the sky. He searched the inner pocket of his vest for a subway token, found only a handful of balloons, then checked his bag for his wallet, but except for his bicycle horn, a marked deck of cards he used in tricks, and an old pack of sugarfree gum, it was bare. There wasn't time to go back to his apartment—Roberto would have to borrow money for a token from a stranger.

Across the street, patrolling his usual spot next to the staircase leading into the station, was George, a black, bearded man who had lost his legs to a land mine in Vietnam. On the seat of his wheelchair, where his legs should have been, was a brown, paper bag full of fortune cookies. The Chinese restaurant in the middle of the block kept him in good supply in exchange for his absence from their storefront. George handed out cookies and greeted passersby with a smooth, baritone "good morning," though it was already Saturday afternoon. When evening's darkness would come, he could still be found wishing everyone he saw a "good morning," even in the fast-approaching winter, sometimes reciting from his stock of Chinese wisdom to those who dropped bills or heavier coins into his cup and stayed long enough to listen.

"Does anyone have a token they can lend me?" Roberto asked after crossing the street. Dozens of people ignored him as they passed—a few went around him and gave George money, collecting their fortune cookies.

"Remember," George told a man who had given him a dollar, "humanity triumphs over inhumanity the way water triumphs over fire. One drop at a time."

The crowd grew thick and Roberto still had no token. The train would be in soon, and he had to be on it. "Please," he shouted, "can't someone lend me money for a token? I'm going to be late for a birthday party."

No one stopped for him.

"All people have a heart which cannot bear the suffering of others," George said to a woman as he handed her a cookie, then smiled wide and yellow and said, "Thank you, and God bless."

I'm going about this all wrong, Roberto thought. He blew up a long, pink balloon, twisted it into a poodle, and handed it to a little girl who was walking by. The girl's mother smacked him in the shoulder with her pocketbook and yelled, "Stay away from her!" She grabbed the balloon from her daughter's hands and threw it to the ground. Roberto picked it up and dusted it off.

"Balloon animals for fifty cents," he announced. "Get your balloon animals before they're gone."

"Hey," George said, "cut that out. You can't do that here."

"I'll be out of your way in just a minute," Roberto said, then to the passing people, "Just fifty cents per balloon. It's a steal." He inflated and manipulated an orange balloon into a giraffe.

"Get your own corner, clown," George said, pushing himself up against Roberto and snatching the giraffe from his hands.

"Give me that," Roberto said, and pulled at the balloon giraffe's head.

George locked the wheels of his chair and tugged on one of the giraffe's legs. Roberto tripped over his own floppy shoe and fell into George, toppling with him to the ground. Roberto landed on the bag of fortune cookies, crushing them, and George tumbled from his chair.

"You want to fight me? I'll get you! Don't think I won't!" George screamed as he dragged himself to his chair on its side.

Roberto had scraped the palm of his left hand but was otherwise unhurt. He knelt to help George who, still screaming, tried to punch him before losing his balance and falling to the ground again.

Someone yelled, "That clown just hit George!" Another joined in, "He decked that cripple!"

A loose circle of people had formed around Roberto, George, the balloon giraffe and poodle, the bag of crushed fortune cookies, and the upset wheelchair. Roberto was about to explain when he heard his train pulling in below. He grabbed his feathered hat and black bag and charged at the people blocking the station's entrance. They fought each other to get out of his way and he had a clear path to the stairs. His sudden ferocity must have frightened them, because no one followed him down. Roberto dodged the people who had exited the train and were working their way up the stairs. He hurdled the turnstile and skipped onto the subway car just before the doors slid closed.

There were about twenty people in the car, and Roberto rested on a plastic seat and tried to catch his breath. The tunnel's evenly spaced lights sped by as the train gained momentum. Roberto was glad he'd decided to run when he had. Nothing good could have come from staying there, and he didn't think anyone would have been much interested in his explanation. There was nothing Roberto could have done for George. It was just an unfortunate accident, a misunderstanding. He had to get it out of his mind, get on with his day. A shaking, flustered clown wasn't what Mrs. Johnston was expecting for Timothy's birthday.

At least Roberto would make the party. If he made this one and found one for next weekend he could catch up. He was going to cut his credit cards in half as soon as he finished using them to pay each other off. The train stopped with a screech and a few people disembarked. A frail, old man in a beige coat carrying two clear plastic bags entered and sat across from Roberto. There were two melons in them, a quart of skim milk, cans of cat food, and a head of lettuce. The train was on its way again, picking up speed as it rounded a turn. Roberto's stop was after the next one.

Three boys, the oldest no more than 15, walked over to the man as he reviewed his grocery receipt. One of them sat next to him, the other two blocked Roberto's view. The boy in the seat spoke softly to him, and Roberto heard only the old man's answer: "I spent it all at the grocery." There was more whispering and Roberto heard him again: "Please don't..."

"Leave him alone," Roberto said, but got no reaction.

One of the boys yanked a plastic bag away from the man, who begged now, "Take it all, but leave me Oscar's food. Please."

Roberto stood. "I said leave him alone," but was again ignored.

He pointed his bicycle horn at them and honked twice. The two boys turned around and the third, the whisperer, got up from his seat.

"Mind your business, clown," he said.

"He isn't bothering anyone," Roberto said. "Leave him alone."

"How 'bout I wipe that smile off your face, huh, clown?"

They had Roberto surrounded now. A few people at the other end of the car went through the connecting door to the next car, but no one came to help. The whisperer boy punched at Roberto's head, and when he ducked to avoid being hit, the other two jumped Roberto and dragged him to the floor. They rolled around once, slamming into the chrome pole in the middle of the car. The whisperer, still standing, kicked Roberto in the ribs, and again, and the other boys threw punches and kicked wildly, and Roberto curled up and covered his head with his hands, blocking his face with his forearms.

Seeing that he wasn't fighting back, they got off of Roberto and took the two bags of groceries from the man. Roberto didn't move or open his eyes. Maybe they would leave if he pretended he was unconscious, or dead. His desire to look at them, to get up and defend the old man, wasn't quite forgotten, but Roberto squeezed his eyes closed and held his breath. One of them laughed, picked up the bicycle horn, and tossed a can of cat food into Roberto's overturned hat. The train stopped at the next station and the boys scrambled off, smashing the melons, lettuce, and milk on the ground, honking the horn and shouting as they headed for the stairs.

Seconds later the train was on its way again, this time to Roberto's stop. He was shaking and nauseous, his hat's plume had snapped in two, he had a bruise above his right eye, and his side hurt like hell, but Roberto didn't think he'd suffered any serious damage. Maybe a broken rib; it was hard to tell. He pulled himself up and sat on the plastic seat. Red streaks of no-streak makeup ran down his face from the upturned corners of his smile.

The old man didn't look at him or say a word, and only stared blankly out the window into the darkness, his lower lip quivering. No one approached their end of the car. The train pulled into the station and the doors opened. Roberto retrieved his black bag, put on his hat with its half of a feather, and, placing the can of cat food on the seat beside the old man, exited the train.

Roberto returned from the party as evening settled in, the makeup scrubbed from his face, the hobo's hat, red wig, and nose in his black bag. Concentrating at the party had been impossible (not one card trick had worked and the kids couldn't have cared less for balloon animals), but at least Timothy's mother had paid in cash. His ribs were sore, but all day he could only think about George, lying on the sidewalk next to his wheelchair, screaming with the rage of helplessness. Roberto couldn't convince himself that their tussle was inevitable, and played the scene over in his mind, trying to imagine it taking place differently. There must have been something he could have done, some way to avoid conflict, and he was angry with himself for not finding it. He emerged from the station into the early December dusk, his ears stinging almost immediately from the chill of the wind.

He saw George across the street, handing out cookies and holding out his cup, and Roberto let out a restrained sigh, wincing as he breathed in again. He smiled at his luck: finding George here, still here. It wasn't often people got a second chance, and Roberto knew it. He could make things right.

At the salad bar of the grocery just up the block, Roberto filled a container with steaming tomato soup. He clamped the lid tight, grabbed a plastic spoon and a wrapped cracker, and paid at the register. Maybe he hadn't saved the old man on the train, maybe he wasn't really a hero, but he could still be one today. Roberto remembered George's earlier words, and he thought, with pride in the species as well as himself, that humanity could still triumph over inhumanity. He crossed the street with his offering, with his flimsy Styrofoam bowl of tomato soup in its paper bag, and handed it to George. George rested the bag on his seat and removed the soup and the spoon.

"Thank you, sir. God bless," he said.

"I just wanted you to know," Roberto said, quietly, but distinctly, "that what happened today was an accident ... I'm sorry."

George didn't at first understand. He squinted as he glanced at Roberto's floppy shoes and striped vest and black bag, then looked up at Roberto. A thin smile of recognition, of redemption, flashed across George's face, and he unsealed the container of tomato soup.

"Thank you," he said, and flipped the hot soup up at Roberto. It splashed Roberto's shoulder and splattered lightly onto his neck. Then George threw the empty container and plastic spoon at Roberto and said, "Go kill yourself."

Roberto pulled his vest and shirt off and wiped his neck dry. His shoulder felt hot, his neck prickly, but most of the soup had missed him, and he didn't think he was burned badly. He thought of striking George, of smacking him in the head until he begged for forgiveness. Roberto wanted to drag him from his chair, to stuff him in a garbage can, to take the fury of today and shove it right down George's throat.

Instead, with great effort and a sense of higher purpose, Roberto turned and half walked, half shuffled cold and bare-chested the five blocks back to his studio apartment, carrying his shirt and vest and telling himself the whole way home, one drop at a time.

Ari McKee
Supreme Being, Your Party Is Waiting for You at Baggage Claim

After a couple of years ensconced in the holy sacrament of marriage, I'm finally beginning to understand my husband's religion. We have a mixed marriage—Jewish and Catholic. Together we picked one religion to commit to and base our lives on, the sacred center of our moral compass. But there's one catch—we won't tell anyone what it is. Not even the kids. They have to guess.

So, it's not the Star-of-David-on-top-of-the-Christmas-tree kind of conflict. It's the other religious tradition that I'm having trouble interpreting—the mysterious rituals, the ironclad commandments, and the exhaustive pilgrimages he makes over and over again. It's not anything the Vatican dreamed up, and you won't find it in any spiritual text. The sacred cow pie we keep stepping in at our house is nothing less than the Holy Land itself: the airport.

This is my side of it: I believe that most people who have the money and time to fly somewhere can figure out how to get themselves to the flying place and back again. End of story.

In my husband's opinion, airplane trips are like outpatient surgery. One needs to be driven there and back, for free, by a relative, no matter what. But that's only the beginning. I think the original Sexton family scripture reads: Thou shalt greet thy cousins at the portal from which they came forth out of their DC-9, not at the place wherein their baggage waiteth, for that is not pleasing to the Lord. Not from the lane of loading outside the Holy Hangar, for that is not pleasing to the Lord. And not from within the ramp of parking, lo, not even in the spot nearest the elevator, because that is way not pleasing to the Lord.

To my husband, denying someone a ride to the airport would be like saying, "Your flying great distances means nothing to me," or "Our kinship is doubtful." It's as bad as saying, in his language, "I don't much feel like being your pallbearer because I'd rather not drive all the way out to the cemetery. There's a hockey game on." It's a bitch slap, man.

So, day or night, he drives 'em. If I'm not home, he'll load up our sleeping children and drive deep into the dark multi-leveled maze of loading and dropping and standing. He'll be forced to park acres away from the terminal in a cold, concrete hell, and then he'll have to drag the kids in and drape their little bodies over internationally unsanitary black vinyl lawn chairs. There he sits, wiping noses, buying three-dollar candy bars, and waiting out a late arrival for some cruddy, ungrateful, able-bodied nephew with a healthy allowance who took the first flight out after finals and charged it to his dad's credit card.

My own sister doesn't call me from the airport unless she's been mugged by a pack of wilding skycaps. She knows she'd hear "What? They don't have overnight parking anymore?" because that's exactly what she'd say to me.

Believe me, it's a mixed marriage. Jesus, schmesus—this airport thing is like a knife in our hearts.

Once—only once—I didn't pick him up. It was late. The baby was sleeping. I was home with a head cold. He'd only been to Chicago for the weekend. It wasn't like his three-month Mount Everest expedition had finally come home, with only four survivors out of the original nine. It was a seminar, for God's sake, an embroidery seminar, if you need to know. It's a seventy-minute flight. He had a ride with his co-worker. He had a ride, oh God, sweet Jesus, please, he had a ride, I thought it was OK.

It was definitely not OK. And I was reminded about the one thing I forgot about Catholics: They enjoy sex as much as the next person, but they can go for a long time—I mean a long time—without it. They're like sex camels, man.

So, we compromise a little bit every day. I'm there if he even does a standing long jump. *I am there.* And he has realized that I won't be scheduling my life around his mother's *Golf Across America* tours or his brother's *Working Is For Suckers* ski trips. We try to meet halfway. And if, God willing, he ends up a fallen-away Airportian, one of those lapsed souls who only show their faces on slow football weekends and holidays—then, praise Kali, I'll have done my job.

Jason Stein
Taxed to the Max

On every paycheck you get, they take out City tax, State tax, and Federal tax. Then on April 15th, you have to pay Federal tax *again*!

What if you're born on April 15th—do you have to pay a Birthday tax? This is unconstitutional, not to mention annoying. There's got to be some kind of double-triple-quadruple jeopardy magna-carta pro-quo clause somewhere.

When you buy food there's a Food tax and when you buy clothing there's a Clothing tax. If you own your home you have to pay a Real Estate tax, and for the land underneath your home, a Property tax. If you own too big a home you have to pay a Luxury tax, and if you have too many rooms in the home, a Mansion tax. If you take too deep a breath, there's a Deep-Breath tax. If you have too many possessions, you have to pay an Envy-Screw-You-Wish-It-Were-Mine tax.

If you want to travel across this great country you have to pay a Travel tax. If you take trips out of your country, then return to your country, you have to pay a Re-Enter tax. The only safe places are those duty-free shops. These should be franchised out.

Oh, don't forget the Franchise tax.

They warn you about staying in the sun too long, not because too much sun is bad for you—they're thinking of the Sunburn tax. Don't have too good a time, or you'll have to pay an Over-Enjoyment tax.

If you park your car on the street, you have to put money in the meter. You're just borrowing a little piece of land for a certain length of time. You have to pay a Please-Can-I-Stay-Here-For-A-While tax. And if you fail to pay this tax someone will take your car away. A meter is nothing more than a satellite tax office.

If you're fortunate enough to have an estate or some inheritance for your children or future generations, watch out for an Estate tax and Inheritance tax. And when we drop the "E" in Estate tax, we find out that the E*state* tax is really just another State tax.

I say remove the "T" from T*ax* and work with an *ax* instead. Let's ax everything.

Jody Lane
Recipe for Holiday Peace

INGREDIENTS
12 hours of football
11 turkey experts
10 idiot uncles
9 whining babies
8 neo-Nazis
7 sassy adolescents
6 religious fanatics
5 Marilyn Manson look-alikes
4 bitching aunts
3 illegal aliens
2 kissing cousins, and
1 really sharp object

C.P. Kaiser and Scott Stein
To email or Not to e-mail

The following was taken from a series of e-mails between **C.P. KAISER** *and* **SCOTT STEIN**, *the two people responsible for editing all of the writing that appears on* When Falls the Coliseum. *Both have worked as professional editors; hence, both know more than anything how little they know about the English language. The below might seem like nitpicking to our readers not engaged in writing and editing, but agonizing over these decisions is part of what online editors do in this brave new world of the Internet, when they aren't working at their real jobs and downloading naked photos of Bea Arthur.*

SCOTT STEIN: House style will be *Web site* and *e-mail*. *Web* is uppercase because there is only one Web, just like there is only one Internet. It is therefore a proper noun. The non-hyphenated *email* is also incorrect. A hyphen is needed. Computer programs like MS Word and sites like Yahoo! are recognizing *email* as correct in a misguided effort to make their lingo part of the larger language and society, ignoring grammatical precedents in the process.

C.P. KAISER: Back in the old days, all nouns were capitalized. That stopped sometime in the 1800s. *Web* and *Internet* are new terms and as such are being capitalized. But I suspect that in time (hopefully sooner than a century) they will not be capitalized, and I am in favor of pushing that agenda ahead.

Concerning house style, I want to engage you in conversation here, not force any of my preferences on you (as if anyone could force anything on you). Even well respected publications differ in house style. I'm all for creating a consistent house style, but when you say that *email* is incorrect, I would say that our house style prefers the hyphenated version. At a previous job, after consulting *The Chicago Manual of Style* and the *Associated Press Style Book,* we (four editors) decided to go with a small *w* in *web* and no hyphen in *email.* Were we incorrect? No, because it became our house style. (If we were incorrect, at least we were consistent.)

If you have any reservations, just remember that this is the web, a very new, very different, and very fast-changing form of communication. The rules are being made and changed continually. Of course, that does not give us license to be careless. I'm not suggesting that. I guess I'm only suggesting that we don't have to follow AP or the *New York Times* because this is different. It's ours. It belongs to the people.

SS: I don't want to be a slave to AP or anyone else's rules either. I think there is good reason to keep the hyphen in *e-mail.* An excellent explanation of this and other matters can be found at Bill Walsh's www.theslot.com. This is what he said about *e-mail:*

> No initial-based term in the history of the English language has ever evolved to form a solid word—a few are split, and

the rest are hyphenated. Look at A-frame, B-movie, C-rations, D-Day, E- (uh, skip that one), F layer, G-string, H-bomb, I-beam, J-school, K car, L-shaped, N-word, O-ring, Q rating, S-connector, T-bill, U-joint, X-ray, Y-chromosome, Z particle and dozens of other such compounds. It doesn't even look right; at first glance, email (the French word for *enamel*, by the way) begs to be pronounced with a schwa (*UH-mail* or maybe even *uh-MAIL*). Setting the letter apart makes it clear that the letter is a letter. *E! E! Eeeeeee!*

So, CPK, if language is like law, with evolving principles based on precedent, not using the hyphen in *e-mail* is incorrect, especially if consistency is desired. Preserving the hyphen helps to convey the word's meaning. It also aids the eye in reading and the tongue in pronunciation. Mail is a separate concept from *e*, or electronic, and there are and will be many more e-things. Removing the hyphen from one will lead to removing it from all eventually. I think this would result in a whole mess of words that become hard to read and understand at first glance: *ecommerce, etrade, elaw* are all hard to read. The e serves a useful purpose.

On to *Web* vs. *web*. If there were many internets, I would lose the uppercase *I*. However, if there is only one Internet, it is incorrect to write *internet*, unless we are writing about a hypothetical situation in which there are many, or more than one, internets. Using a lowercase *i* is like writing *april* to mean the month, when *April* is the name of a specific thing. There are many cars, but only one company called Mercedes. But you know all this.

The question is what does *Web site* mean. There is only one Web, like one Internet (they are the same thing, aren't they?). I see *website* as one word a lot more than *email*, and it doesn't bother me as much, because it seems to be referring more to any one of many generic sites, and less to the Web. Still, I don't see why *Web* isn't referring to a one-of-a-kind item. Therefore, it should be uppercase.

For all of these, I am trying to use reason, make the site easy to read and understand, be internally consistent, and be somewhat in line with accepted usage. As you said in "Getting Laid Was Never So Easy" (p. 222), people not knowing the thinking behind your choice of spelling and usage might think you unschooled. I am not insecure enough to really care, but I tend to buck the Establishment with care and good reason. The site is a showcase for our writing, and we do not want to seem unschooled, though we've obviously given this more thought than some of those who might misjudge us. We also have an obligation to the writers we edit to not make them seem unschooled either. They might not share your agenda of shaping the language at the expense of reputation.

CPK: I don't fully agree that language is like law in that it evolves solely on precedent. I think it's much more malleable than that and evolves on usage as well. Law seems to get ever more complicated, whereas language seems to evolve into a simpler form, because, based on the laws of entropy, everything in the universe eventually slows down, including people's mouths.

I believe the origins of the prefix *co* are from the word *common*, shortened to *com*, then to *co*, meaning *with*. Words such as *coordinate, coworker,* and *cooperate* rarely appear with hyphens (although I have seen it so). I purposely picked these three examples because they could easily be hyphenated for the reader's better comprehension at first glance. I would actually prefer co-worker to be hyphenated. But my point is that over time, hyphenated words lose their novelty and become regular words. The hyphen serves as a blinking red light, warning us of a new use of a word. I admit, my logic is akin to someone asking why he should make his bed when he's just going to sleep in it again tonight. I am asking why use the hyphen now when time will dissolve its use anyway.

At one small publishing house where I worked, I was always searching for space for editorial, so I got into the habit of making decisions for house style based on what would give me a few more picas of space, such as *email* without a hyphen and area codes without parentheses. I guess since the Internet is infinite, we don't need to worry about each pica.

I do agree that the spate of e-words would be better served with a hyphen—all but *email*, only because of its common usage, or *co-usage* (ha ha). As far as my worry expressed in "Getting Laid" about being perceived as unschooled when using less accepted grammatical variations, yes, it's a problem if I am pandering to pedantic pubs that are anal about that stuff.

The Web is different and we are all in on the ground floor of its creation. We don't have to let the status quo rule our every comma or hyphen. Again, I'm not advocating anarchy, just the refreshing pleasure of enjoying something new and recognizing that language is so fluid that it changes on a daily basis. Shakespeare, the acknowledged greatest dramatist ever, has various spellings of the same words from manuscript to manuscript. That bastard had fun!

SS: *E* is different from *co* since *e* is a letter that represents a word. But eventually, and it seems *eventually* in this case means soon, *e* might be like *co* and lose the hyphen. Even if this is true, the hyphen is a necessary and useful phase. If common usage will strip away the hyphen, I see no need for us to push common usage in that direction too quickly. Many people in this country, and abroad, are not yet on the Internet, so it is premature to force the hyphen out. When the language has naturally ejected the hyphen because it is no longer needed or widely used, I will change along with it.

You are probably right that the language will change more rapidly than in the past. It will not take another hundred years. That is not necessarily a good thing. Our being involved so intimately with both language and the Internet does not mean that most people are. Of course, the dictionary can be stuffy and slow to recognize these changes, but I think erring on the side of caution is warranted. Let's not force things. Common usage will do what it is going to do without our help.

A word about Shakespeare: His greatness is due to his beautiful use of language and his genius as a dramatist. He is not revered for his spelling, or his inconsistency. If you are to make your mark as a writer, it will probably not be due to your use of a hyphen, or lack thereof.

CPK: I agree with just about everything you've been saying. I think where we diverge is on how fast each one of us is willing to let change happen. Shakespeare did not wait for words to come into existence. He coined them when he needed them. His beautiful use of language includes all the new words he "forced" into existence. If he had waited for Christopher Marlowe or Ben Johnson to OK his coinage, the Renaissance in England might have been delayed a century or two. I'm advocating not waiting for the rhythms of change to happen to us, but to be an active participant in that dance.

You're willing to err on the side of caution. I'm willing to force the change, push the grammatical envelope. So, in the interest of the English language, care to dance?

SS: Thanks for the offer, but at the moment my dance card is full. For now, the editorial risks we take will be in content. As a writer, I desire to communicate clearly, be understood, and be remembered for the power of my writing and ideas. Let our readers continue to enjoy what our writers are saying and how well they are saying it, without the distraction of any grammatical agenda. House style will be *Web site* and *e-mail.*

CPK: As usual, the visionary must dance alone. So be it. Cue the band, please. . . .

Ari McKee
Help for the Reluctantly Human

There are animal *lovers* and then there are animal *people*. You may be a pet owner, you may be a Sierra Club member, and you may even own a copy of *Free Willy* and be the adoptive mother of a Tibetan yak. But unless you've stepped over the line, unless you view your fellow humans as, well, *not* your fellows, then you're not an animal person.

You've undoubtedly met an animal person—like the vet tech who lovingly fondled your arthritic old housecat and listened, astonished, as you rejected his offer to clean the doddering hairbag's teeth for $450. Or the niece who saw a picture of you in a dyed fox fur and now prefers any other family member (even smelly Uncle Carl) to you. We've all listened to somebody's diatribe on declawing or pinch collars or kennels; and nary a soul has missed hearing the sorriest shampooed bunny story, the ongoing veal/calf tragedy, or the plight of the poultry.

Animal people are out there, all right. They've made some changes in the world, but you can't really say they've been successful as a cultural revolution. In fact, the opposite is true: They're widely ridiculed and ignored, even by die-hard dog lovers like Queen Elizabeth. It's not that we all secretly enjoy electrocuting squirrels with car batteries. No, as a matter of fact, most people love animals.

So what is the problem then? Well, I've been analyzing the animal folks' tactics and I've decided there are myriad reasons why they're monologue magnets instead of revolutionary heroes.

Here's some free credibility advice for the PETA/ASPCA crowd:

1. The first problem is animal rights activists try to talk with people when it's perfectly obvious they don't really *like* people. All the *high-functioning* animal folks are probably in *management*. That's as good as it gets! We get the guy with the "Jesus Was a Vegetarian" (www.JesusVeg.com) tattoo and a full hemp ensemble, the guy who breeds ferrets to save up for Grolights, the guy our dogs badly want a piece of—on our front porch. Is this the face of animal rights? Look, guys, meat is *in*. Can bullfighting be far behind? *You need a sustainable offense!*

2. Forget the celebrities: Bridget Bardot, Doris Day, Chrissie Hynde—all those nutty dog ladies. While we may go see their act at the Mirage, we're not going to sign their petition. Why? Because we know they're nuts. We know they sleep in a great big bed covered with dog hair and feed their mutts out of those thirty-dollar stands that hold the food bowls up to dog-head level. What a rip-off. Answer me this—who props up the dead antelopes so wolves don't have to bend their heads down while they're disemboweling? Helpful badgers?

3. Give up already on the fur thing. Who came up with that issue? "Hey, I know! Let's alienate all the people whom we're absolutely, positively *sure* have lots of money—stylish, influential women with cash." How smart is that? Besides, the argument is kind of lame—why is it worse to kill animals and use their skins than to just to kill them like at the pound? And another thing—why, exactly, is leather OK and fur isn't? Clarification, people.

4. While we're clarifying, let's have a moratorium on lab animal freeings. Everybody knows that most of the lucky parolees of the last well-publicized release left their cages and met their Maker within an hour. Ten quiet years of climate-controlled, well-lit, predictable daily mouse life finished off in thirteen minutes of sheer, hysterical, primal, skittering panic. There's just no positive spin to something like that.

5. In your favor: people *want* to like animals. In *Generation X*, Douglas Coupland calls the phenomenon "bambification." *Dumbo, Sounder, The Secret of NIMH.* Disney and the like have been making us look askance at our steaks for forty years. But now that the activists are taking over, now that there's an official, sanctioned animal rights movement, now that the participants in said movement are the new synonym for "wacko," suddenly everybody's on all-meat diets. Butchers can't keep up with the demand. Coincidence? How could you have let animal sympathy deteriorate so far that nobody is interested in suffering bunnies anymore? This is *not* a hard sell, people. My guess is you're simply pains in the collective meat-eating asses.

6. Save *yourselves*. Hire an actor, a people person, a real personality with a capital *P*. Somebody unknown but good, who makes everyone—even the most rabid rat-releaser among you—feel warm all over. Then pay that guy to be your full-time rep in an exclusive contract, pay him to explain to the general society how you're all a bunch of very nice people who don't want to disrupt the medical trials for little Jimmy's diabetes medication, who don't want us to send back the sausage sampler Grandma gave us for Christmas, and who don't have any immediate plans to liberate the llama exhibit at the State Fair. Just don't pick George Hamilton. He looks like an overdone piece of meat.

In conclusion, stop acting like kids whose 4-H calf just got loaded onto the cattle truck. You really don't have a bad case, but your image needs to be euthanized. Oh, and keep your scary, earnest, vegan animal people and their clipboards off my porch. They're scaring the dogs.

Helen Cates
The Empty Bed

I was driving through the neighborhood when I spotted a cardboard sign propped on the hood of a car. The front door of the house was ajar and people were already milling about. It was an estate sale.

I parked across the street and grabbed my purse. Adrenaline already pumped through my veins. The house was a modest white bungalow in bad need of repair. The yard itself was barren of flowers and attention. By the time I stepped through the foyer, I had already guessed that the resident had been an elderly male. Estate sales can tell a lot about a person.

The gentleman had apparently passed on. Everything was price tagged, personal effects were up for sale—even the paintings adorning the wall. Haste hung over the room like a boiling cloud. Someone wanted the house cleaned out, and quickly.

I stopped to browse at the bookcase. There were ancient leather-bound books and dainty figurines. Either he or his wife had loved to read. I wondered, as I pulled each dusty book from its spot, how long his wife had been dead. He must have missed her. She obviously was gifted with the needle. Embroidered doilies were draped over the furniture. An old worn photo of a young sailor hugging his sweetheart slipped out of one of the books. She was radiant in her bouncy curls and sweater. Was it them? I slipped the photo back into its place and headed for the hallway. The linen closet was open wide and I made a mental note to come back and browse.

The kitchen was a mess. I was surprised to find dirty dishes stacked in the sink.

"If you need any help, I will be in the other room."

I glanced up at the smiling man. He appeared to be in his mid-forties and looked familiar. It dawned on me—he was related somehow to the sailor in the photograph. I mumbled a thank you and continued to dig and sort. I was making quite a racket as I dug through the cabinets.

It looked as if someone were still living in the home. There were hard-boiled eggs soaking in a pan of water. The butter had been left out. I snuck a quick peek in the refrigerator: milk, half a cantaloupe, not-quite-wilted lettuce. Maybe he had died suddenly. I spotted a roasting pan and held it under my arms.

In a bedroom I was greeted by huge smiles and warmth from a photo of the sailor and his sweetheart. It was a vision of matrimony and love contained in a beautifully carved frame. Children and grandchildren were scattered about, each contained in their own special frames. On the table beside the bed there was a cup with a teabag string dangling from its side. There were crumbs—someone had eaten a cracker.

The bed's blankets were pulled back—someone had recently slept there. There were even brown slippers at the side of the bed. I stood there momentarily, eyeing the teacup. I was starting to feel strangely uncomfortable.

The relative appeared in the doorway and was accompanied by another man. They were discussing the closet's contents and I couldn't help but eavesdrop.

"Yes, we need to clear this all out by the end of the day."

The other man kneeled at some boxes and began to attach some more price tags.

The relative kept glancing at his watch. He wore a crisp polo shirt and white cotton shorts. He probably had a golf game. "Now, that box right there is for Dad. He only needs a few undershirts. We can take it to the nursing home later tonight."

The man checked his watch again. I glanced back at the bed. I pictured the elderly man being yanked from his sleep. I wondered if the sheets were still warm. What was he thinking right now? Did he know that strangers were walking through his house?

I was still clutching the roasting pan in my arms. It grew heavy. I placed it on the dresser.

I hastily exited the house. Never had my hands felt so dirty.

Scott Stein
Keep (All) Your Laws Off My Body

Supporters of abortion rights often position themselves as defenders of liberty. Self-determination and personal freedom demand choice, they say. After all, a woman's body belongs only to herself, not to any government official and not to fellow citizens or the god they worship.

One of the main arguments used against pro-lifers is that it is not scientifically possible, at least for now, to determine precisely when a fetus becomes sentient—able to feel and aware of being alive. When does it become a thinking being, with all the rights of any thinking being? Clearly, sentience is not present in a mass of cells in the days following conception.

If a mass of cells cannot think nor feel, what makes pro-lifers call abortion, even at this early stage, murder? It is usually the religious belief in a soul that supports the call for a ban on *all* abortions. God created life and gave the mass of cells a soul, the argument goes, so it is a human being with full rights. Of course, this logic does not sway people who do not believe in gods or souls, or who have different views of what exactly god might be.

Let's not let this essay degenerate into the usual, tired debate over abortion—believe it or not, this isn't even about abortion rights or the lack thereof. The reason I bring all of this up is that the main objection many have to pro-lifers is that no government body should be able to impose the deeply held philosophical or religious views of some people on other people. Creating laws for everyone based on religious morality seems to violate the spirit of the separation of church and state valued by so many. We see bumper stickers that say, "Keep your laws off my body" and "Keep your rosaries off my ovaries." In other words, the pro-choice contingent is saying, your right to believe in religious or philosophical morality is *your* right, but the government should have no right to impose your morality on others who might not share that religious morality.

Many people who are pro-choice for just the above reason also support current taxation policies that take money from some people in order to help others who have less money. Perhaps they do not realize the hypocrisy of holding both positions—hence the need for this essay. Am I saying that imposing taxes on the rich and the not-so-rich to help feed the poor is the same attack on personal freedom, on the principle of the separation of church and state, as banning abortions? Yes, I am. Just as imposed prayer in school or censorship or imposed attitudes on abortion can be seen as the government forcing the morality and religious views of some people on others, so too is the taxation of some to help others an imposition of morality and a religious view by the government.

Unfortunately, anyone who suggests that citizens are overtaxed is automatically called uncaring, as if the government ought to be able to force people to care. You're about to accuse me of being a heartless bastard who wants to see poor people starve. But you don't know me or what I think about the poor, or what I might choose to do to help those in need. The key word here is *choose*. Caring about the poor, or feeding the hungry, is a moral act, a choice. If there is no choice, there is no moral act. By forcing people to help others, our government has denied them the right to even experience the goodness of choosing to be generous and caring. This is a prime cause of both the disconnection so many feel from fellow citizens and the increasing resentment and lack of civility in everyday life.

But the larger issue is one of principle. The values of personal freedom and the control of one's body should resonate with everyone who supports a woman's right to choose an abortion. People who desire to help others do so out of deep philosophical or religious convictions. It is a matter of morality. If by chance some people do not share those convictions, and the government makes them support those convictions anyway, isn't that imposing moral beliefs? Taking money from those who have earned it and redistributing it to those who have not earned it is a violation of personal freedom, and forces some people to be slaves for the moral beliefs of others—some people work 6 out of 12 months just to pay taxes. If the result of the labor of one's mind and body are not one's own—if it belongs without consent to others—then one does not have the right to self-determination of his or her own body. Remember what the bumper sticker says.

Can anyone explain what rational, non-religious principle makes people responsible for the welfare of complete strangers? After citizens have paid enough taxes to cover all of the services they use, what makes those citizens responsible for paying for so many other people? Because they can afford it? What does that have to do with anything? Isn't it their money? Didn't they earn it? If they did not earn it but stole the money, prosecute them. If they earned it, it is theirs and the government has no right to it.

To many people, the right to choose an abortion, even if they oppose abortions for themselves, is an important issue of self-determination and personal freedom; so too is the right to live according to whatever religion they choose, or without religion. Self-determination and freedom also include the right to be free from the morality of the secular religions of economic equality and socialism. The next time you accuse the holier-than-thou crowd of trying to impose its morality on you, think about how your vote imposes your morality on others. Valuing freedom is an either-or proposition. There is no such thing as benign tyranny.

David "Preacher" Slocum
**Screw Who You Want,
But Shoot Who We Tell You**

With a strong economy, no Evil Empire to rally against, and a presidential election sneaking up on us, the controversy over gays in the military has surfaced again in recent political debates, antics, and speeches by our prospective candidates. Some favor opening the military to the openly gay, some hate the idea and want to close the doors, but most agree that the Don't Ask, Don't Tell policy initiated by the Clinton administration is not working. The plan was flawed from the beginning, implemented poorly, and has caused more problems than it has solved.

Some people claim that homosexuals are a disruptive influence and that the outright ban should be restored. Unit cohesion and trust between unit members are absolutely necessary—unlike most civil employees, the people serving in the military might be asked to face situations the rest of America cannot even understand. The job description includes possibly killing, or dying, or both, a pressure not experienced by your average banker. Reliance on fellow members of a unit is crucial, so it is a fair question: Are homosexuals a disruptive influence?

If the majority of a given outfit are homophobic or have religious or moral objections to homosexuals, then yes, they can be a disruptive influence to unit cohesion. But if the majority of the truly disruptive behavior tends to be among a portion of the more religious and homophobic people who show little tolerance, who is to blame for the disruption—gay people or those who refuse to accept them?

Homosexuals are like most of us in that they eat the same things, breathe the same air, and put their pants on one leg at a time. The difference is in their choice of bed partners. Do we oust the homosexuals because they are different or enforce discipline among the dissenters? Keep in mind that the military is NOT a democracy and can never be one. Even if the majority of soldiers are against serving with gay people, should that have any bearing on the policy? At one time, many members of the military might have been opposed to serving with blacks, and many "intellectuals" made the same argument—that integration would be disruptive, that white soldiers wouldn't accept them, and the military would lose efficiency as a result. The military, of course, is not weaker because of integration, and we tend to look back at those who campaigned against racial integration as ignorant.

Retired Infantry Colonel turned columnist Warren H. (Sandy) Anderson wrote, "Nor should we put recognized gay men in showers with heterosexual men." The Colonel's homophobic tendencies aside, he seems to be proposing separate shower facilities for each sexual orientation. It would be fiscally irresponsible for the U.S. military to construct separate and equal bathing facilities for each and every sexual subgroup that exists: one for straight men, one for gay; one for straight women, one for lesbian; a separate shower for each and every bisexual person. What is the logical solution to this quandary?

I think that all boundaries should be erased. I believe that the military should mandate communal showers for all sexes and sexual orientations—men, women, and every variation in between, showering and living together. What could be fairer than that? The military teaches that there is only one color, green (or gray for the navy and blue for the air force) among soldiers. Why not teach that equality in all areas?

What can the military do about the larger problem of discrimination against gays, minorities, women, redheads, and people with zits? The truth of the matter is that every group has its close-minded bigots. There are people who won't like you because you are black, or gay, or redheaded, or Catholic. It happens. Is it right? No, but that's life.

Most of these prejudicial attitudes are brought on by ignorance. Putting diverse groups of people with different backgrounds and beliefs together and getting them to work as a team is what the military does best. The military forces people from every walk of life, every racial and ethnic background, into the same mold, that of a soldier. The system generally works, as evidenced by recent polls that show minorities in the military are the least likely in our society to feel discriminated against and the most likely to feel that they are judged by actions, not skin color or religion.

At its best, the military is about honor, self-confidence, and trust. Clinton's Don't Ask, Don't Tell policy undermines the basic values that are taught to every recruit from the first day they arrive at boot camp. It tells homosexuals that they must live a lie, that they must hide their orientation from others lest they be pulled from their units and ostracized. The military teaches its personnel to be true to themselves and to be honest with each other. Trust is critical between you and the person next to you in battle. Teaching new recruits that they are supposed to lie about something as silly as what makes them horny is just plain stupid. If it is OK to lie about something that unimportant, why isn't it OK to lie about whether you completed the maintenance on that tank, or that rifle?

I don't care any more about having gays in the military than I do about having people from Montana. Clinton should have just ordered the military to accept it and deal with whatever issues came up. It might have been messy for a while but it would have happened and it would be over by now. The bottom line is this: Soldiers follow orders, even those they don't like, but give a soldier a suggestion and he will most likely tell you to go fly a kite.

Robert O'Hara
Six Innings of Freedom

Calvin Williams had loved life, but couldn't enjoy it. As a preacher's son, he spent his youth giving to the Westhill Christian Ministry. Pious standards were unrewarding, charity was futile, so he cheated and stole from the community, until fear controlled his life. There was no freedom for Calvin, so he went to jail where there was at least an end.

Calvin was released twice in four years, only to break his parole both times. The third time he was released to John Burke, a man known for keeping people like Calvin out of jail. Burke invited Calvin to a Yankee game after their first meeting. Calvin was suspicious of his parole officer's intentions, but accepted the invitation anyway, since his love of the game hadn't died with his love of life.

Burke gave Calvin two tickets before they entered Yankee stadium. One was for today, May 30th, and one was dated September 8. Burke promised Calvin that if he could enjoy tonight, then he could enjoy the game in September—a game he could only attend as a free man.

The Yankees were playing the Red Sox, Calvin's favorite team. He went to the concessions before the game to buy a Boston hat. When he put it on he felt like the kid his uncle used to take to Fenway Park.

Burke walked fast, and it was tough for Calvin, a man fifteen years younger, to keep up. Calvin's ticket read Section 33, but Burke turned towards Section 13. Burke scurried until he found a full row of empty seats three rows from the field behind first base. Calvin followed Burke to the middle of the row—both men sat.

Calvin leaned forward, pulled out his ticket, and showed it to Burke. "These aren't our seats," he said.

"The game is a gift, much like life," Burke said. "Don't question it. Enjoy it."

Calvin accepted this advice, and leaned back in his seat. He'd never had this good a view of the field as a boy. He smiled at a brief daydream of running onto the field to join play in the later innings, and felt the growing energy of the crowd—the players would soon be introduced. For the first time in 4 years Calvin wanted something—to enjoy a baseball game.

Before he could, a young couple made their way down the row. Calvin thought to get up, but didn't when the two found their seats before reaching him. Five minutes later a family of four sat in their row. Every minute there was a new threat. By the second inning Calvin thought *this is it* any time someone walked by.

In the third inning Burke summoned an usher to have teenagers seated in front of them removed. He suspected that they were in someone else's seats. Two minutes later he insisted on seeing the tickets of two men sitting next to him to verify that they were allowed to sit there. Calvin was sure it was just a matter of time before he and Burke got discovered and kicked out. He didn't understand how Burke could enjoy the game like this. Maybe Burke felt safe as long as he was making others scared. Calvin told him he was heading for the men's room and set off to find his assigned seat.

Calvin's face sank as he came out of the tunnel into section 33. The ticket Burke had given him was no gift at all. The seat was in the right field upper deck, 15 rows up. Before he sat down an usher ordered him to remove his cap. Someone had deemed it inappropriate to wear Red Sox caps in that section of the stadium because of the fights they had provoked days before. How did the stadium justify selling these tickets? Why not just put him behind a pillar—the view couldn't be much worse. After five minutes of squinting with a mess of hat hair, Calvin decided he would rather spend September 8th in prison than at another game. He ripped up his extra ticket, and made his way to the stadium exit.

Burke was right—the game was like life. You can sit in the bleachers, or sneak behind the dugout, but you will always be in someone else's seat.

Near the concessions on the lower level a stadium usher stopped Calvin as he was leaving. The young man recognized him from somewhere.

The usher's father had been a cancer patient at St. Vincent's Hospital ten years earlier, where Calvin had volunteered two afternoons a week. Calvin remembered that the poor guy's dad had died (like everyone else in that place), and he didn't want to stick around to hear about it. He confirmed who he was, and continued on his way.

Before Calvin could disappear the usher yelled out, "I want to thank you."

Calvin stopped.

"You wouldn't let him give up. You gave him hope in place of death."

"I was useless," Calvin said. "I didn't give him hope. I was just trying to justify my own life. Now your Dad is dead, and I'm going back to prison."

The usher paused. He was for a moment stuck on the part about prison, but then he responded to something else Calvin had said.

"He's not dead—you saved him ... I just want to thank you."

Calvin looked up.

"Please, don't thank me. I regret what I did ... And you can't repay me!"

The usher was confused.

"Don't question it, just enjoy it. That's what my parole officer said about the game tonight. Enjoy what? I can't see from where I sit, and I can't sit where I can see."

Calvin realized he was yelling at a stranger. He apologized, and told the man he was leaving.

The usher put his hand on Calvin's shoulder. "Maybe I *can* make it up to you."

Behind home plate was a single seat that was always open. The usher had worked the section for five seasons, and knew that the row never sold the odd seat on the end. It was an oversight at the box office. There was no ticket for that seat.

The usher brought Calvin down to the seat. "I can get you this seat all the way up until the end of September, when the playoffs begin. Just look for me." Calvin sat back in the seat, and the usher returned to his post.

Calvin wondered if Burke was still kicking people out of their seats, or if he had been kicked out himself. He thought about his seats in the upper deck, and put his Boston cap on proud. He remembered his life in jail and how empty it was. He took in the magnificent view, and laughed. He was enjoying something he loved. It was only the fourth inning. He spent the next six innings as a free man in a seat he was sure he had earned.

Cassendre Xavier
Why Do Gay Men Have Such Small Dogs and Lesbians, Large Ones?

Gay men use small dogs as cruising tools and conversation pieces. Ever notice all the gay guys cruising the park with their Chihuahuas? The smaller and cuter the doggie, the more play the guy gets, because cute, little dogs attract attention. Of course, I know several gay men who are butch, laid back, and, well, "straight-appearing." Some of these guys might have a tiny pooch, but most have a "real" dog.

Lesbians don't cruise. They don't go to parks looking to get laid. They stay at home with their wives that they moved in with after the second date. They don't have sex. They don't go out. And they most certainly don't need cute dogs. If they go to a "picnic" (a potluck dinner, of course), they'll bring a shaggy old mutt.

Gay men are usually all about presentation. Society says men must be big and strong, but gay men eschew this notion. One of the best compliments you can pay a gay man is that he looks *boyish*. Whether he's 20 or 60, he will absolutely beam. Like their dogs, gay men like to be small and cute themselves. They'll spend hours and hours in the gym each week to attain or maintain a tight, small physique. Fifi, too, *must* be tiny, precious, and of course, impeccably groomed.

Society says that women are supposed to be small. Lesbians reject this restriction and strive to be as big and as strong as they can be, and so are their dogs. (Call a dyke a *girl* and get ready for a forty-minute diatribe on how she's a *woman* and not a child and a girl is a child and how dare you call her that and she hopes you remember *never* to say that again to any woman.)

Gay men and lesbians identify with their canine creatures; through them, they project a part of themselves that they wish they could express in society. Gay men can't actually be as small and adorable as a Chihuahua puppy. And a lesbian can't really be as fierce as a defense-trained German shepherd. But it sure is nice to walk next to one, pretending.

Scott Stein
Ask Marilyn About the Big Bang and the Difference Between Faith and Science

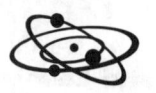

Following the decision by the Kansas State Board of Education to delete evolution from the state's science standards, a *Parade Magazine* reader wrote to "Ask Marilyn," the column written by Marilyn vos Savant (*Parade Magazine*, November 14, 1999, page 20). Marilyn, we are told in a brief bio beneath her column, is listed in the *Guinness Book of World Records* Hall of Fame for "Highest IQ." If you are searching for proof that a high IQ does not guarantee rational thought, look no further.

The reader wanted to know what Marilyn thought of the decision to delete evolution. Marilyn, to her credit, noted that it is "a public-relations setback for the creationists" and that "it doesn't make sense to believe in only those scientific conclusions that don't clash with one's personal faith and then to discourage the teaching of the rest." But Marilyn was certain to mislead *Parade Magazine*'s typical reader with the rest of her answer:

"But before castigating creationists for trying to combine church and state, let's consider just how crazy some 'scientific' theories look.

"Evolution is easy for both scientists and nonscientists to support, but the Big Bang theory, for example, was also an important deletion in the Kansas decision. In essence, the theory holds that, billions of years ago, everything in the universe was contained in an area smaller than the head of a pin (!) and that this minuscule speck of unbelievably dense and incredibly hot matter suddenly exploded violently. That sounds just plain nuts, right?

"But do you believe it? If so, how do you support your belief that the entire cosmos was once smaller than a polka dot? (With a strong line of reasoning? Some solid evidence? Anything at all?) If you cannot, welcome to the world of faith: You're accepting what you've been told by those you respect. And that's just what creationists do. They just respect different folks."

Maybe Marilyn's argument makes complete sense to you, and you are as you read this cheering her for letting those godless scientists have it. Please hold your applause—the show's not over yet.

The main thrust of her argument is that the Big Bang theory defies common sense and is hard for us to even imagine. But most new scientific theories, no matter how well-accepted today, defied the common sense of their times. What nut believed the earth was round, when everyone knew it was flat? And what heretic believed the earth moved when it so clearly was the sun that rose and set? Only a lunatic could believe in gravity, or germs, or atoms, or any number of things that could not be seen or went against current beliefs. Common sense usually offers only common answers. Science is about searching for the truth, and often expands the range of common sense.

And if we are going to use common sense as the criterion for truth, then the creationists have some problems of their own. It is contrary to common sense for people to walk on water, virgins to give birth, bushes to talk, people to live to be 800, seas to part—the list goes on for almost as long as all the books of all the religions. If the Big Bang theory were to be rejected because of a legitimate question of its scientific method, consulting a religious book would not be an appropriate method to find its replacement. Besides, whose would we use? What rational basis is there for choosing one creation myth over another?

Now let's deal with the slant Marilyn's words give the Big Bang theory. It is her choice to refer to the concentration of mass as "unbelievably dense" and the matter as "incredibly hot." These words mean "unable to be believed" and "not credible," so is it any wonder we finish reading her answer and conclude that the theory is not to be believed? My source (*Dictionary of Scientific Literacy*, Richard Brennan, John Wiley & Sons, Inc., 1992, pp. 22-23) uses "infinitely dense" and "infinitely hot." This difference is significant. What religious person can argue with the concept of infinity? It is, after all, used to describe God all the time.

Marilyn also conveys her doubt that the Big Bang theory is indeed "scientific" by placing quotes around the word and telling us it looks crazy and that it "sounds just plain nuts, right?" All of this might help convince those people hoping to be convinced, but it hardly qualifies as a logical argument and is definitely not scientific.

The bias conveyed by her writing style aside, she does raise a valid question: What reason is there to believe something that seems contrary to common sense? As she asks, is there solid evidence? Is there a strong line of reasoning? Anything at all? What follows is the idiot's explanation (the only one I know) of the Big Bang theory. Prepare for immense oversimplification.

In 1929, the American astronomer Edwin Hubble discovered that the universe was expanding—we can see a red-shift of the light that is emitted by the stars that are accelerating rapidly away from us. Almost no one doubts that this is true—it is observable through a telescope. If the universe is expanding at an accelerating rate, it logically follows that it was once much smaller. The more recent discovery of cosmic microwave background radiation is evidence of a massive explosion, or "big bang." The possibility of intense mass occupying a tiny space is supported by observation of gravity's behavior around black holes. Further observation and other experimental and theoretical evidence and computer simulations have added credence to the Big Bang theory, and it is now the most prominent scientific theory on the origin of the universe. That is all I know. I am not a scientist, I don't know the math, and haven't done more extensive reading on the topic.

Now Marilyn thinks she has me. "So you don't really understand the Big Bang theory," she might say, "and you believe it on faith. Your view and the view of creationists are both based on faith, and there is no reason to choose one over the other."

Wrong again, Marilyn. There are crucial differences:

• The scientific method allows for revising beliefs. If contrary evidence is found, if a mistake in interpretation or observation or in the math is discovered, the theory must be revised or discarded. Faith, however, cannot be tested or supported by evidence. Faith is believing in the *absence* of evidence, or, in the case of some creationists who ignore the fossil record or the empirical discoveries of genetics, *despite* the evidence. The Big Bang theory, whether it is true or not, is based on observation and experimentation. The fact that it can be rejected if it fails tests or if a theory more supported by evidence emerges makes it very different from a creation myth, which is believed on faith and can never be tested or observed in any way. In science, we are prepared to reevaluate our belief, if necessary. This alone makes belief in a scientific theory very different from faith, even if we don't understand the specifics of the theory.

- I could learn the math and study cosmological physics. I might not have the background to fully understand the Big Bang theory, but there is nothing about the theory or the scientific method that prevents me from acquiring that background. If I were so inclined, I could become a physicist or buy a telescope or read about the theory, and maybe come to a different conclusion. I could understand it for myself, based on my own observation and experimentation. Faith, on the other hand, doesn't allow for this personal observation or experimentation. Faith demands that one believe without empirical or observational evidence, since religion asserts propositions that cannot be tested or observed. No matter how hard I study a religious book, I am always basing my belief on that book. By choosing a particular book or religion, or being brought up to follow a particular religion, my beliefs have been determined for me.

- Although scientific theories are part of the larger culture and as such often creep into our consciousness without a deliberate critical analysis on our part, people who understand science know that scientific knowledge is provisional. But by the time topics such as the origin of life and the origin of the universe are raised in school, most children have been exposed to religious teachings in church or synagogue on countless Sundays. They have recited the pledge of allegiance with its assumption of God's existence every day, and have heard their parents refer to God as if the existence of a specific supernatural being were as obvious as the sun in the sky. This goes beyond mere faith. The belief in religion is usually not a decision at all. Or is it just a coincidence that the overwhelming majority of people believe in the same religion as their parents? It is not clear to me how the result of this endless cycle of conditioning is different from brainwashing.

- Science is slowly taught in school, usually with an emphasis on method and testing and experimentation. Religious faith is too often taught in a much more oppressive manner—no one is ever told they will go to hell if they disagree with a teaching of science.

- Science does not find threats and guilt to be necessary. No one says, "If we don't believe in evolution the fabric of society will tear." But religious people often point out the social consequences of not believing, as if that has something to do with the validity of a belief.

- Convincing people of a scientific theory involves presenting evidence and perhaps critiquing the foundations of a rival theory. Convincing people that they should give up their religion for yours has traditionally involved the rack, the thumbscrew, and a cauldron of scalding water.

- People tend not to base day-to-day activities and a system of ethics on a scientific theory about the origin of the universe. If it turns out that the particulars of the Big Bang theory are wrong or that the entire theory is mistaken, it would have few practical consequences on our lives. Religion, however, is the overwhelming force in many people's lives. If we have to choose one thing to believe on scant evidence, it would be better to choose a scientific theory like the Big Bang instead of a religion. Because if our choice of religion is wrong, our whole life is based on a lie. If the Big Bang theory is wrong, we'll say, "How about that," look for a better answer, and get on with our day.

If Marilyn disagrees with the Big Bang theory or any other scientific belief, she should challenge the evidence or dispute the interpretation of an observation. That would be an honest attempt to discover the truth. She has not done that. She has instead done what she knows will raise the ire of rationalists more than anything else will: She has accused them of having faith.

Religious people, when asked to prove God's existence or the validity of a particular religion in comparison with another one, often fall back on faith. "You have to have faith," they say. "Some things are beyond science," they say. They say this because religion is not scientific. It doesn't claim to be based on reason. They do not believe it can be tested and, in fact, religious people are often offended by the notion that they should test it.

If Marilyn vos Savant or others want to claim that faith is a valid way of knowing, that it deserves respect as a method of gaining knowledge, that is a matter for another essay, I suppose. But one cannot defend faith as a legitimate means of knowing, distinct from science, while insisting that science is in fact faith. That violates the logical principle of non-contradiction. Apparently, it is a principle some religious people have no trouble violating.

Reader Comments

—Debra Smith responds to "Ask Marilyn About the Big Bang and the Difference Between Faith and Science" by Scott Stein.

One thing I have never understood about the debate over science and religion is just how they got to be in conflict. "Faith is the assurance of things not seen," the Bible says. If it's seen, if it can be proven, it isn't a matter of faith. The faith mentioned in the Bible is also quite specific. Scientific theories aren't the least bit relevant to one's relationship with God. So why all the arguments over evolution or cosmology? No one will be damned for believing in Darwin or the Big Bang. Contrary to popular belief, the Bible is quite science-friendly. The apostle Paul said to "prove all things, and to hold fast to what is good." Isn't this the goal of science?

—Scott Stein responds to Debra Smith's comments on his "Ask Marilyn About the Big Bang and the Difference Between Faith and Science."

The problem is that if a religious book makes any claims about physical reality that science can show to be incorrect, that religious book and the religion based on it lose their claims to infallibility, to the status of God-inspired, literal truth. If the Bible is wrong about one thing, how can believers be sure it is right about anything? How can it be the word of an omniscient God and be wrong? These are natural questions some would prefer people not ask. To prevent the questions from coming up, some would be happy to see science stay out of what they see as religion's exclusive business of explaining things. Just ask Galileo. Or Kansas. (But don't ask Marilyn.)

—Keith Whaley responds to "Ask Marilyn About the Big Bang and the Difference Between Faith and Science" by Scott Stein.

I had some thoughts that have plagued me since I was about 9, I guess. I was raised in a Christian religion from whatever "day one" I can remember. I started becoming an agnostic (generically speaking) when I couldn't get answers I could believe in catechism classes. I had questions that were profound, to me as an insatiably curious 13-year-old, but all I got in response was "have faith." In other words, *trust me*. Things logical made much more sense to me.

I find no credible evidence for the existence of a Supreme Being. I know of no supportable evidence of the hand of a god being responsible for anything. Whatever happens to a believer that is wonderful and marvelous must be because s/he was being smiled upon by God and s/he was living or acting in a moral, religious (God-fearing?) way. And if it was a bad thing, ipso facto, it was because s/he didn't have a strong enough faith or wasn't worthy, ad infinitum. Sorry, that flies in the face of rationality. And science. Not once have any of the formal religions come up with one scintilla of evidence of a Supreme Being. It's always been 100% *trust me*.

Show me something tangible, something I can see and touch and hear for myself, and I'll take pause and consider it. That very statement rouses rancor in those whose faith (alone) supports them. To them, it's too obvious that I don't have any faith (belief in unsupportable contentions) and am a godless person.

Regarding science and the Big Bang, it's almost as incredible to me, because I have the same questions as most other folks have. I can imagine and almost accept a neutron star, where the neutrons and other particles are so closely packed that there's (relatively) little space left between them, and the density of this star is of itself stretching credibility. Still, it seems it might be real, with what my basic understanding of science supports. Yet, a neutron star is very, very much larger than the original particle from whence came the universe as we know it today. The original matter source is unimaginably smaller than can be believed, since that's supposed to be that from which all of the universe we "know" today came. Uh huh.

Ignoring for the moment the supposed validity of that theory, from where did this primordial singularity come? How did it come to exist? And into what is it expanding, pray tell? Empty space? Does that space exist into infinity? That would indeed be world without end, for me. These are the questions that boggle my mind!

Scott Stein has said, "But one cannot defend faith as a legitimate means of knowing, distinct from science, while insisting that science is in fact faith." Perhaps some more scientifically grounded person than I am can explain how my last few questions require any less a leap of faith than those of religious followings require.

—Scott Stein responds to Keith Whaley's comments on his "Ask Marilyn About the Big Bang and the Difference Between Faith and Science."

I do not think it takes a scientist to answer Mr. Whaley's final concern. It is not a leap of faith to hold no opinion on a matter. If there is no evidence or scant evidence for what the universe is expanding into, or what existed before the Big Bang, we would be wise not to believe anything about it. This is difficult to do, and might be what made religion so popular in the first place. There were so many questions about everything a few thousand years ago, and religion offered people answers (never mind the sense of those answers). People don't like to accept "we don't know." That is what drives science—the desire to eliminate "we don't know."

Unlike religion, science is not free to make up an answer to fill every void. If we don't know, then we don't know. Is there evidence about what we are expanding into, or what started it all prior to the Big Bang? If not, it is best to not believe anything about it. Or if we must speculate and our curious natures force us to believe something, at least we should understand that the belief lacks proper support and should not be taken too seriously, for when new evidence arrives, it might prove us wrong. Does this sound like faith? No. In the absence of evidence and reason, faith allows people to have convictions about all sorts of propositions that cannot be verified. Belief in some primordial pre-Big Bang scenario and even the Big Bang itself would be provisional and, unlike faith, would not gain prominence if it could not be supported by evidence and reason.

Some readers have suggested that the Big Bang's support is not very strong. That does not make it faith. If strong enough arguments are presented, and a stronger competing scientific theory is postulated, the Big Bang might one day lose its position as the dominant theory. Change might not be as forthcoming as all would like—scientific revolutions do not come easily. But the capacity for change based on evidence makes it unlike faith.

It is true that some people defend specific theories with an almost religious zeal and that some scientists have political or other agendas that give us reason to regard their findings with a healthy skepticism. In the end, though, what matters is that we base our beliefs on reason and evidence. The strength of our belief should be proportional to the support that exists for that belief.

Let's remember that even many of the accepted theories today will be revised and refined in future years. Some might be discarded. There are many things we just don't know yet. There are many that we will not know in any of our lifetimes, and others we might never know. It is not faith to withhold judgment, to the extent our curious natures let us, on matters that are not supported.

—Bloodhunter responds to "Ask Marilyn About the Big Bang and the Difference Between Faith and Science" by Scott Stein.

Actually, Marilyn is exactly right, but you're just not grasping what she is trying to say. She has simply stated that science, too, requires faith, because in reality even the most seemingly proven scientific theories really have no evidence for or against them. In a nutshell, all aspects of the universe have infinite factors affecting them, so all possible events have the exact same chance of occurring. Thus, faith and science are the same, because both involve believing something without a reason.

—Scott Stein responds to Bloodhunter's comments on his "Ask Marilyn About the Big Bang and the Difference Between Faith and Science."

If you think the Big Bang might not be good science, then make your case, offer a competing theory. But to say that faith and all science are the same thing? Maybe I was aggressive in attacking her famed IQ in my essay, but Marilyn does not say *this*. Try defending "all possible events have the exact same chance of occurring" and "even the most seemingly proven scientific theories really have *no* evidence for or against them." But even those who say they agree with these absurd statements do not really believe what this reader has claimed, as proven by their actions. If they did, then when driving it would make no sense to step on the brake pedal instead of using the horn to stop the car. All events have the same chance of occurring, right, so why believe the brakes will stop the car and the horn will not? Why use antibiotics when a tall glass of milk has the same chance of curing an infection? Why not jump off of a building's roof ... there is the same chance of flying like Superman as there is of falling to one's death, right?

The scientific method helps us avoid these obviously false beliefs, by subjecting claims to a high standard that includes testing by experimentation and examining the evidence. The world is not so fickle as this reader suggests ... cause and effect might be battered in some circles, but it still applies to the world we see and live in. None of us would survive beyond a minute in a world without somewhat predictable and consistent physical "laws." The uncertainty that seems to exist on the quantum level and in chaos theory does not mean that we cannot know *anything*. Look at daily life ... it is astounding how many things we *do* know, and take for granted every day.

It is this kind of thinking that made me respond so strongly to Marilyn's equating of a theory with faith. Whatever her intentions, she hurt the scientific method's credibility with her readers. *It sounds weird, so it isn't true* is what I think lots of people reading her column came away with. That, and, *Whatever book I choose to believe this week is just as valid an explanation of the physical world as a scientific theory that I do not fully understand.*

Suzanne Hakanen
**Acting Assistant Executive
Associate Manager**

McDonald's was revolutionary in creating a work caste system in which everyone felt useful and safe. You were cook or cashier. Then assistant shift manager. Then shift manager. Then assistant manager. Then a job in purchasing or office management ... the possibilities were endless. One day you were a sixteen-year-old kid working weekends for gas and movie money, and a few years later you could end up as an executive for one of the most successful corporations in the world.

How did Ray Kroc do it? Simple. The company offered its employees a sense of accomplishment: When workers did their jobs correctly, arrived at work on time, and were generally good team players, they assumed a few more responsibilities and earned a few more dollars each week. They learned new skills. Perhaps they weren't learning the most valued skills around, but they could do something concrete: whip up a Big Mac with special sauce on the side. And people were happy with promotions, complete with a small upward creep in their paycheck amounts.

It wasn't a bad system, and one might be hopeful that these employee management techniques would still be working in the 21st century. But it seems that today's managers have gotten things turned around. The person's work title is now the focus instead of the increased responsibility or compensation.

Every time I walk into Home Depot, Sears, or my local paint store, I am inundated with Sales Associates. What the hell does this title mean? Is the Sales Associate one who associates with sales? Who is a "friend" with sales? And if so, why doesn't he know where any of the items I am attempting to purchase—that he is attempting to sell me—are?

My other favorite title is Customer Service Representative. I'm not even going to try to decode the meaning of that. It makes no sense. These people are not representative of ideal service, if that was the idea in creating the title. Aren't these the same cashiers who can't sell me a two-dollar pack of nails for lack of a UPC code? And aren't these the same people who are powerless to give me a (reasonable) discount when I find a tear in the clearance-rack jacket I want to buy, or refund my money when my purchase turns out to be defective, or open their own cashier drawers to void a mistyped amount? What type of service do they profess to represent?

On a short trip to the SuperFresh during which there was a power surge, I was horrified to find that the young man operating the cash register could not make change for a $20 bill. The customer in front of me, an elderly woman, made no attempt to hide her disgust as she told the worker, "Just count out to a dollar. The total is $8.78, so get coins for 79 cents, 80 cents, ninety, a dollar. Now count the bills out to 20."

The young man was obviously perplexed.

"Don't they teach you math in school?" the woman demanded.

The young man hung his head.

"Yeah, I have math analysis," he mumbled, still fumbling for the correct bills.

The woman turned to me. "We studied arithmetic," she said. "What the hell is math analysis?"

"It's what the Sales Associates take," I replied. "It's for people who failed the regular math class, and the teachers don't want to make them feel bad, so they made up a name to make the basic course sound like the advanced course."

The woman laughed, and finally got her change and left.

I handed the boy a $12 roast and a $10 bill.

"Please," I urged, "keep the change."

His bright smile made my day.

Bob Sullivan
Making the Most of Your Take-Home Pay

Most people work because they need to earn money. And most people vote because they want to have some say in how federal and local governments spend their money. But don't look to political candidates to inform you on the best ways to maximize your tax dollar. Not in an electoral process as corrupt as the one currently operating in this country.

It's the same old shell game: The two sides offer two conflicting points of view, and argue them so vehemently that the average voter completely forgets that there is a third choice, a third possibility. The Democrats claim they want to spend our budget surplus on entitlement programs and the infrastructure, while Republicans claim they want to give the money back to the American people. What the politicians lose sight of in their rhetoric (on purpose) is that, from an accounting standpoint, there is no money to spend or give back.

The national debt as of December 1999 was $5,703,684,230,138—that's not 5.7 billion with a *b* but 5.7 trillion with a *tr*. And let's not kid ourselves: If we the American people are, in fact, the government, then this is, in fact, our debt. The estimated population of the United States is 274,224,926, so the debt works out to about $21,000 per man, woman, and child.

If you or the company you own owes over a trillion dollars, and one year you make a little more than you spend, you can hardly claim that you are now in the black—in a position to either hold onto the money or spend it—since it's not really your money to begin with. Anyone in debt knows that, except for necessities like housing and food, there is no better way to spend what money you may receive than on retiring your debt; you'll never have any real buying power if you have this never-ending interest payment to shell out every month. Interest payments are payments for which you get absolutely nothing in return, so those to whom the money is owed make pure profit. Due to the interest, the national debt is currently growing at the rate of $3,517 per second.

But the moneymen—with the financial means to make or break candidates—want to make sure that the debt is never retired because it is literally money in the bank. They purchase their candidates (in ways that are currently legal) to ensure that the partisan bickering preceding elections focuses on two opposing ways—a tax cut or government spending—to guarantee that the debt is never retired.

The reason the national debt is so easily forgotten is because we all have this feeling that, well, it's always been here and it's always going to be here. But the vast majority of the debt accumulated in the not-so-distant past; nine out of every ten dollars of national debt was incurred during the Reagan Era. As any financial adviser will tell you, now is exactly the right time to start retiring the country's debt because the country, at least for the moment, is doing quite well financially. No less a light than Alan Greenspan, the chairman of the Federal Reserve, calls this course of action "an extraordinarily effective force for good in this economy." He reasons that reducing the debt will both free funds for private investment and lower government spending.

Vice President Al Gore has pledged to retire some of the national debt every year he is President, but he doesn't give specifics, and his overall message is attracting comparatively few moneymen. Gore claims the tax policies of both Bill Bradley and Republican presidential front-runner George W. Bush would put America "at risk," adding, "Those who forget recessions of the past are doomed to repeat them."

The fact is, while both the Republican and the Democratic plans remove the possibility of paying down the debt, they also stand a good chance of busting the budget completely. Each side has already promised to devote two-thirds of the government's projected $3-trillion, 10-year surplus to shoring up Social Security and Medicare; the dispute centers on that last $1 trillion. But if that last trillion is spent or returned to the American people now and then the economy hiccups, or emergency spending increases, or something unexpected develops, that $1 trillion—heck, that entire $3 trillion—could vanish in the blink of an eye.

It seems our political process has evolved beyond such reasoned arguments. This situation is caused by a combination of lack of meaningful campaign finance reform and a national shortsightedness best typified by U.S. upper management types: individuals who only worry about the next quarter's bottom line, never taking into account the big picture or long-range plans. After all, it's the bottom line that determines their next few bonuses, their instant gratification. If lack of foresight means the company is unable to stay competitive and falters in a few years, by then a new executive will be in charge and that'll be his problem.

So before you decide whether to opt for the spending or the tax cut, just remember: the best way to make the most of your take-home pay is "None of the above."

Scott Stein
Boos for the Boss?

A good friend and equally big Bruce Springsteen fan e-mailed me to get my thoughts about the hubbub over Bruce's new song, "American Skin (41 Shots)," about the Amadou Diallo shooting in New York City. The Fraternal Order of Police has taken issue with the song for reopening wounds it thinks are healing, and has called for a boycott and made some remarks about Bruce that I will not dignify by repeating here. My friend, having read my "Bruce Springsteen's 'The Ghost of Tom Joad' and the Problem of Barbra Streisand" (p. 115), in which I criticize society for letting celebrities dictate political and legislative decisions, was curious to know whether I agreed with the venom aimed at the song and Bruce's stance, or whether, like him, I thought the police were overreacting.

I have been accused on occasion of sitting on the fence, of trying to have it both ways. Democrats and liberals sometimes applaud my acceptance of people different from me, my criticism of religion, and my defense of freedom of expression. Republicans and conservatives have thanked me for defending the free market, pointing out excesses of governmental power, and demanding individual freedom and responsibility. I suppose that here, again, I am taking both sides. Or, more correctly, neither side. But I do not apologize for doing so. If more people saw the complexity of this and other situations instead of blindly following some dictate of loyalty to party or religion or ethnicity, we'd have a better planet.

I support Bruce on this one. I think this is the proper role for an artist: not being didactic or supporting legislation without all the facts or letting emotion sway public policy, but shedding light on the reality of the world. A bad artist would be campaigning for specific policies (as Bruce did, noted in the *New York Times Magazine* cover story "The Pop Populist," a few years back). Good artists make us understand and empathize with the experiences of others (as Bruce did on "The Ghost of Tom Joad").

Regarding the new song, Bruce is right. In America you can get shot in part because of the color of your skin. As an artist, if he brings us closer to understanding the sadness of that reality, good for him. If that understanding of the experiences of people different from ourselves makes us as individuals even a little better able to get along with each other, then art has served one of its elevated purposes.

But that does not necessarily mean that in this specific case the cops committed a criminal act, or that in the big picture law-abiding black people (the vast majority) aren't better off because aggressive police tactics have removed violent criminals from black neighborhoods. It could be argued that part of why you can get shot by cops for being black in some neighborhoods is because of the very real risk of being killed that cops face in those neighborhoods—officers are on edge, with good reason. Is racism a factor?

Sometimes, I'm sure (and sometimes is too much). But not necessarily, and not in every case, as Al Sharpton and the Clintons and Jesse Jackson would have us believe. Understanding the impossible situations the police face every day is important too.

The uncomfortable truth is that when cops were less aggressive, black people in poor neighborhoods were being murdered by black criminals at unprecedented rates. Can you have it both ways: low violent crime and aggressive policing with no terrible incidents or innocent deaths? I don't know. I do know that New York is now a very different, much safer place than I remember it being. It isn't just hype.

But conservatives angry with Amadou Diallo's mother, who's trying to make sense of what happened to her dead son, are also misguided. They criticize her for not understanding that it was an accident, that the police didn't commit murder as defined by our laws, and in fact, according to them, acted appropriately given what they thought was occurring. Whether they are right about this or not, can anyone expect a mother to accept it when her son is dead? My mother wouldn't. Would yours? Some are too quick to say, "These things happen, let's move on."

A man is dead. A man who posed no threat, who was not committing a crime. The horror of a life lost should not be so easily forgotten, and if questions should be asked, let us not be afraid to ask them. If Springsteen's song helps listeners feel that horror to some degree, if it reminds us that we live in a sometimes very ugly world, then he has done his job as an artist. And if it pisses off politicians and bureaucrats and callers to radio talk shows, even better.

Jared Boshnack
America's Sport

Over the past century, three sports have dominated American culture: baseball, football, and basketball. Each sport has a claim to being the national pastime.

Baseball had its greatest years earlier in the 20th century. During wartime, it was clearly America's sport. The New York Yankees were at the center of baseball's success as they continually fielded competitive teams that contended for or won championships. In the process, personalities like Babe Ruth, Lou Gehrig, Joe DiMaggio, and Mickey Mantle became national icons and were able to transcend sport. As pitchmen for national products, their popularity crossed over into the American mainstream.

Integration and talent brought Jackie Robinson to the Brooklyn Dodgers as the first black player in the Major Leagues. Jackie Robinson's success meant that baseball was a game to be played by everyone.

It is to baseball's advantage that its regular season is more (in terms of games played) than 10 times the length of football's and more than twice the length of basketball's. Baseball's exposure year round is far greater and teams draw between 2 million to 4 million fans to the stadiums per season.

Football exploded onto the scene with the creation of the Super Bowl. Prior to that, teams from the old NFL league would play a championship game. The difference was that the Super Bowl allowed for a neutral site, and the league could market the game for the entire year. Super Bowl Sunday is now the most watched of any single sporting event, and enables the league to spend millions of dollars to promote itself and expand.

Of the three sports, football is the most dangerous to play, because there is physical contact on nearly every play. The intensity and action breed loyal fans. Due to football's short season, every game is a sellout, and because each team plays only one game a week, steady anticipation builds.

Basketball is easily the most accessible of the sports. In nearly every city, suburb, or farmland, a hoop and a ball can be found. Unlike baseball and football, it is the only sport that can be played, in some form, alone, or in groups of up to 10 people.

In the 1980s, three athletes helped take the game to another level. Magic Johnson, Larry Bird, and Michael Jordan performed jaw-dropping feats on the court that made children and grown men alike all over the country want to emulate them. Their success helped take basketball games from a tape-delayed afterthought to a primetime match. Clever marketing and an aggressive commissioner helped push basketball to new heights (no pun intended).

Basketball fans pay more for tickets because the arenas are all indoors and seating is limited to twenty thousand per game. In contrast, baseball stadiums seat fifty thousand and football stadiums seat eighty thousand.

Basketball players make the most money in endorsements because they reach the largest and most attractive group of spenders.

An argument can be made for each of these three sports as the national pastime. Baseball fans have a rich history, which can be rewritten on any given night or in any given year. Football fans have an event to plan for once a week for five months, with each game growing more in importance as the short season winds down. Finally, basketball fans have the ability to root as if they were playing themselves, and in the case of some courtside fans (Spike Lee), they do. But those of us who dabble in playing these sports and follow the games know what is closest to America's collective heart.

The real national pastime is sitting in the air-conditioned comfort of your living room on a hot summer day with a beer in one hand and the clicker in the other as you rhythmically flip through the stations to find the most competitive game on at the moment. There is drama and excitement to be had, and breaking a sweat is never required. The end result is always gratifying. If your team's season ends in victory or failure, glory or embarrassment, a simple truth remains:

Win, lose, or draw, there is always tomorrow, another cold beer, same reliable clicker, and a competitive dog show on the USA network.

C.P. Kaiser
I Thank God the Tornado Didn't Suck Me Up ... Too Bad About My Neighbors, Though

Sometimes (really all the time) I just can't understand how so-called people of faith rationalize their god's presence in and purpose for natural and "unnatural" disasters. Take for instance the shooting spree at Columbine High School in 1999. Those who survived thanked—most likely—the Christian biblical god for their lives; relatives of those who didn't survive cursed—most likely—the same god.

Well, *almost* all relatives.

Darrell Scott, the father of Rachel Scott, a victim of the Littleton, Colorado, shootings, addressed Congress during gun-control legislation hearings. He said, in part, "We all contain the seeds of kindness or the seeds of violence. The death of my wonderful daughter and the deaths of that heroic teacher, and the other eleven children who died must not be in vain. Their blood cries out for answers." And his answer, no less, is to allow public schools the right to have prayer services.

A friend of mine said that Scott's message "needs to be heard by every parent, every teacher, every politician, every sociologist, and every so-called expert!" and then added, "There is no doubt that God sent this man as a voice crying in the wilderness."

Am I missing something here? Must the Christian god ruin so many lives just to send us a messenger? If he knows all, doesn't he know that this type of messaging hasn't worked for over five thousand years? His one best-seller, the Bible, is filled with failed examples of his slash-and-burn messaging style. At Columbine, he sent two hormonally-challenged teenage soldiers into a defenseless school armed to the pimples with ammunition and bombs, with the sole purpose of killing as many of his so-called precious creatures as possible, and for that we're supposed to thank him for sending us Rachel Scott's father to teach us the value of being holy and human and forgiving, especially toward the National Rifle Association?

In Scott's address, he referenced "the first recorded act of violence": the story of Cain and Abel. Scott told Congress that *Cain* was responsible for Abel's murder, not the NCA (National Club Association). Accordingly, the NRA was not responsible for his daughter's death, but neither were shooters Dylan Harris and Eric Klebold. The real culprit, he asserted, is the lack of prayer in our schools (actually, I think he meant the lack of school-sponsored prayer).

(Do you think Congress, which basically suckles at the NRA's teats, knew Scott's message before they invited him to speak? Do you think that an NRA lobbyist lobbied for Scott's appearance or was it, say, the work of some god? Do you think an atheist (or any other religionist) who blamed the NRA would have been given the red carpet up the Capitol steps?)

Again, I have to ask: Am I missing something here? Cain was *fourth* in line to the so-called creator. Even Kevin Bacon can't match that! It's closer than the papacy is to secret Swiss bank accounts; closer than Richard Nixon is to Lucifer; even closer than Divine Brown was to Hugh Grant. If anyone had all the cards he needed to be nonviolent, it was Cain. And if anyone could've guessed and helped prevent a brother's animosity toward his brother, it was the Hebrew monolithic god. But neither of those two possibilities occurred, and we've been plagued ever since with similar tragedies, which, based on the logic that the Christian god is all-everything, should have been remedied sometime after the last ice age. But alas, they are not. So, today, we are subjected to asinine opinions of righteous people who rationalize that their god allowed a school population to teeter on the brink of extinction because he wanted to send us a messenger heralding the need for prayer in our public schools.

Wouldn't it have been easier for this god to wiggle his nose to wish peace and prosperity for all peoples in the Milky Way?

Scott told Congress that the answer is *not* more restrictive gun laws that erode our personal and private liberties, but rather the need for a "change of heart and a humble acknowledgment that this nation was founded on the principle of simple trust in [the Christian] God." I beg to differ. My take is that this nation was founded on the best *mistrust* of the gods and of their prized primates. Our forefathers created a system of government that checks and rechecks each branch because they distrusted human, and therefore divine, nature. (If a bunch of farmers could figure this out, why can't the so-called Supreme Being?) Our forefathers also included in the Constitution a provision for a well-armed militia, certainly not because they trusted in god the way Jesus Christ did. And Thomas Jefferson and the gang also constructed provisions to keep the church and state separate, precisely because one's trust or *no* trust in god is a personal relationship, not to be supported or denied in any way by the state.

Scott's son Craig, while hidden under a table in the school library that day, saw his two friends murdered. "He did not hesitate to pray in school," the elder Scott told Congress. "I defy any law or politician to deny him that right." Like I said previously, one's relationship with a god is a personal matter. If children want to hide under desks and whisper ejaculations to their high commander, that's their business, but the school cannot require nor sponsor them to do so.

I'm sorry for Scott's loss, but his support of the NRA contributes to my loss—my continued loss of freedom to engage in the world with fellow humans without the fear of being shot for little or no reason. I do hope the public is smart enough to forgive Scott this bit of eccentricity. After all, he's a man spurned. Having been forsaken by his supreme lover, he's on the rebound, clouded, confused, in denial, and looking for any way to ease his pain. We can only hope that he comes to his senses soon. If by some odd and remote chance the courts vote to install school-sponsored prayer, I hope students pray for the dissolution of the NRA and a constitutional amendment banning the ownership of all firearms. That move could (*almost!*) make me a believer in Scott's god.

Reader Comments

—Suzanne Hakanen responds to "I Thank God the Tornado Didn't Suck Me Up ... Too Bad About My Neighbors, Though" by C.P. Kaiser.

I think C.P. Kaiser's message can't be repeated often enough: Those who attribute actions to "God" usually are completely lacking in ability to think logically. I mean, why *would* God send two depressed rat finks in grunge down to kill innocent students, the ultimate message being that God wants the U.S. government to sponsor prayer in the public schools? Don't you think our most gracious God might find a non-violent vehicle for this mandate?

One of my favorite lines from *The Simpsons* is "guns don't kill people; physics does." It's a thought that always elicits a chuckle, but when compared to the NRA's message it becomes a deeply troubling thought. If I ever have a renewed interest in "God," I'll find an organization that believes in a nice one who likes peace and despises violence. My guess is that he won't be the God of the NRA.

—Chuck Sheehan responds to "I Thank God the Tornado Didn't Suck Me Up ... Too Bad About My Neighbors, Though" by C.P. Kaiser.

As a society, we tend to focus on the symptoms and not the disease. Even before any of the facts about the tragedy at Columbine were known, the media zeroed in on the availability of guns and the power of the NRA. Later, parents, teachers, and students talked about prayer and bringing God back into schools. I readily admit that both of these issues deserve attention. Unfortunately, I do not have the answers to those social questions and I'm pretty sure that no one will find the answers to these dilemmas in this diatribe. Rather, I pose the question: Are we focusing on the right issue? Shouldn't we be looking at what drove those two children to such depths?

The media mentioned that Eric Klebold and Dylan Harris were the brunt of jokes, taunts, and physical attacks by Columbine's student-athletes. Where is the investigation into the motive for the star quarterback's/pitcher's/center's need to dominate and degrade another human being? Isn't there the bigger question of man's inhumanity to man?

True, without guns the slaughter might not have been as widespread. Maybe guns should be outlawed, but I promise that the next time a person is pushed beyond his or her limits, he or she will still strike back. Then national attention will shift to the banning of knives, screwdrivers, cars, rocks, sticks, and anything else that can be used as a weapon. But, unfortunately, when the world is turned into a soft-cornered, weapon-free place, Johnny Quarterback will still ride little Billy for being queer or a wimp or a nerd or a Jew or black. Whatever the taunt, eventually, without intervention, it will go too far and as a result, by law, we will be surgically removing every baby's hands at birth to keep people from using fists to hurt each other.

So what if Eric and Dylan prayed? Does that stop the teasing? What if the jocks prayed? Does that stop their need to control and dominate? The answer to all of the above is maybe, maybe not. But it has been my experience that if the words do not have the heart behind them, you might as well remain silent.

Trying to find the answer of why man needs to dominate and control is too overwhelming. Instead, after the next massacre, riot, and cold-blooded murder/suicide, we will continue to lament that God has been removed from our lives and guns have been placed in his/her stead. Or we will find something else to blame. Something tangible. Something that we can hold hearings about and pen laws to ban or promote. Either way, eventually, we will have to face the fact that some people are evil. No doubt evil has touched the soul of the people who pulled the triggers. But what is that evil? Maybe the truly evil are the people who create a world where the shooters see no other solution to end their pain. And what law can we write to prevent that?

—Scott Stein responds to "I Thank God the Tornado Didn't Suck Me Up ... Too Bad About My Neighbors, Though" by C.P. Kaiser.

Of course, I agree wholeheartedly with C.P. Kaiser's take on the tendency to look to God for answers, to thank or blame God depending on which side of the carnage one's luck fell. The living didn't deserve to live any more than the dead deserved to die. There is no making sense of these things. And prayer in school is a ridiculous solution. In the thousands of years of religion, or as some would call it, the Judeo-Christian tradition, I see no evidence of a less violent and more caring world. How many have killed or been killed in the name of some religion or god, or because of the artificial differences religions create? The concept of an afterlife, where one is rewarded for strapping a bomb to oneself for some holy cause, is part of the problem. Wouldn't it be great if instead of being conditioned to believe in heaven and hell, people instead were taught the truth: that life here on earth is the only life, that what we have on this planet is what needs to be valued?

But I cannot agree with C.P. Kaiser's call for a constitutional amendment banning guns. I am not exactly a card-carrying member of the NRA (I avoid carrying cards of any sort), and I find the notion that "guns don't kill people" to be laughable (wiffleball bats are far less dangerous). Guns certainly make killing easy and efficient. But when killers are as motivated as the punks at Columbine, I wonder what law is going to stop them.

It is not as easy to dismiss the NRA's other slogan, "When guns are outlawed, only outlaws will have guns." Criminals do not obey laws (that is what makes them criminals, and most of them already have illegal guns), so such an amendment would succeed only in disarming the law-abiding population. The mistrust of government Mr. Kaiser mentions above is not only related to the separation of church and state, but also the right to bear arms. If a button could be pressed that would disarm the entire world, magically, without exception, maybe I would press it myself. Perhaps no guns *at all* would be for the larger good. However, no such magic button exists, and never will, so a law banning all guns would leave the government and police armed, the armies of other nations armed, and the criminals who do not care about laws armed. Only the rest of us would be unarmed. I don't like those odds. I wonder how China's recent history might have been different if in Tiannamen Square and the population at-large the tyrannical government had to worry about a well-armed citizenry.

I understand the desire for discussion about some regulation of guns. After all, we do not allow citizens to fly around in Apache helicopters or drive tanks down Main Street. Even Charlton Heston would probably not really want people walking down the street with missile launchers on their shoulders. But it is the call for a total ban (which of course could never be enforced and would result in a lack of freedom far greater than any Mr. Kaiser seems to think has resulted from the existence of guns in law-abiding hands) that gives the NRA its power. Would Mr. Kaiser like to see the government start searching homes for weapons? Should my father go to jail if he has a shotgun for self-defense in his own home? Does Mr. Kaiser want a not-so-civil war? Does he think people are simply going to hand their guns in because the government says so? And will he feel safer when the government has all of the guns, and the people have none? How strong of a democracy is there when the power flows not from the governed but from the government?

This kind of extremism is what makes sensible compromise impossible. People are fearful that the government's attempts at "common sense" gun control are just a precursor to a total ban, so they fight even supposedly sensible measures at every step. That is why the NRA is experiencing such a boom in membership. It seems that the paranoia is well founded, based on Mr. Kaiser's proposal and the activism of Rosie O'Donnell and others.

Perhaps most disturbing, though, is the impulse, on the part of many who would see all guns banned, to blame everyone and everything but the criminal for the crime. Instead of focusing on a ban, what if crimes committed with a gun were treated more seriously? What about holding people accountable for their behavior? We actually have people on the street who once committed murder. There is time off for good behavior, and repeat crime is a big problem. If judges and legislators would do their duty and protect the public welfare, if every crime committed with a gun resulted in real jail time, I think you would see a greater reduction in violent crime than any unenforceable ban or lawsuit could ever create.

—C.P. Kaiser responds to Scott Stein's comments on "I Thank God the Tornado Didn't Suck Me Up ... Too Bad About My Neighbors, Though."

I have to chuckle when Scott Stein asks if I would "feel safer when the government has all of the guns and the people have none," because *the government already has all of the guns!* And they can keep them as far as I'm concerned because my reading of the Constitution calls for a well-armed militia with the President as its commander (not a well-armed neighborhood with my local mechanic's greasy fingers manning the Bat Phone). My .38 or your shotgun or her 9 mm semiautomatic or his .357 or Harris and Klebold's arsenal will never stop the government's violent intent—whether lawful or unlawful.

In the 1930s, the government was a pawn to Big Business when unions were trying to organize. Why didn't the citizenry's legal gun ownership stop their abuses? In the 1950s, the government trampled all over the rights of Americans in its zeal to quash a legitimate political voice—communism. Why didn't the legal ownership of handguns help the citizens against a government gone mad? In the 1960s, the government forcefully and stealthily dismantled the Black Panthers, despite the arsenal they had amassed. And how did legal gun ownership protect the four students killed at Kent State University from their heavily armed government? And in the 1990s, the tremendous firepower of the Branch Davidians couldn't keep the government at bay. Even the Confederate South in the 1860s with all its guns lost to the federal government. Does Mr. Stein actually believe that a community armed with legal handguns will be able to stop a government gone (noticeably) treasonous? If that's the crux of his argument, disarm America now. Believe me, the government isn't afraid of your Uzi or my high-powered rifle. It's more wary of the "bullets" flying from "radical" pens or from union organizers attempting to empower workers to even question the omnipotence of Big Business.

Mr. Stein wonders what law is going to stop killers as motivated as the punks at Columbine. What motivation do teenagers need to be depressed? To quote Lisa Simpson: "Trying to make a teenager depressed is like shooting fish in a barrel." The problem is that when teenagers today weigh their options for relief, one of those options *is*, unfortunately, to randomly or non-randomly *shoot* all those who have "aggrieved" them because of the ease with which they can obtain guns. When I was in high school, many kids got teased, left out of sporting activities, dissed by the pretty girls. When they searched for options of relief, guns was *not* one of the first things to enter their minds because the proliferation of such weaponry had not become commonplace. (A sophomore did shoot the floor during math class once. We never saw him or a gun again.) More likely, those kids would fight hand-to-hand, bury themselves in their books to later become millionaire computer programmers, or adjust in some way. Adaptation is the cornerstone of all things living. Guns seem to circumvent that natural adolescent process.

And how about the countries with no so-called legal constitutional right for its citizenry to own firearms? Don't their low murder rates count for anything? Can we not see that 1+1 = 2? Or are we brainwashed by the NRA's brand of arithmetic: 1+1 = *minus* 2?

I disagree with Mr. Stein's sentiments that a total ban on guns would result in a far greater lack of freedom. We're already subject to legal searches and the only time our freedom is compromised is when the authorities step outside the legal bounds. And there are already many things outlawed that do not infringe upon my freedom, including driving at high rates of speed, jaywalking, and peddling child porn. I would welcome *legal* searches by the government for illegal firearms in the case of a total ban. I believe in our government's system of checks and balances. I'm not so libertarian as Mr. Stein to believe that the cream of humanity will always rise to the top without government "guidance" of itself and of the people. I believe in the distrust of god and country that our forefathers had when drafting and ratifying the Constitution.

And as far as China goes, it's just an all-around bad example because in the U.S. government's eyes, China can do no wrong, since it represents untold billions of dollars for corporate America and, by extension, its politicians. The massacre at Tiannamen Square was truly a tragedy, but a greater tragedy is the continued support of Chinese leaders despite the known human rights abuses, which far outnumber the dead at Tiannamen Square. If that were Castro, we'd have nuked him.

Mr. Stein asks: "Wouldn't it be great if instead of being conditioned to believe in heaven and hell, people instead were taught the truth: that life here on earth is the only life, that what we have on this planet is what needs to be valued?" Yes, I say to Mr. Stein, yes, yes, yes, and let's begin valuing those lives by re-interpreting the Constitution and getting guns out of the general populace's hands. What better way to say "I value you" than by not pointing a gun at me?!

—Scott Stein responds to C.P. Kaiser's rebuttal on "I Thank God the Tornado Didn't Suck Me Up ... Too Bad About My Neighbors, Though."

The essential weakness of C.P. Kaiser's extreme stance is demonstrated by the very existence of this, my second response to his essay. As I previously stated, I am not exactly a gun-toting member of a militia, yet here I am making the NRA's case. I would normally be willing to engage in discussion of gun-safety policies that would make it harder for criminals to hurt others and had respect for privacy, freedom, and defense of self and family. (I think that all but the most detached-from-reality libertarians would not want people strolling through residential neighborhoods with machine guns or bazookas. It is not a violation of individual freedom to prohibit people from carrying personal nuclear arsenals.)

But Mr. Kaiser's position does not allow for such a discussion. If he is correct in his belief that thousands of deaths are attributable to the lack of gun-control legislation, then I am forced to conclude that these deaths are caused in part by his position, and Rosie O'Donnell's. The NRA welcomes Rosie and C.P. Kaiser. They are wonderful recruitment tools. The threat of a total ban gives the NRA more members and power, which in turn prevents any change in gun laws, which in turn, if Mr. Kaiser is right, leads to death. It is ironic—those most opposed to guns have helped create an environment that ensures their continued proliferation.

But before we agree to start passing new laws, let's look at them carefully, and let's look at current laws and the way we sentence criminals who use guns in a crime. And let us ask why such laws, when indeed necessary, cannot be enacted locally. Hunting rifles might not be relevant to Mr. Kaiser, who lives in a city, but not all people lead the same existences. Why does Washington D.C. decide how guns should be regulated in the mountains of Montana? The arguments for some of the gun laws are suspect. Politicians have argued that the six-year-old girl killed last year by a classmate would be alive today if only there were mandatory gunlocks. They conveniently ignore that the weapon in question was owned by a drug dealer and was left loaded on a bed in plain sight of the six-year-old shooter. Criminals do not obey laws. Criminals will not use gunlocks, or obey a ban. No law would've stopped that tragedy.

Mr. Kaiser is exaggerating, of course—the government doesn't already own *all* the guns. It certainly has overwhelming power, which it wields on occasion. Why give it more? I am not suggesting that Joe Farmer is going to keep out the federal troops seizing his land. He is not. But a nation of Joe Farmers, a hundred million armed law-abiding citizens, if the need ever arose, would give any tyrannical government something to think about. There are lines it will not cross. The duration of our democracy is not based merely on the good-natured intentions of our leaders. Yes, the government is not afraid of segments of the population or their arms, Mr. Kaiser is right. But ultimately the rights of any people come from their willingness to fight for freedom if necessary, not from the government or the Constitution.

That is why I mentioned China in my above comment. Mr. Kaiser used the occasion of that mention to lambaste U.S. policy toward China and Big Business. I am not concerned with that diatribe here. I simply was pointing out that when the Chinese people tried to fight for freedom, they did it unarmed, and failed. The Cuban people are similarly not armed. Mr. Kaiser points to European nations as examples of free lands that do not have firearms. But they are free (to the extent they are), and their people choose their leaders, because the United States *was* armed, and *did* fight the American Revolution for freedom in the first place. We cannot separate our freedom so easily from modern democracy's violent beginnings.

McCarthyism is a bad example. The general public was supportive enough of the government's inquiries until McCarthy collapsed under the weight of his obsession and tried to take on the army. The right to bear arms was irrelevant here—fortunately, it never got that far. Had the government defied the will of the people and continued in its witch-hunt, if the tyranny had increased in scope to touch many more ordinary citizens, I don't know what would have happened. But in the case of a tyrannical government out of control on a large scale, which, despite the examples Mr. Kaiser provides, none of us have ever really seen (try being a journalist in Iraq, or China, or Cuba), I believe the right of the people to bear arms is nothing to chuckle about.

What is laughable is the notion that communism is anything as benign as a "legitimate political voice." I disagree with McCarthy, and with the suppression of ideas or speech of any kind. But communism, by its definition, is about denying the rights of other people. I am tired of the cliché that communism is nice in principle but bad in practice. It is bad in principle too. Communism means that you get what I earn, that the state, not the individual, is the foundation of society. I will not argue here against *voluntary* communism, within groups, families, castaways on *Survivor*. But don't claim that communism is merely another political voice, as long as we live in a society that allows a persuaded majority to force others to live under it.

The sad truth is, the government does not fear radical pens of any kind. That is because of the view of democracy that too many people, including it seems Mr. Kaiser, embrace. The government has merely to make a 30-second TV spot, or a good speech, and persuade 51% of voters to do things this way or that. There is no discussion of principles, or rights, or freedom. All that matters is the majority's opinion. That might be democracy, but we should be wary of it.

Mr. Kaiser doesn't think the many laws that have been enacted have infringed on freedom? He should explain that to the thousands of non-violent people in prison right now for drug offenses in this country (and if you really want to reduce gun deaths in America, first look at this nation's unprincipled drug laws, which create profit-motive that leads to killing). Mr. Kaiser would gladly subject himself to a search for weapons if a ban were enacted, because he in this case would be in the 51% that supported the ban. But when elements in the population or the tiny minority of lawmakers decide that they want to ban something else, I wonder how warmly he would welcome federal agents into his home to have a look around. If 51% of the people or their representatives ever managed to outlaw and vigorously search for alcohol again, or homosexuality, or premarital sex, or atheism or a particular religion, or a certain book, I think Mr. Kaiser would be among the first to protest, and would agree that the government has no business invading homes, no matter what the new law or amended Constitution might say.

It is easy to support freedom when it is about a matter with which you sympathize, a much more difficult task when you do not agree and see no ill effects for your own lifestyle. Let's stop talking about majorities and minorities, and blocks of voters each haggling for their own special interest, and let's begin talking about the importance of individual freedom, the right to privacy and self-determination, to live as one chooses and not according to this month's whim of the tyrannical majority. This might include sensible gun laws, especially on the local level. It depends on who is defining sensible, I guess.

I am trying to see the balance of things here. When I lived in Miami I knew people who were irresponsible gun owners, who treated them like toys and handled them after drinking. They were just college students, not even really Florida residents, but could buy guns without much trouble. I felt safer back home in New York City than in Miami, where I sensed that everyone was armed and a little angry (though some say that violent crime in Florida actually decreased when gun control laws were relaxed).

In any case, I don't want losers like Harris and Klebold to have guns. I do not deny that guns are partly to blame for their actions. But to chalk up the enormity of their violence to access to weapons, to teenage angst, is ridiculous. Something more was going on with those two. Let's not simplify it by pointing to the need for prayer in school as a solution, but let's not be equally reductive and say, "All teenagers would do this if they had access to the guns." These were highly motivated killers, who spent months building bombs and planning their attack. They didn't turn to guns because they happened to be handy, in a rage; they sought the weapons out and planned the massacre methodically. A simple combination of weapons and adolescence? Come on now.

Finally, Mr. Kaiser did not answer my questions about self-defense. Given the reality that, even with a ban, criminals in this country will continue to be armed, no government should have the power to prevent me from protecting myself with a weapon in my own home. It was reported that Rosie O'Donnell's bodyguard had applied for a firearm permit, despite her well-publicized call for a ban. I want my family to be as safe as Rosie's. That might include responsible ownership of a gun, it might include no gun. Do not give me the statistics about how many guns in the home are used in domestic violence and suicides and all the rest. There are also many stories about storeowners and homeowners who are alive today because their guns saved their lives. Statistics are used by both sides to keep all of us from thinking. And I am not a statistic. I am a person.

I have been inside a home while it was being broken into. After kicking in the front door, had the criminals decided to make their way upstairs (instead of quickly exiting after leaving a threatening note for the first floor resident who owed them money), they would have met my heavily armed Italian uncle. Fortunately, it didn't come to that—there was no dramatic confrontation. But it is not a stretch to imagine them coming up those stairs, is it? I thought they were going to. People are killed every day by criminals who don't stop on the first floor. Your Constitution and your arm-twisting 51% mean nothing next to the right of people to defend themselves in their own home.

—*C.P. Kaiser responds to Scott Stein's rebuttal on "I Thank God the Tornado Didn't Suck Me Up ... Too Bad About My Neighbors, Though."*

First of all, Mr. Stein, if my stance is extreme, I stand in good company because I am in line with the Constitution and its creators and signers. I ask for nothing except for the dynamic process of democracy to continue, which means endless debates about and interpretations of the Constitution. The framers of that document actually set it up so that you and I can debate such nuances. To me there is nothing extreme about wanting the process of democracy to happen.

Second, it's interesting that in the beginning of your rebuttal you choose to align me only with machine guns, bazookas, and personal nuclear arsenals, when, in fact, I didn't mention any of those by name (very extreme examples on your part). My argument is simply for the process of democracy to go forward, for the Supreme Court and state supreme courts to continue to debate and interpret the Constitution. I support a reading of the Second Amendment that bears little reality to how it is applied by the NRA and other like-minded people, but I also support the NRA's right to debate.

Next, you say that my position does not allow for such a discussion. Excuse me, but what are we having here?

I understand what Mr. Stein is saying about my so-called extreme stance on gun control giving the NRA more power. However, what I hope to do is continue the dialogue about this issue. It took decades before the truth about Big Tobacco was revealed. Those who kept that debate alive are to be commended. Just because I disagree with the NRA doesn't mean I disagree with their right to their opinions. They are doing what I am doing: playing with the malleability of the Constitution. Just like Big Tobacco, they have a lot more power and money than I do; it's gonna be a long debate and I have no intention of shying away from it.

Here's a conversation I imagine you having with the "extreme" American Revolutionaries fighting against English tyranny. "King George welcomes extremists like Kaiser and Jefferson. They are wonderful recruitment tools for the English army. The threat of America's total secession gives the British army more members and power, which in turn prevents any change in taxation without representation for the colonies, which in turn, if

Mr. Washington is right, leads to more repression. It is ironic—those most opposed to remaining a British colony have helped create an environment that ensures its continued proliferation." As my satire indicates, a good fight is worth fighting.

To quote Thomas Paine: "A thing moderately good is not so good as it ought to be. Moderation in temper is always a virtue; but moderation in principle is always a vice."

Your argument about passing new gun control legislation is quite nice but irrelevant to my discussion. I was not calling for any such change. I want the Supreme Court to reinterpret the Second Amendment so that the United States doesn't allow ordinary citizens to own any guns. Militias will be defined as military units headed by the President. That's all I want.

I still have to chuckle when you talk about a tyrannical government being kept at bay by 100 million law-abiding armed Joe Farmers. First of all, give 100 million law-abiding citizens firearms and I would bet the number of law-abiding citizens drops by half in no time. Second, our government is already tyrannical. The stranglehold that Big Business has on our democracy is so insidious that I truly believe you (and millions of others) don't see it. The guns and gun issues are a distraction and the government welcomes that distraction, because while U.S. citizens are being gunned down daily, our politicians are pocketing more and more money from corporations allowed to pollute, cheat taxation, exploit workers, and wreak havoc on majority rule.

Mr. Stein, I simply must disagree with you when you downplay the tyranny of McCarthyism because it doesn't compare to the tyranny of Iraq. Tyranny in a democracy seems to wear a smiley face. The U.S. government is the best propagandist in the world. The real tyranny is to lull Americans into a sense of worthlessness, into a sense of apathy and lethargy. You say that had the tyranny of McCarthyism "increased in scope to touch many more ordinary citizens, I don't know what would have happened." I say that it DID touch many more citizens; it touched all of us and continues to have its effect on us today. That the FBI was allowed to abuse the rights of citizens since its inception contributed to the McCarthy hearings, contributed to the smuggling of Nazis to North and South America, contributed to the overthrow of Allende and the atrocities in Central America and elsewhere in the world by the United States. I don't take lightly the abuses against all American citizens perpetrated by McCarthy because I know it's the tip of the Cuban cigar.

Whether you or I agree with the tenets of communism is irrelevant to my argument. In America, we are supposed to allow for multiple voices, multiple political ideas. If some Americans want to belong to the Communist party, it is their right as Americans. I am merely defending their right as Americans to do so under the Constitution the same as you are defending the rights of Americans to own guns under the current interpretation of the Constitution.

You lambaste me for feeling my freedom has not been infringed by a myriad of enacted laws. However, in my argument, I make a distinction between legal searches and those that step outside such bounds. I'm not such a fool to believe that everything granted by the Supreme Court or any court is going to be the last word on justice and democracy. I only have to look at *Dred Scott.* Our prisons are pathetic, the so-called war on drugs is a joke. This is the democracy I live in and these are the debates I participate in and the fights I choose to fight. I'm not afraid of the malleability of our system of government. It's a works-in-progress. I happen to believe we'd be a better nation if guns were illegal.

You say it's ridiculous to chalk up the enormity of Harris and Klebold's violence to access to weapons and teenage angst. You ask us to not simplify it as such. I say your conclusion that "something more was going on with those two" is equally as simple. You don't know and neither do I what was going on with those two. "A simple combination of weapons and adolescence?" you ask. Who knows...? All I'm asking is for the Constitution to be reinterpreted by the Justices to confine gun ownership to a well-regulated militia with the President as its commander-in-chief.

Rosie O'Donnell is Rosie O'Donnell. I don't have her poster hanging next to my copy of the Constitution. I don't know what her agenda is. I only want to contribute to the checks and balances system of government set up in the 18th century by a band of revolutionaries separating themselves from the financial and religious tyranny of England. I don't consider my desire to see our three branches of government to work as they were designed as "arm-twisting" as you call it.

> "The Revolutionaries believed that every citizen was responsible not just for his freedom, but for the liberty of the generations to come. They fought for the principle that a people who have no power to curb government's appetite for money and power would soon be reduced to servitude." — Matthew Robinson

You may consider guns in the hands of commoners to be the best power to fight a corrupt government. I don't. I think full participation in choosing government officials and holding them accountable for their honest representation is the best way to hold a government in check.

—Scott Stein responds (again) to C.P. Kaiser rebuttal on "I Thank God the Tornado Didn't Suck Me Up ... Too Bad About My Neighbors, Though."

Mr. Kaiser's latest response belies misunderstanding of my position and statements, so let me clear up a few things and try to have *my* last word.

I am not aligning Mr. Kaiser with machine guns or bazookas. I am directing that comment to a small minority of NRA members, libertarians, and others who believe there is *no* role for government in regulating weapons *at all*. My point, which I thought was clear, is that most people, including vocal supporters of gun rights, *do* believe that the government has a role in regulating weapons, evidenced by their desire to not have people toting heavy artillery through school zones in public view. How much regulation will be debated forever. That is the dynamic flow of democracy Mr. Kaiser values that is *not* happening. And it is *that* discussion Mr. Kaiser's position makes impossible.

I believe that reasonable people, who would otherwise be willing to discuss reasonable gun-safety measures, which did not interfere with their rights to own a weapon for legitimate purposes, are now unwilling to discuss measures with which they might agree, because of all this talk of a ban. I said that Mr. Kaiser's position prevented discussion of *gun-safety measures*, and he asked, What are we having here, if not a discussion? We are having a discussion about a hypothetical ban, not gun safety. As long as that is what is being discussed, there is no hope for a real discussion of gun-safety measures. Our lawmakers will not succeed in discussing it either, because of positions like Mr. Kaiser's that have given the NRA more members, power, and incentive to prevent any legislation on any level.

I do not take McCarthy's attack on freedom lightly at all. I am merely claiming that most ordinary Americans were not fearful of McCarthy and in fact supported him for some time. When they saw he had gone too far, as he certainly did, they no longer supported him, and he soon lost power. It did not come to a point that might bring law-abiding citizens to raise arms against their government. All of the examples Mr. Kaiser provided are similar. They involved relatively small groups, easily defeated and not supported by large numbers of Americans. I am talking of an obvious tyranny, of police busting into people's homes at high rates, of a suspension of individual rights on a large scale. It is that potential tyranny that makes the right to bear arms important. The tyranny that Mr. Kaiser points to (Big Business and all the rest) is not relevant, because most people do not perceive it as tyranny. If enough did, if they believed it were necessary, that is when the right to bear arms against a government out of control would come into play.

While Mr. Kaiser is discussing legitimate political voices, I have a question to pose. What if some group wanted to advocate slavery? What if, in present-day America, enough people got together and were able to change the Constitution and pass laws that made slavery legal again? At what point would Mr. Kaiser say that, though these people are entitled to their opinions, and even to the right to speak their sickly minds, they are *not* entitled to impose that view on others just because they have enough votes. There are some principles that must stand above even democracy. That is what I am clearly saying. If 99% of the people are in favor of enslaving the other 1%, we ought to have principles and rules that prevent it.

By making *legal* the highest standard, you open the door for Prohibition, and the current war on drugs, and government censorship, and criminalizing sexual conduct between consenting adults, and even enforced religion. I am asking that we agree that there are some matters over which we as a tyrannical voting mass should not have authority. There are laws we should not be able to make. Belong to any party you want, communist or otherwise. But no party, no matter how many votes it gets, ought to have the power to take what others have earned.

The influence of special interests and Big Business and religious groups that Mr. Kaiser often rails against is possible in part because our system has given lawmakers too much power. There will always be abuses from those in power. I am suggesting that reconceptualizing the role of government, empowering lawmakers to regulate only those matters that are truly public, holding individual freedom and responsibility to be the highest value, is the best way to combat the abuses of power and money. We might not always agree on what counts as public, and there is plenty of room for the discussion and dynamic flow of opinions that Mr. Kaiser values. Our gun debate would continue. It is clearly a public matter, to some degree. But there would be lines the government could not cross, no matter the will of the easily persuaded majority.

—C.P. Kaiser responds to Scott Stein's rebuttal on "I Thank God the Tornado Didn't Suck Me Up ... Too Bad About My Neighbors, Though."

Mr. Stein and I could debate the finer points of our arguments endlessly. In that case, I would like to conclude my comments simply with some thoughts on the Second Amendment, supporting a Supreme Court interpretation I seek. After all, I did not begin the debate on gun legislation; I only asked for a constitutional amendment, which, I understand, doesn't come lightly. In my original essay, I mention that "our forefathers ... included in the Constitution a provision for a well-armed militia" and that "if for some odd and remote chance the courts vote to install school-sponsored prayer, I hope students pray for the dissolution of the NRA and a constitutional amendment banning the ownership of all firearms."

The Second Amendment: A well-regulated militia, being necessary to the security of a free State, the right of the people to keep and bear arms, shall not be infringed.

It seems that the Second Amendment controversy is with the word *militia*. Author Bob Sullivan in "Have Guns, Will Travel" (p. 29) says we can look for clues to the Founding Fathers' meaning by noticing how the word *militia* is used elsewhere in the Constitution.

> *Militia* appears four times: once in Section 2, which names the President as the Commander-in-Chief of the militia of the several states when it's called into national service, and three times in Section 8, which says that Congress can call for the militia to execute the laws of the union, suppress insurrections, and repel invasions; that Congress should provide for the militia's organizing, arming, and discipline; and that the states should appoint officers and train the militia according to the discipline prescribed by Congress.

Contrary to the gun lobby's propaganda, the Second Amendment guarantees the people the right to be armed only in connection with service in a "well-regulated Militia." Courts consistently have ruled that there is no constitutional right to own a gun for private purposes unrelated to the organized state militia. They have unanimously rejected the National Rifle Association's view that the Second Amendment is about self-defense or sporting uses of guns.

"The purpose of the Second Amendment is to restrain the federal government from regulating the possession of arms where such regulation would interfere with the preservation or efficiency of the militia" and the "Second Amendment guarantees no right to keep and bear a firearm that does not have some reasonable relationship to the preservation or efficiency of a well-regulated militia" (*U.S. v. Hale*, 978 F.2d 1016, 8th Cir. 1992).

At the time the U.S. Constitution was adopted, each of the states had its own military force, or militia, comprised of ordinary citizens who were required to report for training several days a year and to supply their own equipment for militia use, including guns and horses. The original intent of the Second Amendment was to prevent the federal government from passing laws that would disarm the state militia.

However, the militia was not, as some gun control opponents have claimed, simply another word for the armed citizenry. It was an organized military force, "well regulated" by the state governments. Even modern dictionaries retain the essence of that meaning, for example, this definition from *Merriam Webster's Collegiate Dictionary, Tenth Edition:* "The whole body of able-bodied male citizens *declared by law* as being subject to call *to military service*" (emphasis mine).

As former Harvard Law School Dean Erwin Griswold put it, "To assert that the Constitution is a barrier to reasonable gun laws, in the face of the unanimous judgment of the federal courts to the contrary, exceeds the limits of principled advocacy. It is time for the NRA and its followers in Congress to stop trying to twist the Second Amendment from a reasoned (if antiquated) empowerment for a militia into a bulletproof personal right for anyone to wield deadly weaponry beyond legislative control."

Scott Stein
An Open Letter to the Dirty Bastard Who Stole My Car

Two days ago I had a car. Not a great one, I guess. It didn't talk and help me fight crime. It didn't have welded doors and the ability to jump cars with no ramp in sight, like the General Lee. I never even once slid over the hood à la Starsky and Hutch.

No, it was a simple 11-year-old beige Honda Civic hatchback with more than 111,000 miles. A four-speed. No power locks. No power windows. No power steering. Hell, no power anything. No CD player either, and only two stereo speakers—backseat passengers don't need to hear the music.

It did have, though, a recent oil change. It still got good mileage, well in the thirties on the highway. And nothing could fit into smaller city parking spaces. Nothing. That car was supposed to last me another couple of years, maybe. Yes, on very hot days in stop-and-go traffic, it was necessary to use the air conditioner with care—overheating was a threat. But it did have air-conditioning, so it wasn't exactly a piece of junk (no matter what my wife might say).

But you dirty bastards stole it. Or maybe there was only one of you, you dirty bastard. I saw my car outside my apartment on Sunday night, and when I dragged myself away from the computer and out of doors late Monday morning, it was gone. At first I thought I had misplaced it. I looked in two nearby sections of the parking lot, but no car.

Once, about four years ago in Miami Beach, I thought my car had been stolen, but it turned out to have been merely towed (unbeknown to me at the time, a resident sticker was required to park on certain city streets). So I didn't rush to judgment about my fellow man this time. Maybe no one had stolen my car.

Could it have been towed? No, of course not, you say. How do you know? Because you stole it, you dirty bastard. I had to face facts. You had stolen my car.

A nice police officer came and told me that cars stolen from this area often end up dumped in Philadelphia or Trenton. It was possible I would get a call in a few days. Though, he said, I might not like what they tell me. Apparently, Hondas, even old ones, are valued for their parts by car thieves—but you, you dirty bastard, already knew that, didn't you?

The prospect of recovering my car in pieces did not improve my day, but I thanked the officer and then called my insurance company. They were sympathetic. Maybe in a couple of weeks I'll get a few bucks from them. How much could my car be worth?

According to the most reliable Internet sources, my car might be worth $1,000. Maybe less. I guess I won't be using my insurance windfall for a down payment on that new yacht I've had my eye on. My car was worth a lot more than $1,000 to me. It was my car, you dirty bastard.

Now I am sharing a car with my wife until we figure out how to replace my fuel-efficient and generally reliable piece of junk. Her car isn't exactly new, but now we are using the Club on it even when it is parked in front of our home in the middle of the day.

But this isn't a story about the loss of trust in people or society. I haven't had that for a long time now. You haven't succeeded in making me cold and jaded—been there, done that. I'm not even that upset. Annoyed, definitely. Inconvenienced, absolutely. But you haven't hit a nerve or left me fearing for my life, you dirty bastard. You are insignificant.

I would leave you with a moving statement about how in all of this what I really feel is sadness for your pathetic life, pity for your empty heart, that all I really want is to reach out to you with these words to convince you to take a more righteous path, but that would be a lie. You did, after all, steal my car, you dirty bastard.

Besides, I'm pretty sure you can't read.

Editor's note: The dirty bastard in this essay is no relation to rap star Old Dirty Bastard. Please don't sue us.

Ari McKee
In Praise of Short Men

George over Jerry. Starsky over Hutch. Kirk over Spock. Davy over Mike. It goes back pretty far. I don't know how it all started. It doesn't make evolutionary sense. It's a thing. Everyone's got one. For mustaches, connected earlobes, Speedos. I don't ask why. If there's one thing I've learned about this, and others, it's that a fetish needs no raison d'être.

A *person*, on the other hand, rationalizes.

- Short men smell better. They do! Don't send me scratch & sniff cards with the scent of your unwashed, under-height neighbor on it, but hear this: It is a well-known and unproven fact that shorter men don't produce the waves of B.O. that their taller brothers emit. Is it the smaller skin surface area, is it the vertical placement of their armpits in relation to your nose? I don't know and I don't care, I just *like* it.

- Short men can usually dance. Check out any dance floor—who's shaking it and who's holding up the bar? Eight out of 10 couples have a short guy—you can't get him off the floor! Riverdancing, macarena-ing, moshing, swinging, whatever. It's almost annoying. But not so annoying as that tall dude with feet as long as your shins doing such a sad, self-conscious little white boy shuffle that you can't even look at him. If you need a helpful reminder, think *Fred*—Fred Astaire (5'9") was the one who could dance; Fred Gwynne (6'5") was Herman Munster. Plus, my dad's name is Fred (5'8") and he married my mom even though she couldn't lindy.

- With short men you can wear their clothes—to lounge in, as well as to the office. Maybe I miss my old boyfriend, maybe *not*, but I'm keeping the gray Scottish cashmere V-neck his mother gave him because it fits, suckah!

- Short men don't take up the whole couch-bed-Barcalounger-bathtub-double sleeping bag. With tall guys, you can't even fit in the bathroom with their *shoes*.

- Here's another dancing thing—there's nothing weirder than slow dancing with a tall guy who's, well, let's say, happy to see you, and his glee is hitting you pretty much directly in the sternum. It's like wearing a necklace with a rubber-handled socket wrench hanging off it. Even a girl madly in love will run giggling into the ladies' room after that dance, if only to pry the Playtex underwires out of her breastbone.

- Short men look better in a beard—tall guys always end up looking Lincolnesque.

- Men's Olympic gymnastics. The rings. Oh, baby, the rings.

- Short men have more energy. You know it and I know it—big guys wear out. Put a beagle and a Great Dane in the same room and see who runs demented in a circle until his toenails snap off and see who lies down even before he's technically entered the room. Tall guys are only human—they're moving those big old limbs and those big old muscles around on those big old bones all day, fighting a gravitational pull the rest of us can only imagine. Wears a person out. They make up for it by being good relaxers. Like we need more of those.

- With a short guy, you don't get half the Adam's apple issues. You ever watch a guy shave one of those goiter-sized ones? It's bad enough being eye level with some big growth on your man's neck, but having to watch it moving up and down, up and down, swimming its endless futile lap against the throat currents, bobbing and weaving, riveting your gaze, throbbing like the swollen glands of a bubonic plague victim, and all the while he's chasing after it with a wet razor blade. You can't help but wonder what would happen if he sliced into it and the whole time everything around you is all wet and fluid and steamy and flecked with white foam until you finally scream, "Cough it up! Cough it up, you tubercular bastard!"
- You don't seem to hear so much from short men about lower back pain. Or about knee pain or neck pain. And they don't make a big stink at the ticket counter about sitting in the bulkhead on every damn flight, so as to minimize their back pain and knee pain and neck pain.
- It's a mistake to underestimate "cute." Tom Cruise. Kevin Spacey. Robert Carlyle. James Cagney. Spencer Tracy. Prince. *Cute.*

In the interests of fraternal brotherhood and global self-esteem, it needs to be said that when the lights are out and the lovin's begun, darn it, height just doesn't matter. Unless you're standing up. Like in the shower. But that hardly ever happens. Forget I even said anything about it.

It's true that I might be missing out on my chance to give birth to the biggest fish in the gene pool. If I keep chasing after guys who use a chair to put the wine glasses away, I'll someday have to explain to my children why I chose cute little chromosomes instead of large, lumbering ones.

"Kids," I'll say, "Once there was this ballgame called evolution. The great big dinosaurs played against the adorable little monkeys. Guess who won?"

Maybe size *does* matter.

Willie, for C.P. Kaiser
If I Had Balls, I'd Be Licking Them

Hi. My name is Willie and I'm a dachshund. (Stop laughing, it's not my fault I'm built like this. If I could change history, believe me, I'd maim those damn 17th-century German breeders who created us with long torsos and short legs simply to ferret out badgers from holes in the Schwartzwald. OK, maybe in the old country we were valued, but who in this civilized North American continent in the 21st century has the slightest idea what a badger is? Do we still need to resemble mutant hot dogs? No, it's evolutionarily wasteful, somewhat akin to Donald Trump washing dishes at his own casino, or Alan Greenspan owning a game of Monopoly minus Park Place and Boardwalk, or Julia Roberts taking acting lessons—OK, maybe the Julia Roberts scenario isn't evolutionarily wasteful. Anyway, you get my point. This is my body so I do the best I can with it. But I digress.)

My master, C.P. Kaiser, is so busy and stressed out searching for employment since he moved to the Bay Area, that he barely has the time to wipe my ass let alone write an essay for *When Falls the Coliseum*. Not like I've got "all the time in the world," as he muttered one night when he thought I wasn't listening. But he paid for that slip of the tongue: I spit up on the carpet after eating Styrofoam. Just because my work doesn't look like work doesn't mean I'm not on the payroll.

Anyway, I've taken it upon myself as his trusted, faithful companion (what else can I be without any balls?) to write this essay for him. I hope it makes him happy, lest he force me to do that tennis ball trick for onlookers. You know the one where I balance it on the end of my nose, then catch it in my mouth. I hate that! What the fuck am I, a freak show? We're not in the Schwarzwald anymore, my friends. I expect a little dignity.

So, my day starts like everyone else's, sort of. I awake from my so-called bed, a pockmarked pillow on the cold, hard floor covered with an old Mexican blanket from the Eisenhower administration. Do my masters care? No. They're quilted from head to toe. But I digress.

As with humans, I can't go to work until my morning weedle. But I have to wait for C.P. to get up, make coffee, scan the morning news, weedle, check e-mail, toast an English muffin, etc., etc., all the while I'm doing a Bavarian pee-pee dance in the corner, with kidneys swelling like Ball Park franks. Just because I look like a giant bladder doesn't mean I have one.

You see, back on the East Coast, I could slip out the back door and pee with impunity in fenced-in security. Here, on the second floor, I need human support to navigate the stairs (damn those 17th-century German breeders) and human supervision lest I stray into the middle of traffic or over to Penelope Poodle's pen. Can you blame me for straying? Better than 70% of my brain is olfactory related. If I smell a hot dish, I'm outta there (too bad about my lack of certain equipment, though). But alas, equipment or no, my master is slowly sipping coffee, with lip-smacking satisfaction and not a whit wiser about my urinary urgency.

When C.P. does take me out for my morning constitutional (ah, sweet revenge), instead of going just once, I break it up into two, sometimes three, separate movements, forcing him to cart around a super pooper-scooper the size of a small bulldozer. When I'm finished with that business, we head home where I eat my so-called food: dried slaughterhouse scraps that couldn't get respect at an Oscar Meyer plant. But I digress.

When my two masters leave for the day, I finally go to work, sniffing around the kitchen for morsels of bread crumbs, cookie crumbs, or olive pits (if I don't learn to recognize them soon, I'll have no teeth left). Then I'll check out the sweet aroma coming from the trashcan. If there's sufficient bag-hangover that I can grab with my teeth, I'll pull it down and rummage through. Thanksgiving trash was an especially tasty meal. When my masters came home from their Thanksgiving movie, they actually blamed themselves for leaving the garbage can on the floor. Stupid humans! Who do they really think is more evolved? After all, *they're* picking up *my* turds! But I digress.

After my work in the kitchen, it's still early and I usually like to nap. If I had any balls, this would be the perfect time to lick them. But alas, I was stripped of my alpha status years ago because I couldn't stop humping the Queen Anne dining set. In the absence of scrotal authority, I'll head for the pockmarked pillow in the bedroom and snooze for a couple hours, always on the alert for UPS drivers, trash men, and utility workers. Once the doggie hotline begins, I've got to join in or my hairy brethren will shun me. It's hell! I can't get any decent REM action going.

After that barking splurge, I'll often tour the kitchen again, licking other parts of the floor, then head back to the bedroom where I'll sleep until the U.S. postal service arrives. Back in Philly, the mail had to be slipped right through the front door, causing a ruckus a deaf muskrat could hear a mile away. Here, the mail arrives silently, shoved into a clump of boxes downstairs, away from the keen earshot of canine cunning. Even so, if it's past 3 o'clock, I'll give a five-minute perfunctory barking performance just to stay in shape.

After that workout, I'll swing by the kitchen, sniffing the crevices, licking the floor. Maybe now I'll tour the living room, smell the pair of socks by the sofa, sniff the front door, smell the laundry basket, stuff like that. I'd lick my balls, but you know that story. So, exhausted from all this work, I head for bed and dream of doing it all over again tomorrow.

Scott Stein
The Stacker

The stack was developing as a sort of snowflake, with a symmetry as unconventional as it was unconditional. The columns at the snowflake's outer tips consisted of the rectangular crates, which grew larger as they neared the ceiling, and the crates with still more sides also grew progressively larger throughout the stack. The stack was sorted by code in a diagonal pattern, both alphabetically and numerically, and a chessboard arrangement had also emerged, with the alternation of light and dark wood crates throughout.

Had the Stacker intended all of it? Any of it? He didn't understand how it had worked out to such perfection. The pieces had just fallen into place. He couldn't believe the beauty he had brought into the world, and stood for a moment, still and silent and wondering how it had all happened. Finally, he had a stack that he wanted people to see, that people were capable of seeing. The other stackers would never tell him they liked it, he knew that. They would resent his accomplishment; their blind jealousy wouldn't allow them to acknowledge the greatness of his art. He didn't need them anyway. A stack as important as this one could not be long ignored.

With a synthesized chime and a flashing red light, the freight elevator's doors parted. For a full minute, the automated treadmill churned loudly as it steadily spewed more crates into the room. The Stacker laughed for a second. This was clearly a joke. There was never more than one delivery per day. Someone was having fun at his expense. Who could be playing games like this? No one. It was no joke. He had no friends, no one who would trouble with such childishness. And tampering with crates was a serious offense. No, this was a real shipment, and he would have to assimilate it into the rest of the stack. How could they do this to him? He looked at the perfection of the stack he had constructed, marveled at its purity, and was afraid to disturb it, to introduce new crates that might upset the harmony it embodied.

But looking upon it made him know that he had nothing to fear. He was now one of the Masters. The finest stack in history stood before him, fashioned by his own hands, and this new challenge could only result in further greatness. He strapped a crate and maneuvered it into position, and another, and another. The stack reached nearly to the ceiling. He worked even more frantically than he had the first time, and the stack grew in size and beauty. The symmetry continued, and the top half of the stack mirrored the lower, with the new crates now getting smaller as they approached more glorious heights. Certainly it would be the subject of numerous papers and articles. Probably the University would offer research grants to study it at length. The Stacker was sure to be made a supervisor. He would likely tour the country, speak to panels, help with important decisions and policies.

He swung and hooked and strapped until his hands burned and his back ached. He ran and leapt and nearly danced as he became one with the stack, until he understood each crate as if he had built it himself, until his clothes were wet and his arms were heavy. Then, still sweating and panting, he realized that it was done. The stack was complete. Its giant shadow drowned out the light, and he stood, shivering in awe. He wished it weren't so dark. He couldn't get a good look at the stack, and turned toward the wall to brighten the light, but bumped into a crate instead. He was inside the stack, in the center of the immense snowflake, which was everywhere flush with the ceiling. The Stacker had walled himself in. He couldn't get out and couldn't see the stack from the outside, as it was meant to be seen. He had to find a way out. The collators would be by soon, there would be transfer requests, and he couldn't be found in this ridiculous position, trapped by his own creation. The greatness of his stack would be lost if it got out that he had imprisoned himself. The first thing one learned as a stacker was to leave a way out. The fundamentals had eluded him.

Just then there was a knocking from the hall. He didn't answer. A banging. He held his breath and was motionless. More banging, and the Stacker heard a sheet of paper being slipped under the door and then withdrawing footfalls. He was saved. He had bolted the door, and no one would be able to enter until he unlocked it himself.

The Stacker grabbed a crate and slowly began shimmying it loose. He had designed the stack so that he could remove crates when called upon without disturbing the integrity of the overall structure. True, he had intended to remove them only from the outside (after he'd shown the stack to the proper persons and had it photographed), but that shouldn't make any difference. He slid the crate from side to side before finally pulling it through.

There was a distant creak and a rumble, and the giant shadow wavered. The columns swayed slightly, and the Stacker ran to one and tried to hold it in place. There was a perfectly square hole where he'd pulled the crate loose, large enough for him to escape from the deteriorating stack, but he made no move toward it. He ran from one column to another, but the rumble grew louder and the wavering more severe. As the crates toppled from their height, he made no effort to evade them but struggled to brace the stack, still pitifully leaning into a trembling column when the first crate came down on his head. The entire stack followed. A deafening crash of wood sprayed throughout the room as the Stacker was crushed to death and buried beneath tons of plain, ordinary crates. On the floor next to the steel door, half-covered with dust and shards of wood, was a sheet of paper. It read: Crates sent in error. Do not stack.

About the Contributors

Alastair MacDonald Black is an architect and holds a master of regional planning degree from the University of Pennsylvania. Careers already mined include farming, metal fabrication, industrial design, folk singing, residential construction (all trades), and pedagogy (business English). He preceded John McCain in navy aviation, but he spent his entire career in training, thus avoiding capture by hostiles. Alastair used to march and lead protest songs; the FBI still maintains a file on him, including photos at anti-Vietnam War rallies as he made Sicilian gestures at Bureau photographers.

Kevin Bolshaw is a miscreant and ne'er-do-well who occasionally writes prose and poetry to discharge mega-joules of angst. Read some at http://home.att.net/~k.bolshaw. He would like to gather together members of the boards of directors for BASF, Dow Chemical, and DuPont (and subsidiaries), along with the CEOs from both Champion and International Paper and a few members of the Department of the Interior and bang their heads à la the *Three Stooges*. He will gladly include a gratuitous eye-poke for executives of Pfizer Inc. for strip mining lime in Adams, Massachusetts, and despoiling the romping ground of his youth.

Amy Boshnack is *the* media. She began her career in television news and helped launch MSNBC before moving on to the magazine industry. She graduated with a double major in public relations and political science and a minor in marketing from the University of Miami. Amy also studied at the University of Essex in England for a semester with a focus on British and American history.

Jared Boshnack holds a bachelor of arts from Queens College. He has been employed in production for television and radio up and down the East Coast of the United States. Jared is currently working for ABC Sports. Don't touch his remote.

Helen Cates was raised around the Lake of the Ozarks and now resides in the Austin, Texas, area. She loves the great outdoors and likes to reminisce about the good-ole days back in hillbilly country. She joined the navy upon graduation, and has had the opportunity to serve this great nation and also to mop a few floors. Helen daily juggles home-schooling her two children, managing a writer's forum for America Online as a short story contest judge, as well as being a freelance writer, playwright, stage manager, and actress for the local theatres. Her most recent theatrical involvement was for *Chicago*.

Suzanne Hakanen is not ashamed to admit she is from New Jersey. In a haze of deluded post-high school dreams of a corporate job and a 401(k), she completed a bachelor of science in chemistry at The College of New Jersey. Fearing employment, she prolonged her education at Drexel University and received her master of science in technical and science communication. She spends most of her time complaining and devising ways to avoid doing any real work.

Robert L. Hall is a trained musician with a bachelor of music degree from the University of Memphis and a master of music from Florida State University. Robert is a Christian and an aspiring writer of mainstream fiction and crime novels. His work on *When Falls the Coliseum* has attracted attention, and the editors of southernscribe.com, an online magazine for Southern writers, have asked him to write for them as well.

Katherine Hauswirth is a full-time medical writer and editor and a freelance essayist. She has been published in *Pilgrimage, Clever Magazine,* and *Living for the Whole Family.* Katherine is also the author of the book, *Things My Mother Told Me.* Although her work is generally soft and sentimental, occasional binges on large doses of caffeine generate cyclical fits of indignation in which Katherine skewers cell phones, managed care, arrogant academics, and change in general. Katherine hails from Long Island, home of Joey Buttafuco, which explains a lot. She has retreated to the quiet shoreline of Connecticut, where the coffee is good and the living easy.

Alex Joseph's work has appeared in *The New York Times, The Evergreen Chronicles, Blythe House Quarterly, XConnect,* and many other places. He holds a master of fine arts in writing from Sarah Lawrence College. Alex teaches at the Gotham Writers' Workshop in Manhattan, and works as a staff writer at the Fashion Institute of Technology. His home on the Web is http://members.aol.com/BSALJO/index.html.

C.P. Kaiser earned a master of arts in theatre from the very Catholic Villanova University, not the most liberal-minded place to honestly explore the human condition. However, he managed to ruffle more than a few Augustinian robes with his one-act play *Gender Bender,* which explored relational dynamics when one partner decides to have a sex change. He recently won an Orgasmic Writing Contest for his story, "The Beeper," and is currently the associate editor for Diagnostic Imaging, a news magazine covering diagnostic radiology issues.

Jody Lane, an art school dropout, lives somewhere in the Midwest with her two children, the Antichrist and Rosemary's baby. After a brief hiatus that included a year of aimless surfing on the 'net, researching the effects of faith healing on diaper rash, and opening a halfway house for her insane relatives, Jody has returned to the ranks of those who actually have a life, and got a job as the advertising manager for a daily newspaper. Jody would like to become the champion of the common man, the voice of average middle-class Americans, but they are not taking applications or returning her phone calls.

Ari McKee learned a lot in college, but not enough to entirely escape graduate school. Now that she's a writer and humorist, she utilizes her hard-won comparative religion degree and therefore justifies her crippling student loan payments by dropping theological themes into her otherwise fluffy and lowbrow satirical sketches. Saint Paul, Minnesota, is the hub of her ever-expanding wheel of influence, not unlike the karmic wheel of Samsara in Hinduism or the Great Circle Mandala found in many aboriginal cultures, or like the *Wheel of Fortune* found every night at 6 p.m. on Channel 9. You, too, can contribute to her inflated sense of cultural and spiritual relevance by visiting her Web site http://arimckee.iwarp.com or by reviewing aforesaid Web site positively in numerous local and national publications, or by waving signs with her name on them at large, televised sports events.

Robert O'Hara was born in and still resides in Norwalk, Connecticut. He holds a bachelor of science in communication from the University of Miami. An advocate of personal improvement through self-education, Robert's interests include foreign languages, geography, metaphysics, fiction writing, performing, and travel. In his spare time, he torments white people with his fade-away jumper and coaches at a local boxing club in South Norwalk.

Jeff Podell is an American. He remembers the Alamo, would have fought for 54/40, loves his mother, and eats apple pie. Jeff started a speaker bureau, was program director, and sat on the board of one of the largest political clubs in an unidentified major metropolis. He has appeared on cable talk shows as an advocate of law and order. A CPA and graduate of Washington University in St. Louis, Jeff has worked for Price Waterhouse's Investment Company Group and the Soros Fund Management. He is now the Chief Financial Officer of a hedge fund, and recently moved with his family to an environment more conducive to raising children, just north of Dixie.

Jeffrey Scheuer, a writer, leads a quiet life in Greenwich Village and rarely ventures north of 14th Street. He is the author of *The Sound Bite Society: Television and the American Mind* (Four Walls Eight Windows, 1999), a comic look at how television simplifies political discourse and thus serves the right and hurts the left. *The Chicago Tribune* described it as "lively and invigorating ... delicious writing style." He did not collaborate with Al Franken or anyone else, but steals some material from Jackie Mason.

Ron Schorr is critical and cynical by birth. He uses these "God-given" talents to manage a software testing team in Bucks County, Pennsylvania. Ron's interests include music, sports, and board games; he is a particular fan of backgammon, for its mix of skill and probability. A former member of Mensa, Ron quit because of the intellectual inferiority of the other members.

Marni Schwartz is currently attending the Ferkauf School of Psychology, part of Yeshiva University in New York. After five years of romping in this intellectual playground, Marni will emerge with a Doctorate in Psychology (Psy.D). She is a recent graduate of Sarah Lawrence College and is happy to use academia as an excuse to spend a few more years dodging the real world.

Marni has been known to enjoy a bowl of cereal while watching Saturday morning cartoons, but that is off the record.

Chuck Sheehan is a graduate of the University of Miami. In addition to his tuition, Chuck donated his liver to Miami's medical school for "alcoholic research." Chuck is a card-carrying rabble-rouser known for his shenanigans. Unlike your average paranoid, he is comforted by the knowledge that everyone is indeed out to get him. At present, Chuck is serving time in Alabama as a result of a failed attempt to expose professional wrestling as fake.

David "Preacher" Slocum is a municipal underwriting specialist for a major bank (remember, the longer the title, the less important the job). A 10-year military veteran and graduate of Ft. Benning's University of Gravity, his hobbies include trucks, dogs, guns, and ridiculing political correctness in all of its hideous forms. His humorous (and often mindless) writings can be sampled on his anti-PC Web site: www.BASTAARDS.org (Brotherhood Against Social Trends Aimed At Restructuring Democratic Society).

Jason Stein is a Java developer, mostly because he wanted to do something that started with the first letter of his own name and he heard Java is paying more than Janitor. He is also an entrepreneur; his latest venture is www.nudewear.com, where you will find his humorous T-shirts along with many other outrageous goodies. Jason has performed standup comedy around New York City. As the only American in the British sketch comedy group Bangers n' Mash, the *New York Post* described him as bringing "engaging freshness" to his work. Jason holds a bachelor of arts from the University of Maryland, but has since put it down because it was accumulating dust and getting heavy.

Scott Stein's first novel, *Lost*, was published by Free Reign Press in 2000. *The Philadelphia Inquirer* said he "has a keen eye for the details of our cultural landscape." The same review described *Lost* as "wonderfully comic ... a page-turner ... insightful tweaking of city living and modern times." Scott is an assistant professor at Drexel University. He received his bachelor of arts in English and master of fine arts in creative writing from the University of Miami and his master of arts in liberal studies from New York University. His short fiction has been published in *The G.W. Review*, *Art Times*, and *Liberty*. You might not think he is funnier than you, but you are wrong.

Bob Sullivan is a writer who received a bachelor of arts in creative writing from Purdue University and attended the University of Southern California graduate film school in the immediate wake of George Lucas. He also did three years postgraduate work at The Actors and Directors Lab under Jack Garfein and wrote film reviews for the *L.A. Free Press* for five years. Bob wrote the B-movie sci-fi classic *Clonus* starring Peter Graves, Keenan Wynn, and Dick Sargent. He is currently working on more screenplays, and is a major contributor to the *Saint James Encyclopedia of Popular Culture* and

The International Dictionary of Films and Filmmakers.

Rev. Angeline E.M. Theisen, a born and raised Michiganian, is a major fan of Midwestern Americans, once described by radio commentator Garrison Keillor's New York character Gloria as, "really calm, really happy people—like trees with hair." With a BA in English from Barry University in Miami, Rev. Angie spent 10 years in advertising—most notably at New Woman Magazine, Young & Rubicam Advertising/Atlanta, and Women's Wear Daily/Atlanta Bureau. When she became disillusioned with the artificiality necessary for a career in advertising, she returned to the University of Chicago for her masters in divinity and doctor of ministry degrees, before entering a new phase of the persuasion business—parish ministry. All along Rev. Angie has been a nonfiction writer, editor, and the book reviewer for WritersHome.com. Her essays have been published in several collections of Michigan women writers. She currently lives with her husband in Atlanta, Georgia.

Eva Marie Tremoglie would prefer it if the rabble knew nothing about her.

Andrew Turner ... Hi. You've reached Andrew's bio. Sorry, I can't take your call right now, but if you leave a brief message, I'll get back to you as soon as I can. Thanks.

Cassendre Xavier is an American writer. Her poetry, journalism, humor, and spiritual essays have appeared in numerous publications including *We'Moon: Gaia Rhythms for Womyn, Goddessing Magazine, sub/vertical: for queer black wimmin and our allies,* and *Dykes with Baggage: a Lighter Look at Lesbians in Therapy* (Alyson). She loves lesbian culture but only dates bald actors. Her proudest accomplishments are having hundreds of books and no cavities. When she grows up, Cassendre wants to marry Penn Jillette of Penn & Teller. Of course, she'd have to overlook his irreverent lack of baldness. Word to your mother.

Read more by these and new contributors to
When Falls the Coliseum on **www.WFtheColiseum.com**.

If you enjoyed this book, turn the page to find
out more about other Free Reign Press titles.

Also from Free Reign Press

Lost
a novel by Scott Stein

"It was the truth and there was no denying it. Jeremy Keller was being followed. At first he didn't quite believe it. Who gets followed in real life?"

Welcome to Jeremy's world: New York City at the end of the 20th century. Yes, Jeremy is being followed, but he doesn't mind. He is, after all, destined for great things. A little being followed is to be expected.

And yes, he doesn't know why he is being followed. And his job is nothing to brag about either. And a certain police detective has it in for him. And the love of his life doesn't know he exists. And he thinks he's responsible for the death of an innocent man. And his rent is late. And he lost the mysterious envelope that just might have the answers he's looking for. And New York can't seem to leave him in peace.

But at least he is being followed. Not everyone can say that. But then, not everyone is destined for great things.

Reviews

Lost
a novel by Scott Stein

"There are a million laughs in the big city, as a sharp-eyed writer shows ... wonderfully comic ... a page-turner ... Stein has a keen eye for the details of our cultural landscape. And he sprinkles his scenes with deadpan one-liners and cultural reference points. Theme restaurants, bomb scares, video games, voice mail, and even flesh-eating viruses are stitched into amusing sitcom-style situations ... Jeremy's daily life is a set of wacky misadventures. He gets clobbered by bureaucracy and basic technology and even has a few brushes with the law, all with great comic effect ... Even workplace violence – or the perceived threat of it – makes a great punch line ... insightful tweaking of city living and modern times."
–*The Philadelphia Inquirer*

"It is American conspiracy theory run riot in hilarious premises that no sitcom can match ... *Lost* is a funny book, turning sacred cows upside down, sometimes more than one to a page, explosive, insightful, and with language that's sharp and crackles like the twists of Stein's plot."
–Lester Goran, author of *Tales from the Irish Club*

"This urban comic novel is an entertaining view of a lost soul in the big city ... it's a furious romp well worth reading."
–*The Queens Courier*

"A humorous look at the human condition as it exists in today's cities."
–*The Bucks County Courier Times*

"Scott Stein takes on the inanities, barbarities, and pretensions of modern urban life in this winning first novel. *Lost* is what happens to an ordinary guy when an ordinary day turns into an existential car chase through the subways of New York City. The book is packed with hilarious, deadpan descriptions of brushes with bureaucracy, technology, insanity."
–Valerie Block, author of *Was It Something I Said?*

www.freereignpress.com
Available from the publisher and wherever books are sold.

Also from Free Reign Press

No-Nonsense Parenting, Common Sense Schools
by Dom Giordano

"As the parent of two teenagers, I recognize the critical difference good parenting or indifferent parenting can be in shaping the direction of a child's life. That is why Dom Giordano's message of involved, common-sense parenting is so timely and important. He can provide parents with a clear roadmap to ensure that their children follow the right path, with an approach that blends values with academic achievement."
—Larry Mendte, News Anchor, NBC-10 Philadelphia

"Raising an educated, achievement-oriented child is no easy task today. Dom Giordano brings a unique perspective to this effort as a parent, former teacher, and no-nonsense radio talk show host. Whether it's government officials, out-of-touch education bureaucrats, or burned-out teachers, Dom tackles these problems head-on to deliver powerful, common-sense solutions to the challenges parents face today."
—Tom Marr, Talk Show Host, WCBM Radio Baltimore

Dom Giordano is heard each weekday on 1210 AM WPHT in Philadelphia, New Jersey, and Delaware. In his fifteen-year career as a radio talk show host, he has earned a reputation for honesty and integrity, and never shying away from controversy in search of answers that make sense.

No-Nonsense Parenting, Common Sense Schools offers anecdotes, analysis, and practical solutions to some of the most pressing and prevalent challenges facing parents and educators today. The book blends Dom Giordano's in-the-trenches teaching career, his own experiences as a parent, and his talk radio background, where he has interviewed some of the leading experts in education, child psychology, social services, and parenting.

www.freereignpress.com
Available from the publisher and wherever books are sold.